# THE SHAKEN LANDS

VIOLENCE AND THE CRISIS
OF GOVERNANCE
IN EAST CENTRAL EUROPE,
1914–1923

Lithuanian Studies without Borders
Series Editor
**Darius Staliūnas (Lithuanian Institute of History)**

**Editorial Board**
Zenonas Norkus (Vilnius University)
Shaul Stampfer (Hebrew University)
Giedrius Subačius (University of Illinois at Chicago)

**Other Titles in this Series**
*The Storytelling Human: Lithuanian Folk Tradition Today*
Compiled and edited by Lina Būgienė

*Entangled Interactions between Religion and National Consciousness in Central and Eastern Europe*
Edited by Yoko Aoshima

*The Lithuanian Metrica: History and Research*
Artūras Dubonis, Darius Antanavičius, Raimonda Ragauskienė, and Ramunė Šmigelskytė-Stukienė

*Between Rome and Byzantium: The Golden Age of the Grand Duchy of Lithuania's Political Culture. Second half of the fifteenth century to first half of the seventeenth century*
Jūratė Kiaupienė

*The Literary Field under Communist Rule*
Edited by Aušra Jurgutienė & Dalia Satkauskytė

*The Creation of National Spaces in a Pluricultural Region: The Case of Prussian Lithuania*
Vasilijus Safronovas

*Spatial Concepts of Lithuania in the Long Nineteenth Century*
Edited by Darius Staliūnas

*The Art of Identity and Memory: Toward a Cultural History of the Two World Wars in Lithuania*
Edited by Giedrė Jankevičiūtė & Rasutė Žukienė

*For more information on this series, please visit:*
*academicstudiespress.com/lithuanianstudies*

# THE SHAKEN LANDS

VIOLENCE AND THE CRISIS
OF GOVERNANCE
IN EAST CENTRAL EUROPE,
1914–1923

Edited by Tomas Balkelis
and Andrea Griffante

BOSTON
2023

**Library of Congress Cataloging-in-Publication Data**

**Names:** Balkelis, Tomas, editor. | Griffante, Andrea, 1980- editor.
**Title:** The shaken lands: violence and the crisis of governance in East Central Europe, 1914–1923 / edited by Tomas Balkelis and Andrea Griffante.
**Other titles:** Violence and the crisis of governance in East Central Europe, 1914–1923
**Description:** Boston: Academic Studies Press, 2023. | Series: Lithuanian studies without borders | This volume emerged from the online conference "Violence and the Crisis of Governance in East Central Europe, 1905–1925" held in November 2020, organized by the Lithuanian Institute of History in Vilnius. | Includes bibliographical references.
**Identifiers:** LCCN 2023001380 (print) | LCCN 2023001381 (ebook) | ISBN 9798887191737 (hardback) | ISBN 9798887191744 (adobe pdf) | ISBN 9798887191751 (epub)
**Subjects:** LCSH: Europe, Eastern--History--1918–1945. | World War, 1914–1918--Europe, Eastern--Influence. | Europe, Eastern--Politics and government--1918–1945. | Europe, Eastern--History, Military--20th century. | Civilians in war--Europe, Eastern--History--20th century. | Violence--Europe, Eastern--History--20th century.
**Classification:** LCC DJK49 .S54 2023 (print) | LCC DJK49 (ebook) | DDC 940.3/47--dc23/eng/20230210
LC record available at https://lccn.loc.gov/2023001380
LC ebook record available at https://lccn.loc.gov/2023001381

Copyright © 2023 Academic Studies Press
All rights reserved

ISBN 9798887191737 (hardback)
ISBN 9798887191744 (adobe pdf)
ISBN 9798887191751 (epub)

Book design by PHi Business Solutions
Cover design by Ivan Grave
On the cover: German Postcard from WWI "After the storming of Vilna, 18 September 1915"

Published by Academic Studies Press
1577 Beacon Street
Brookline, MA 02446, USA
press@academicstudiespress.com
www.academicstudiespress.com

# Contents

Acknowledgments — vii

Introduction — 1
*Tomas Balkelis and Andrea Griffante*

1. The Evolution of Wartime Criminality in Lithuania, 1914–1920 — 15
   *Vytautas Petronis*
2. War Violence and Its Representation: A Comparison of Civilian Experiences of the Great War on Both Sides of the Former Russian-German Border — 42
   *Vasilijus Safronovas, Vygantas Vareikis, and Hektoras Vitkus*
3. The Military Pogroms in Lithuania, 1919–1920 — 83
   *Darius Staliūnas*
4. Scandinavian Volunteers as Perpetrators of Violence and Crime in the Estonian War of Independence — 103
   *Mart Kuldkepp*
5. The Rich and the (In)famous: Social Conflicts and Paramilitary Violence in Hungary during the Counterrevolution, 1921–1923 — 136
   *Béla Bodó*
6. The Polish Central Government, Regional Authorities, and Local Paramilitaries during the Battle for the Western Borderlands, 1918–1921 — 161
   *Jochen Böhler*
7. *Eisenbahnfeldzug*: Railway War in East Central Europe — 188
   *Maciej Górny*
8. Beyond Comparison? The Challenges of Applying Comparative Historical Research to Violence — 211
   *Julia Eichenberg*

Contributors — 237
Index — 241

# Acknowledgments

This volume has emerged from a collective effort of an international team of historians who in November 2020 gathered at the online conference "Violence and the Crisis of Governance in East Central Europe, 1905–1925," organized by the Lithuanian Institute of History in Vilnius. Firstly, the editors would like to thank all the participants and commentators who shared their critical input. We are grateful to the director of the Institute Professor Alvydas Nikžentaitis for the administrative and logistical assistance of the Institute. Neither the conference nor the publication of this book would have been possible without the generous funding provided by the Lithuanian Historical Institute and the German Historical Institute in Warsaw. Our special gratitude goes to Darius Staliūnas and Vytautas Petronis who helped to organize the conference and were among the first readers of the following chapters. We also want to thank Professor John Horne of Trinity College, Dublin and Professor Ronald Suny of the University of Michigan, Ann Arbor for their intellectual inspiration, encouragement, and active participation in the conference—they were our guides in helping discuss key concepts of the project and to define its limits. Finally, we want to thank those participants of the conference who shared their research with us: Claire Morelon, Gergely Bödők, Łukasz Mieszkowski, and Raul Cârstocea.

# Introduction

## Tomas Balkelis and Andrea Griffante

This book deals with one of the most violent periods in modern European history, which lasted almost a decade: from the start of the Great War in 1914 until 1923 when Europe, finally, achieved peace after a series of civil conflicts and interstate wars.[1] The violence unleashed during this period transformed the political landscape of the continent beyond recognition. This change was especially drastic in the vast East Central European region stretching from the White to the Black Seas and from Germany to Soviet Russia. By 1918, four major European empires were in ruins as they were replaced by a number of new nation states and the revolutionary Soviet state.

Today there is a growing consensus among historians not to seek a traditional caesura between the Great War and the postwar conflicts that have swept the region after 1918, but to consider the whole period as a single "continuous cycle of violence," variously described as the "Greater War," an international civil war, and even the second Thirty Years War.[2] Contributors to this volume support this paradigm. We seek to explain how the Great War transformed itself into the "Greater War" by focusing on the relationship between violence and the crisis of state governance in East Central Europe.

Recent scholarship made a strong case that the erosion of the old state system in Europe began well before 1914. In the case of the Romanov state, the unsuccessful Russo-Japanese war (1903–1904) led to the revolution of 1905 that subsequently forced the Russian government to reform the empire. Similarly, the Bosnian crisis (1908) and the Balkan wars (1912–1913) had a destabilizing impact on the southern part of East Central Europe and significantly weakened

---

1   By 1923, the last two major post-WWI conflicts had ended: the Russian Civil War and the Turkish War of Independence.
2   Peter Holquist, "Violent Russia, Deadly Marxism? Russia in the Epoch of Violence, 1905–1921," *Kritika: Explorations in Russian and Eurasian History* 4, no. 3 (Summer 2003): 630; Robert Gerwarth and Erez Manela, eds., *Empires at War, 1911–1923* (Oxford: Oxford University Press, 2014), 16; Jochen Böhler, *Civil War in Central Europe, 1918–1921: The Reconstruction of Poland* (Oxford: Oxford University Press, 2018), 59–60; Winston Churchill, *The Gathering Storm (The Second World War)* (Boston: Houghton Mifflin Co., 1948), 12.

the Ottoman Empire. Austria-Hungary became directly involved in both conflicts, while Russia and Germany also became entangled. A number of researchers argued that violence did not necessarily originate in the trenches of the Great War but was rather ingrained in the institutional weakness of empires and their cultures of violence that existed prior to 1914.[3]

However, none of these early conflicts had such a devastating impact on the old political system and civilian populations as the Great War and its aftermath. In her influential work *On Revolution* (1963), Hannah Arendt wrote that "the seeds of total war developed as early as the First World War when the distinction between soldiers and civilians was no longer respected."[4] In fact, in the decades prior to the outbreak of WWI, the legal distinction between combatants and civilians had experienced a slow but significant development. In the second half of the nineteenth century, some major military events—such as the Battle of Solferino in 1859 and the Prussian siege of Paris in 1870–71—resulted in an increasing search for shared norms regulating warfare. The Geneva Conventions of 1864 and 1906 guaranteed a neutral status for those caring for military wounded. The Hague Conventions of 1899 and 1907 enshrined legal protection for civilians under military occupation by an enemy power.

However, these early guarantees of the international law provided little protection to civilians in wartime. Germany proved to be extremely reluctant to absorb these norms in its military culture and entered the war without automatically recognizing the protection afforded to civilians of the occupied territories by the Hague Convention.[5] The victimization of civilians became its basic strategy of war both on the Western front and even more intensively in the East.[6] Russia and the Ottoman Empire pursued the same strategy as several ethnic groups of their populations (Germans, Jews, and Armenians) became targets of state repressions and systemic displacement from the early years of war.[7] In the post-WWI period, the civilian/combatant distinction became even less

---

3   Dietrich Beyrau, "Brutalization Revisited: The Case of Russia," *Journal of Contemporary History* 50, no. 1 (2015): 17; Robert Gerwarth and John Horne, eds., *War in Peace: Paramilitary Violence after the Great War, 1917–1923* (Oxford: Oxford University Press, 2012), 7.
4   Hannah Arendt, *On Revolution* (London: Penguin Books, 1990), 15.
5   Isabel V. Hull, *Absolute Destruction: Military Culture and the Practices of War in Imperial Germany* (Ithaca: Cornell University Press, 2005), 226–27.
6   Alexander B. Downes, *Targeting Civilians in War* (Ithaca: Cornell University Press, 2008), 83–114.
7   Eric Lohr, *Nationalizing the Russian Empire: The Campaign Against Enemy Aliens During World War One* (Cambridge, MA: Harvard University Press, 2003); Ryan Gingeras, *Sorrowful Shores: Violence, Ethnicity, and the End of the Ottoman Empire 1912–1923* (Oxford: Oxford University Press, 2009).

significant as revolutionary, counter-revolutionary, and nationalist terror campaigns swept across East Central Europe.[8] From this point of view, one may consider the Great War and its aftermath as reflecting the singular tendency that would be entrenched in the history of the twentieth and twenty-first centuries: the international laws that tried to protect civilians grew alongside the piling numbers of civilian casualties and refugees.[9]

Today, we know that the scale of destruction brought by the Great War and the postwar conflict was tremendous. Millions of soldiers died on battlefields or ended up in captivity. Those who survived suffered from physical and psychological traumas. East Central Europe—and especially the zones of occupation—experienced massive losses of population. At the same time, equally sizable numbers of civilians found themselves in war displacement. Most were able to come back to their newly transformed homelands only after the violence subsided.[10] In WWI alone, there were more than eight million military casualties and, according to some estimates, a further five million civilians perished as a result of war, civil conflicts, and famine.[11] In Russia alone, more than five million soldiers died in battle and from wounds and illness.[12] Between four and five million Russian soldiers were captured by the enemy.[13] By July 1917, more than seven million refugees were displaced from their homes.[14] In Germany, there were more than 1.7 million war dead, more than a million Germans became prisoners of war, and about eight hundred thousand civilians were displaced in East Prussia alone.[15] Estimates of the total losses of the Austro-Hungarian armed forces ranged from 1.1 to 1.2 million, while there were about half a million of

---

8   Heather Jones, "The Great War: How 1914–18 Changed the Relationship between War and Civilians," *The RUSI Journal* 159, no. 4 (2014): 86–87.
9   Daniel Rothbart, Karina Korostelina, and Mohammed Cherkaoui, eds., *Civilians and Modern War: Armed Conflict and the Ideology of Violence* (London: Routledge, 2012), 3–4.
10  Nick Baron and Peter Gatrell, eds., *Homelands: War, Population, and Statehood in Eastern Europe and Russia, 1918–1924* (London: Anthem Press, 2004).
11  Robert Gerwarth, ed., *Twisted Paths: Europe 1914–1945* (Oxford: Oxford University Press, 2007), 1.
12  Alexander Sumpf, "War Losses (Russian Empire)," *International Encyclopedia of the First World War: 1914–1918 Online*, accessed on April 2, 2022, https://encyclopedia.1914-1918-online.net/article/war_losses_russian_empire.
13  Beyrau, "Brutalization Revisited: The Case of Russia," 17.
14  Peter Gatrell, *A Whole Empire Walking: Refugees in Russia during WWI* (Bloomington: Indiana University Press, 1999), 212.
15  "World War I Casualty and Death Tables," Public Broadcasting System (US), based on US Justice Department statistics, accessed on April 2, 2022, http://www.pbs.org/greatwar/resources/casdeath_pop.html; Alexander Watson, *Ring of Steel: Germany and Austria-Hungary in World War One* (New York: Basic Books, 2014), 209.

refugees.[16] In many cases the displacement of civilians continued after the Great War, as new civil and interstate wars generated terror campaigns and new waves of refugees. Overarchingly, the period of 1914 to 1923 saw the value of human life and moral standards drastically decline as collective bonds and old social structures ruptured and social alienation became a norm.[17] This was particularly visible in the rise of criminality, paramilitaries, and mob violence, one of the key themes for the contributors of this volume.

Arendt also noted that "since the First World War, all governments have lived on borrowed time."[18] As old political structures and their leaders lost their authority, socialist and nationalist revolutionaries as well as counter-revolutionaries adopted the use of violence against civilians in the name of realizing their new ideologies. The gradual decline and then eventual collapse of empires spelled the end to the old imperial forms of government and led to what Joshua Sanborn had described as a "state failure" and "social disaster."[19] Both processes went hand in hand and catalyzed each other: the collapsing state structures fostered social disorder, while the remaining state institutions became powerless in the face of social collapse. This crisis of governance resulted in a post-WWI power vacuum, which created an ideal space for a variety of violence-oriented groups and actors that tried to enforce their own political and often, simply, criminal agendas.

Regarding Russia, Dietrich Beyrau argues that the breakdown of the state "marks the essential difference between the institutionalized violence of the Great War and the deinstitutionalized spaces of the Civil War."[20] This argument may be extended to the whole East Central European region where violence took place in three key stages: 1) violent decomposition of empires, 2) short period of de-institutionalized violence produced by the lack and weakness of state governance, and 3) institutionalized violence by the new states. In all cases, violence represented a means to contest and reshape territoriality—that is, to delimit and assert centralized power over former imperial spaces.[21]

---

16  Anatol Schmied-Kowarzik, "War Losses (Austria-Hungary)," *International Encyclopedia of the First World War: 1914–1918 Online*, accessed on April 2, 2022, https://encyclopedia.1914-1918-online.net/article/war_losses_austria-hungary.
17  Piotr Wróbel, "The Seeds of Violence. The Brutalization of an East European Region, 1917–1921," *Journal of Modern European History* 1, no. 1 (2003): 126.
18  Arendt, *On Revolution*, 15.
19  Joshua Sanborn, *Imperial Apocalypse: The Great War and the Destruction of the Russian Empire* (Oxford: Oxford University Press, 2014), 6.
20  Beyrau, "Brutalization Revisited: The Case of Russia," 17.
21  Deborah Cowen and Emily Gilbert, eds., "The Politics of War, Citizenship, Territory," in *War, Citizenship, Territory* (London: Routledge, 2008), 16.

The crisis of governance soon unleashed a frenzy of new armed conflicts among newly born state actors. The emerging national and revolutionary states turned out to be even more belligerent and violent than old empires. The civil wars in Russia, Ukraine, Latvia, Finland, and Hungary especially stand out for their bloody Red and White terror campaigns that targeted civilians. Between 2.5 and three million people were killed in the Russian Civil War alone.[22] In Finland (which had a population of 3.2 million), a civil war caused the death of more than thirty-eight thousand people.[23] From 1918–1921, the newly formed Polish nation-state became involved in no less than six military conflicts with its neighbors,[24] while adjacent Lithuania and Latvia had to fight three wars to ensure their survival.[25] Violence was not simply an outcome but also a tool in the hands of nation-makers to define their new state borders, to mobilize populations, to impose new social and national identities, and to filter out undesirable ethnic or social foes. Civilians were caught in the middle of this struggle for power and control. For them, the war did not end in 1918 and, depending on the country, continued for another four or five years.

Violence represents a fundamental feature for the creation and identity-making of modern statehood. Scholarly literature has widely pinpointed that modern statehood has emerged from and has constantly pursued a process of "denaturalization" of violence.[26] An expression of nature-dominated barbarian entities and epochs, in "civilized" modern statehood violence, freed from ritual and metaphysical restrictions, was blamed and reduced to a *means* state's authorities can employ for the achievement of *moral* goals.[27] Reorganized around the legitimate–illegitimate dichotomy, violence—to be more precise,

---

22  Jochen Böhler, "Enduring Violence: The Postwar Struggles in East-Central Europe, 1917–21," *Journal of Contemporary History* 50, no. 1 (2015): 63.
23  Tuomas Tepora, "Finnish Civil War 1918," *International Encyclopedia of the First World War: 1914–1918 Online*, accessed on April 2, 2022, https://encyclopedia.1914-1918-online.net/article/finnish_civil_war_1918.
24  Böhler, "Enduring Violence," 66.
25  For the wars in the Baltics see Tomas Balkelis, "War, Revolution and Terror in the Baltic States and Finland after the Great War," *Journal of Baltic Studies* 46, no.1 (2015): 1–9.
26  Anthony Giddens, *The Nation-State and Violence* (Cambridge: Polity Press, 1985); Reinhart Kössler, "The Modern Nation State and Regimes of Violence: Reflections on the Current Situation," *Ritsumeikan Annual Review of International Studies* 2 (2003): 15–36; James Ryan, *Lenin's Terror: The Ideological Origins of Early Soviet State Violence* (London: Routledge, 2012); Charles Tilly, *Coercion, Capital, and European States, AD 900–1990* (London: Blackwell, 1990).
27  Bernd Hüppauf, "Introduction: Modernity and Violence: Observations Concerning a Contradictory Relationship," in *War, Violence, and the Modern Condition*, ed. Bernd Hüppauf (Berlin: De Grutyer, 1997), 14.

the centralization and monopolization of it—has become the fundament upon which modern territorial state authorities have grounded their legitimacy. Max Weber's famous dictum is quite clear in this regard: the state is a human community that successfully claims the monopoly of the legitimate use of physical force within a given territory.[28] Against this background, warfare has been indicated as a possible catalyzer of modernity. Analyzing the process of modern state making, Charles Tilly has stressed that warfare proved to be the most efficient mechanism of social control and state expansion, and the monopoly over the legitimate use of violence tended to develop as the direct outcome of war making.[29]

The contributors of the volume aim to detect the centrality and meanings of violence during the breakdown and decomposition of East Central European states in the context of the political turmoil of the period of 1914–1923. Our broad thesis has two crucial dimensions. The first is that disintegration of state power brought by the Great War was a key condition that produced violence. In other words, widespread violence was a symptom of state weakness. Yet the process of post-WWI state building was equally or more violent as nascent East Central European states institutionalized the use of violence to achieve their political agendas. Emerging states acted violently to ensure a monopoly of violence against other violent paramilitary, para-state, and state actors in their projected borders. Civilian populations became subject to institutionalized military policies of political, social, and economic control, and, under conditions of state failure and social disaster—to the deinstitutionalized and indiscriminate violence of paramilitaries, mobs and often criminals.

This long-standing wave of violence entailed a profound renegotiation and reassessment of the relation among territoriality, state power, and citizenship. But what kind of states *did* emerge from the violent period of 1914–1923? Firstly, there were several states that simply did not survive the cauldron of imperial collapse, revolution, and nation-state building (specifically, Belarus and Ukraine). Those that did survive empowered their titular national groups and, to various degrees, became exclusionist to their national minorities. Some of the states remained revisionist (namely, the Soviet Union, Lithuania, Hungary, and Bulgaria) due to their lost and unsuccessfully contested territories. Others, like Poland and Romania, turned out to be quite expansionist as their new territorial

---

28 Max Weber, "Politics as a Vocation," *From Max Weber: Essays in Sociology*, ed. H. H. Gerth and C. Wright Mills (London: Routledge, 1991) [first edition 1948], 78.
29 Charles Tilly, *The Politics of Collective Violence* (Cambridge: Cambridge University Press, 2003), 55.

acquisitions extended far beyond the lands inhabited by the majorities of their titular nations. In many cases, the states that have emerged from the maelstrom of imperial collapse and war remained partly militarized as their citizens became accustomed to and prepared for "the production of violence."[30] Although their armies were to some extent demobilized, after the postwar conflicts they continued to heavily influence local political cultures. Wartime deeds of the military forces were turned into rituals of nationalist or revolutionary commemoration. In addition, many military laws and institutions remained in place for years after the wars, while local paramilitary organizations expanded their memberships among civilians and became massive armed proxies of national armies. It is no wonder that war veteran movements and wartime leaders (together with a new generation of right-wing radicals) played a key role in militarizing interwar politics and dismantling fragile East Central European democracies: starting with Poland and Lithuania in 1926 and ending with Hungary in 1931, Estonia, Latvia, and Bulgaria in 1934, and Romania in 1937. This military heritage of 1914–1923 in many forms survived the interwar period and played a key role in the historical unraveling of World War II.

To define violence in a narrow and one-dimensional way (for example, by focusing only on physical violent acts) is an insufficient strategy because violence necessarily produces a highly charged emotional and psychological dimension that affects human behavior. During the aforementioned period, physical acts of violence were as important as threats and fear of violence, fantasies and symbols of violence, and rituals of atonement and commemoration produced by violence.[31] Trying to mobilize people and create a palpable caesura between the self and the enemy, state and social actors actualized violence-related *lieux de mémoire* and mythologized ongoing events. In turn, while becoming catalysts of additional violence, mythologies of violence helped fix new boundaries of

---

30  We borrowed the term *militarization* from Michael Geyer who defines it as "the social process by which civil society organizes itself for the production of violence." His understanding of *militarization* is broader than is commonly meant as simply the dominance of military organizations in a society. For Geyer, *militarization* is, first of all, "mobilization of people and resources for war" and the process through which "societies remake themselves and their social-political orders for the purpose of organizing destruction." See Michael Geyer, "The Militarization of Europe, 1914–1945," in *The Militarization of the Western World*, ed., John R. Gillis (New Brunswick: Rutgers University Press, 1989), 79–80.

31  On the fantasies and fears of violent Bolshevism see, Robert Gerwarth and John Horne, eds., "Bolshevism as Phantasy: Fear of Revolution and Counter-Revolutionary Violence, 1917–1923," in *War in Peace: Paramilitary Violence in Europe after the Great War* (Oxford: Oxford University Press, 2012), 40–51.

citizenship and reshape long-lasting friend-foe distinctions.[32] State policies of massive expulsions or requisitions that led to displacement, economic destruction, hunger, and the spread of epidemics and criminality were also forms of "structural" violence that impacted the political, ethnic, and social make-up of societies.

That is why we chose a broad definition of violence as "the deliberate infliction of harm on people," proposed by Stathis Kalyvas and widely used by other scholars.[33] As historians, we are always aware that violence is a recurrent human condition that is produced by the search for security. Still, we direct our efforts, as Geyer wrote, "to understanding the reining in of violence."[34] This understanding is possible because, in most cases, violence is always premeditated, orchestrated, instrumentalized, and therefore, political. Recognizing the political circumstances under which violence takes place is our major task. However, in this volume we are interested not only in political violence but also in criminal violent acts produced as a result of the lack of state power and social disorder.

Violence is always contextual and although it takes place locally, it may be studied as a transnational phenomenon. Recently, there were a number of studies that adopted the transnational and comparative approaches to the study of violence in East Central Europe.[35] These perspectives challenged the nationalist one-country accounts of the post-1918 period that still dominate in many East European countries. This volume is also intended as a contribution to the growing transnational field. Since violence is deeply contextual, most of our contributors chose to deliver a series of case studies on separate countries where

---

32  Cowen, Gilbert, *The Politics of War, Citizenship, Territory*, 2.
33  Stathis Kalyvas, *The Logic of Violence in Civil War* (Cambridge: Cambridge University Press, 2006), 19. For a similar definition see also Julia Eichenberg and John Paul Newman, "Introduction: Aftershocks: Violence in Dissolving Empires after the First World War," *Contemporary European History* 19, no. 3 (2010): 188.
34  Michael Geyer, "Some Hesitant Observations Concerning 'Political Violence,'" *Kritika: Explorations in Russian and Euro-Asian History* 4, no. 3 (Summer 2003): 695.
35  Gerwarth and Horne, eds., *War in Peace*, 2012; Robert Gerwarth, *The Vanquished: Why the First World War Failed to End, 1917–1923* (Falkirk: Allen Lane, 2016); Böhler, *Civil War in Central Europe, 1918–1921*; Jochen Böhler, Ota Konrád, and Rudolf Kučera, eds., *In the Shadow of the Great War: Physical Violence in East-Central Europe, 1917–1923* (New York, Oxford: Berghahn Books, 2021); Eichenberg and Newman, eds. "Introduction: Aftershocks"; Tim Wilson, *Frontiers of Violence: Conflict and Identity in Ulster and Upper Silesia, 1918–1922* (Oxford: Oxford University Press, 2010); Alexander Prusin, *The Lands Between: Conflict in the East European Borderlands, 1870–1992* (Oxford: Oxford University Press 2010); Włodzimierz Borodziej and Maciej Górny, *Forgotten Wars: Central and Eastern Europe, 1912–1916* (Cambridge: Cambridge University Press, 2021); Omer Bartov and Eric D. Weitz, eds., *Shatterzone of Empires: Coexistence and Violence in the German, Habsburg, Russian and Ottoman Borderlands* (Bloomington: Indiana University Press, 2013).

violence took place: Poland, Lithuania, Estonia, Hungary and the eastern part of Germany (Prussia). Yet we tried to answer the same set of questions on political contexts, role of state structures, motives and aims of violence, and profiles of victims and perpetrators that would make those cases comparable. Despite contextual specifics, we suggest that during 1914–1923 in East Central Europe, similar violent actors engaged in similar types of violence because of similar causes and under similar historical circumstances. In the final chapter, Julia Eichenberg reflects on the history and the current state of affairs of historical comparison in studies of violence and discusses where and when it is useful to apply it with regard to the case studies of Eastern Europe in the first quarter of the twentieth century.

What was specific about the violence during 1914–1923? Arendt was also one of the first to suggest that at the time "wars had become politically, though not yet biologically, a matter of life and death."[36] Robert Gerwarth argued that from 1917, when the dismantling of the empires became a war aim, conventional conflicts changed into "existential conflicts fought to annihilate the enemy, be they ethnic or class enemies," adding to them "genocidal logic."[37] Recently, there was also a lively debate between those scholars who, in explaining the explosion of violence, offered the "brutalization" thesis and those who criticized it for its limited application to all belligerents.[38] Limited demobilizations that have led to remobilizations after the Great War,[39] "cultures of defeat,"[40] warlordism,[41] imperial collapse and the crisis of governance,[42] ethnic conflict and (counter)revolutions emerged as alternative explanations of the persistence of

---

36 Arendt, *On Revolution*, 15.
37 Gerwarth, *The Vanquished*, 13.
38 For the "brutalization" thesis see, George Mosse, *Fallen Soldiers. Reshaping the Memory of the World Wars* (New York, 1990) and Wróbel, "The Seeds of Violence. The Brutalization of an East European Region, 1917–1921." For its criticism see, Robert Gerwarth and John Horne, eds., "Paramilitarism in Europe after the Great War. An Introduction," in *War in Peace: Paramilitary Violence in Europe after the Great War* (Oxford: Oxford University Press, 2012), 2–4.
39 Böhler, "Enduring Violence"; Tomas Balkelis, "Demobilization and Remobilization of German and Lithuanian Paramilitaries after the First World War," *Journal of Contemporary History* 50, no. 1 (2015): 38–57.
40 Gerwarth, *The Vanquished: Why the First World War Failed to End, 1917–1923*.
41 Joshua Sanborn, "The Genesis of Russian Warlordism: Violence and Governance during the First World War and the Civil War," *Contemporary European History* 19, no. 3 (August 2010): 195–213.
42 Beyrau, "Brutalization Revisited: The Case of Russia"; Joshua Sanborn, *Imperial Apocalypse: The Great War and the Destruction of the Russian Empire* (Oxford: Oxford University Press, 2014).

violence after the Great War.[43] The wealth of these interpretations clearly suggests that monocausal explanations of the violence during this period are simply inadequate.

The contributors to this volume offer their case studies by building on these explanations and debates. They explore different forms of violence that may be grouped into three broad categories. Firstly, there was state-sanctioned violence against civilians perpetrated by regular troops. They actively engaged in summary executions, requisitions, forced mobilizations, expulsions, punitive expeditions, hostage taking, but also in pillaging, pogroms, and debauchery. Terror campaigns carried by regular revolutionary, counter-revolutionary or national armies were among the most devastating and appalling forms of this type of violence that resulted in massive numbers of civilian victims.

Secondly, there was non-state or semi-sanctioned violence performed by various paramilitary or para-state actors. These violent entrepreneurs flourished especially after 1918 in the postwar power vacuum due to the destruction or weakness of state institutions. Some of these paramilitaries (various warlords, volunteer corps, civil militias, self-defense, and "green" bands) acted independently and even tried to create their quasi-statelets in the shape of various "republics." Yet the majority were (or in the long run became) proxies to the regular armies. They engaged in beatings, summary executions, requisitions, intimidation of civilians, expulsions, destruction of their properties, robberies, pogroms, and banditry. The fact that their actions remained in the shady zone between state-sanctioned and non-state violence added additional swagger of brutality to their violent acts and often gave them impunity.[44]

Thirdly, there was communal violence performed by civilians against their civilian neighbors. The crisis of governance and social disaster that followed (or precipitated) it led to the general disorder and lawlessness that created the conditions for growing criminality, banditry, and mob violence. Most of such violent acts (robberies, arsons, acts of personal vengeance, pogroms, land grabs) took place far from the political centers in the countryside within local communities where state power was at its weakest.[45] Yet many of these violent acts also happened in towns and cities where especially Jewish communities became

---

43 See several chapters on ethnic conflict and (counter-)revolutions in Gerwarth and Horne, eds., *War in Peace*; Eichenberg and Newman, eds. *Aftershocks: Violence in Dissolving Empires after the First World War*.
44 On the close connection between paramilitarism and the state see, Uğur Ümit Üngör, *Paramilitarism: Mass Violence in the Shadow of the State* (Oxford: Oxford University Press, 2020).
45 Eichenberg and Newman, "Introduction: Aftershocks," 188.

targets of pogroms, robberies, and mob violence. In general, anti-Jewish excesses became one of the most visible forms of this type of violence during 1914–1923.

Finally, it is important to note that these three types of violence often overlapped and stimulated each other. Thus, often requisitions or pogroms initiated by regular troops or paramilitaries were followed by mob violence, banditry, and theft that involved civilians, while often paramilitaries were turned into regular troops and their violence became state sanctioned.

The geographical and thematic coverage of the volume has been shaped by an international team of historians who in November 2020 gathered at the online conference "Violence and the Crisis of Governance in East Central Europe, 1905–1925," organized by the Lithuanian Institute of History in Vilnius. With a relatively small team of specialists, we could not cover all East Central European countries. Yet we hope that our volume will considerably expand the geography of the field by including four chapters on two of the Baltic states (Lithuania and Estonia). Usually, the Baltics are rarely included in similar thematic studies of violence, even though the violent processes of imperial disintegration and state building followed similar patterns there as they did in Russia, Poland, Ukraine, and other Central and East European countries. The Baltic region is also important for the key reason that it faced almost all types of violent developments of the period: military occupations, population displacement, social disorder, banditry, civil conflicts, revolutionary and counter-revolutionary terror, interstate wars, and foreign military incursions. Here the notion of all-encompassing Russian Civil War is only partly useful to convey the scope, variety, and complexity of the conflicts. Thus, in the Baltic states, lines of confrontation ran not only along the revolutionary (Reds) and counter-revolutionary (Whites) axis, but also along nationalist lines (Germans and Whites versus Lithuanians, Latvians, and Estonians; Poles versus Lithuanians). Moreover, the belligerents often switched sides, making the conflict even more complex.

We also hope that this volume will stand out for its special attention to communal violence, that is, violence committed by civilians onto their neighbors. Thus far, only a few studies paid closer attention to various gangs of "greens," prisoners of war, freebooters, and simply criminals who briefly flourished in the social chaos and disorder produced by the crisis of governance by the end of the Great War.[46] Some of our contributors pay close attention to this communal

---

46  Jakub Beneš, "The Green Cadres and the Collapse of Austria-Hungary in 1918," *Past & Present* 236, no. 1 (2017): 207–41; Serhy Yekelchyk, "Bands of Nation Builders? Insurgency and Ideology in the Ukrainian Civil War," in *War in Peace: Paramilitary Violence in Europe After the Great War*, ed. Robert Gerwarth and John Horne (Oxford: Oxford University Press,

violence in the shape of banditry (see the chapter by Vytautas Petronis) as well as the surge in antisemitic riots that took place during the period (chapters by Darius Staliūnas and Béla Bodó). They demonstrate that there was a close link between communal violence produced by the occupation regimes during the Great War and later forms of violence that took place after 1918. They also show that antisemitic violence was an inherent element of the crisis of governance and nation-building during the period. Jews turned out to be the first "minority" whose political rights were formulated and safeguarded by the treaties imposed by the western Allies on emerging nation-states such as Poland, Lithuania, Hungary and others. However, Jews often became the targets of antisemitic attacks and campaigns that went parallel with state-building in these states.

Some of the contributors to this volume focus their attention on the modern networks that facilitated the expanding geography of violence (Maciej Górny), while others explore the complex and fluid relationship between violent parastate and state actors (Jochen Böhler), the ideological mindsets and criminal activities or foreign paramilitary volunteers (Mart Kuldkepp), and how the civilian experiences of the Great War became represented and instrumentalized in interwar political contexts of different countries (Vasilijus Safronovas, Vygantas Vareikis, and Hektoras Vitkus). In the final chapter, Julia Eichenberg surveys the approaches taken by all authors in their case studies and the merits and challenges of comparative or transnational study of violence.

Today, the study of violence against civilians and its relationship with the state remains as important as ever. Numerous war crimes committed against civilians by Russian troops in Ukraine testify that modern states continue to use violence to achieve their political objectives or are unable to control it due to the weakness of state power. As civilian casualties continue to pile up in our century, Hannah Arendt reminds us that "violence can be justifiable, but it never will be legitimate. Its justification loses in plausibility the farther its intended end recedes into the future. No one questions the use of violence in self-defense, because the danger is not only clear but also present, and the end justifying the means is immediate."[47]

---

2012), 107–25; Christopher Gilley, "Pogroms and Imposture: The Violent Self-Formation of Ukrainian Warlords," in *In the Shadow of the Great War: Physical Violence in East-Central Europe, 1917–1923*, ed. Jochen Böhler, Ota Konrád, and Rudolf Kučera (New York: Berghahn Books, 2021), 28–44.

47   Hannah Arendt, *On Violence* (London: Harcourt Brace Jovanovich Publishers, 1969), 52.

# Works Cited

Arendt, Hannah. *On Revolution*. London: Penguin Books, 1990.
———. *On Violence*. London: Harcourt Brace Jovanovich Publishers, 1969.
Balkelis, Tomas. "Demobilization and Remobilization of German and Lithuanian Paramilitaries after the First World War." *Journal of Contemporary History* 50, no. 1 (2015): 38–57.
———. "War, Revolution and Terror in the Baltic States and Finland after the Great War." *Journal of Baltic Studies* 46, no. 1 (2015): 1–9.
Baron, Nick, and Peter Gatrell, eds. *Homelands: War, Population and Statehood in Eastern Europe and Russia, 1918–1924*. London: Anthem Press, 2004.
Bartov, Omer, and Eric D. Weitz, eds. *Shatterzone of Empires: Coexistence and Violence in the German, Habsburg, Russian and Ottoman Borderlands*. Bloomington: Indiana University Press, 2013.
Beneš, Jakub. "The Green Cadres and the Collapse of Austria-Hungary in 1918," *Past & Present* 236, no. 1 (2017): 207–41.
Beyrau, Dietrich. "Brutalization Revisited: The Case of Russia." *Journal of Contemporary History* 50, no. 1 (2015): 15–37.
Böhler, Jochen, "Enduring Violence: The Postwar Struggles in East-Central Europe, 1917–21," *Journal of Contemporary History* 50, no. 1 (2015): 58–77.
———. *Civil War in Central Europe, 1918–1921: The Reconstruction of Poland*. Oxford: Oxford University Press, 2018.
Böhler, Jochen, Ota Konrád, and Rudolf Kučera, eds. *In the Shadow of the Great War: Physical Violence in East-Central Europe, 1917–1923*. New York: Berghahn Books, 2021.
Borodziej, Włodzimierz, and Maciej Górny. *Forgotten Wars: Central and Eastern Europe, 1912–1916*. Cambridge: Cambridge University Press, 2021.
Churchill, Winston. *The Gathering Storm (The Second World War)*. Boston: Houghton Mifflin Co., 1948.
Cowen, Deborah and Emily Gilbert. "The Politics of War, Citizenship, Territory." In *War, Citizenship, Territory*, edited by Deborah Cowen and Emily Gilbert, 1–30. New York: Routledge, 2008.
Downes, Alexander B. *Targeting Civilians in War*. Ithaca: Cornell University Press, 2008.
Eichenberg, Julia, and John Paul Newman. "Introduction: Aftershocks: Violence in Dissolving Empires after the First World War." *Contemporary European History* 19, no. 3 (2010): 183–94.
Gatrell, Peter. *A Whole Empire Walking: Refugees in Russia during WWI*. Bloomington: Indiana University Press, 1999.
Gerwarth, Robert. *The Vanquished: Why the First World War Failed to End, 1917–1923*. Falkirk: Allen Lane, 2016.
———. *Twisted Paths: Europe 1914–1945*. Oxford: Oxford University Press, 2007.
Gerwarth, Robert, and John Horne. "Bolshevism as Phantasy: Fear of Revolution and Counter-Revolutionary Violence, 1917–1923." In *War in Peace: Paramilitary Violence in Europe after the Great War*, edited by Robert Gerwarth and John Horne, 40–51. Oxford: Oxford University Press, 2012.
Gerwarth, Robert, and Erez Manela, eds. *Empires at War, 1911–1923*. Oxford: Oxford University Press, 2014.
Geyer, Michael. "Some Hesitant Observations Concerning 'Political Violence.'" *Kritika: Explorations in Russian and Euro-Asian History* 4, no. 3 (Summer 2003): 695–708.

———. "The Militarization of Europe, 1914–1945." In *The Militarization of the Western World*, edited by John R. Gillis, 65–102. New Brunswick: Rutgers University Press, 1989.

Giddens, Anthony. *The Nation-State and Violence*. Cambridge: Polity Press, 1985.

Gilley, Christopher. "Pogroms and Imposture: The Violent Self-Formation of Ukrainian Warlords." In *In the Shadow of the Great War: Physical Violence in East-Central Europe, 1917–1923*, edited by Jochen Böhler, Ota Konrád, and Rudolf Kučera, 28–44. New York: Berghahn Books, 2021.

Gingeras, Ryan. *Sorrowful Shores: Violence, Ethnicity, and the End of the Ottoman Empire 1912–1923*. Oxford: Oxford University Press, 2009.

Holquist, Peter. "Violent Russia, Deadly Marxism? Russia in the Epoch of Violence, 1905–1921." *Kritika: Explorations in Russian and Eurasian History* 4, no. 3 (Summer 2003): 627–52.

Hull, Isabel V. *Absolute Destruction: Military Culture and the Practices of War in Imperial Germany*. Ithaca: Cornell University Press, 2005.

Hüppauf, Bernd. "Introduction: Modernity and Violence: Observations Concerning a Contradictory Relationship." In *War, Violence, and the Modern Condition*, edited by Bernd Hüppauf, 1–31. Berlin: De Grutyer, 1997.

*International Encyclopedia of the First World War: 1914–1918 Online*. Accessed on April 2, 2022. https://encyclopedia.1914-1918-online.net/home/

Jones, Heather. "The Great War: How 1914–1918 Changed the Relationship between War and Civilians." *The RUSI Journal* 159, no. 4 (2014): 84–91.

Kössler, Reinhart. "The Modern Nation State and Regimes of Violence: Reflections on the Current Situation." *Ritsumeikan Annual Review of International Studies* 2 (2003): 15–36.

Lohr, Eric. *Nationalizing the Russian Empire: The Campaign against Enemy Aliens During World War I*. Cambridge, MA: Harvard University Press, 2003.

Prusin, Alexander. *The Lands Between: Conflict in the East European Borderlands, 1870–1992*. Oxford: Oxford University Press, 2010.

Ryan, James. *Lenin's Terror: The Ideological Origins of Early Soviet State Violence*. London: Routledge, 2012.

Rothbart, Daniel, and Karina Korostelina, Mohammed Cherkaoui, eds. *Civilians and Modern War: Armed Conflict and the Ideology of Violence*. London: Routledge, 2012.

Sanborn, Joshua. *Imperial Apocalypse: The Great War and the Destruction of the Russian Empire*. Oxford: Oxford University Press, 2014.

Tilly, Charles. *Coercion, Capital, and European States, AD 900–1990*. London: Blackwell, 1990.

———. *The Politics of Collective Violence*. Cambridge: Cambridge University Press, 2003.

Üngör, Uğur Ümit. *Paramilitarism: Mass Violence in the Shadow of the State*. Oxford: Oxford University Press, 2020.

Watson, Alexander. *Ring of Steel: Germany and Austria-Hungary in World War One*. New York: Basic Books, 2014.

Weber, Max. "Politics as a Vocation." In *From Max Weber: Essays in Sociology*, edited by H. H. Gerth and C. Wright Mills, 77–128. London: Routledge, 1991.

Wilson, Tim. *Frontiers of Violence: Conflict and Identity in Ulster and Upper Silesia, 1918–1922*. Oxford: Oxford University Press, 2010.

Wróbel, Piotr. "The Seeds of Violence. The Brutalization of an East European Region, 1917–1921." *Journal of Modern European History* 1, no. 1 (2003): 125–49.

CHAPTER 1

# The Evolution of Wartime Criminality in Lithuania, 1914–1920

## Vytautas Petronis

In the official "Note on Banditry" from August 27, 1918, the Lithuanian State Council, the highest national institution of the newly established independent Lithuania, complained to the German military administration about the intolerable situation in the country. Besides pointing out heavy requisitions, robberies, and executions carried out by the Germans, Lithuanian representatives also pleaded to combat the widespread banditry, which became, as they noted, a "profitable and not that dangerous business."[1] But having no power to stop the perpetrators, the state council was fully dependent on the German military force.

The phenomenon of wartime criminality, and especially banditry, has not yet received sufficient scholarly attention, even though it became an integral part of the overall violence during WWI. The Lithuanian lands, which during the German occupation from 1915 until 1919 were known as the Ober Ost,[2] were no exception to that. However, when other warring powers, for example, Austro-Hungary, were less oppressive against the civilian population in the occupied territories, the German military authorities conducted a methodical, harsh, and violent policy.[3]

---

1 "Lietuvos Valstybės Tarybos prezidiumo 'Raštas dėl banditizmo,'" in *Lietuvos valstybės tarybos protokolai, 1917–1918* (Vilnius: Mokslas, 1991), 305–07.
2 Full name: *Oberbefehlshaber der gesamten Deutschen Streitkräfte im Osten*. The territory also included Kurland, the western part of present-day Latvia and parts of northwestern Poland.
3 Jonathan E. Gumz, "Losing Control: The Norm of Occupation in Eastern Europe during the First World War," in *Legacies of Violence. Eastern Europe's First World War*, ed. Jochen Böhler,

The system of the Ober Ost has been already analyzed in historiography.[4] Perhaps the most relevant analysis for our topic may be found in Abba Strazhas' study that discussed Russian plans from 1914 to 1915 to start a partisan war in the occupied territories.[5] At the same time, a somewhat different picture of wartime criminality can be gathered from accounts of witnesses and victims. For this reason, memoirs and periodical press are used here as the main source of information, because archival materials on the topic are scarce, fragmented, and usually do not reflect the point of view of the local population. Unfortunately, I could not find any accounts either of German soldiers who served in the Ober Ost and fought criminals, people who were involved in criminal activities, or recollections of those Russian soldiers who escaped German prisoner of war camps and spent the war living in the Lithuanian forests.[6]

Moreover, military censorship prohibited publishing reports on any disorder in the country during most of the war. The restrictions became looser after Lithuania declared its independence on February 16, 1918, and the Lithuanian administration and newspapers were established. Still, the prohibition remained until November 1918.[7] After that, reports on the desperate criminal situation in the country almost immediately appeared in the press, predominantly in liberal and leftist periodicals.

Therefore, this chapter will primarily focus on the rise and evolution of wartime criminality, especially banditry, and its containment during the early

---

Wlodzimierz Borodziej, and Joachim von Puttkamer (Munich: de Gruyter Oldenbourg, 2014), 69–87.

4   See, for example, Börje Colliander, *Die Beziehungen zwischen Litauen und Deutschland während der Okkupation 1915–1918* (Åbo/Turku: Åbo Akademi, 1935); Abba Strazhas, *Deutsche Ostpolitik im Ersten Weltkrieg: Der Fall Ober Ost 1915–1917* (Wiesbaden: Harrassowitz Verlag, 1993); Vejas G. Liulevicius, *War Land on the Eastern Front: Culture, National Identity and German Occupation in World War I* (Cambridge: Cambridge University Press, 2000); Christian Westerhoff, *Zwangsarbeit im Ersten Weltkrieg. Deutsche Arbeitskräftepolitik im besetzten Polen und Litauen 1914–1918* (Padeborn: Ferdinand Schöningh, 2011); Vasilijus Safronovas, Vytautas Jokubauskas, Vygantas Vareikis, Hektoras Vitkus, *Didysis karas visuomenėje ir kultūroje: Lietuva ir Rytų Prūsija* (Klaipėda: Klaipėdos universiteto leidykla, 2018); Kai-Achim Klare, *Imperium ante Portas. Die deutsche Expansion in Mittel- und Osteuropa zwischen Weltpolitik und Lebensraum (1914–1918)* (Wiesbaden: Harrassowitz Verlag, 2020), especially 315–488.

5   Strazhas, *Deutsche Ostpolitik im Ersten Weltkrieg*, 13–24; 208–11.

6   Literary depiction of the life of a runaway Russian prisoner of war can be found in Arnold Zweig's famous novel *Der Streit um den Sergeanten Grischa* (1928). The material for the book came from Lithuanian lands, where from 1917 Zweig worked as a censor at the Ober Ost Press department in Kaunas.

7   See the editorial note for the article: A., "Apie plėšimus ir plėšikus," *Darbo balsas*, November 26, 1918, 1. For more on the censorship of the wartime publications, see Marija Urbšienė, "Vokiečių karo meto spauda ir Lietuva," *Karo archyvas* 7 (1936): 143–48.

postwar years. A few dozen recorded and relevant memoirs allow us to provide a view from below. I argue that wartime banditry evolved and was closely connected not only with the repressive policies of both Russian and German military regimes, but most of all with the emergence of numerous groups of Russian prisoners of war, who, having escaped from the German internment camps, hid in forests, and together with local criminals engaged in robbing and murdering the local civilian population.

## Military Violence against Civilians at the Beginning of the War

With the outbreak of World War I in August 1914, the Russian Empire quickly delved into chaos. Large numbers of troops were moved to the western borders of the state. But from the very beginning, the Russian General Staff encountered a number of significant hindrances: among many others, the lack of discipline and morale among its troops. This caused massive surrendering of soldiers to the enemy, when—in an attempt to escape death—whole detachments and platoons voluntarily went into captivity.[8] Also, there were many cases of desertion. Soldiers ran away, alone and in groups, not only from their units on the frontline but also on the way to the front. There were cases when trains, fully loaded with troops, reached the frontline half-empty. Some of the deserters attempted to return home, but many hid in forests or lurked in the pre-front territories. The need for food and money quickly turned them into criminals. Naturally, their primary target became the civilian population.[9]

Remaining in the army did not guarantee full provisions either. Often, soldiers at the frontlines found themselves in similar situations when, due to poor roads and overloaded railways, the arrival of ammunition and supplies was delayed. They were forced to provide food for themselves, which meant requisitioning it from the locals. According to Mikhail Lemke, who from 1915–1916 served as

---

8   Aleksandr B. Astashov, *Russkii front v 1914—nachale 1917 goda. Voennyi opyt i sovremennost'* (Moscow, Novyi khronograf, 2014), 416–66.
9   According to the calculations of the Russian historian A. Astashov, during the whole period of the war, the number of deserters could have been close to 1–1.5 million. By the end of 1915, gangs of armed deserters appeared in the Moscow military district and other internal provinces. Mostly they were preoccupied with banditry, pillaging, and murdering of civilian population (Aleksandr B. Astashov, "Dezertirstvo i bor'ba s nim v tsarskoi armii v gody Pervoi mirovoi voiny," *Rossiiskaia istoriia* 4 [2011]: 44–52; Astashov, *Russkii front v 1914— nachale 1917 goda*, 466–95).

censor at the General Staff of the Russian Imperial High Command, such disorder started at the very beginning of the war. He claimed that some low-rank military officials considered pillaging and marauding to be an easy source of wealth. They even took short holidays to go robbing in the occupied or pre-frontline territories. The Russian High Command was greatly concerned about such malicious tendencies among the ranks, but the measures they took to prevent them had no effect, because, as Lemke put it, a criminal mindset rested at the core of the Russian army.[10]

Even high-ranking field commanders tolerated and sometimes encouraged the demoralizing behavior of their soldiers. This can be seen from the Russian invasions into Prussia during the first months of the war. Officially, the terror they caused was a "response" to the supposed or real atrocities that the German army committed during its brief invasion into Russia.[11] Soldiers were allowed to terrorize, deport, and even murder the civilian population. According to the order from August 5, 1914, issued by General Zhilinskii, the commander of the northwestern front, the military was instructed to capture six to ten high-valued civilian hostages and demand ransom from their communities. Similar orders were given by General Samsonov, the commander of the Second Army, who, regardless of his initial prohibition for his soldiers to carry out requisitions from the "brotherly Slavic nations" (for example, from the Prussian Poles), soon allowed requisitions. His successor General Rennenkampf also at first ordered punishing the marauding soldiers, but already in September he and all the high commanders authorized the appropriation of any civilian property in exchange for so-called requisition notes. Locals who attempted to resist the soldiers had to be executed without a trial.[12]

Pillaging in Prussia opened Pandora's box. Russian military terror against the civilian population peaked during the so-called "Great Retreat" of 1915. This time, the victims were subjects of their own empire. To stop the advancement of the Germans, the imperial army was ordered to implement the "scorched earth" policy, which meant that any material property, food supplies, grain, and even entire villages and towns had to be destroyed.[13] Cossack troops were especially noted for their cruel treatment of civilians both in Prussia and during the retreat.

---

10 Mikhail Lemke, *250 dnei v tsarskoi stavke (25 sent. 1915–2 iiulia 1916)* (Petrograd: GIZ, 1920), 268–72.
11 Astashov, *Russkii front v 1914–nachale 1917 goda*, 530–36.
12 Lemke, *250 dnei v tsarskoi stavke*, 269.
13 Gabrielė Petkevičaitė-Bitė, *Karo metų dienoraštis*, vol. 1 (Panevėžys: E. Vaičekausko knygyno leidykla, 2010), passim. Retreating Russian soldiers (interestingly enough of Polish origin) bragged to Petkevičaitė-Bitė that while setting fires to the buildings in the town of Šiauliai,

It is interesting to note that German propaganda skillfully exploited the terror caused by Russians in Prussia, and during most of the German occupation of the Lithuanian lands, the "revenge for Prussia" was used to justify their own atrocities.[14]

Especially painful for the Germans was the Russian raid on Memel (Klaipėda) in March 1915. It was carried out by a newly formed, but already quite demoralized military unit. Later, the Russian High Command admitted that the raid had no strategic value and caused more problems than gains. Drunken Russian soldiers murdered civilians, plundered houses, and took the booty back to their positions. Among the official 200 Russian casualties, many were those who, due to drunkenness, could not find the way back to their positions in Libau (Liepaja) and remained in Memel. It was believed that because of the raid, the Germans deployed a large number of regular troops in the region, who began threatening not only Libau, but also Mitau (Mintauja) and Riga. A report from an investigation of the incident also noted that the Russian soldiers' demoralized behavior had a negative impact on the local Lithuanian and Latvian populations.[15]

Starting from the beginning of 1915, the German army gradually pushed the Russians to the east. The Germans demonstrated greater discipline and organization, although their behavior with the civilian population was not very different. The occupied territories faced immediate cattle and food requisitions, people were forced to dig trenches, transport provisions, and so on. When a Lithuanian priest asked the German officers to explain their cruel behavior, he was told that it was not the regular army but some *Landsturm* unit composed of criminals conscripted from the German prisons doing it.[16]

It seems that criminal behavior of the military against the civilian population was largely due to demoralization and disorder within the ranks. The Russian army especially suffered from a lack of discipline. Its high command was not innocent either, because the use of terror and violence against the civilians were officially sanctioned acts of retaliation. For the Russians, just as for the Germans, the official excuse was taking revenge for the atrocities that the enemy had committed against their civilians. However, it did not hold for the Russians because during the retreat of 1915, they plundered and murdered subjects of their own empire.

---

    they did not allow Jews to escape the burning houses and those who did were backed into the fire (Petkevičaitė-Bitė, *Karo metų dienoraštis*, 163–64).

14    A. Juozapavičius, "Vokiečių okupacija Varniuose," *Karo archyvas* 9 (1938): 186; Kazimieras Pakalniškis, "Rusų-vokiečių karo užrašai," *Karo archyvas* 11 (1939): 136, passim.
15    Lemke, *250 dnei v tsarskoi stavke*, 569–71.
16    Juozapavičius, "Vokiečių okupacija Varniuose," 187–88.

## The Rise of Criminality among the Civilian Population

It is not surprising that in the face of the war and terror from the military, daily life in local communities changed dramatically. Alienation among the people grew. The prevailing chaos released old interpersonal and intercommunal tensions, which started taking new forms. Common people were also affected by newspapers and official propaganda and their intense use of descriptors such as "enemies." While to the Russian authorities the word primarily meant military enemies and anyone who hindered their power or disobeyed orders, on the local level, the definition of an "enemy" acquired a much broader definition. Often the "enemy" carried not only the official but also specific national, religious, and economic connotations. Therefore, the call to search for "German spies" became an excuse for getting back at the long tolerated "others." For example, close to the Prussian border Catholics tended to inform on their long-time Protestant neighbors, claiming that they were German sympathizers. This often resulted in deportations of the accused and in the worst cases—in death penalties. There were incidents when overactive individuals went on "spy-hunts" and brought the so-called "enemies of the state" to the authorities. For the most part, such acts had nothing to do with politics or war, but were driven by personal revenge or gain, because houses of the deported or executed became easy prey for their plundering neighbors.[17]

A similar behavior was noted after the arrival of the Germans. Wealthier or undesirable people were reported as "Russian spies," knowing very well that this carried grave consequences. German soldiers—just as the Russians before them—together with the local looters plundered abandoned houses. According to a witness, some of the local fourteen- and fifteen-year-old Lithuanian boys were especially involved in such "spy-hunts"; they voluntarily passed information about their neighbors to the Russians and Germans alike.[18]

A much greater rise in criminality among civilians was closely related to the Russian army's pillaging in Prussia. News about "abandoned wealth" in nearby territories spread very fast. This information primarily came from those locals who were forced to transport (the so-called wartime *stuika* duty) the booty from Prussia to the nearest railway stations. From there, loaded trains took the stolen goods to Russia. Often, however, they also had to transport things from

---

[17] Andrius M. Martus, *Lietuvoje Europos karės metu* (Worcester: Amerikos lietuvio spauda, 1916), 16–17, 20–21.

[18] Kazimieras Jokantas, "Suv. Kalvarijoje vokiečių okupacijos metu (1914–1918)," *Karo archyvas*, 8 (1938): 133, 135.

plundered houses on this side of the border. In some cases, these were goods from their own neighbors' houses.[19]

It seems that the amount of stolen goods was huge. There were not enough train carriages to bring everything back. Therefore, the Russian military opened improvised marketplaces, where Prussian livestock, clothes, agricultural machinery, furniture, and so on were sold for half-price or less. For example, after the first Russian retreat from Prussia in 1914, such markets appeared in the Kaunas fortress' barracks. The sale was open for everyone and those who were still uncomfortable about buying stolen goods were reminded that plundering and pillaging in Prussia was a justifiable act of retaliation for German brutality.[20]

The existence of such wealth nearby resulted in the rapid growth of looting among civilians. Disregarding prohibitions to enter Prussia, hundreds of Lithuanians headed across the border and collected everything they could find. When all the valuable things were gone, the looters started dismantling lids from fireplaces, taking out window and door locks, tiles, and so on.[21] Catholic priests unsuccessfully tried to convince their parishioners against such immoral behavior, but for many this was an opportunity to compensate for their own losses caused by war and requisitions. For others, however, looting and plundering became a new wartime occupation. The most desperate even reached the front line, where they hoped to discover untouched households. It was claimed that numerous border villages were filled with stolen goods.[22] Interestingly enough, after the German invasion in the beginning of 1915, their army was followed by the Prussian civilians, who, just as their Russian counterparts a few months earlier, came to the occupied territories driven by the same reasons. Usually dressed in military uniforms, they joined their own soldiers in looting, plundering, and pillaging. However, German military authorities were much stricter in eradicating such disorder.[23] On one occasion plunderers were caught and "crucified" by tying them to trees.[24]

It is no wonder that mass pillaging in Prussia gave birth to larger and more organized criminal structures. Networks of looters, contrabandists, and resellers started to appear, covering not only the territory of present-day Lithuania, but also stretching into Prussia and Latvia as well. Even some Catholic priests

---

19 Martus, *Lietuvoje Europos karės metu*, 23.
20 Antanas Vireliūnas, "Atsiminimai iš Didžiojo karo," *Karo archyvas* 1 (1925): 109.
21 Henrikas Baltrušaitis, "Vokiečių okupacija Saudarge," *Karo archyvas* 8 (1938): 188.
22 J. Pikčilingis, "Pergyventos valandos," *Karo archyvas* 3 (1926): 92.
23 S. Narušis, "Didžiojo karo metai Kidulių-Kaimelio apylinkėje," *Karo archyvas* 7 (1936): 308; Baltrušaitis, "Vokiečių okupacija Saudarge," 191.
24 Pranas Žadeikis, *Didžiojo karo užrašai* (Klaipėda: Rytas, 1921), 64.

were corrupted by the easy possibility of enrichment. On one occasion, a priest, together with local petty criminals, formed a network that transported Prussian livestock, furniture, and other things to Lithuania. His relatives' homes in other districts of the country acted as warehouses. Interestingly, under German rule the same priest did not stop his "business" and started smuggling goods from the Ober Ost back to Prussia.[25]

Looting in Prussia was mostly carried out by inhabitants who lived close to the border. Another "source of wealth" was located nearby—large numbers of unguarded homesteads of the displaced, deported, or executed people. At first, the criminals were halted by the presence of state structures (military or police). However, when the Russians left, and the Germans had not arrived yet— criminality flourished. This was especially visible in towns. In Šiauliai, for example, such period of "rule by criminals" lasted for two days on April 17–18, 1915.[26] A similar situation happened in Kaunas. The power vacuum there resulted in a large-scale plundering of closed shops, warehouses, and apartments. An observer noted a peculiar pattern of escalation: first, the alcohol shops were attacked; then, watch and jewelry parlors; after that, shoe and leather shops, and so on. Several hours before the appearance of Germans, many Kaunas' shops were robbed. The most active plunderers were Russian deserters, but townsfolk from all social groups also took the opportunity. Even after the arrival of the German authorities, the plundering did not stop. In fact, some German soldiers also joined in.[27] A similar situation was recorded in other places too.[28]

I will try to explain the progression of the wartime banditry in the Lithuanian lands by briefly discussing four relative phases of the escalation. Their main distinguishing characters were the gangs' level of organization and the violence they used against the civilian population. I argue that even though the fourth phase (which started in mid-1918) did not differ mechanically from the third, its specificity rested in the bandits' widespread adoption of the Bolshevik outlook and phraseology. In turn, part of the German and Lithuanian state authorities as well as the public began perceiving and associating the bandits with the left-wing political current—an association that had significant impact on the postwar sociopolitical landscape.

---

25 Pakalniškis, "Rusų-vokiečių karo užrašai," 119, 144.
26 Martus, *Lietuvoje Europos karės metu*, 33–34.
27 Pikčilingis, "Pergyventos valandos," 98–100.
28 For example, in Panevėžys. See "Vinco Jonuškos dienoraštis (1915–1917)," *Karo archyvas* 7 (1936): 251.

## Phase 1: The Appearance of Fugitive Russian POW Groups (Second Half of 1915 to the Beginning of 1916)

The growth of banditry during the German occupation was a result of several factors. Some contemporaries indicated that among the main causes were the demoralization of society and the oppressive regime of occupying authorities. There is no doubt that requisitions of food, grain, and livestock caused large-scale hunger and poverty, while the requisition of horses—the main instrument in agricultural production—resulted not only in the decrease of arable land but also in growing unemployment. For example, without horses, farmers could not work their land and had to find other ways to survive and provide for their families. All this directly or indirectly complemented the growth of criminality.[29]

A somewhat different interpretation of the emergence of banditry can be found in a document produced by the Lithuanian Council in 1917. The third paragraph of the memorandum to the German authorities on banditry (*Bandenunwesen*) described it as an act carried out mostly by fugitive Russian prisoners of war:

> It began with the Russian captives, who either escaped from the internment camps, or stayed behind their military units. They were joined by German deserters. At first, they only asked for food, but when the German police began hunting them, and here or there [locals] reported [them to the authorities]—they took revenge. Willingly, unwillingly those gangs were joined by the [civilian] fugitives from the forced labor [camps], also all kinds of vagabonds. A 'guerrilla' fight sprung up in villages—a small war with robberies, burnings, and murders. In some places, such gangs consisted of a hundred men, some had commanders and lieutenants. They organized assaults, staged trials, carried out executions. In 1917, banditry spread across the whole of Lithuania. Assaults were carried out even during daytime. The occupying authorities forced inhabitants to report and betray bandits and punished not just the bandits but the locals too. We have presented many cases when policemen or gendarmes

---

29 Stefanija Jablonskienė, "Didžiajam karui siaučiant," *Karo archyvas* 6 (1935): 300. For one of the best analyses on the German economic exploitation of the country see: Marija Urbšienė, "Vokiečių okupacijos ūkis Lietuvoje," *Karo archyvas* 11 (1939): 19–100.

dressed as bandits, provoked peasants, later punishing them for not reporting [to the authorities]. They even offered weapons. If somewhere a gendarme was killed, the whole village was punished.[30]

Both explanations complement each other. Demoralization of society and rise of criminality started at the beginning of the war, but only with the German occupation and appearance of the new group—the fugitive prisoners of war, or as people commonly called them *plienniki* or *plienchiki*[31]—banditry became one of the biggest burdens in wartime Lithuania.

As mentioned earlier, the lack of discipline and order in the Russian Imperial Army resulted in large numbers of deserters and prisoners of war. In the beginning of the war, the German authorities managed to accommodate many of the captives by employing them in different support spheres. They were used as a cheap labor in factories, hospitals, agriculture, forestry, and elsewhere. At first, Russian and other prisoners of war did not try to escape, hoping for a quick end to the war. However, their increasing numbers worsened the situation. Poor living conditions deteriorated even further.[32] Hard work, malnutrition, illnesses, cruel behavior of German soldiers, and other hardships soon revealed that the only outcome for a prisoner of war was a slow and painful death from exhaustion and hunger.[33]

---

30  Petras Klimas, *Iš mano atsiminimų* (Vilnius: Enciklopedijų redakcija, 1990), 170.
31  The name is derived from the Russian words *plien* (captivity) and *plienniki* (captives). *Plienchiki* was a Lithuanianized colloquial form of the word.
32  In the words of a runaway Russian prisoner of war: "The first to be captured—those lived better. They were taken to tend after the ill, or in some other institutions ... We were taken to build a railway. It was not that bad during the day; despite being hungry like a wild animal, one received close to half-a-cup of bean porridge for lunch and half-a-pound of bread, and in the mornings and evenings—a cup of coffee without sugar or anything. At night [the Germans] crammed around thirty men into a small room, which was barely fit for six ... We did not see any sauna. Fleas, the size of a chicken, have beset us ..." (Gabrielė Petkevičaitė-Bitė, *Karo metų dienoraštis* [Panevėžys: E.Vaičekausko knygyno leidykla, 2011], 2:435–36).
33  See, for example, numerous reports from Russian prisoners of war in "Cherezvuchainaia sledstvennaia kommisiia," in *Nashi voenno-plennye v Germanii i Avstro-Vengrii (po dopolnitel'nym svedeniiam)* (Petrograd: Senatskaia tipografiia, 1917). Accounts of Russian medical doctors, former prisoners at the German and Austro-Hungarian internment camps: M. Bazilevich, M. *Polozhenie russkikh plennykh v Germanii i otnoshenie germantsev k naseleniiu zaniatykh imi oblastei Tsarstva Pol'skogo i Litvy* (Petrograd: n.p., 1917). Of course, such situations were not everywhere. In Germany, especially in the camps for the officer staff, the conditions were somewhat better. However, as many reported, prisoner of war labor camps in Prussia, Poland and Ober Ost were the worst, where captured soldiers of all nationalities lived and worked like slaves.

Historian Strazhas indicated that in 1915–1916, the Russian Imperial High Command planned organizing partisan resistance against the German occupation. Special military units were dispatched behind enemy lines where they sabotaged communication lines, attacked patrols, and so on. However, according to Strazhas, from June 1916 until February 1917, these partisan units lost contact with the Russian military and were forced to operate independently. While hiding in forests, they were joined by the fugitive prisoners of war and some civilians.[34] Supposedly, at first locals called these partisan units the "forest brothers" (*miško broliai*), and only after the prisoners of war started dominating the groups, their name changed into plienniki.[35]

From the very beginning of the occupation, the German authorities were aware of the deserters living in forests. On November 1, 1915, local priests were instructed to announce during Sunday services that parishioners had to tell the hiding Russians either to surrender and register at gendarmeries or to report them to the authorities. If the Germans discovered the Russians before they registered, the whole district was to be fined with a large penalty. Moreover, those who hid or helped the soldiers had to be imprisoned or executed.[36] A few months later, the head of Ober Ost, general Hindenburg, increased the penalties for civilians and legalized collective responsibility and punishments.[37] Even very fragmented statistics on death penalties carried out in the Mažeikiai military prison show the methodical and uncompromising way that the German administration approached eradicating the threat. Together with the Russians, many of those who helped them were also executed. It is interesting to note that most of the civilians punished by death were reported by people from their own communities.[38] One of the attending priests at the Panevėžys town prison noted that most of the prisoners of war he encountered were of the Orthodox faith. In the

---

34 Strazhas, *Deutsche Ostpolitik im Ersten Weltkrieg*, 13–24.
35 Ibid., 24. The name "forest brothers," however, is absent from all the memoirs used in current investigation. Even the wartime diaries mention only plienniki, which was the common term used for all the Russian soldiers living in the forests.
36 Žadeikis, *Didžiojo karo užrašai*, 86; Antanas Gintneris, ed., *Lietuva caro ir kaizerio naguose. Atsiminimai iš I Pasaulinio karo laikų, 1914–1918 m.* (Chicago: Spausdino ViVi Printing,1970), 346.
37 Ibid., 57. Paliepimas and Verordnung "Rusų kareivijos asmenims, kurie nekareiviškuose rūbuose užsilaiko Vokiečių užimtuose kraštuose apie priedermę maldavimosi ir gi apie pranešimo priedermę krašto gyventojų ir tųjų apsiėjimą su Rusų kareivijos asmenimis," *Paliepimų laiškas vokiečių valdžios Lietuvoje*, no. 2 (1916): 9–10.
38 Stasys Ličkūnas, "1915–1918 m. vokiečių okupacijos karo teismas Mažeikiuose," *Karo archyvas* 7 (1936): 220–25.

absence of an Orthodox priest, he took their confessions; some even converted to Catholicism before execution.[39]

It is hard to assert definitively, but as a distinctive and noticeable group, the fugitive plienniki appeared sometime during the second half of 1915. Before the stabilization of the frontline in 1916, some of the prisoners of war tried reaching and crossing the frontline.[40] However, many more decided to stay in forests, perhaps, expecting the return of the Russian army. Local population helped them, because even though being "Russians" (for example, strangers from ethnic and confessional points of view), they were still considered "ours." At first, the fugitives acted with caution: hiding during daytime and only at night visiting nearby villages and farmsteads, begging for food or offering to buy it. In some places, locals even established a special warning system: a red cloth on the fence meant the presence of the Germans, white—the absence of danger. Moreover, some of the plienniki even managed to get work for food and shelter. They disguised themselves as locals by learning a few phrases in Lithuanian, wearing Catholic attributes, and successfully avoiding capture.[41] Since this was a huge risk for everyone, it can be presumed that such success stories were very few. Most, however, remained living in forests.

To some extent, topographical and geographical situations played an important part in the relations between the locals and the prisoners of war. For example, in the north, close to the border with Kurland (present-day Latvia), many Lithuanian villages were surrounded by swamps and dense forests. German patrols visited there rarely. For quite some time, a fragile equilibrium of cohabitation between the locals, the plienniki and even the Germans was established.

In 1916 in a village close to the river Nemunėlis (Latvian: Mēmele), local peasants became involved in the illegal production of alcohol. The Russians and the Germans (separately, of course) were frequent consumers of the product. Together with the farmers, plienniki worked the land and produced alcohol. Villagers also assisted the travelling fugitives in crossing the river into Kurland. Only after an accidental fire caused by the Russians did someone report them to the authorities. Even though the assistance from locals continued, it was done with greater caution. However, when the Germans deployed regular troops in towns and villages and began hunting the plienniki, this cohabitation came to

---

39 Juozas Stakauskas, *Trys lietuvių tautos pagrindai. Iš atsiminimų* (Vilnius: Lietuvos istorijos instituto leidykla, 2014), 218–19.
40 Priest K. Pakalniškis personally encountered such prisoners of war in September 1915. He was also told by his parishioners, that there were many more of them travelling across the Žemaitija region (Pakalniškis, "Rusų-vokiečių karo užrašai," 164).
41 Stakauskas, *Trys lietuvių tautos pagrindai*, 217–18.

an end. Armed conflicts between the Russians and the Germans, and the rise of violence against the civilian population caused people to fear both sides.[42]

German authorities also acknowledged that there was a specific geographical spread of the plienniki gangs in the Ober Ost. According to some, the most affected regions were the Panevėžys and Ukmergė districts.[43] This is hard to verify because no information remains about the territorial spread and numbers of the fugitive prisoners of war. Judging from other memoirs, they were living all around the Ober Ost.

## Phase 2: The Organization of Armed Gangs and the Beginning of Robberies (1916–1917)

The first relatively calm period of relations between the civilian population and plienniki ended in the spring of 1916. From this time on, reports about the armed prisoners of war assaulting gendarme and police units increased, although German authorities did not differentiate between the assailants: deserters, fugitive prisoners, Russian military partisans (if any), local criminals and others—all were considered outlaws. However, the insufficient network of gendarmes—on average, every 173 square kilometers populated by 4,173 inhabitants were covered only by one patrolling gendarme—could not contain the growing threat. According to the official statistics, until January 31, 1917, the Germans captured four thousand fifty former Russian soldiers and their supporters.[44]

In parallel to attacking the Germans, plienniki started robbing local inhabitants too.[45] It can be assumed that from this time on, banditry reached a qualitatively new—armed and organized—phase. The plienniki gangs were also joined by locals, especially the youth. For the latter, banditry gradually became not just means for survival, but one of the sources of income and, as the Lithuanian Council complained, a profitable business. Despite that during 1916–1917 additional gendarmerie units were deployed in every major town and strategic locations, this solution did not have a greater positive effect.

---

42 Juozas Audickas, "Didžiojo karo atsiminimai," *Karo archyvas* 9 (1938): 204.
43 Gabrielė Petkevičaitė-Bitė, *Karo metų dienoraštis* (Panevėžys: E. Vaičekausko knygyno leidykla, 2008), 3:156.
44 *Das Land Ober Ost. Deutsche Arbeit in den Verwaltungsgebieten Kurland, Litauen und Bialystok-Grodno* (Stuttgart und Berlin, n.p., 1917), 149–50.
45 The first records of such robberies in Panevėžys district were from January 1916 (Petkevičaitė-Bitė, *Karo metų dienoraštis*, 2:259).

It must be noted that not all gendarmes regarded plienniki as a threat. There were cases when local authorities demonstrated greater leniency towards the captured Russians than did the locals. For example, a Lithuanian village elder, who captured several Russian prisoners of war, was punished by a gendarme for his actions and the Russians were released. However, the elder reported the gendarme to his commanding officer, which resulted in his deployment to the front.[46] Generally, however, the provincial gendarmes were much more afraid of the fugitive prisoners of war than receiving punishment from their superiors: sometimes the captured plienniki were released or allowed to escape out of a fear of revenge from their comrades.[47]

The ineffective combat with the rapidly growing banditry suffered even a greater setback with the beginning of the forced labor campaign. Local civilians were forcefully taken to build roads, railroads, cut forests, work land, and so on in the Ober Ost and Germany. Conditions in the labor camps were almost the same as in the internment camps, therefore, many chose to hide or run away from the new form of serfdom or even slavery. Unable to return home, they hid in forests and in order to survive some joined the plienniki gangs.[48] Later, after the war, there were attempts to present those people as the first Lithuanian fighters against the German occupation.[49] This is true only in part. Indeed, some consciously resisted the Germans, but there were also those who joined or even formed bandit gangs themselves. Unfortunately, such information is very scarce and does not allow making even general conclusions about the involvement of locals in banditry during this stage. To some extent, the growing problem can be seen in the German administration's attempts to discourage people from becoming bandits. One of the main lines of communication between the authorities and the local population—the Catholic clergy—were ordered to announce the names of the captured and/or killed bandits.[50] Supposedly, this should have had a preventive effect, especially, when hearing the names of familiar persons.

In parallel, the collective responsibility of civilians for the captured bandits in the vicinity of their villages or the failure to report them was also widely used. This, in turn, produced more negative than positive effects for the containment of criminality. It also increased the alienation and degradation of community

---

46 Petkevičaitė-Bitė, 299–300.
47 Ibid., 420–21.
48 Urbšienė, "Vokiečių okupacijos ūkis Lietuvoje," 35–60.
49 Antanas Urbelis, "Vokiečių okupacijos laikai," *Karo archyvas* 3 (1926): 126–27.
50 Kazimieras Pakalniškis, "Rusų-vokiečių karo užrašai," *Karo archyvas* 12 (1940): 110–11.

bonds. The fear of one's neighbor became paranoia because no one could be sure what grudges the neighbor had or whom he or she talked with. According to a witness, "people got accustomed to hiding everything, not only from the Germans, but also from those closest to them, and wanting to deflect the occupants' attention from themselves, or bearing grudges, or, out of revenge, informing on their neighbors, acquaintances, and even relatives. They reported who and where hid goods."[51] Moreover, the presence of two opposing forces—the German military and the bandits—gave an opportunity to manipulate them for gain. For example, traders could report their competitors either to the Germans or plienniki. Usually, the former were told that the accused helped the fugitive Russians, while the latter were told that they were German informants. Still, asking for the plienniki to help was more dangerous, because if the assailant survived, he or she could have informed the Germans about who collaborated with the bandits.[52]

## Phase 3: Armed Robberies with Torture, Killings, and Burnings (1917–1919)

The transformation of banditry in the third phase—armed robberies with murdering of witnesses and destruction of crime scenes—started to intensify at the end of 1916 and beginning of 1917.[53] From this time onwards, after committing a crime, the bandits often killed everyone and the whole crime scene (a house, a farm, or even a village) was usually torched. The Lithuanian writer and politician Gabrielė Petkevičaitė-Bitė, who throughout the war lived in her manor in the Panevėžys district, recorded:

> "For two years people sheltered, fed, and took care of those fugitives as the greatest sufferers, every time showing the kindness of their hearts. To tell the truth, even the Germans not just once took pity on these unlucky ones; but all that came to an end. They [the Russians] decided to lurk around with guns. Here, on this side of the front, a civil war started. Those who refuse to give the armed Russians food or reports them to the Germans—get

---

51  Jablonskienė, "Didžiajam karui siaučiant," 299.
52  Petkevičaitė-Bitė, *Karo metų dienoraštis*, 2:391–92.
53  Ibid., 3:35.

their revenge. How they discover who informs on them—that is their secret, but I am convinced that there are those among the Germans who collaborate with them."[54]

From June 1917, she decided to stop calling the Russians as prisoners of war, only the bandits.[55]

There are many recorded cases, when the plienniki gangs murdered people who worked for or were loyal to the German regime, like, for example: foresters, millers, village elders, administrators of state manors, and assistants to the police.[56] The extermination of the collaborators went hand in hand with the killings of innocent parties, like foresters or millers who were just doing their job. Of course, there were those (especially among the youth), who for money or other benefits, voluntarily served the new regime.[57]

The extent of involvement of locals with the plienniki becomes somewhat clearer thanks to the short notices about their apprehension. For example, in 1918, in Joniškėlis district (near the town Panevėžys), gendarmes arrested a fugitive prisoner of war, a former junior officer of the Russian imperial army Ivan Morozov, who was a leader of a local bandit gang. The interrogation revealed that he collaborated with close to forty locals, who even though not being part of the gang, acted as its informants. In his hideout, the gendarmes discovered not only large sums of different currency, jewelry, and other stolen items, but also lists of robbed and murdered people, as well as lists of those who had to be robbed and murdered in the future.[58]

It is quite clear that by 1918, banditry became a profitable "business." The fear and terror of plienniki was so great that even a single individual could exploit it for his own benefit, like, for example, a young village worker who, masquerading as a Russian soldier, assaulted and robbed travelers. He claimed that he was a member of the supposed plienniki group from the nearby forest.[59] In another place, the apprehended bandit was the son of a farmer, who robbed his neighbors and kept stolen goods at home.[60] Moreover, in spring 1917 in the Panevėžys district, people started noticing a new sort of bandits. They were described as

---

54   Ibid., 52.
55   Ibid., 66.
56   "Vinco Jonuškos dienoraštis (1915–1917)," 295–96.
57   Petkevičaitė-Bitė, *Karo metų dienoraštis*, 3:21–22.
58   Petraitis, "Krukiai (Joniškėlio apskr.)," *Tėvynės sargas*, September 28, 1918, 14.
59   Kaukys, "Gegužynas (Kaišiadorių aps.)," *Lietuvos aidas*, October 18, 1917, 4.
60   Erškėčių vainikas, "Viekšniai," *Darbo balsas*, December 20, 1918, 4.

well-fed, dressed, and armed young Lithuanian men. It was presumed that they were the town youth, who for one or another reason became criminals.[61]

The uncontrollable malady reached its peak during the last year of the war. Masked and armed peasants in wagons raided neighboring villages, as it happened in the Liškiava district.[62] They often even contracted plienniki to murder a rival, a collaborator, or a wealthier person.[63] Banditry also crossed administrative borders—in northern Lithuania, local inhabitants were frequently visited by Latvian criminals.[64]

## Phase 4: Bandits Turn "Bolsheviks" (Spring of 1918–1919)

In spring and summer 1918, an unexpected qualitative shift occurred—a political dimension got introduced. After the Bolshevik coup of October 1917, some of the Russian prisoners of war started calling themselves Bolsheviks, thus disguising their criminal activities as a class struggle. The signing of the Treaty of Brest-Litovsk on March 3, 1918 might have also played an important role for the change of self-identification. It is quite possible that some of them conformed to the Bolshevik ideals; however, when in the beginning of 1919 the Red Army invaded the country and invited some of the "Bolshevik" gangs to join them, very few took the offer.[65] It is not surprising that soldiers of the proper Red Army were quite suspicious about the "ideological sincerity" of their local comrades, as, for example, in the case of the so-called "Samogitian Regiment," which operated as part of the invading Red Army in 1919. In the words of the Russian Bolsheviks, this regiment largely consisted of clearly criminal elements, who for their violence and crimes against the civilian population had to be shot.[66]

This qualitative turn played an important role not only in the evolution of banditry, but even more so in the ideological polarization of Lithuanian society. In the memoirs and periodical press of the time, one can find many examples when Lithuanian right-wing politicians and conservative intelligentsia (especially the provincial Catholic clergy) used the "Bolshevik equals bandit" formula to strike even more fear into the uneducated, terrified, and hungry local population.

---

61   Petkevičaitė-Bitė, *Karo metų dienoraštis*, 3:32–33.
62   Garsas, "Lyškeva (Alytaus apskr.)," *Tėvynės sargas*, October 16, 1918, 10.
63   Gintneris, *Lietuva caro ir kaizerio naguose*, 348.
64   Šingalis, "Naujoji Žagarė," *Lietuvos aidas*, February 24, 1918, 3.
65   Kaimietis, "Lietuvos bolševikai dirba," *Tėvynės sargas*, December 19, 1918, 6.
66   LSB, "Iš Šiaulių padangės," *Lietuva*, March 20, 1919; Petkevičaitė-Bitė, *Karo metų dienoraštis*, 3:364.

They explained that this socio-political rift appeared as a consequence of the brutality of the occupying regime, requisitions, terror, and murders of the civilian population, which led some Lithuanians to support the Bolsheviks.[67] This was only partially true, but the main reason for making the analogy between the bandits and the Bolsheviks, or virtually anyone with the leftist worldviews, was to discourage voters against the support of the Lithuanian left-wing parties. This became especially apparent during the elections to the Constituent Assembly, which took place in 1920.[68]

The newly acquired "ideological" colors were quite beneficial for the bandits-turned-Bolshevik gangs too. For instance, in mid-1918 in northern Lithuania, a large armed group operated, which consisted of plienniki and fugitives from the neighboring German prisons. The gang identified themselves as "Bolsheviks who returned from Russia." This might have been true, although it is doubtful that apart from primitive banditry they were involved in any kind of ideological propaganda.[69]

In another place, people were terrorized by a gang of locals, whom the gendarmes located and eliminated in June 1918.[70] However, later in a brief note to one of the Lithuanian newspapers, a local priest stated as a matter of fact that among the bandit leader's possessions, the gendarmes supposedly discovered leftist periodicals, which, as the priest implied, indicated the gang's political standing.[71] It is hard to say whether this was true, but with the beginning of political struggle between the Lithuanian left- and right-wing parties, this small episode might have been important for setting up the minds of the voters. In parallel to that, almost every refugee who returned from Russia at that time was strongly suspected of being a Bolshevik spy.[72]

The image of a "terrible Bolshevik" was a convenient masquerade for local criminals too. In May 1918 in northern Lithuania, near the town Skaudvilė, twenty to thirty armed "Bolsheviks" surrounded and robbed a manor house, which was temporarily administered by a Jewish family. Despite being severely

---

67 Žadeikis, *Didžiojo karo užrašai*, 53.
68 Vladas Sirutavičius, "Lithuanian administration and the participation of Jews in the elections to the Constituent Seimas," in *A Pragmatic Alliance: Jewish-Lithuanian political cooperation at the beginning of the 20th century*, ed. Vladas Sirutavičius and Darius Staliūnas (Budapest: Central European University Press, 2011), 181–205; Vytautas Petronis, "Neperkirstas Gordijo mazgas: valstybinės prievartos prieš visuomenę Lietuvoje genezė (1918–1921)," *Lietuvos Istorijos Metraštis*, no. 1 (2015): 69–95.
69 Adomas iš Rojaus. "Ukrinai (Sedos aps.)," *Darbo balsas*, June 6, 1918, 10.
70 Siūnas, "Plungė," *Tėvynės sargas*, July 16, 1918, 12.
71 Kun. Pūkys, "Plungė," *Tėvynės sargas*, October 5, 1918, 10.
72 Juozas Dagilis, "Kaip gintis plėšikams apipuolus," *Darbo balsas*, September 27, 1918, 2.

beaten and threatened with execution, the family was left alive. Later the victims told the gendarmes that even with facemasks and acting as Bolshevik "plienniki," the bandits spoke poor Russian and between themselves communicated in Lithuanian. Also, they knew members of the family by name, which indicated that the perpetrators were local. Keeping up appearances, the "Bolsheviks" also warned the victims that such "redistribution of wealth" awaited other local manors too.[73]

The Lithuanian State Council—the highest authority of the newly established state—was aware of the problem that the politicization of criminality introduced. In July 1918, one of the leaders of the Lithuanian left Steponas Kairys complained that "the name of the Bolsheviks is given to many things, even bandits. Indulged by the Germans, all those wild forces consciously work together. I know many cases when those whom priests named as 'Bolsheviks,' were detained; they [refugees returning from Russia] were treated differently in quarantine."[74] Left-wing politicians desperately tried to persuade their counterparts not to lump bandits and Bolsheviks together with people who had leftist worldviews, but, judging from reports from the provinces, this plea was not successful.[75] Also, it has to be noted here that in mid-1918 the Lithuanian left did not regard Bolshevism negatively; this changed with the invasion of the Red Army into Lithuania in late 1918.

Bolshevik or not, banditry remained a grave problem for the newly established state. In the note addressed to the German Military Governor from August 27, 1918, the Lithuanian State Council urged him to take immediate steps to fight the malady. First, it asked to allow civilians to arm and defend themselves. Secondly, banditry could not have been stopped without eradicating its roots: the large numbers of the fugitive Russian prisoners of war; the still existing system of forced civilian labor; the continuing requisitions and impoverishment of population, and the general demoralization of society by the oppressive system of governance. To resolve this, the Council suggested to open the frontline with Russia and announce that during a one-month period every Russian prisoner of war in hiding would be allowed to safely return to Russia. Those who refused to comply were to be considered criminals. Moreover, the Council also demanded to abolish all forced labor and allow civilians to return home; to declare amnesty for those who assisted the prisoners of war, hid weapons or were arrested for

---

73  Kaributas, "Stulgiai (Skaudvilės apskr.)," *Tėvynės sargas*, May 8, 1918, 9.
74  After crossing the border, the returning refugees had to undergo several weeks of quarantine due to the bad epidemic situation in Russia.
75  "Protokolas nr. 78," in *Lietuvos valstybės tarybos protokolai*, 262–63.

political reasons; to allow local population to organize its own militia; and so on.[76] However, this Council's note had no consequences.

In the meantime, the deteriorating German military and police supervision allowed the criminals to expand by constructing large underground networks. For example, close to the border with Prussia, the German police managed to track down a large ring of horse thieves. They were organized in a set of so-called "agencies," which operated on a particular territory and transported stolen animals across the border to Prussia. Perhaps unsurprisingly, most of the apprehended were well-to-do medium scale farmers, who were involved in stealing only for profit.[77] As it was mentioned earlier, such networks of looters appeared at the beginning of war, but, presumably, only cooperation with bandits allowed them to establish a stronger organization, where bandits acted as "security" for the thieves and terrorized or killed anyone who informed on them to authorities.[78]

In 1918, some gangs started taking part in the contract killing business. In spring 1918 near Kaunas, an infamous bandit gang operated led by a Russian prisoner of war nicknamed Grishka (Grigorii Petrov). On March 23, they assaulted farmer Klebinski's household. The farmer was taken to his house and shot in the head in front of his family. The bandits' intention was to murder everyone, but the farmer's daughter managed to convince the bandits to leave the rest of the family alive. Before leaving the place, the bandits revealed that the assault was not a personal matter; rather, they were contracted to kill everyone by the farmer's neighbor. Moreover, Grishka's lack of fear of being apprehended can be seen in a note he left for the police in which he not only revealed details of the hit but also the intentions of the gang to move to the neighboring district.[79] Obviously, it is hard to say whether it was just a brag or a cunning plan to throw the police from their scent, but it's no secret that since 1918, many bandit gangs moved almost freely around the country.

The appearance of the Lithuanian national press in 1918 became one of the main sources to provide the public with information about the grave situation in the country, especially pointing to the business side of criminal associations.

---

76 "Protokolas nr. 1027," and "Lietuvos Valstybės Tarybos prezidiumo 'Raštas dėl banditizmo,'" in *Lietuvos valstybės tarybos protokolai*, 305–07.
77 Vrgs., "Nemakščiai, Skaud. apskr.," *Darbo balsas*, September 12, 1918, 13.
78 "Kodiškiai (Marijampolės aps., arti Zapyškio)," *Lietuvos aidas*, December 13, 1917, 3.
79 A. Žansparnis, "Nuo Panevėžninko padangės (Kauno aps)," *Darbo balsas*, April 4, 1918.

POWs and all kinds of old "natural born" thieves and vagabonds—all work in the same organization, but they are still not the worst leaders and managers of this terrible business. Their leaders are our new petty individuals—degenerates, the products of the war. They are the "completely innocent" people, our respected brethren; and they live right here, among us. The only reason for their wicked craft is the unstoppable greed and desire to abuse. . . The quieter and wealthier ones provide alcohol for the poor; and they drink, play cards and learn how to steal and rob.[80]

There were cases when local bandit gangs were led and managed by people who could hardly be suspected of any criminal activities. For example, near the town Kavarskas, a father and his sons formed a gang. Elsewhere, a group of bandits were led by an old man who was primarily known as a funeral mourner.[81]

The beginning of 1919 was the high time for bandits. The remainder of the German military was forced to engage and hold back the advancing Red Army, almost completely abandoning the policing of the country. In the absence of Lithuanian state power structures, the containment of banditry became largely the matter of people themselves, although it was very difficult, especially in places where the German military and criminals collaborated. For example, in 1919 in the vicinities of the town Veliuona, a well-organized and armed bandit gang struck an accord with the locally stationed German military unit. In exchange for not attacking the Germans, the military not only refused to persecute the criminals but also sold them weapons, ammunition, and explosives. A small detachment of poorly armed local militia could not do anything, while the local population was passive, fearing revenge.[82]

Arguably, during the first half of 1919, the Bolshevik disguise gradually lost its appeal. Instead, reports about robberies masked as "official" searches for illegal items started to appear. Usually, such bandits wore corresponding military uniforms (German, Russian, or Lithuanian), sometimes identifying themselves as Lithuanian militia and presenting appropriate insignias and identification documents. They usually followed the same scheme: first, a "search" for weapons and other illegal items was conducted and then transformed into an open robbery, torture, and murder. Even if the victims did not have money or valuables, they

---

80  Vargovaikis, "Vagys, plėšikai ir kova su jais," *Darbo balsas*, August 30, 1918, 2–3.
81  Gintneris, *Lietuva caro ir kaizerio naguose*, 349.
82  A., "Veliuona," *Lietuva*, June 19, 1919, 3.

were still mutilated or killed so that no one could report or identify the perpetrators. It was presumed that some of those criminals might have belonged to one or another legal military or police organization: either they joined them after the official end of the war, or it was the new recruits who turned onto the path of banditry.[83]

## The Dissolution of Wartime Criminality

By the end of 1919, most foreign military units and individuals—chief among whom were the Germans and the White Russians—had left Lithuania. Gradual strengthening of the local police force began the containment process of criminality, but stabilization was not easy, especially due to the bad economic situation in the country.

The Lithuanian State Council's idea to arm the population and defend themselves, which was proposed to the German authorities at the end of the war, materialized in September 1919.[84] In May, the new law of state militia was passed.[85] This institution had to be developed under the strict supervision of state authorities; therefore, all previously established local self-defense units had to be disbanded. However, in some places, the disarmament of the self-defense units began even prior to the official creation of a state militia, which negatively impacted the process of containing criminality. For example, in the town Pasvalys, the abolishment of armed self-defense resulted in the almost immediate reappearance of gangs in neighboring forests. A small number of the new militiamen could not resist the criminals.[86] The situation was resolved with the help of the army but not without additional victims. It is interesting to note that a few years later, it was reported that the former wartime bandits still lived prosperously and unpunished in the town vicinity.[87]

Lithuania's war with Poland, which started in 1919, also contributed to the prolongation of banditry. Moreover, the Red Army's successful advance through Lithuania into Poland the same year worsened the situation. As a consequence of the new military actions, a new kind of plienniki appeared in the Lithuanian forests. This time they mostly consisted of fugitive Polish prisoners of war and

---

83   See, for example: "Kazlų Rūda," *Lietuva*, March 14, 1919, 2; "Kelmė," *Lietuva*, May 15, 1919, 3.
84   "Leidimo ginklams laikyti davimo taisyklės," *Vyriausybės žinios*, October 1, 1919, 2–3.
85   "Milicijos įstatymas," *Vyriausybės žinios*, May 20, 1919, 1.
86   Mažilius, "Kelionės įspūdžiai," *Lietuva*, March 30, 1920, 2–3.
87   Žaliosios Nykštukas, "Žalioji Giria," *Lietuvos žinios*, July 27, 1922.

deserters who escaped either from the Bolshevik or Lithuanian internment camps. Just as the Russians before them, the Polish soldiers robbed surrounding farms and villages.[88] One of their differences with the World War I plienniki was that the Poles mostly stayed in and operated from the so-called neutral zone—a stretch of land that separated Lithuania from the Polish-controlled Vilnius region.

In the summer of 1920, numerous incidents were reported of plienniki dressed in the Red Army's uniforms who came from the Bolshevik occupied territories and conducted "requisitions" from the local population.[89] Now dressed in the Lithuanian military uniforms, they went on robbing the civilian population in the Bolshevik-controlled Vilnius region.[90] Later, after Polish annexation of the Vilnius in October 1920, the Lithuanian authorities accused Poland of the acts of banditry, although it is difficult to distinguish whether it was a state-supported banditry or it was criminal gangs of locals. Most likely, it was both. The Lithuanian government was not without blame itself—according to some, there were special state-run secret agents who agitated and organized criminals at the demarcation line and directed them to terrorize and murder wealthier farmers and landlords in the Polish-controlled Vilnius region.[91] Therefore, it can be supposed that during the first postwar years, some wartime bandits might have been used (or even unofficially employed) by the new governments to continue their work of terrorizing to prolong the unstable situation on both sides of the demarcation line. Arguably, in the mid-1920s, such a state of affairs was useful for all the conflicting parties. The criminals benefitted from all of them.

Lithuania introduced martial law on July 23, 1920.[92] To some extent this helped to combat banditry thanks to the involvement of the military as a policing force. Occasionally, it informed the society about the successful operations in eliminating banditry. However, it seems that former World War I bandits, thieves, and other criminals who had ceased their activities after the war remained unpunished. Some hid under false passports or changed names, others might have "redeemed" their crimes by joining military or paramilitary forces, emigrating, or simply returning home.

---

88  Kapso sūnus, "Kazlų Rūda," *Lietuvos ūkininkas*, October 28–November 2, 1922, 10.
89  "Rusų okupuotoj Lietuvoj", *Lietuva*, August 27, 1920, 3.
90  M., "Iš Vilniaus," *Lietuva*, August 4, 1920, 2–3.
91  Antanas Pauliukas, *Dienynas 1918–1941 m. I knyga. 1918 m. rugsėjo 1-oji–1926 m. birželio 30-oji* (Vilnius: Lietuvos istorijos instituto leidykla, 2017), 366.
92  "Nr. 430. Įstatymas karo stoviui įvesti," *Vyriausybės žinios*, July 24, 1920, 1.

## Conclusion

The emergence of the specific criminality in Lithuania (looting, pillaging, marauding, and so on) can be traced back to the very beginning of World War I and the demoralizing environment that was created by Russian troops plundering in Prussia. This malicious example was very quickly picked up by locals, who due to heavy material losses from military actions and especially from requisitions saw an opportunity (albeit illegal) to replenish their lost property. Naturally, the relative ease of the whole endeavor strengthened the basic instinct of greed in some. After the Russian army's retreat from Prussia, the looters turned to the abandoned households of retreated, deported, or executed fellow citizens.

The German occupation introduced a highly oppressive regime. Its approach was much more methodical and uncompromising. It stopped or significantly reduced certain forms of illegal activities like looting and pillaging. However, a new group of criminals emerged—the bandits, the main representatives of whom were fugitive Russian prisoners of war commonly described by Lithuanians as plienniki. Living in forests, outlawed by the German authorities, and not wishing to die from hunger and exhaustion in the internment camps, they chose to resist the gendarmes and resorted to banditry, which was their only means of survival. However, this meant that they had to force local inhabitants into giving them food and sustenance. Moreover, heavy requisitions, penalties, forced labor, and other kinds of oppression that the German military authorities imposed on the civilian population resulted in a rapid growth in banditry among civilians. Separately or together with the Russian prisoners of war, local criminals terrorized, robbed, and murdered people, more often than not out of greed.

I attempted to structure the evolution of wartime banditry into four relative and interconnected phases. During the first that began in the second half of 1915 and continued until the beginning of 1916, the numbers of Russian deserters and fugitive prisoners of war in the Lithuanian forests grew. Before the stabilization of the Russian-German front, they must have waited for the return of the imperial army and looked for peaceful cohabitation with the locals. Soon, however, this came to an end, mostly thanks to the German administration which introduced heavy penalties and collective responsibility for not reporting and helping the fugitives.

The second phase started in the beginning of 1916 and continued until 1917, during which the Russians armed themselves and started resisting the Germans. In parallel to that, they resorted to armed robberies of civilians, although, mostly refraining from excessive killings. This approach changed in spring 1917 (the third phase), when cases of robberies with murders increased significantly. This trend during the last year of the war, when the bandits started killing their witnesses, followed by torching their crime scenes.

Overlapping with the third phase, the fourth phase shows an important qualitative change, which, arguably, had a deeper impact on society and the political landscape of the country. Chronologically, it started in spring 1918, when numerous bandit gangs began calling themselves Bolsheviks. Presumably, after the Bolshevik coup of October 1917, some of the prisoners of war associated themselves with the new political trend. The signing of the Treaty of Brest-Litovsk on March 3, 1918 might have also played an important role for their change of self-identification. Very soon, both Russian and local criminals adopted the label and used the ideologically loaded phraseology while committing the crimes. Arguably, such masking started to wane with the invasion of the Red Army in late 1918 and the beginning of 1919, though identification of criminals with Bolsheviks continued even longer. With the strengthening of the Lithuanian state structures and after the introduction of martial law in mid-1920s, the new authorities were able to contain the criminal situation in the country.

The toll that wartime criminality and especially banditry took on society is difficult to measure, but it is quite clear that for five years, hundreds and thousands of families were terrorized, robbed, starved, or killed. There is no doubt that alongside heavy oppression from the German occupation, the terrible criminal situation was a major cause for the post-traumatic condition of Lithuanian society after the war. The absence of punishment for the wartime bandits indicates that officially it was chosen to forget the dark times. Perhaps justice was brought quietly on the local level because many of the perpetrators were people from the same communities.

# Bibliography

Astashov, Aleksandr B. "Dezertirstvo i bor'ba s nim v tsarskoi armii v gody Pervoi mirovoi voiny." *Rossiiskaia istoriia* 4 (2011): 44–52.

———. *Russkii front v 1914–nachale 1917 goda. Voennyi opyt i sovremennost'*. Moscow: Novyi khronograf, 2014.

Audickas, Juozas. "Didžiojo karo atsiminimai." *Karo archyvas* 9 (1938): 198–211.

Baltrušaitis, Henrikas. "Vokiečių okupacija Saudarge." *Karo archyvas* 8 (1938): 187–97.

Bazilevich, M. *Polozhenie russkikh plennykh v Germanii i otnoshenie germantsev k naseleniiu zaniatykh imi oblastei Tsarstva Pol'skogo i Litvy*. Petrograd: n.p., 1917.

Cherezvuchainaia sledstvennaia kommisiia. *Nashi voenno-plennye v Germanii i Avstro-Vengrii (po dopolnitel'nym svedeniiam)*. Petrograd: Senatskaia tipografiia, 1917.

Colliander, Börje. *Die Beziehungen zwischen Litauen und Deutschland während der Okkupation 1915–1918*. Åbo/Turku: Aktiebolag, 1935.

*Das Land Ober Ost. Deutsche Arbeit in der Verwaltungsgebieten Kurland, Litauen und Bialystok-Grodno*. Berlin: Verlag der Presseabteilung Ober Ost, 1917.

Gerwarth, Robert. *The Vanquished. Why the First World War Failed to End, 1917–1923*. London: Penguin Books, 2017.

Gintneris, Antanas, ed. *Lietuva caro ir kaizerio naguose. Atsiminimai iš I Pasaulinio karo laikų, 1914–1918 m*. Chicago: ViVi Printing, 1970.

Gumz, Jonathan E. "Losing Control: The Norm of Occupation in Eastern Europe during the First World War." In *Legacies of Violence. Eastern Europe's First World War*, edited by Jochen Böhler, Wlodzimierz Borodziej, and Joachim von Puttkamer, 69–87. Munich: Oldenbourg Wissenschaftsverlag, 2014.

Jablonskienė, Stefanija. "Didžiajam karui siaučiant." *Karo archyvas* 6 (1935): 298–300.

Jokantas, Kzaimieras. "Suv. Kalvarijoje vokiečių okupacijos metu (1914–1918)." *Karo archyvas* 8 (1938): 117–86.

Juozapavičius, A. "Vokiečių okupacija Varniuose." *Karo archyvas* 9 (1938): 183–91.

Klare, Kai-Achim. *Imperium ante Portas. Die deutsche Expansion in Mittel– und Osteuropa zwischen Weltpolitik und Lebensraum (1914–1918)*. Wiesbaden: Harrasowitz Verlag, 2020.

Klimas, Petras. *Iš mano atsiminimų*. Vilnius: Lietuvos enciklopedijų redakcija, 1990.

Lemke, Mikhail. *250 dnei v tsarskoi stavke (25 sent. 1915–2 iiulia 1916)*. Petrograd: GIZ, 1920.

Ličkūnas, Stasys. "1915–1918 m. vokiečių okupacijos karo teismas Mažeikiuose." *Karo archyvas* 7 (1936): 220–25.

*Lietuvos valstybės tarybos protokolai, 1917–1918*. Vilnius: Mokslas, 1991.

Liulevicius, Vejas G. *War Land on the Eastern Front: Culture, National Identity and German Occupation in World War I*. Cambridge: Cambridge University Press, 2000.

Martus, Andrius M. *Lietuvoje Europos karės metu*. Worcester, MA: Amerikos lietuvis, 1916.

Narušis S. "Didžiojo karo metai Kidulių-Kaimelio apylinkėje." *Karo archyvas* 7 (1936): 300–19.

Pakalniškis, Kazimieras. "Rusų-vokiečių karo užrašai." *Karo archyvas* 11 (1939): 101–76.

———. "Rusų-vokiečių karo užrašai." *Karo archyvas* 12 (1940): 95–147.

Pauliukas, Antanas. *Dienynas 1918–1941 m. I knyga. 1918 m. rugsėjo 1-oji–1926 m. birželio 30-oji*. Vilnius: Lietuvos istorijos instituto leidykla, 2017.

Petkevičaitė-Bitė, Gabrielė, *Karo metų dienoraštis*. Vol. 1. Panevėžys: E. Vaičekausko knygyno leidykla, 2010.

———. *Karo metų dienoraštis*. Vol. 2. Panevėžys: E. Vaičekausko knygyno leidykla, 2011.

———. *Karo metų dienoraštis*. Vol. 3. Panevėžys: E. Vaičekausko knygyno leidykla, 2008.

Petronis, Vytautas. "Neperkirstas Gordijo mazgas: valstybinės prievartos prieš visuomenę Lietuvoje genezė (1918–1921)." *Lietuvos Istorijos Metraštis* no. 1 (2016): 69–95.

Pikčilingis, J. "Pergyventos valandos." *Karo archyvas* 3 (1926): 90–111.

Safronovas, Vasilijus, Vytautas Jokubauskas, Vygantas Vareikis, and Hektoras Vitkus. *Didysis karas visuomenėje ir kultūroje: Lietuva ir Rytų Prūsija*, Klaipėda: Klaipėdos universiteto leidykla, 2018.

Sirutavičius, Vladas. "Lithuanian administration and the participation of Jews in the elections to the Constituent Seimas." In *A Pragmatic Alliance: Jewish-Lithuanian political cooperation at the beginning of the 20th century*, edited by Vladas Sirutavičius and Darius Staliūnas, 181–205. Budapest: Central European University Press, 2011.

Stakauskas, Juozas. *Trys lietuvių tautos pagrindai. Iš atsiminimų*. Vilnius: Lietuvos istorijos instituto leidykla, 2014.

Strazhas, Abba. *Deutsche Ostpolitik im Ersten Weltkrieg. Der Fall Ober Ost 1915–1917*. Harrassowitz Verlag: Wiesbaden, 1993.

Urbelis, Antanas. "Vokiečių okupacijos laikai." *Karo archyvas* 3 (1926): 112–27.

Urbšienė, Marija. "Vokiečių karo meto spauda ir Lietuva." *Karo archyvas* 7 (1936): 143–219.

———. "Vokiečių okupacijos ūkis Lietuvoje." *Karo archyvas* 11 (1939): 19–100.

"Vinco Jonuškos dienoraštis (1915–1917)." *Karo archyvas* 7 (1936): 226–99.

Vireliūnas, Antanas. "Atsiminimai iš Didžiojo karo." *Karo archyvas* 1 (1925): 107–20.

Westerhoff, Christian. *Zwangsarbeit im Ersten Weltkrieg. Deutsche Arbeitskräftepolitik im besetzten Polen und Litauen 1914–1918*. Padeborn: Ferdinand Schöningh Verlag, 2011.

Zweig, Arnold. *Der Streit um den Sergeanten Grischa*. Potsdam: Kopenhauer Verlag, 1928.

Žadeikis, Pranas. *Didžiojo karo užrašai*. Klaipėda: Lituania, 1921.

CHAPTER 2

# War Violence and Its Representation: A Comparison of Civilian Experiences of the Great War on Both Sides of The Former Russian-German Border

Vasilijus Safronovas, Vygantas Vareikis, and Hektoras Vitkus

Schirwindt, a small parish center on the Russian-German border, which was, in the early twentieth century, known as the easternmost town of the German Reich and the smallest town of the East Prussia province, had a population of around one thousand three hundred people and more than one hundred residential dwellings in the period before World War I. There were just four undamaged dwellings left in Schirwindt after the front line reached it several times in the first years of the war, and the editor of the Königsberg-based newspaper *Hartungsche Zeitung* described it as "a dead town" in 1919: the war refugees still lived in the temporary barracks four years after returning from temporary evacuation.[1]

Vladislavov, which was located just across a stream on the Russian side of the border, had a prewar population of over five thousand six hundred people,

---

1  Ludwig Goldstein, *Der Wiederaufbau Ostpreussens* (Königsberg: Hartungsche Zeitungs- und Verlagsdruckerei, 1919), 52–53.

with nearly half of them being Jews. In 1920, this town was still described as a "destroyed town."[2] Today it is known by the name Kudirkos Naumiestis. In 1914–1915, Vladislavov changed hands several times between the Russians and the Germans. Besides the material damage it sustained, it lost nearly 70 percent of its population, as evidenced by data from 1916.[3] Schirwindt and Vladislavov, located right on the Russian-German border in 1914, are perhaps extreme examples. However, they illustrate that the First World War affected civilians on both sides of the border between the countries at war.

While civilian experiences—material damage, forced displacement, and food shortages brought on by the Great War—can no longer be regarded as a new topic for research, violence perpetrated against civilians is still under-researched. Given that civilians accounted for as many as 40 percent of those killed during World War I,[4] this lack of research in the field can hardly be justified. There have been a number of efforts by historians to discuss the violence committed against civilians as a pan-European experience of the World War I.[5] Nonetheless, giving a generalized view of specific cases is still challenging as there is a great shortage of comparative studies.

This chapter explores the violence experienced by civilians during the First World War from at least two perspectives.[6] Covering the territories of East Prussia (part of the German Reich) and future Lithuania (part of imperial Russia in 1914), for example, the northern section of the former Russian-German border area, it not only seeks to contribute to creating a more comprehensive picture of the forms of violence perpetrated against civilians but also to compare the different acts of violence and its subsequent representation.

The chapter is comprised of three parts. The first part aims to shed light on the current state of research, that is, what we learned from the historical studies

---

2   Ministry of the Interior to the Executive Committee of the Lithuanian American Community, 5 March 1920, col. 377, inv. 7, file 231, p. 15, *Lietuvos centrinis valstybės archyvas* (Lithuanian Central State Archives, hereafter cited as *LCVA*).

3   *Verwaltungsbericht der Militärverwaltung Litauen für die Zeit vom 1. April bis 30. September 1917*, vol. 7 (Kowno: Militärverwaltung Litauen, 1917).

4   Rüdiger Overmans, "Kriegsverluste," in *Enzyklopädie Erster Weltkrieg*, ed. Gerhard Hirschfeld et al. (Paderborn u.a.: Ferdinand Schöningh, 2009), 665.

5   Just one of the examples: Oswald Überegger, "'Verbrannte Erde' und 'baumelnde Gehenkte' Zur europäischen Dimension militärischer Normübertretungen im Ersten Weltkrieg," in *Kriegsgreuel. Die Entgrenzung der Gewalt in kriegerischen Konflikten vom Mittelalter bis ins 20. Jahrhundert*, ed. Sönke Neitzel, Daniel Hohrath (Paderborn u.a.: Ferdinand Schöningh, 2008), 241–78.

6   A large portion of the ideas discussed in this chapter were first published in the Lithuanian language. See Vasilijus Safronovas et al. *Didysis karas visuomenėje ir kultūroje: Lietuva ir Rytų Prūsija* (Klaipėda: Klaipėdos universiteto leidykla, 2018).

published so far on the use of violence against the civilians during the First World War in East Prussia and Lithuania, what forms of violence were identified in those studies, and how the researchers explained the motives behind this violent behavior. The second part covers the process of gathering information on civilian experiences. It will confirm what we already know from previous historical research—that the process of gathering information on the acts of violence was, from the outset, not only driven by the goal of documenting them but also by the hope of being able to use this information for a variety of pragmatic purposes. At the same time, however, it will demonstrate the long-lasting nature and relevance of this goal even two decades after the war. The third part will focus on the representation of violence in the period up to World War II. It is aimed at exploring the depiction of perpetrators of violence against civilians. Our underlying goal is to shed light on the impact that the representation of violence had on the understanding of what actually happened—what remained from the multiple forms of violence after subjecting them to a number of filters of representation before they reached the audience and were translated into public opinion perceptions.

## Forms of Violence: State of Research

Unlike battlefield casualties which included killed, wounded, or incapacitated soldiers, violence against civilians during World War I manifested in more diverse forms. Most of these forms involve the acts that the army invading the enemy's territory perpetrated against civilians. They are often described as atrocities or reprisals, thereby referring to a number of different acts ranging from civilian executions to the destruction of civilian property or looting, and terrorizing civilians. Moreover, a distinction is made between the violence of invasion and the violence of occupation. We also know that the invading army or the occupying military power were not the only parties to perpetrate violence against civilians. If forced displacement is also to be treated as a form of violence against civilians, we can see clear manifestations of violence committed against civilians in 1914–1915 in the eastern part of Europe. Unlike millions of "voluntary" migrants who fled from their homes to escape war hostilities, Jews and Germans in Russia became victims of deportations conducted by the Russian military on the western peripheries of the Romanov Empire. Some of them also experienced acts of terror and looting from other groups of civilians.

From 1914 onwards, the areas on the northern section of the former Russian-German border became the parts of Europe where these multiple forms of violence unfolded. We can learn a lot about this from previous studies discussed below. East Prussia was the hotbed of hostilities and violence for the period of seven months from mid-August 1914 to mid-March 1915. The first invasion by Russian troops—the First Army and the Second Army—to the easternmost province of Prussia took place on August 17, 1914. Within several weeks, the armies advanced almost eighty to one hundred seventy kilometers inland, occupying nearly three quarters of the province's territory. In the first half of September, the Germans pushed Russian forces out of East Prussia. However, a repeated invasion by the Russian Tenth Army and other units took place in November to the border regions lying ten to seventy kilometers inland from the border. It was only in February 1915 that hostilities from East Prussia moved to the Russian territory as a consequence of the Winter Battle of the Masurian Lakes. However, the residents of Memel (Klaipėda), a city in the northern part of East Prussia, witnessed another short invasion by the Russian army on March 17–21, 1915.

In the areas on the Russian side of the border, the first German troops appeared as early as August 1914. However, the German Eighth Army penetrated further inland into Russian territory on the northern section of the border for the first time during the First Battle of the Masurian Lakes in September 1914. It was then that some parts of the Kovno (Kaunas) Province and of Suvalki (Suwałki) Province experienced a short-lived invasion by German troops. In February 1915, the Eighth Army and Tenth Army once again set foot in Suvalki Province and advanced twenty to seventy kilometers inland. However, the main offensive effort in the direction of Libava (Liepaja) and Shavli (Šiauliai) started on the night of April 26 to April 27, 1915 and continued intermittently until late autumn. During the Great Retreat of the Russian army, the German troops seized Shavli on July 21, Mitava (Jelgava) on August 1, Kovno Fortress on August 18, Grodno (Hrodna) on September 2, and Vilna (Vilnius) on September 18. It was only in October that the front line was established along Western Dvina (Daugava) River and the western border of present-day Belarus. The occupied territory remained in German hands for a period of three to four years. Although the occupying troops stationed in Ober Ost began to retreat after the Armistice of Compiègne in late 1918, they were partly replaced by the new German volunteer units that participated in the war against the advancing Red Army in Lithuania until the summer of 1919. Therefore, in the memoirs of many residents, 1919 was still considered a year of German occupation to a certain degree because they also regarded the West Russian Volunteer Army, a formation made of the Freikorps volunteers, Baltic Germans, and the White Russian forces in the Baltic provinces, as Germans. For many, the incursion of this formation into northwestern Lithuania (July–December 1919) was merely a continuation of the "same" German occupation and endless violence.

Published in 1931, *The Russians in East Prussia* compiled by historian Fritz Gause and commissioned by the Chairman (Landeshauptmann) of the Landtag (Diet) of East Prussia, remains the most extensive study shedding light on the actions of the Russian army and the policies of the occupying regime. Relying mostly on official records, recollections, and contemporaries' accounts, Gause described in great detail the requisitions, contributions, lack of discipline within the ranks of the occupying army, and looting that affected different economic sectors and civilians, as well as property destruction and arson, destruction of works of art, and other villainies. Moreover, the book discusses the civilian casualties attributed to the Russian occupying regime (Gause estimated a total of 1,491 civilians were killed in the province)[7] and forced migration of civilians from the Russian-occupied East Prussian border regions further into Russian territory (13,566 deportees).[8]

Later, German historians expressed more moderate views. They pointed out that a considerable amount of information on the behavior of the Russian army in East Prussia was collected for propaganda purposes.[9] Recent studies, however, seek to reassess these events. Russian historian Konstantin Pakhaliuk, drawing both on German and Russian sources, presented a more balanced picture.[10] He discovered data confirming the above mentioned behavioral characteristics of the

---

7   Fritz Gause, *Die Russen in Ostpreußen 1914/15* (Königsberg: Gräfe und Unzer, 1931), 229.
8   Gause, *Die Russen in Ostpreußen*, 246, 359. For more recent studies on this topic see Sergei Nelipovich, "Pereselenie nemtsev iz Vostochnoi Prussii v Rossiiu: 'vol'noplennye,' ili zlokliucheniia vostochnoprusskikh nemtsev v Rossii (1914–1917)," in *Migratsionnye protsessy sredi rossiiskikh nemtsev: istoricheskii aspekt. Materialy mezhdunarodnoi nauchnoi konferentsii, Anapa, 26–30 sentiabria 1997 g.* (Moscow: Gotika, 1998), 173–83; Sergei Nelipovich, "Naselenie okkupirovannykh territorii rassmatrivalos' kak rezerv protivnika," *Voenno-istoricheskii zhurnal* 2 (2000): 60–69; Serena Tiepolato, "'. . . und nun waren wir auch Verbannte. Warum? Weshalb?' Deportate Prussiane in Russia 1914–1918," *Deportate, Esuli, Profughe. Rivista telematica di studi sulla memoria femminile* 1 (2004): 59–85; Serena Tiepolato, "La deportazione di civili prussiani in Russia (1914–1920)," in *La violenza contro la popolazione civile nella grande Guerra. Deportati, profughi, internati*, ed. Bruna Bianchi (Milan: Unicopli, 2006), 107–25; Charles Perrin, "Eating bread with tears: Martynas Jankus and the deportation of East Prussian civilians to Russia during World War I," *Journal of Baltic Studies* 48, no. 3 (2017), 363–80; Charles Perrin, "Forgotten Prisoners of the Tsar: East Prussian Deportees in Russia during World War I," in *An International Rediscovery of World War One. Distant Fronts*, ed. Robert B. McCormick, Araceli Hernández-Laroche, and Catherine G. Canino (Abington, New York: Routledge, 2021), 5–34.
9   Imanuel Geiss, "Die Kosaken kommen! Ostpreußen im August 1914," in Imanuel Geiss, *Das Deutsche Reich und der Erste Weltkrieg* (München, Zürich: R. Piper, 1985), 58–66.
10  Konstantin Pakhaliuk, "Russkii okkupatsionnyi rezhim v Vostochnoi Prussii v 1914–15 gg.," *Voenno-istoricheskii arkhiv* 6 (2012): 160–178; 9 (2012): 107–30.

Russian invading army in historical records on the Russian side. He attempted, however, to explain this behavior by arguing that it was primarily a response to the actions of the residents of the Russian-occupied regions which in turn resulted from the fact that civilians were living in fear for their lives, that they were suspicious and harbored hatred toward their enemy. This caused paranoia among the Russian army and provoked retaliatory and punitive operations that had a direct effect on civilians. Placing greater emphasis on nuances and details (as compared to, for example, John Horne, who speaks solely of the spasmodic nature of the brutality of the Russian troops in East Prussia),[11] Pakhaliuk, drawing upon Russian sources, insisted that it was important to make a distinction between the acts of the occupying authorities and those of ordinary soldiers. Taking into account the circumstances of the war period, the former's actions are to be treated as retaliatory, including the Tenth Army commander's order issued in November 1914, which required that all adult men be removed from the occupied territory due to the antagonistic attitudes of local Germans and Jews. Ordinary soldiers, in turn, used violent force and engaged in looting in the regions that were not yet controlled by the occupying authorities; there were also occasional cases of vandalism and violence against peaceful civilians which Pakhaliuk explained by the lawlessness among the troops in the face of a power vacuum.

British historian Alexander Watson presented a similarly balanced picture of these issues.[12] Revisiting many of the same documents once used by Gause as a reference, he did not raise doubts as regards to the massacres of civilians, use of violent force, mass deportations, or other cases of violence documented by the Germans. However, Watson also underscored the fact that the documentary material on the atrocities of the Russian army was collected for propaganda purposes. Just like Pakhaliuk, Watson attempted to explain the actions of the Russian occupying authorities; he tried to make a distinction between the regime's intention to discipline the occupying army and to maintain order, which usually produced tangible results in urban areas, and the actions that could take place under less strict control, especially in rural areas. Watson proposed that the violence of occupation was brought about by several factors: a) information that the Russian government had accumulated on East Prussia during the

---

11  John Horne, "Atrocities and war crimes," in *The Cambridge History of the First World War*, ed. Jay Winter (Cambridge: Cambridge University Press, 2014), 1:571.

12  Alexander Watson, "'Unheard-of Brutality': Russian Atrocities against Civilians in East Prussia, 1914–1915," *The Journal of Modern History* 86, no. 4 (2014): 780–825. See also Alexander Watson, "Ego Documents from the Invasion of East Prussia, 1914–1915," in *Inside World War One? The First World War and its Witnesses*, ed. Richard Bessel and Dorothee Wierling (Oxford: Oxford University Press, 2018), 83–101.

prewar period (and that information led them to expect animosity from civilians); b) individual attitudes of ordinary (often poorly educated) troops which, due to a lack of information and encounters with otherness, were permeated with paranoia, fear, and antagonism (thus provoking violence); c) specific data either on the actual resistance of East Prussian civilians or resistance "attributed" by Russian officers to them which provoked violence and punitive campaigns. For Watson, this suggested that the violent behavior of the occupying authorities was, to a large extent, determined by encounters with a different culture and the way they perceived that culture.

Watson makes an interesting statement (on which he did not elaborate further) that looting was not only characteristic of the Russian troops but also of East Prussian civilians who had lost their homes and wandered around the province; there were also cases where such acts against German subjects were perpetrated by German troops in East Prussia.[13] This form of violence against civilians on home territory and its extent requires a more detailed analysis. Moreover, recollections and accounts published in Lithuania in the period between the two world wars suggest that not only Russian troops but also civilians from the Russian Empire's border area engaged in looting in East Prussia: these involved not only officials but also farmers who were obliged to deliver food, ammunition and other supplies to the front line.[14] They travelled to East Prussia in the footsteps of the invading Russian army to steal farm animals, farming implements, furniture, and other household items. Neither recollections nor historians provided any explanations for this phenomenon except for the fact that the civilians followed the example set by the actions of the Russian troops.

The actions of the German army while invading the Lithuanian-inhabited western provinces of the Russian Empire, and the later policies of the occupying regime had also first attracted historians' attention in the period between the two world wars. In Lithuania, Marija Urbšienė showed great interest in this topic during that period. Although she was unable to complete her monograph,[15] she published some of her research in separate articles.[16] Urbšienė mostly relied on

---

13  Watson, "'Unheard-of Brutality,'" 788.
14  Antanas Vireliūnas, "Atsiminimai iš Didžiojo karo," *Karo archyvas* 1 (1925), 109; J. Pikčilingis, "Pergyventos valandos," *Karo archyvas* 3 (1926), 92; Kazimieras Jokantas, "Suv. Kalvarijoje vokiečių okupacijos metu (1914–1918)," *Karo archyvas* 8 (1937), 128–130; Kazimieras Pakalniškis, "Rusų-vokiečių karo užrašai," *Karo archyvas* 11 (1939), 119.
15  For the contents of the planned monograph by Urbšienė see F14-26, *Lietuvos nacionalinė Martyno Mažvydo biblioteka, Retų knygų ir rankraščių skyrius* (Martynas Mažvydas National Library of Lithuania, Rare Books and Manuscripts Section).
16  Marija Urbšienė, "Vokiečių karo metų spauda ir Lietuva," *Karo archyvas* 8 (1937): 71–116; "Vokiečių okupacijos ūkis Lietuvoje," *Karo archyvas* 10 (1938): 7–94; 11 (1939): 19–100;

official reports of the German military authorities and used the German military press, propaganda publications, and other sources. The author did not intend to look specifically at violence against civilians; instead, she was more guided by the goal of shedding light on adversities brought by the "German occupation in Lithuania." While she mostly focused on the economic exploitation of the country, administrative restraints, and control of civilians by occupying authorities, Urbšienė was among the first to provide generalized accounts about requisitions, contributions, and forced labor. Stefan Glaser was another author who explored the legal aspects of requisitions and contributions before Urbšienė.[17] Later, different forms of violence perpetrated against civilians by the German army in what subsequently became the territory of Lithuania were explored by Abba Strazhas,[18] Christian Westerhoff,[19] Klaus Richter,[20] Vėjas Liulevičius,[21] Isabel V. Hull,[22] Tomas Balkelis,[23] and other authors.

---

"Susisiekimas, paštas ir pasai Lietuvoje Didžiojo karo metu," *Karo archyvas* 12 (1940): 63–84; "Sveikatos priežiūra vokiečių okupuotoje Lietuvoje Didžiojo karo metu," *Karo archyvas* 12 (1940): 85–94.

17   Stefan Glaser, *Okupacja niemiecka na Litwie w latach 1915–1918. Stosunki prawne* (Lwów: Drukarnia L. Wiśniewskiego, 1929), 131–42.

18   Aba Strazhas, "Kolonial'nyi rezhim germanskikh imperialistov v Litve v gody pervoi mirovoi voiny," *Voprosy istorii* 12 (1958): 67–85; Aba Strazhas, *Deutsche Ostpolitik im Ersten Weltkrieg. Der Fall Ober Ost 1915–1917* (Wiesbaden: Harrassowitz, 1993), 13–42.

19   Christian Westerhoff, "Deutsche Arbeitskräftepolitik in den besetzten Ostgebieten," in *Über den Weltkrieg hinaus. Kriegserfahrungen in Ostmitteleuropa 1914–1921*, ed. Joachim Tauber (Lüneburg: Nordost-Institut, 2009), 83–107; Christian Westerhoff, *Zwangsarbeit im Ersten Weltkrieg: Deutsche Arbeitskräftepolitik im besetzten Polen und Litauen 1914–1918* (Paderborn u.a.: Ferdinand Schöningh, 2011); Christian Westerhoff, "'A kind of Siberia': German labour and occupation policies in Poland and Lithuania during the First World War," *First World War Studies* 4, no. 1 (2013): 51–63; Christian Westerhoff, "Rekrutierung und Beschäftigung jüdischer Arbeitskräfte im besetzten Polen und Litauen während des Ersten Weltkriegs," in *Arbeit in den nationalsozialistischen Ghettos*, ed. Jürgen Hensel and Stephan Lehnstaedt (Osnabrück: Fibre, 2013), 33–51.

20   Klaus Richter, "'Seit einer Woche brennen Sumpf und Wälder.' Der Krieg in den Gouvernements Suwałki, Kovno und Kurland in der Erfahrung der Zivilbevölkerung 1915/16," in *Wielka Wojna poza linią frontu*, ed. Daniel Grinberg, Jan Snopko, Grzegorz Zackiewicz (Białystok: Instytut Historii i Nauk Politycznych Uniwersytetu w Białymstoku, 2013), 117–31; Klaus Richter, "'Go with the hare's ticket' mobility and territorial policies in Ober Ost (1915–1918)," *First World War Studies* 6, no. 2 (2015): 151–70.

21   Vejas Gabriel Liulevicius, *War Land on the Eastern Front. Culture, National Identity, and German Occupation in World War I* (Cambridge: Cambridge University Press, 2000), especially 54–112.

22   Isabel V. Hull, *Absolute Destruction. Military Culture and the Practices of War in Imperial Germany* (Ithaca: Cornell University Press, 2005), 243–48.

23   Tomas Balkelis, *War, Revolution, and Nation-Making in Lithuania, 1914–1923* (Oxford: Oxford University Press, 2018), 14–34.

In attempting to explain the behavior of the German army and the military occupying authorities, Strazhas put forward a thesis in 1958 that this behavior was contingent upon the fact that the occupied country was regarded as a colony.[24] The author supported his argument by citing accounts from German politicians and soldiers,[25] and by mentioning specific actions having analogies with the colonial regime in Africa. However, it seems that the forms of military violence against civilians that the German army used in the Ober Ost hardly differed from those practiced in Northern France and Belgium.[26] Requisitions of resources and food, material damage sustained by civilians as a result of hostilities, penalties that civilians were subjected to, looting by the troops, mobilization of civilians for forced labor and deportations related to forced labor or otherwise, sexual violence, and creation of conditions that subjected civilians to food shortages and infectious diseases as well as many other forms of violence were not solely the characteristics of the occupying regime in the Ober Ost. Despite this, we can hardly refute the claim that many of these forms of violence were impacted by earlier German colonial practices.[27] The slogans *Ordnung, Arbeit* and *Kultur*, which were actively used as part of the colonial language in Wilhelmine Germany, became what Germans proudly tried to "teach primitive natives" in Russia's western provinces occupied during World War I. From the construction of new railway lines and openings of schools to the introduction of fire escape ladders on the buildings, outdoor toilets, or saunas—all this was expected to strengthen the German missionary self-image. Forced labor practices (or "educating for work"—*Erziehung zur Arbeit*) were also present. From the perspective of the occupying authorities, most of these practices were justified as tools to bring the situation under control in a region inhabited

---

24  Strazhas, "Kolonial'nyi rezhim."
25  For example, in March 1918, a member of the Polish fraction in the Reichstag, Wojciech Trąmpczyński, spoke of *Militärgewalt* and *Zwangsverwaltung* in Lithuania and complained that in Lithuania the opinion that the Germans aimed "at making Lithuania an empty land for settlement" had prevailed (*aus Litauen ein menschenleeres Siedelungsland zu Machen*) (*Verhandlungen des Reichstags* 311 [1918]: 4303). In the same month, a member of the Reichstag for the Social Democratic Party, Eduard David, addressed members of the Reichstag asking rhetorically whether they believed that they would actually "set up in Lithuania one east-of-the-Elba-River military colony" (*eine ostelbische Militärkolonie in Litauen einrichten*) (*Verhandlungen des Reichstags* 311 [1918]: 4436).
26  Cf. Bruno Cabanes, "Violence and the First World War," in *The Cambridge World History of Violence*, ed. Louise Edwards, Nigel Penn, Jay Winter (Cambridge: Cambridge University Press, 2020), 4:289; Annette Becker, *Les cicatrices rouges, 14–18: France et Belgique occupées* (Paris: Librairie Arthème Fayard, 2010); Horne, "Atrocities and war crimes," 573–76.
27  Cf. Sebastian Conrad, *Globalisierung und Nation im Deutschen Kaiserreich* (Munich: C. H. Beck, 2006).

by "primitive natives" where the occupants could see nothing but "chaos" and "disorder" and which suffered considerable population losses.

Surely, this is not the only explanation of violence perpetrated against civilians. Previous stereotypical knowledge and behavioral models did play some part, like in the case of the actions of Germans in Belgium.[28] However, they impacted German troops and their military authorities along with additional factors. Among them was the simple bureaucratic adherence to the rules of the Prussian army as to how the military authorities should treat civilians in the rear areas (*Etappengebiet*), or "standard procedures"—the military culture that emerged in Wilhelmine Germany.[29] The violence perpetrated by ordinary troops against civilians was also driven by attempts to demonstrate their power in areas occupied by the enemy. Those which could not defend themselves were chosen for this end. The effect of capturing war trophies, that is, a desire to get immediate material gain also probably played an important role. Finally, just like in East Prussia, troops and military authorities perpetrated violence against civilians due to interactions with them: acts of violence were not only pre-programmed or psychologically motivated but also occurred as a response to civilian actions.

Compared to East Prussia, the violence committed against by the tsar's army against its own civilians in the western provinces of Russia has been researched more extensively. As demonstrated by the studies of Sergei Nelipovich, Peter Gatrell, Semion Goldin, Eric Lohr, Joshua A. Sanborn, and others,[30] violence primarily took the form of mass forced displacement of civilians. In the western peripheries of the Romanov Empire, the subjects of Germany and its allied countries (Austria-Hungary and the Ottoman Empire) were the first to experience mass displacements. In addition, the Russian troops—using the authority granted to military authorities by the military rule regulations approved by

---

28  Cf. Stéphane Audoin-Rouzeau and Annette Becker, *1914–1918: Understanding the Great War* (London: Profile Books, 2002), 50–51.
29  Cf. Hull, *Absolute Destruction*, 226–30.
30  Sergei Nelipovich, "Repressii protiv poddannykh 'tsentral'nykh derzhav,'" *Voenno-istoricheskii zhurnal* 6 (1996): 32–42; Peter Gatrell, *A Whole Empire Walking. Refugees in Russia during World War I* (Bloomington and Indianapolis: Indiana University Press, 1999); Semen Goldin, "Deportation of Jews by the Russian Military Command, 1914–1915," *Jews in Eastern Europe* 41, no. 1 (2000): 40–73; Eric Lohr, "The Russian Army and the Jews: Mass Deportation, Hostages and Violence during World War I," *The Russian Review* 60, no. 3 (2001): 404–19; Eric Lohr, *Nationalizing the Russian Empire: The Campaign against Enemy Aliens during World War I* (Cambridge, MA: Harvard University Press, 2003); Joshua A. Sanborn, "Unsettling the Empire: Violent Migrations and Social Disaster in Russia during World War I," *The Journal of Modern History* 77, no. 2 (2005): 290–324; Semen Gol'din, *Russkaia armiia i evrei 1914–1917* (Moscow: Mosty kul'tury, 2018), 157–206.

Emperor Nicholas II on July 16 (29), 1914,[31] including the right to deport any residents from the zone affected by hostilities—began applying it to Russian subjects as well. As a result, the first deportations of civilians began as early as the autumn of 1914 in the Suvalki Province. In September, a corps commander ordered the deportation of "German colonists" in the Suvalki Province from the areas where his troops were stationed. Towards the end of the year, these measures were applied to all Germans who lived in the so-called Vistula Land (*Privislinskii Krai*). Although army commanders did not provide clear guidelines as to the implementation of these displacements,[32] they affected a large number of the Germans living in Suvalki Province as well as Lithuanian Lutherans (who could be easily identified as "Germans" by Catholics). Jews were the other group of residents subjected to deportations. While the displacement of individual Jews from the frontline area took place as early as 1914, it was not until January 25, 1915 (February 7 in the Gregorian calendar) that it began taking place on a larger scale after the Chief of the General Staff, General of the Infantry Nikolai Ianushkevich ordered the displacement of "all Jews and suspect individuals" from the areas in which the army operated.[33] After a few months, when all these processes were well under way, an order was issued specifically targeting what later became the territory of Lithuania, whereby all the Jews who lived to the west of the line Riga-Ponevezh (Panevėžys)-Kovna had to be displaced. Some one hundred fifty thousand to one hundred sixty thousand Jews were displaced from the Kovno Province alone during the two-week operation which took place in May 1915. This displacement of Jews was often accompanied by the use of violent means, which sometimes ended up in pogroms (for example, in Suboch' [Subačius], Trashkuny [Troškūnai], Vishinty [Viešintos], Onikshty [Anykščiai], Debeiki [Debeikiai], Vobol'niki [Vabalininkas], Rakishki [Rokiškis] and Vidziuny [Vidžiūnai][34]) or led to the spread of rumors about Jews allegedly helping the Germans to find out Russian positions (for example, in Kuzhe [Kužiai]).[35] The displaced Jews, like Germans, generally had to move to

---

31   For more information about this authority, see Daniel W. Graf, "Military Rule Behind the Russian Front, 1914–1917: The Political Ramifications," *Jahrbücher für Geschichte Osteuropas* 22, no. 3 (1974): 390–411.
32   Gatrell, *A Whole Empire Walking*, 23–25; Lohr, *Nationalizing the Russian Empire*, 129–32.
33   Lohr, "The Russian Army," 409.
34   Anatolii Khaesh, "V prifrontovoi Litve 1915 goda. Rasskazy evreev-ochevidtsev," *Arkhiv evreiskoi istorii* 2 (2005): 371–406.
35   Word spread in Russia about the so-called "rumors of Kuzhe" (*Kuzhskii navet*) where the Jews of Kuzhe were accused of giving a sign to the Germans before they seized this settlement and pushed out the Russian unit. Cf. "Iz 'chernoi knigi' rossiiskago evreistva. Materialy dlia istorii voiny 1914–1915 g.," *Evreiskaia Starina* 10 (1918): 236–40, 252; Gatrell, *A Whole*

the inner provinces of Russia. The Jews of Kovno and Kurlandiia Provinces who had moved to Vilna, for instance, were ordered explicitly to leave the city in May 1915.[36] Given the impact the Jewish businesses had on economic sectors, local governments understandably complained of the adverse effects of the deportations. In some cases, the orders of the army were even sabotaged. Despite this, the forced displacements only intensified when the Russian army began retreating after the breakthrough by the Germans in the spring and summer of 1915. Among the main motives for the displacements were alleged betrayals, espionage, support for the enemy, and other assumptions based on stereotypes that found a breeding ground in the crisis-ridden war situation.

Regardless of the arguments sometimes reported in scholarly literature,[37] the displacement of civilians from the western territories of the Russian Empire in 1914–1915 not only included deportations but also forced the evacuation of civilians and their "voluntary" migration to flee hostilities. Although "Germans" and Jews were the populations most affected by deportations, the majority of war refugees from Lithuania were in fact ethnic Lithuanians.

This state of research review has revealed that violence against civilians on the northern section of the former Russian-German front took many different forms. While the violence primarily inflicted by the troops and military authorities was present on both sides of the front line, mass deportations of civilians and persecution of "spies" were mostly characteristic of the Russian army. However, not only the German and Russian armies or occupying authorities acted violently. In the course of the war, civilians perpetrated violence against other civilians. Also, people (both military and civilian) committed acts of violence not only in the enemy's territories but also in their home territories. The violence was not targeted at individual victims only; the acts of violence took place on a massive scale and affected thousands or even hundreds of thousands of civilians.

---

*Empire Walking*, 22; Lohr, "The Russian Army and the Jews," 404–19; Lohr, *Nationalizing the Russian Empire*, 138–40; Frank M. Schuster, *Zwischen allen Fronten: Osteuropäische Juden während des Ersten Weltkrieges (1914–1919)* (Köln: Böhlau, 2004), 203–09; Semion Goldin, "Ot Novoaleksandrii do Belostoka: deportatsii evreiskogo naseleniia pol'skikh zemel' russkoi armiei v 1914–1915 gg.," *Studia Judaica* 17, no. 2 (2014): 5–33; Anatolii Khaesh, "Navet 1915 goda na evreev mestechka Kuzhy," in *Evrei Rossii, Evropy i Blizhnego Vostoka: istoriia, kul'tura i slovesnost'. Materialy mezhdunarodnoi nauchnoi konferentsii 14 aprelia 2019 g.*, ed. Varvara Vovina, Maksim Mel'tsin (St. Petersburg: Peterburgskii institut iudaiki, 2019), 220–227, 374.

36 "Del žydų gabenimo," *Viltis*, May 15 (28), 1915, 1.
37 For comparison, see Alan Kramer, "Combatants and Noncombatants: Atrocities, Massacres, and War Crimes," in *A Companion to World War I*, ed. John Horne (Oxford: Wiley-Blackwell, 2010), 192.

## Gathering Information, Framing the Representation

Although violence against civilians took many forms, later representations of this violence in East Prussia and in the future state of Lithuania portrayed the stories of violence and their victims selectively. There was a prevalent trend of narrating experiences of the Great War that were national or regional, at best. For this reason, the diverse picture of victims and perpetrators was presented in a strict frame. The victim was depicted in national terms; the violent experiences were narrated as the experiences of the whole community. Thus, the victim's role was often attributed to the whole community. The perpetrator was also considered in a collective sense. In general, the "enemy" or "the occupying force" of the war period played perpetrator's role, often failing to emphasize that the acts of violence were committed by individual soldiers and simplifying the portrait of the perpetrator to mere "Russians" or "Germans."

This representational mode of depicting violence was impacted by the practices used for gathering information on both sides of the border and later on both sides of the front line. The data on the behavior of the enemy or occupying force in both cases was also collected intentionally, encouraging witnesses to share their accounts, to write, and to record their experiences. Furthermore, the publication of this material was selective and often driven by propaganda or other purposes.

In East Prussia, residents were also encouraged to recall and document their experiences of encounters with the enemy by the local government. It primarily targeted two categories of residents: those residents who witnessed the "Russian atrocities" in East Prussia and war refugees. The collection of accounts of the former began as early as September 1914.[38] The latter attracted attention as a potential source of information in January 1915 when the chief officer (*Oberpräsident*) of the Province of East Prussia called, for the first time, upon the districts that had accommodated refugees to "collect refugee accounts that should be concise and accurate, to the maximum extent possible, on their experiences during the enemy's invasion."[39] At that time, they had several ideas as to the use of that material. This data collection effort was justified as a typical historian of the nineteenth century would have justified it: it was the duty of contemporaries to document the most important events of their era. The gathered accounts, rather

---

38 See, "Russische Grausamkeiten und Verwüstungen sind anzuzeigen," *Königsberger Hartungsche Zeitung*, September 3, 1914, 2.
39 A[lbert] Brackmann, "Die Sammlungen zur ostpreußischen Kriegsgeschichte," *Ostpreußische Kriegshefte* 5 (1917): 105.

than putting blame on or vindicating specific people, were expected to shed light on what actually happened.[40] However, there is little doubt that they intended to use the collected material for war propaganda. The first reports on the behavior of the Russian army in East Prussia and the ravaged territories occupied by the army appeared in the press in early September 1914.[41] In Germany, both regional (East Prussian) and national press eagerly snapped up various pieces of information related to this topic. This information also appeared in the newspapers of other countries such as Italy or Sweden. During the same period, special committees were set up in the province for the purpose of gathering information on the "Russian atrocities" in East Prussia.[42] The collected information was published in March 1915 in the special report titled "Atrocities of Russian Troops against German Civilians and German Prisoners of War" compiled by the Ministry of Foreign Affairs.[43]

However, the use of information for propaganda purposes was not the sole goal of these efforts to gather materials. There were also merely pragmatic interests for gathering recollections on the civilian experiences of war, for example, concerning property-related matters as the state institutions wanted to accurately register the property losses of residents, businesses, and establishments as well as the circumstances of the property loss. Eventually, assessments based on people's accounts were necessary to evaluate the actions or omissions of the administrative bodies in the face of a critical situation while taking care of citizens' needs.

The processes that took place for a while seemingly without greater ambitions for coordination acquired a more systematic form after engaging professional historians. Albert Brackmann who had previously worked on preparing medieval sources for publication and was invited for the position of Ordinary Professor at the University of Königsberg in 1913, was not mobilized into the army upon the outbreak of the war and, for some time, assisted at a military hospital and also

---

40  Cf. [Adolf] von Batocki, "Vorwort," *Ostpreußische Kriegshefte* 1 (1915): 7.
41  Cf. "Wie die Russen in Tapiau hausten!" *Königsberger Hartungsche Zeitung*, September 2, 1914, [3]; "Erzählungen ostpreußischer Flüchtlinge," *Königsberger Hartungsche Zeitung*, September 4, 1914, [5]; "Russengreuel in Ostpreußen . . ." and "Russische Schandtaten in Ostpreußen. Amtlich beglaubigte Fälle," *Königsberger Hartungsche Zeitung*, September 6, 1914, 1–2.
42  For more on this issue, see Fritz Gause, "Die Quellen zur Geschichte des Russeneinfalls in Ostpreußen im Jahre 1914," *Altpreußische Forschungen* 7 (1930): 87.
43  *Greueltaten russischer Truppen gegen deutsche Zivilpersonen und deutsche Kriegsgefangene* (Berlin: s.n., 1915). Cf. Watson, "'Unheard-of Brutality,'" 789–97.

helped refugees.[44] It was this activity that probably led him to start documenting the experiences of refugees, and before long, he was mandated to organize the activities of the special commission for East Prussian war history. The first meeting of the commission on September 28, 1915 was formally chaired by the *Oberpräsident* of the Province of East Prussia, Adolf von Batocki. Brackmann cooperated with state institutions and historians on the issues examined by the commission. On September 30, the commission sent circulars to the district administrative chiefs (*Landrats*) and burgomasters calling upon them to collect information on the experiences of war and Russian occupation from the communities, parishes, and schools in the coming winter months. School teachers were expected to become the key assistants in these efforts. Instructions were developed as to the appropriate method of writing and the kind of materials that had to be collected to gather the war survival accounts in villages, manor estates, parishes, schools, and districts.[45] A decision was made to publish a portion of the materials in the special *East Prussian War Issues* (Ostpreußische Kriegshefte). Five such issues were published in 1915–1917. They depicted different experiences of war in East Prussia through official documents and personal accounts.

However, they did not leave much space for the voices of ordinary people. On the one hand, during the implementation of this campaign of collecting detailed information, residents were given the opportunity to share stories about their hardships which, in a sense, provided them with an outlet to vent their grievances. On the other hand, the publishing of the War Issues also represented a form of control as it allowed the coordinators to make sure that only the information that they regarded as important reached the publicity. It must be added that the specific data collection criteria were set right from the start: already in early 1915 it was recommended that the material be collected from the refugees "who could be expected to produce reasonable, accurate, and non-exaggerated accounts."[46] The major portion of the material collected ended up in the special Provincial Commission Military Archives. The first references to the creation of these archives probably appeared in 1917.[47] This collection of documents later

---

44  Michael Burleigh, "Albert Brackmann (1871–1952) Ostforscher: The Years of Retirement," *Journal of Contemporary History* 23, no. 4 (1988): 573.
45  Brackmann, "Die Sammlungen," 105–111. See also Barbara Sapała, "Organisierte Erinnerung. Ein Beitrag zu Entstehungsgeschichte und Funktionen der Kriegschronik der Provinz Ostpreußen," *Studia Ełckie* 17, no. 3 (2015): 255–68.
46  Brackmann, "Die Sammlungen," 105.
47  Ibid., 111.

became part of the Königsberg State Archives before these archives were lost by Germany in 1945.[48]

The process of data collection was also conducted within the army. The collection and publishing of accounts were also encouraged among priests and schoolteachers.[49] However, also in this case, the collection and publishing of information created an "elite" narrative about the war where the data was mostly gathered (and at the same time "filtered") by priests and schoolteachers who, along with other public leaders, were themselves usually involved in publishing this data. Using witness accounts, an illusion was, in a sense, created of incorporating the voice of "ordinary people" in the narrative. However, many such accounts, especially those published during the war, were greatly imbued with propaganda; they contained not only personal experiences of the publications compilers who had survived the war, but also rumors.[50]

Also, in the territory of what later became Lithuania, data on World War I events, encounters with the enemy, and the damages caused by the enemy and the occupying regime were collected during the war. The church also played some role in collecting such materials, though probably to a lesser extent than in the case of East Prussia. We know that in some Roman Catholic rectories of the Diocese of Samogitia, the most important events were documented daily from

---

48   Gause, *Die Russen...*, 7; Fritz Gause, *Die Geschichte der Stadt Königsberg in Preußen*, 2nd ed. (Köln u.a.: Böhlau, 1996), 3:4. At least some of the materials from these archives are currently kept in the Russian State Military Archives.

49   For more on that issue, see Gause, "Die Quellen." The first publications of this kind appeared already in 1914. Selected accounts of priests were published by General Superintendent, Hans Schöttler (*Aus Ostpreußens Kriegsnot: schlichte Bilder aus schwerer Zeit* [Potsdam: Stiftungsverlag, 1915]) and the priest of Gumbinnen Carl Moszeik (*Kriegserlebnisse ostpreußischer Pfarrer* [Berlin-Licherfelde: Edwin Runge, 1915]). Bruno Schwark collected the accounts of the Catholic priests of the Diocese of Warmia (*Der Feind im Land: Berichte ermländischer Geistlicher über Ostpreussens Russenzeit 1914/15* [Braunsberg: Ermländische Zeitungs- und Verlagsdruckerei, 1915]). In addition, Königsberg Cathedral priest Albert Nietzki published the accounts of priests for the series of pamphlets on East Prussian war history launched by specially created Synod Commission (*Was wir in der Russennot 1914 erlebten* [Königsberg: Kommissionsverlag Ferd. Beyers Buchhandlung Thomas & Oppermann, 1915]; *Was wir in der Russennot 1914–15 erlebten* [Königsberg: Gräfe & Unzer, 1916]). The accounts of schoolteachers, as commissioned by the Teachers' Association of the Province of East Prussia, were collected and published in three volumes by Schmelz School (Memel district) teacher Carl Beutler (*Erlebnisse ostpreußischer Lehrer in der Kriegs- und Russenzeit* [Königsberg: Verlag des Ostpreußischen Provinzial-Lehrervereins, 1916]).

50   For comparison, see the five parts of *War Experiences of East Prussians* published during the war in Angerburg: Hermann Adalbert Braun, *Ostpreußische Kriegserlebnisse* (Angerburg: Druckerei der Krüppel-Lehranstalt, 1914–1915). The first part was titled *Kriegs-Kreuz und Liebe: als Zeichen innigsten Dankes für die unserem Krüppelheim erwiesene Wohltat*. It was largely focused on describing the encounters with "Russians."

the outset of the war "as observed through one's own eyes and heard through one's own ears."[51] However, ordinary residents were also encouraged to collect materials and to document accounts relating to various war events.

Perhaps the first such call appeared in September 1914 in a newspaper published specifically for Lithuanians. It was motivated by the fact there was not only the necessity to remember the events but also to "leave them for our history." The author of the article proposed sending the materials to the Lithuanian Learned Society in Vilna where the Great War Archives were to be created.[52] Later, more detailed guidelines appeared specifying what kind of information (the situation before the war, rumors, mobilization, requisitions, the relationship between the army and civilians, battles and their descriptions; spies and intelligence agents; duties; and losses) and what type of documents (newspapers, photographs, diaries, solders' letters, songs and poems of the war years, and so on) had to be collected.[53] It is not entirely clear what effect this public call had on its audience. However, the manuscript collection of the Lithuanian Learned Society currently kept in the Wróblewski Library of the Lithuanian Academy of Sciences contains handwritten memoirs from the second half of 1914 which were likely included in the collection during that same period.[54]

Similar public calls to document the events of that time also appeared in the Lithuanian press in 1915. In one public call from May 1915, readers were encouraged to write about their encounters with the Germans:

> I have lived under German rule two times already and I have witnessed with my own eyes and was fascinated by how our wives, suffering beatings, and kicking that Germans inflicted upon them, made every effort to reach the soldiers, who were kept in starvation as prisoners of war, and deliver them food so that they do not die from starvation. The Germans would try to stop our

---

51 "Karo istorijai medžiaga," *Lietuva*, November 20, 1921, 3.
52 [Peliksas Bugailiškis] GK, "Rinkime karo meto medžiagą!" *Lietuvos ūkininkas*, September 18 (October 1), 1914, 350.
53 [Peliksas Bugailiškis] GK, "Karo istorijos medžiaga," *Lietuvos žinios*, November 1 (14), 1914, 1–2.
54 For example, K. Norkus, "Iš Kalvarijos padangės. Pasakojimas apie karo veiksmus tarp Vokietijos ir Rusijos," second half of 1914, F 255–221, *Lietuvos mokslų akademijos Vrublevskių biblioteka, Rankraščių skyrius* (The Wroblewski Library of the Lithuanian Academy of Sciences, Manuscript Section, hereafter cited as *LMAVB RS*); Jackus Sondeckas, "Europos karo istorijai medžiagos žiupsnelis, Žemaičių Kalvarijoje," November 6–10, 1914, F 255–375, *LMAVB RS*.

gracious women and curse at them ... It is unfortunate that these good deeds, however small some of them may have been, will be left undocumented.[55]

After the Kaiser's troops occupied Lithuania in 1915, there could be no talk of public calls to collect materials of a similar nature as the occupying authorities considered any data collection effort as espionage and it was punishable by death. Despite this, information on German occupation was collected and documented even during the war. This is evidenced by many sources. Peliksas Bugailiškis later wrote: "I have documented the actions of the German occupants as much as I could in my dairy-chronicle ... The chronicle paints a very vivid and accurate picture of the occupying regime and the hardships that people experienced."[56] Without the collection and documentation of this material, the memoranda compiled by the Lithuanian intelligentsia for the occupying authorities of Ober Ost and the lecture given by Jonas Basanavičius in 1916 (which was later published as a brochure) would not have been possible.[57] In terms of content, they were comparable to *The Memorial of the Great Lithuanian Perils* handed over by the Council of Lithuania (*Lietuvos Taryba*) to the chancellor of the German Reich on October 20, 1917. It aimed at drawing the attention of Germany's central government to the major economic challenges and losses caused by the occupying authorities to the residents of Lithuania (forced labor, requisitions, deforestation, looting, crimes of mobsters and prisoners of war who were hiding in forests, crimes against civilians, and so on).[58]

However, the materials on occupation collected by Lithuanians during the war could not be published in the Ober Ost owing to censorship and other reasons. Therefore, a considerable portion of the memoirs and accounts written during that time never made their way from manuscripts to readers. Other materials

---

55 [Antanas Šmulkštys] Papentis, "Rašykime karo istoriją!" *Šaltinis*, May 30 (June 12), 1915, 137–38. This public call was soon repeated in the Riga Lithuanian newspaper: J[uozas] Tumas, "Rinkkime žinias karo istorijai Lietuvoje!" *Rygos garsas*, June 6 (19), 1915, 1.
56 Peliksas Bugailiškis, *Gyvenimo vieškeliais: medžiaga istorijai*, ed. Vigintas Bronius Pšibilskis (Šiauliai: "Aušros" muziejus, 1994), 204–05. Some of the personal writings of Bugailiškis were published as an introductory text to the diary by Petras Klimas (*Dienoraštis 1915–1919* [Chicago: AM & M Publications, 1988], 13–44).
57 Jonas Basanavičius, *Iš lietuvių gyvenimo 1915–1917 m. po vokiečių jungu* (Vilnius: Švyturys, 1919).
58 *The Memorial of the Great Lithuanian Perils* by the Provisional Presidium of the Lithuanian Council [*Lietuvos Taryba*], October 20, 1917, in *Lietuva vokiečių okupacijoje Pirmojo pasaulinio karo metais 1915–1918. Lietuvos nepriklausomos valstybės genezė*, ed. Edmundas Gimžauskas (Vilnius: Lietuvos istorijos instituto leidykla, 2006), 171–90.

that reached the activity centers of Lithuanians in neutral countries, for instance, in Switzerland, were published for propaganda or opinion-forming purposes by Lithuanian activists such as Juozas Gabrys.[59] Meanwhile, it was not until 1919, that is, after the withdrawal of the German army, that the publishing of the materials on German occupation intensified in the former Russian territories inhabited by Lithuanian speakers.

The texts on the hardships and suffering of Lithuanians under German occupation published in French by Juozas Gabrys in Switzerland primarily targeted an international audience. Gabrys, who was "undoubtedly the best known Lithuanian political figure on the Europe scene before 1916", according to Alfred E. Senn,[60] had a very specific goal in mind—to raise internationally the issue of the political future of Lithuanians. The material on the violence against civilians had to serve as a trigger inducing empathic concern for Lithuanians.

The Jews pursued a very similar goal during the war. The Jewish War Relief Committee and the so-called Political Bureau collected documents and materials on their suffering in Russia, especially in the Pale of Settlement, from the onset of war until the Revolution of 1917.[61] The Political Bureau was an assembly of the leaders of different Russian Jewish movements and political activists who operated in the capital city of Russia in close cooperation with three Jewish deputies of the state Duma. The Political Bureau published a portion of the materials collected including official documents, reports, and witness accounts, during the war. The deputies used the tribune of the state Duma for this purpose.[62]

---

59  Cf. [Juozas Gabrys] C[harles] Rivas, *Ober-Ost. Le plan annexionniste allemand en Lithuanie (Extrait de "Pro Lithuania", № 1, 1917)* (Lausanne: Bureau d'Information de Lithuanie, 1917); [Juozas Gabrys] C[harles] Rivas, *La vie publique en Lituanie occupée par les Allemands* (Genève: n.p., 1917); [Juozas Gabrys] C[harles] Rivas, *"Justice" allemande en Lituanie occupée* (Genève-Nancy: n.p., 1918); [Juozas Gabrys] C[harles] Rivas, *La Lituanie sous le joug allemand 1915–1918. Le plan annexioniste allemand en Lituanie* (Lausanne: Librairie Centrale des Nationalités, 1918); [Juozas Gabrys] C[harles] Rivas, *Occupation allemande en Lituanie* (Genève-Nancy: n.p., 1918); [Juozas Gabrys] C[harles] Rivas, *Visées annexionistes allemandes sur la Lituanie* (Lausanne: Librairie Centrale des Nationalités, 1918); [Juozas Gabrys] C[harles] Rivas, *Lituanie et Allemagne. Visées annexionistes allemandes sur la Lituanie à travers les siècles* (Lausanne: Librairie Centrale des Nationalités, 1919).

60  Alfred Erich Senn, "The Activity of Juozas Gabrys for Lithuania's Independence, 1914–1920," *Lituanus* 23, no. 1 (1977): 16.

61  Simon Dubnov wrote in 1922: "I would receive copies of reports sent to our bureau by the representatives of the Jewish War Relief Committee who could lawfully enter the front-line area": Semen Dubnov, *Kniga zhizni. Vospominaniia i razmyshleniia: materialy dlia istorii moego vremeni* (St. Petersburg: Peterburgskoe Vostokovedenie, 1998), 342.

62  For instance, in August 1915, the Jewish deputies organized a protest against "the internal war against Jews" in the state Duma. See Semen Dubnov, *Noveishaia istoriia evreiskogo naroda ot frantsuzskoi revoliutsii do nashikh dnei* (Riga: Dzive un kultura, 1938), 3:401.

They published the materials on the violence against Jews in pursuit of the wider goal of improving the conditions of Jews (the abolition of the Pale of Settlement, among others) focusing primarily on Russia. However, war censorship hindered the publication of the materials in Russia on the deportations of Jews and their situation. Thus, it was not until 1918 that the Jewish Historical-Ethnographic Society (co-founded by Simon [Semion] Dubnov in 1892) was able to publish these materials.[63] While it was supposed to be an ongoing effort, *Evreiskaia Starina* published only the first part of the *Black Book* in 1918 (the publication was not continued in a subsequent volume of 1924).[64]

Thus, the great wave of collecting and gathering accounts of civilians in East Prussia about their encounters with the "enemy" and violence they had experienced occurred during the war.[65] Given the intensity of the war years, the texts on this topic were far less numerous in later years. In general, the same could be said about the issue of East Prussian refugees the relevance of which dwindled in Germany around 1916. This shows that the representations of a violent enemy were most relevant during the time when Russia still posed an actual threat to Germany. At the time when public opinion still counted for something, besides more general propaganda interests to "balance out" the "damaged" reputation of the German army by exposing the behavior of the Russian army (due to its behavior in Belgium),[66] the interest in depicting "Russian atrocities" clearly stemmed from the belief that this would help attract more German support for rebuilding East Prussia. This was particularly evident in East Prussia where, according to one eyewitness, local people were not interested in the military success of Germans on the Western Front due to the threat from Russians; all eyes were on the fate of East Prussia.[67] Understandably, with this level of concern, East Prussians tried to influence their fellow citizens in the rest of Germany.

In turn, Lithuanian and Jewish political actors collected materials on violence against civilians and published them during the war with the former specifically

---

63 "Iz 'chernoi knigi' rossiiskago evreistva," 195–296. See also Dubnov, *Noveishaia istoriia*, 400–401.

64 Cf. Polly M. Zavadivker, *Blood and Ink: Russian and Soviet Jewish Chroniclers of Catastrophe from World War I to World War II* (PhD diss., University of California Santa Cruz, 2013), 128–57.

65 Cf. Hektoras Vitkus, "*Die Russen in Ostpreussen*: Rusijos ir rusų įvaizdžiai 1914–1939 m. Vokietijoje publikuotuose atsiminimuose apie Didįjį karą Rytų Prūsijoje," *Darbai ir dienos* 67 (2017): 47.

66 For more, see John Horne and Alan Kramer, *German Atrocities, 1914: A History of Denial* (New Haven: Yale University Press, 2001).

67 Margarete Poehlmann, "Aus Tilsits Russenzeit," *Die Lehrerin: Organ des Allgemeinen Deutschen Lehrerinnenvereins*, November 7, 1914, 242–43.

targeting the international audience, and the latter targeting the Russian domestic audience depending on the type of audience from whom they expected empathy and support. The voices of both actor groups fed into the general discourse of "subjugated nations" concerning new political hopes generated by the Great War.

Meanwhile, in Lithuania, it was not until after the war that the collection and publication of the materials on the violence perpetrated by the occupying force intensified. From 1918 onwards, the *Lietuvos Taryba* began focusing on the collection of data on the material damage caused by the war. In 1918–1920, the governments of Lithuania called upon civilians to register the property losses they had experienced due to the war. It was expected that this information could be used for negotiations with Bolshevik Russia and later with Germany, regarding the compensation for war damage. The collection of memoirs and experiences on the violence perpetrated during the war was also carried out in connection with this issue.

After returning from Russia to Lithuania in 1918, Jaroslavas Rimkus came up with an idea to use drawings to depict German occupation, which he himself, in principle, did not experience. To create these drawings, he most likely relied on the accounts he collected from the residents. This is evidenced by the lines appearing in the introduction to the album of drawings published by him as a teacher at Šiauliai Gymnasium in 1922: "It was a very easy matter to collect material for this book because every Lithuanian who [had] lived under German occupation seemed an unending source of information about German cruelty and misdeeds."[68]

The end of the war marked the start of the publication of the first "egodocuments" written during the war. These publications primarily included diaries and writings produced in the war years.[69] In 1921, Pranciškus Žadeikis, a priest from Skuodas, published his writings (the second part of his texts was released in 1925),[70] where he set the goal of documenting war events so that the citizens of Lithuania, having read them, could understand "the horrific times and

---

68 *Vokiečių okupacija Lietuvoje 1915–1919 m. paveikslėliuose ir trumpuose jų aprašymuose*, ed. J. Šilietis [Jaroslavas Rimkus] (Kaunas: J. Šilietis, 1922), iii.
69 Liūdas Gira, "Vilniaus gyvenimas po Vokiečiais. 1916 m.," *Mūsų senovė* 2 (1921): 21–38; "Vilniaus gyvenimas po Vokiečiais. 1917 m.," *Mūsų senovė* 1, no. 3 (1922): 410–24; A[leksandras] Dambrauskas, "Mano užrašai," *Mūsų senovė* 1, no. 3 (1922): 398–409; no. 4–5 (1922): 796–807; P[etras] Klimas, "Mano kelionė po Lietuvą 1915 metais," *Mūsų senovė* 1, no. 4–5 (1922): 545–56.
70 Pr[anciškus] Žadeikis, *Didžiojo karo užrašai*, vol. 2: *1917–1918–1919 metai* (Klaipėda: Rytas, 1925).

the hardships we went through before Lithuania won back freedom."[71] The majority of those publications including the album of drawings by Rimkus were published in 1921–1922, at the time when the government of Lithuania had already lost hope that Bolshevik Russia would compensate for war damages and expected to obtain this compensation from Germany. Rimkus even sent his album of drawings to Georges Eybert, the French consul in Kaunas, and to Raymond Poincaré, the Prime Minister of France, clearly with the hope of finding solidarity with France.[72] But the negotiations between the Lithuanian and German governments concerning compensation of war damages in 1922–1923 did not end as the Lithuanian government had expected. Burdened by war reparations, Germany made a counterclaim to Lithuania for German "investments" into the Lithuanian infrastructure during the occupation and the postwar military and financial support provided to Lithuania. Eventually, both parties simply withdrew their claims for damages to each other.

Following these negotiations, only sporadic accounts of the German occupation were published for some time.[73] They conveyed the everyday life under German occupation, so they were hardly suitable for primitive propaganda.

During this period, the documentation of experiences of German occupation was essentially supported by the Lithuanian army alone. These initiatives continued until World War II. They were covered by journals published by the Lithuanian army: *Mūsų žinynas* and especially *Karo archyvas*. Both journals were edited by Vytautas Steponaitis in 1921–1925 and from 1925 respectively. Therefore, more consistent collection of materials of World War I was related to his activities. As soon as a separate division for research on military history, the so-called Military History Section, emerged in the military headquarters in 1936, a call for accounts on World War I was issued to the public. The first

---

71  Pr[anciškus] Žadeikis, *Didžiojo karo užrašai*, vol. 1: *1914–1915–1916 metai* (Klaipėda: Rytas, 1921), 4.
72  In his letter, he noted that "by defeating the Germans in the fields of the homeland, France also gave freedom to Lithuania" and his artwork bore evidence to the suffering of the Lithuanian people during the occupation. *Ištraukos iš laikraščių recenzijų apie J. Šiliečio albumą "Vokiečių okupacija Lietuvoje 1915–19 m."* (Šiauliai: Savičo ir Šumkauskio spaustuvė, 1923), 5.
73  Mikas Gudaitis, *Lietuva 1917 metais. Kelionės po Lietuvą vokiečių okupacijos metu* (Klaipėda: Rytas, 1925); G[abrielė] Petkevičaitė, *Karo meto dienoraštis*, vol. 1 (Kaunas: Varpo spaustuvė, 1925); vol. 2: *1915–1916 metų okupacija* (Kaunas: Varpo spaustuvė, 1931). The third part was not published during the interwar period. In 1966, the diary was republished with the third part integrated, but parts of the text itself were cut out. The full edition of the diary was first published in 2008–2011: Gabrielė Petkevičaitė-Bitė, *Karo meto dienoraštis*, vols. 1–3 ([Panevėžys]: E. Vaičekausko knygyno leidykla, 2008–2011).

address of the Military History Section said: "Accounts on the German occupation and the periods of other occupations are also welcome."[74]

In the 1930s, ethnographers joined the initiative of collecting the accounts. In 1935, this task was undertaken by the Lithuanian Folklore Archive established by Jonas Balys. In the instructions for collection of people's accounts approved by Jonas Balys himself, "The Great War and the German Occupation" were singled out as a separate subject in the section of historical accounts. The instructions, among other things, noted that the interviewers had to make sure that the speaker had not learned their stories from books or at school.[75] School textbooks also encouraged to record the experiences of World War I and in particular of the Lithuanian people during the German occupation.[76] A textbook issued in 1928 was one of the first to ask the junior pupils the following: "Write down your family's memories about the rule of German soldiers in your vicinity."[77] In the 1930s, such requests became more common in both elementary and high school textbooks.

However, the publishing of materials gathered for the most part in the period between the two world wars intensified only after the relations between Lithuania and Germany became more complicated. Publishing memoirs of the German occupation and the violence against civilians in Lithuania became particularly extensive in 1933–1935. Several Lithuanian newspapers and magazines published individual memoirs or their sets much more often than before. The answer as to why the publication of such memoirs intensified specifically in 1933–1935 is suggested by the changes in Lithuanian foreign policy. At the time, foreign trade and foreign policy of Lithuania were shifting away from Germany.[78] Implementing a rigorous integration policy in the Klaipėda (Memel) territory, Lithuania faced great pressure from Germany. Therefore, the period of 1933–1935 was the peak of propaganda upsurge between the two countries. To consolidate the public perception of the German threat and justify Lithuanian policy, a variety of mental images from the Great War were used to portray the "true German face" to the Lithuanian people.

---

74  "Karo istorijos reikalu," *Karys*, April 16, 1936, 388.
75  Instructions: Collection of Folklore No. 2. Collection of people's accounts, February 20, 1936, col. 391, inv. 4, file 1015, p. 47, *LCVA*.
76  World War I was not an exceptional event; pupils were equally encouraged to take interest in the old people's stories about other recent events in the Lithuanian history.
77  P[eliksas] Šinkūnas, *Krašto mokslo vadovėlis (istorijos pradžiamokslis)*, third ed. (Kaunas: Varpo spaustuvė, 1928), 121
78  For more on that issue, see Vasilijus Safronovas, "Neumann-Sass-Prozess als Ausdruck fundamentalen Wandels in den Beziehungen zwischen Litauen und Deutschland," *Annaberger Annalen* 21 (2013): 9–34.

In a similar way, another collection of war memoirs was also inspired by the change of relations with Germany. The idea to collect and publish Lithuanian accounts in the book titled "The Great War" was proposed by the Reserve Officers Association (*Atsargos karininkų sąjunga*). In March 1935, at the peak of the relationship crisis between Germany and Lithuania, retired Major Petras Ruseckas addressed the public, encouraging citizens to write down accounts and giving an example of how to do so. The example described the "inhumane" conduct of Germans during the occupation.[79] It was expected to publish the collected materials or at least part of them as the first volume of the *Memoirs of the German Occupation* in 1935.[80] However, the book was published only in 1939 under a much broader title of *Lithuania in the Great War* (Lietuva Didžiajame kare).[81] Although the name of the book no longer mentioned the Germans, the content still had anti-German motifs: regardless of a broader title, the publication covered mostly the German occupation. However, at that time, in 1939, this had to be concealed, as problems with Germany was the last thing Lithuania wanted. According to some witnesses, this was one of the reasons why the book was published in Vilnius: there were concerns that publishing in Kaunas could provoke a German reaction.[82] This book compiled by Ruseckas was the only collection of this scale comprised of accounts collected in an organized way in Lithuania in the inter-war period. It consisted of recollections and accounts of thirty witnesses recorded in 1929–1939 and one diary that was written in 1915–1919. Geographically they covered a large part of the Lithuanian territory and, in particular, the former Kovno province.[83]

These arguments should not create the impression that war victims recalled the violence they experienced solely for pragmatic reasons, that is, to ensure support for rebuilding East Prussia or to maintain Lithuania's stance in its relations with Germany. In fact, a number of factors stimulated their recollections, including people's desire to name the perpetrators and their atrocities, their wish

---

79 For comparison, see Petras Ruseckas, "Kaip rašyti į Didįjį Karą," *Lietuvos aidas*, March 14, 1935, 6.
80 See the advertisement about the forthcoming books by Petras Ruseckas in: Petras Ruseckas, *Išniekintos vėliavos: Lietuvos atgijimo novelės* (Kaunas: Varpo spaustuvė, 1935).
81 Petras Ruseckas, ed., *Lietuva Didžiajame kare* (Vilnius: Vilniaus žodis, 1939).
82 Cf. Julius Būtėnas, *Lietuvos žurnalistai* (Vilnius: Žurnalistika, 1991), 161.
83 Another attempt of a similar scale to collect and publish Lithuanian eyewitness recollections of World War I had to wait for three decades. This initiative belonged to Antanas Gintneris, a Lithuanian journalist in the US. See his *Lietuva caro ir kaizerio naguose. Atsiminimai iš I Pasaulinio karo laikų 1914–1918 m.* (Chicago: ViVi Printing, 1970). Unlike Ruseckas' collection, Gintneris' book consists not only of eyewitness accounts, but also of his own essays depicting the events of World War I.

to vent out their traumatic experiences and the loss of their loved ones, and the gathering of the documentary evidence of war losses that was necessary in order to obtain the long-promised compensations (the latter was especially relevant during the war and in the first years thereafter).

However, the intentional collection and publishing of these recollections of the Great War were contingent upon pragmatic causes. In Lithuania, these causes went beyond anti-German propaganda. The demonization of Germans, and specifically of German occupation, added the significance to the political involvement of the Lithuanian intelligentsia during the war. It contributed to the understanding that the precious value of independence was achieved thanks to Lithuanian political elites. And, since some of these figures, especially Antanas Smetona, held the highest official post in the 1930s, it added political legitimacy to the "Leader of the Nation."

In Germany, too, some pragmatic factors played a role after 1918 or even after the announcement in 1925 that the postwar rebuilding of East Prussia was completed. The depiction of "Russian invasions" in as negative light as possible during or after the war added more legitimacy to the members of the military elite (Paul von Hindenburg, Erich Ludendorff, among others) some of whom, as we know, remained active in the postwar German political scene. For instance, the representative book dedicated to the eightieth anniversary of Reich President Paul von Hindenburg and published in a huge print run still featured several propaganda images produced during the war.[84]

## Who Committed Violence? Some Notes on the Image

How were the actors, to whom the violence against civilians was attributed, represented? If we look at the images that were targeted at the East Prussian and Lithuanian societies, we notice several similarities. The perpetrator's image was hardly ever nuanced or subtle. In nearly every case, it was depicted as a force from beyond the border. Moreover, the violence was attributed to the countries at war rather than their armies. As a result, the actors involved were usually represented as the source of evil, an elemental and chaotic force which befell the entire country rather than having specific and distinctive violent characteristics. In both cases, to create the image of such an elemental force, an "inhumane" behavior that was against socially accepted norms (morale, religious ethics,

---

84 See Paul Lindenberg, ed., *Hindenburg-Denkmal für das deutsche Volk. Eine Ehrengabe zum 80. Geburtstage des Reichspräsidenten* (Berlin: Vaterländischer Verlag C. A. Weller, 1927).

culture) was used, putting it in stark contrast with the image of "own people" or their "humanity."

In Germany, an important contributing factor that has created such an attitude was the fact that, unlike on the Western Front which was portrayed as the space of "modern warfare" with dominant industrialized technology and new military methods, the Russian front (along with hostilities in East Prussia) was represented as the space of archaic ("medieval") warfare where cultural advantage of German troops triumphed over "Eastern barbarians."[85] The images of Russian cavalry and scorched-earth tactics employed by the Russian troops were particularly suited to reinforce this image.[86] The cavalry was seen as an attribute of "archaic warfare" and, at the same time, "backward society," while setting wooden huts or even whole farms on fire (which was a common practice of preparing the areas close to the frontline for military action)—as a "medieval custom of Russian troops." A teacher from East Prussia later wrote in his memoirs: "What the Russians have really mastered over hundreds of years of war was burning, burning, and burning, in the land of the enemy and in the own land alike."[87] According to his account, once the Russians came, the majority of farm and town buildings in East Prussia were swallowed by a sea of fire.[88] Portraying the clash with the Russians in East Prussia through the lens of a "disaster" was quite common.[89] The recollections of the "East Prussian" stage of the Great War often contained the narrative of fire ("the war of fire") as a metaphor of the beginning of war ("coming of the Russians.") It was conveyed using the images of the "bright skies of East Prussia darkened by the glow of fire and a fog of smoke."[90] "From the north to the southeast, the horizon was glowing with unending fire; it was a sign of the coming war," wrote another teacher of the eastern province of Prussia in his memoirs about the beginning of war.[91]

---

85  Cf. Oscar Usedom, *Im Kampf mit dem russischen Koloß* (Leipzig: Hesse & Becker, 1916).
86  See, for example, [Carl] Moszeik, "Kriegserlebnisse," in *Kriegserlebnisse ostpreußischer Pfarrer*, ed. C[arl] Moszeik (Berlin-Licherfelde: Edwin Runge, 1915), 1:1–53.
87  [George] Reżat, *Meine Erlebnisse in der Kriegszeit und mir authentisch mitgeteilte Geschehnisse* (Tilsit: J. Reylaender & Sohn, 1917), 23.
88  Reżat, *Meine Erlebnisse*, 24.
89  The East Prussian Oberpräsident Ludwig von Windheim used this metaphor in an interview as early as September 1914: "Oberpräsident von Windheim über Ostpreußens Notlage," *Königsberger Hartungsche Zeitung*, September 5, 1914, 2.
90  M[ax] Brügmann, *Aus Ostpreußens Russennot* (Berlin: Verlag des Evangelischen Bundes, 1916), 13–14.
91  Rudolf Müller, *Drei Wochen russischer Gouverneur. Erinnerungen an die Besetzung Gumbinnens durch die Russen August–September 1914*, 4th ed. (Gumbinnen: Verlag von C. Sterzels Buchhandlung, 1915), 6.

German wartime publications retelling the invasion of the Russian army into East Prussia were abundant with images of "Russian atrocities" committed against civilians. They often wrote about the "inhumanity of invaders,"[92] "a surge of Russians,"[93] their "dreadful domination,"[94] being under the "Russian whip,"[95] the rule of "Russian hordes,"[96] "the Russian economy" (*Russenwirtschaft*)[97] (an analogy of the "Polish economy," *polnische Wirtschaft*, which was better-known to Germans).[98] The Russians were portrayed with barbarian or even zoomorphic characteristics: the authors were astonished that they buried people "where they fell" and even when they were "still alive,"[99] were "prone to drunkenness," "depraved," "thieves" and "marauders,"[100] able to "brutally shredding civilians to pieces with their spears."[101] All this, of course, was especially applicable to the unfamiliar but exotic sounding category of the "Cossacks." During the war, "Cossack" to some extent became synonymous with "Russian" and, in general,

---

92  The Russian soldiers are always "cruel and insidious, but stupid and exclusively hideous to the last one," wrote M. Felchner in his memoirs. See M. Felchner, *Unter Russenhorden. Schilderungen aus der Zeit der Russenherrschaft in Masuren* (Reutlingen: Enßlin & Laiblins Verlagsbuchhandlung, 1915), 21. "Many women have stopped bathing because of the fear of being suddenly assaulted by Russian soldiers. Some of them did not take their clothes off for the night so as to not create additional temptation for Russian rapists. For the same reason, women did not undo their hair for the night," said a priest of Stallupöhnen in his memoirs. See Moszeik, "Kriegserlebnisse," 18–19.
93  K[arl] O[tto] Leipacher, *Die Russenflut in Ostpreußen. Nach amtlichen Berichten, zuverlässigen Schilderungen und eigenem Erleben*, vol. 1: *Kämpfe um die Heimaterde*, 2nd ed. (Würzburg: Curt Kabitzsch, 1916); vol. 2: *Schicksal und Anteil*, 2nd ed. (Leipzig und Würzburg: Curt Kabitzsch, 1918).
94  Paul Hurtzig, *Russische Schreckensherrschaft in Ostpreußen. Selbstgesehenes*, 5th ed. (Schwerin i. Mecklb.: Friedrich Bahn, 1916).
95  Chr. Grigat, *Unter russischer Knute im deutschen Gebiet nördlich der Memel. Erinnerung an die Zeit der beiden Russeneinfälle in den nördlichen Teil der Kreise Ragnit und Tilsit* (Tilsit: J. Reylaender & Sohn, 1916).
96  Felchner, *Unter Russenhorden*.
97  A[xel] Kuhn, *Die Schreckenstage von Neidenburg in Ostpreußen. Kriegserinnerungen aus dem Jahre 1914* (Minden, Leipzig: Wilhelm Köhler, 1914), 39.
98  Cf. Hubert Orlowski, *"Polnische Wirtschaft." Zum deutschen Polendiskurs der Neuzeit* (Wiesbaden: Harrassowitz, 1996).
99  Cf. Liedtke, "Erlebtes und Erfahrenes," in *Kriegserlebnisse ostpreußischer Pfarrer*, 2:31–32, 36. Cf. Danielowski, "Erlebnisse," in *Kriegserlebnisse ostpreußischer Pfarrer*, 1:59.
100 Cf. e.g., the testimonies of Axel Kuhn, burgomaster of Neidenburg, and Carl Beutler, teacher of Schmelz (suburb of Memel): Kuhn, *Die Schreckenstage*; C[arl] Beutler, "Erlebnisse aus Memels Kriegs- und Russentagen," in *Erlebnisse ostpreußischer Lehrer in der Kriegs- und Russenzeit*, ed. C[arl] Beutler (Königsberg: Verlag des Ostpreußischen Provinzial-Lehrervereins, 1916), 1:24; S. J. Siegfried-Jäglack, *Aus der Russenzeit Ostpreußens. Erlebnisse einer Gutsfrau* (Berlin: Hapke & Schmidt, 1915), 20, 25.
101 [Friedrich] Angermann, "Auf der Flucht," in *Kriegserlebnisse ostpreußischer Pfarrer*, 2: 100–01. The testimonies provide much more evidence of "Cossack brutality."

became a mythical figure representing the clash of civilians with the "Russians": the exclamations "Cossacks are coming! Cossacks are here!" (*Die Kosaken kommen! Die Kosaken sind da!*) became generic leitmotifs in painting the picture of encounters with the enemy. Such emphasis on the Cossacks is understandable, given the fact that they inspired terror by their unusual appearance and armament alone. Cossacks were portrayed armed with sabres (*shashkas*), spears, bows, wearing "nomadic clothes" and special belts for whipping people.[102] Their behavior was also hardly understandable for the people of East Prussia.[103]

The memoirs set the "inhumane" policy of the occupying authorities in stark contrast with relations and conduct of the people of East Prussia and Germans in general. The stories told that East Prussians humanely treated the enemy troops: organized "humane" burial of Russian soldiers and supported Russian captives with food and necessary items. "When the first Russian captives appeared in Memel (and there were thousands of them), everyone tried to give them a piece of bread or sausage—this was probably their only meal after captivity," one resident of Memel said in his memoirs and added that he also met an "intelligent Russian captive, who turned out to be a German of Russia [*Deutschrusse*] from Estland. Who would believe this? A German of Russia was taken captive near Tilsit, though along with his military unit he was brought to the German border for 'spring maneuvers' in March 1914. He was very pleased with his situation in captivity and confirmed that the Germans in Russian captivity are also being treated well."[104]

In Lithuanian publications, Germans were also portrayed as "antihuman" at the beginning of the war, partly under the influence of tsarist propaganda. This was done using the images of "crusaders" rooted in the Lithuanian national culture, where the crusader had been portrayed as a medieval torturer and killer of the Lithuanian people and the plunderer and burner of their lands and property since the nineteenth century.[105] According to the research carried out by Andrea

---

102 Kuhn, "Insterburg unter russischer Herschaft," in *Kriegserlebnisse ostpreußischer Pfarrer*, 1:64; Siegfried-Jäglack, *Aus der Russenzeit*, 11.
103 For more, see Peter Jahn, "'Zarendreck, Barbarendreck'–Die russische Besetzung Ostpreußens 1914 in der deutschen Öffentlichkeit," in *Verführungen der Gewalt. Russen und Deutsche im Ersten und Zweiten Weltkrieg*, ed. Karl Eimermacher, Astrid Volpert, Gennadij Bordjugow (München: Wilhelm Fink, 2005), 223–41; Peter Jahn, "Befreier und halbasiatische Horden. Deutsche Russenbilder zwischen Napoleonischen Kriegen und Erstem Weltkrieg," in *Unsere Russen, unsere Deutschen: Bilder vom Anderen 1800 bis 2000*, ed. Peter Jahn, Philip Springer (Berlin: Christoph Links, 2007), 28–29.
104 Beutler, "Erlebnisse," 12–13.
105 Cf. Vasilijus Safronovas, *The Creation of National Spaces in a Pluricultural Region: The Case of Prussian Lithuania* (Boston: Academic Studies Press, 2016), 174–86.

Griffante, at the beginning of the war, the Lithuanian intelligentsia supported the image of the new "Teutonic" attack, which was intended to agitate the public, and mythologized the Germans and their occupation using the images related to the "crusaders," the Battle of Grunwald, and so on. However, news and testimonials from the front area published in newspapers created another narrative, only partly related to the first one, telling about the destruction of the Lithuanian economy and the moral decline of its people due to cruel and predatory behavior of the German troops.[106] For understandable reasons, these images were first revealed in the recollections published after the war, although their origins in many cases lie in the opinions published in the Lithuanian press in 1914–1915.[107]

The image of German "inhumanity" was consolidated in Lithuanian society due to the prolonged German occupation. A grim impression was left and later, recollections often mentioned the looting, requisition of livestock by the German troops, constant demands for food, destruction of property, and attempts to seduce local women. Forced military recruitment, capture of people, and forced labor imposed by the German occupation authorities left a particularly negative impression that remained in the collective memory for a long time. The memories also revealed the moral decline of the Lithuanian people because of the war: reporting to the occupation authorities, loose sex behavior and the spread of venereal diseases, resignation, and a drop in living standards.

Naturally, the formation of the image of German "inhumanity" in the memory of the Lithuanian people was influenced by both their experience of the war period and propaganda and stereotypes of that time. For example, one priest testified that when asked why civilians were being transported from East Prussia to the depths of Russia in December 1914, a Russian subordinate-officer answered: "they are not human beings, but more vile than dogs."[108] Even twenty years after the war, the perpetrator of the Great War was almost always associated with the Germans in the memoirs of Lithuanian authors. The violence of Russian troops

---

106 Cf. Andrea Griffante, "La Prima guerra mondiale e l'uso pubblico della storia in Lituania: i nuovi Cavalieri teutonici," *Storicamente: laboratorio di storia. Studi e Ricerche* 10 (2014): 1–25; "Gemeinschaft und Mythos. Zwei litauische Narrative über den Ersten Weltkrieg," in *Der Große Krieg beginnt: Sommer und Herbst 1914*, ed. Joachim Tauber (Lüneburg: Nordost-Institut, 2016), 97–113.
107 See, for instance, "Pasisaugokime!" *Šaltinis*, May 14 (27), 1915, 113; P. V., "Vokiečiai Lietuvoje," *Šaltinis*, May 19 (June 1), 1915, 123–25; May 25 (June 7), 1915, 130–32; "Užkrečiamosios ligos ir kova su jomis," *Šaltinis*, May 25 (June 7), 1915, 130; SG, "Vokiečių nežmoniškumas," *Viltis*, June 25 (July 8), 1915, 1; reprinted in: *Šaltinis*, June 30 (July 13), 1915, 173.
108 Pakalniškis, "Rusų-vokiečių karo užrašai," 119.

was hardly ever mentioned, so the wartime propaganda and the roles of "our own" and "stranger" were still effective.

However, the "inhumanity" of the Germans and their comparison with the medieval crusaders was brought up again and again in postwar Lithuania, especially in the cases mentioned above, when publishing the information about violence against civilians had to serve as additional propaganda in mobilizing public opinion against Germany. The Rimkus' aforementioned album published in 1922 became a quintessence of violent experiences during occupation. In this album, the invasion of the Germans was also equated to the medieval crusader attacks, and some drawings used drastic imagery of the occupation: a German soldier shooting at Lithuanian civilians, the Germans ploughing land using harnessed war prisoners, the Germans looting the churches, defiling women, and so on. Of course, many Lithuanian memoirs opposed this "antihuman" behavior to the "humane" Lithuanian customs and virtues.

In 1933–1935, these images were brought up again. Publications reproduced the imagery of violence against civilians during World War I, where the actors were the "Lithuanian people" and the "Germans."[109] The Germans were still portrayed as murderers, who robbed the poor farmers from the last farm animal and the last piece of bread.[110] Some publications pointed out that during the war, the Germans in Lithuania deliberately pursued a policy where they needed "to be feared" rather than "be loved by others."[111] "At first our people were happy with the coming of the Germans, because from them they expected more cultured conduct than from Russians. But having experienced their 'culture,' they were deeply disappointed," wrote a Catholic priest in his memoirs, "the Russian soldiers stole in secret, while the Germans looted in the middle of the day. Out of fear, women offered them eggs, butter and fatback . . . And when rumors spread about women raped by soldiers, 'our people began seeing the Germans as real animals.'"[112] He continued, "the farmers became slaves to the Germans."[113] Naturally, the people were sharing their own experiences of the war in these recollections. However, the increased publication of such memoirs in 1933–1935 had obvious propaganda objectives, sometimes beyond the control of the

---

109 See, for example: J. Dovydaitis, "Vokiečių okupacija Lietuvoje," *Karys*, May 30, 1935, 515–17.
110 J. M., "Už Lietuvos duoną. Vokiečių okupacijos laikų kruvini pėdsakai," *Jaunoji karta*, April 8, 1934, 217–18.
111 J. Strimaitis, "Vokiečių okupacija Kaune," *Lietuvos aidas*, March 24, 1934, 14.
112 [Antanas Pauliukas] A. Uzinas, "Didžiojo karo nuotykių atsiminimai," *Panevėžio garsas*, March 17, 1935, 3.
113 [Antanas Pauliukas] A. Uzinas, "Didžiojo karo nuotykių atsiminimai," *Panevėžio garsas*, April 14, 1935, 3.

authors of the memoirs. This is illustrated, for example, by the headlines given to the memoirs, such as "Civilized predators rob Lithuania," although the content did not match the headline at all.[114]

In 1933–1935, the violent experiences of World War I once again became proof of German incivility and brutality and associations with the crusaders were remembered again. Even a textbook for elementary school students encouraged: "if you can find any old photographs" from the times of the Great War, take a look "what those descendants of the crusaders who took over Lithuania looked like."[115] Another example was the pamphlet "German Horror" published in 1934 with the following subheading: "What the Germans have done wrong for Lithuania and what else they are going to do." The pamphlet recounted the evils done by the Germans to Lithuania from the "crusaders" to Adolf Hitler, and a large chapter was understandably dedicated to the experiences of World War I. It said: "The Germans have devastated and slaughtered Lithuania during the Great War and their goal was clear: the more of the Lithuanian people they destroy, the more free space there will be for the German colonists... and an old dream of the crusaders will come true: all of Lithuania will be taken over."[116] The introduction of the aforementioned book by Ruseckas, whose anti-German title was toned down in 1939, read:

> Read the recollections speaking of how the Germans repaid the trust in them: with superficial and empty politeness and greeting and immediate and cruel looting, robbery, pointless ruining of farms and crops, shooting livestock, requisitions, contempt towards the people, beatings and even killings. Like clouds of locusts, wave after wave the Germans came, bringing ever more destruction. The flowering and satiating land inhabited by quiet and hard-working people soon was turned into a country of poverty, misery, and hunger.[117]

However, neither the "inhumane Russian" in East Prussia, nor the "inhumane German" in Lithuania were the only attributes. The relationship with the invading army or occupying force was conveyed by more than just supporting the

---

114 Kaz[imieras] Pakalniškis-Dėdė Atanazas, "Civilizuoti grobuonys plėšia Lietuvą," *Jaunoji karta*, November 12, 1933, 757–58.
115 P[aulius] Šležas and V[aclovas] Čižiūnas, *Lietuvos istorija šeštam pradžios mokyklų skyriui* (Kaunas: Sakalas, 1936), 126.
116 [Balys Sruoga] Jurgis Plieninis, *Vokiškasis siaubas. Teisybė apie vokiečius* (s.l.: n.p., 1934), 27.
117 *Lietuva Didžiajame kare*, 3–4.

image of the other as the antithesis of self. Margarete Poehlmann who had suffered the hardship of the "Russian rule" in Tilsit, northern part of East Prussia, challenged the propagandist portrayal of Russians in the autumn of 1914. She argued that claims of Russian brutality have been determined by imagination stirred by natural human fear and uncertainty; in many cases, it was only rumors spread by people, who themselves had not seen any Russian crimes.[118] In the areas at the German border, where the people had more contact with those living on the other side of the border, such as Memel, the witnesses believed in the humanity of the "enemy." According to one teacher from Memel, before facing the Russians they expected that "not all Russians are barbarians. Many of them are just as humane as we are."[119] Some testimonies of positive personal contacts with the enemy also cast doubt on the image of the "Russian barbarians." This is especially noticeable in the descriptions of contacts with Russian army officers. In East Prussia, they were often portrayed as people of "higher culture:" speaking German, literate, relatively polite, and with basic hygiene habits. Many written recollections about the events of war recounted the "higher morals" of the Russian officers (they were seen as religious, because they did not take part in the destruction of churches and cemeteries) and a different mindset compared to their subordinates.[120]

Respectively, the recollections of the Lithuanian people told more than only about negative traits of German soldiers and officers and negative characteristics of the occupation. Some conveyed the ambiguous feelings in captivity: "the German soldiers surrounded the two of us. They were so merry and kind, gave us cigars, bread and said: see, we are kind, whereas Russian soldiers cut the ears off the heads of captive German soldiers."[121] Petras Klimas, a Lithuanian politician and diplomat, was impressed that "there was hardly any difference between German soldiers and officers: they all sat down at a table to drink a beer or coffee as equals, talked and joked amongst themselves, read their newspapers."[122] Another witness wrote that at the end of July 1915, in the eastern part of Kovno Province, although the mood of the people was very depressed, the Germans left a great impression on the locals, because they were merry, sang songs, smoked cigars, drank rum, and were eating well from outdoor kitchens. Among the German soldiers, the witness noted stricter military discipline and obeying the

---

118 Poehlmann, "Aus Tilsits Russenzeit," 245–46.
119 Beutler, "Erlebnisse," 24.
120 For comparison, see Braun, "Unter der Russen," in *Kriegserlebnisse ostpreußischer Pfarrer*, 1:90–111
121 Žadeikis, *Didžiojo karo užrašai*, 1:27.
122 Petras Klimas, *Iš mano atsiminimų* (Vilnius: Lietuvos enciklopedijų redakcija, 1990), 42.

orders compared to the Russian soldiers, and the "greatest impression was that if a German platoon stopped for at least half an hour, almost everyone took out the newspapers, were reading and sharing them and discussing. In all this time, I had not seen a Russian officer reading a newspaper, let alone the soldiers."[123] In addition, there were not only closer short-term contacts between the German soldiers and the Lithuanian girls, but also deeper emotional ties between the locals and the soldiers who had been stationed in the rear area for a long time.[124]

It is also noticeable that part of the Lithuanian accounts to some extent adopted the self-image that the Germans created and spread about themselves and their "mission" of dissemination of *Kultur* in the east during the war. For example, when criticizing poor work organization of the Lithuanian militia in 1921, a member of the *Steigiamasis Seimas* (Lithuanian Constituent Assembly) gave an example from the times of the occupation: "two German gendarmes had huge areas to cover and managed to do it well. This is an example for us: they knew how to write a report and the order was good."[125] Presumably, this image of the German "order" (*Ordnung*) referred to their own understanding of their civilizing mission to educate the chaotic and barbaric East during the Great War. Although not predominant, all these cases challenged the "typical" image of those who were associated with wartime violence.

## Implications and Conclusions

Our general understanding of the civilian experience during the Great War is still greatly affected by the images of the "national goals" and the "national suffering." These images come from the period before World War II. In Lithuania, they are still relevant, because the references to World War I often focus on the story of gained independence. In Germany, they were relevant for nearly a half century (at least until the academic interest in East Prussia was covered with the veil of political incorrectness). In these images, the perpetrator had a very clear label: for the Germans it was "Russians" and "Cossacks," for the Lithuanians— "Germans" and "crusaders."

---

123 Juozas Audickas, "Didžiojo karo atsiminimai," *Karo archyvas* 9 (1938): 201.
124 This is how Petkevičaitė described the emotional farewell to the German soldiers in her diary at the end of November 1917, in the vicinity of Puziniškis: "We said goodbye forever. We saw them off, the soldiers who had become unexpected loyal friends in this terrible time. These lads did not leave any dark memories behind": Petkevičaitė-Bitė, *Karo meto dienoraštis*, 3:183.
125 *Steigiamojo Seimo darbai* 13 (1921): 621.

In this chapter, we have argued that even during World War I, these images served the pragmatic objectives of their creators. It also showed that these objectives were not only short-term expectations of German wartime propaganda machine. Lithuanians and Jews generated very similar expectations during the war. Moreover, the expectations related to the use of the information about violence against civilians did not end in 1918. This information supported the image of the "enemy" and added extra legitimacy to political decisions, for example, in Lithuania during the 1930s.

We have also argued that the current understanding of the violence suffered by civilians during World War I does not represent the diversity of actual experiences of civilians both in East Prussia and future Lithuania. Many forms of violence were neglected due to later adoption of "appropriate" narratives and victims of violence. Civilian violence against other civilians and the violence of fellow countrymen against each other that did not cross the borders or the front-line remained completely underrepresented. After the war, in the modern Lithuanian nation-state, virtually no-one wrote about the forced deportations of the Jews and Germans, and the Russian government and troops were much less often remembered as perpetrators of violence compared to the "Germans." The personal nature of violence, violence against specific people, rape of women, and other themes were hardly reflected on both sides of the border of the former empires. The importance of these themes was shrouded and sunk into oblivion by the stories of the "national suffering." We will probably never be able to accurately, beyond any possibility for counterarguments, measure to what extent this was proof of brutalization of society or a collective displacement reaction to uncomfortable experiences.

Finally, this chapter revealed the importance of comparative research into World War I. Comparative studies allow to see that the perpetrators were not just the "Germans" or the "Cossacks," and that violence against civilians was a massive phenomenon in World War I. This, of course, provides new arguments for a broader question whether the violence suffered by civilians during World War II was essentially unique and different compared to World War I.

## Bibliography

Angermann, [Friedrich]. "Auf der Flucht." In *Kriegserlebnisse ostpreußischer Pfarrer*, edited by C[arl] Moszeik. Vol. 2, 93–102. Berlin: Edwin Runge, 1915.
Audickas, Juozas. "Didžiojo karo atsiminimai." *Karo archyvas* 9 (1938): 198–211.
Audoin-Rouzeau, Stéphane, and Annette Becker. *1914–1918: Understanding the Great War*. London: Profile Books, 2002.

Balkelis, Tomas. *War, Revolution, and Nation-Making in Lithuania, 1914–1923*. Oxford: Oxford University Press, 2018.

Basanavičius, Jonas. *Iš lietuvių gyvenimo 1915–1917 m. po vokiečių jungu*. Vilnius: Švyturys, 1919.

Batocki, [Adolf] von. "Vorwort." *Ostpreußische Kriegshefte* 1 (1915): 7–8.

Becker, Annette. *Les cicatrices rouges, 14–18: France et Belgique occupées*. Paris: Librairie Arthème Fayard, 2010.

Beutler, C[arl]. "Erlebnisse aus Memels Kriegs- und Russentagen." In *Erlebnisse ostpreußischer Lehrer in der Kriegs- und Russenzeit*, edited by C[arl] Beutler. Vol. 1, 5–36. Königsberg: Verlag des Ostpreußischen Provinzial-Lehrervereins, 1916.

Beutler, Carl, ed. *Erlebnisse ostpreußischer Lehrer in der Kriegs- und Russenzeit*. Königsberg: Verlag des Ostpreußischen Provinzial-Lehrervereins, 1916.

Brackmann, A[lbert]. "Die Sammlungen zur ostpreußischen Kriegsgeschichte." *Ostpreußische Kriegshefte* 5 (1917): 105–12.

Braun, [Erich]. "Unter der Russen." In *Kriegserlebnisse ostpreußischer Pfarrer*, edited by C[arl] Moszeik. Vol. 1, 90–111. Berlin-Licherfelde: Edwin Runge, 1915.

Braun, Hermann Adalbert. *Ostpreußische Kriegserlebnisse*. Angerburg: Druckerei der Krüppel-Lehranstalt, 1914–1915.

Brügmann, M[ax]. *Aus Ostpreußens Russennot*. Berlin: Verlag des Evangelischen Bundes, 1916.

Bugailiškis, Peliksas. *Gyvenimo vieškeliais: medžiaga istorijai*, edited by Vigintas Bronius Pšibilskis. Šiauliai: „Aušros" muziejus, 1994.

———. "Rinkime karo meto medžiagą!" *Lietuvos ūkininkas*, September 18 (October 1), 1914.

———. "Karo istorijos medžiaga." *Lietuvos žinios*, November 1 (14), 1914.

Burleigh, Michael. "Albert Brackmann (1871–1952) Ostforscher: The Years of Retirement." *Journal of Contemporary History* 23, no. 4 (1988): 573–88.

Būtėnas, Julius. *Lietuvos žurnalistai*. Vilnius: Žurnalistika, 1991.

Cabanes, Bruno. "Violence and the First World War." In *The Cambridge World History of Violence*, edited by Louise Edwards, Nigel Penn, Jay Winter. Vol. 4: *1800 to the Present*, 286–303. Cambridge: Cambridge University Press, 2020.

Conrad, Sebastian. *Globalisierung und Nation im Deutschen Kaiserreich*. München: C. H. Beck, 2006.

Dambrauskas, A[leksandras]. "Mano užrašai." *Mūsų senovė* 1, no. 3 (1922): 398–409; no. 4–5 (1922): 796–807.

Danielowski, [Alfred]. "Erlebnisse." In *Kriegserlebnisse ostpreußischer Pfarrer*, edited by C[arl] Moszeik. Vol. 1, 54–62. Berlin-Licherfelde: Edwin Runge, 1915.

"Del žydų gabenimo." *Viltis*, May 15 (28), 1915. Dovydaitis, J. "Vokiečių okupacija Lietuvoje." *Karys* 22 (1935): 515–17.

Dubnov, Semen. *Kniga zhizni. Vospominaniia i razmyshleniia: materialy dlia istorii moego vremeni*. St. Petersburg: Peterburgskoe Vostokovedenie, 1998.

———. *Noveishaia istoriia evreiskogo naroda ot frantsuzskoi revoliutsii do nashikh dnei*. Vol. 3: *Epokha antisemitskoi reaktsii i natsional'nogo dvizheniia (1881–1914) s epilogom (1914–1938)*. Riga: Dzīve un kultūra, 1938.

["Evreiskaia Starina"]. "Iz 'chernoi knigi' rossiiskago evreistva. Materialy dlia istorii voiny 1914–1915 g." *Evreiskaia Starina* 10 (1918): 195–296.

Felchner, M. *Unter Russenhorden. Schilderungen aus der Zeit der Russenherrschaft in Masuren*. Reutlingen: Enßlin & Laiblins Verlagsbuchhandlung, 1915.

[Gabrys, Juozas] C[harles] Rivas. *"Justice" allemande en Lituanie occupée.* Genève-Nancy: n.p., 1918.

———. *Lituanie et Allemagne. Visées annexionistes allemandes sur la Lituanie à travers les siècles.* Lausanne: Librairie Centrale des Nationalités, 1919.

———. *La Lituanie sous le joug allemand 1915–1918. Le plan annexioniste allemand en Lituanie.* Lausanne: Librairie Centrale des Nationalités, 1918.

———. *Ober-Ost. Le plan annexionniste allemand en Lithuanie (Extrait de "Pro Lithuania," no. 1, 1917).* Lausanne: Bureau d'Information de Lithuanie, 1917.

———. *Occupation allemande en Lituanie.* Genève-Nancy: s.n., 1918.

———. *La vie publique en Lituanie occupée par les Allemands.* Genève: n.p., 1917.

———. *Visées annexionistes allemandes sur la Lituanie.* Lausanne: Librairie Centrale des Nationalités, 1918.

Gatrell, Peter. *A Whole Empire Walking. Refugges in Russia during World War I.* Bloomington: Indiana University Press, 1999.

Gause, Fritz. *Die Geschichte der Stadt Königsberg in Preußen.* Vol. 3: *Vom Ersten Weltkrieg bis zum Untergang Königsbergs.* 2nd ed. Köln u.a.: Böhlau, 1996.

———. "Die Quellen zur Geschichte des Russeneinfalls in Ostpreußen im Jahre 1914." *Altpreußische Forschungen* 7 (1930): 82–106.

———. *Die Russen in Ostpreußen 1914/15.* Königsberg: Gräfe und Unzer, 1931.

Geiss, Imanuel. "Die Kosaken kommen! Ostpreußen im August 1914." In Imanuel Geiss. *Das Deutsche Reich und der Erste Weltkrieg,* 58–66. Munich: R. Piper, 1985.

Gimžauskas, Edmundas, ed. *Lietuva vokiečių okupacijoje Pirmojo pasaulinio karo metais 1915–1918. Lietuvos nepriklausomos valstybės genezė.* Vilnius: Lietuvos istorijos instituto leidykla, 2006.

Gintneris, Antanas. *Lietuva caro ir kaizerio naguose. Atsiminimai iš I Pasaulinio karo laikų 1914–1918 m.* Chicago: ViVi Printing, 1970.

Gira, Liūdas. "Vilniaus gyvenimas po Vokiečiais. 1916 m." *Mūsų senovė* 2 (1921): 21–38.

———. "Vilniaus gyvenimas po Vokiečiais. 1917 m. "*Mūsų senovė* 1, no. 3 (1922): 410–24.

Glaser, Stefan. *Okupacja niemiecka na Litwie w latach 1915–1918. Stosunki prawne.* Lwów: Drukarnia L. Wiśniewskiego, 1929.

Goldin, Semen. "Deportation of Jews by the Russian Military Command, 1914–1915." *Jews in Eastern Europe* 41, no. 1 (2000): 40–73.

———. "Ot Novoaleksandrii do Belostoka: deportatsii evreiskogo naseleniia pol'skikh zemel' russkoi armiei v 1914–1915 gg." *Studia Judaica* 17, no. 2 (2014): 5–33.

———. *Russkaia armiia i evrei 1914–1917.* Moscow: Mosty kul'tury, 2018.

Goldstein, Ludwig. *Der Wiederaufbau Ostpreussens.* Königsberg: Hartungsche Zeitungs- und Verlagsdruckerei, 1919.

Graf, Daniel W. "Military Rule Behind the Russian Front, 1914–1917: The Political Ramifications." *Jahrbücher für Geschichte Osteuropas* 22, no. 3 (1974): 390–411.

*Greueltaten russischer Truppen gegen deutsche Zivilpersonen und deutsche Kriegsgefangene.* Berlin: n.p., 1915.

Griffante, Andrea. "Gemeinschaft und Mythos. Zwei litauische Narrative über den Ersten Weltkrieg." In *Der Große Krieg beginnt: Sommer und Herbst 1914,* edited by Joachim Tauber. Vol. 24 of *Nordost-Archiv,* 97–113. Lüneburg: Nordost-Institut, 2016.

———. "La Prima guerra mondiale e l'uso pubblico della storia in Lituania: i nuovi Cavalieri teutonici." *Storicamente: laboratorio di storia. Studi e Ricerche* 10 (2014): 1–25.

Grigat, Chr. *Unter russischer Knute im deutschen Gebiet nördlich der Memel. Erinnerung an die Zeit der beiden Russeneinfälle in den nördlichen Teil der Kreise Ragnit und Tilsit.* Tilsit: J. Reylaender & Sohn, 1916.

Gudaitis, Mikas. *Lietuva 1917 metais. Kelionės po Lietuvą vokiečių okupacijos metu.* Klaipėda: Rytas, 1925.

Horne, John. "Atrocities and war crimes," in *The Cambridge History of the First World War*, edited by Jay Winter. Vol. I: *Global War*, 561–84. New York: Cambridge University Press, 2014.

Horne, John, and Alan Kramer. *German Atrocities, 1914: A History of Denial.* New Haven: Yale University Press, 2001.

Hull, Isabel V. *Absolute Destruction. Military Culture and the Practices of War in Imperial Germany.* Ithaca: Cornell University Press, 2005.

Hurtzig, Paul. *Russische Schreckensherrschaft in Ostpreußen. Selbstgesehenes.* 5th ed. Schwerin i. Mecklb: Friedrich Bahn, 1916.

*Ištraukos iš laikraščių recenzijų apie J. Šiliečio albumą „Vokiečių okupacija Lietuvoje 1915–19 m."* Šiauliai: Savičo ir Šumkauskio spaustuvė, 1923.

Jahn, Peter. "Befreier und halbasiatische Horden. Deutsche Russenbilder zwischen Napoleonischen Kriegen und Erstem Weltkrieg." In *Unsere Russen, unsere Deutschen: Bilder vom Anderen 1800 bis 2000*, edited by Peter Jahn, Philip Springer, 14–29. Berlin: Christoph Links, 2007.

———. "'Zarendreck, Barbarendreck'–Die russische Besetzung Ostpreußens 1914 in der deutschen Öffentlichkeit." In *Verführungen der Gewalt. Russen und Deutsche im Ersten und Zweiten Weltkrieg*, edited by Karl Eimermacher, Astrid Volpert, Gennadij Bordjugow, 223–41. München: Wilhelm Fink, 2005.

Jokantas, Kazimieras. "Suv. Kalvarijoje vokiečių okupacijos metu (1914–1918)." *Karo archyvas* 8 (1937): 117–86.

["Karys"]. "Karo istorijos reikalu." *Karys* 15–16 (1936): 388.

Khaesh, Anatolii. "Navet 1915 goda na evreev mestechka Kuzhy." In *Evrei Rossii, Evropy i Blizhnego Vostoka: istoriia, kul'tura i slovesnost'. Materialy mezhdunarodnoi nauchnoi konferentsii 14 aprelia 2019 g.*, edited by Varvara Vovina, Maksim Mel'tsin. Vol. 15 of *Trudy po iudaike: istoriia i etnografiia*, 220–227, 374. St. Petersburg: Peterburgskii institut iudaiki, 2019.

———. "V prifrontovoi Litve 1915 goda. Rasskazy evreev-ochevidtsev." *Arkhiv evreiskoi istorii* 2 (2005): 371–406.

Klimas, Petras. *Dienoraštis 1915–1919.* Chicago: AM & M Publications, 1988.

———. "Mano kelionė po Lietuvą 1915 metais." *Mūsų senovė* 1, no. 4–5 (1922): 545–56.

["Königsberger Hartungsche Zeitung"]. "Erzählungen ostpreußischer Flüchtlinge." *Königsberger Hartungsche Zeitung*, September 4, 1914.

["Königsberger Hartungsche Zeitung"]. "Oberpräsident von Windheim über Ostpreußens Notlage." *Königsberger Hartungsche Zeitung*, September 5, 1914.

["Königsberger Hartungsche Zeitung"]. "Russengreuel in Ostpreußen . . ." *Königsberger Hartungsche Zeitung*, September 6, 1914.

["Königsberger Hartungsche Zeitung"]. "Russische Grausamkeiten und Verwüstungen sind anzuzeigen." *Königsberger Hartungsche Zeitung*, September 3, 1914.

["Königsberger Hartungsche Zeitung"]. "Russische Schandtaten in Ostpreußen. Amtlich beglaubigte Fälle." *Königsberger Hartungsche Zeitung*, September 6, 1914.

["Königsberger Hartungsche Zeitung"]. "Wie die Russen in Tapiau hausten!" *Königsberger Hartungsche Zeitung*, September 2, 1914.

Kramer, Alan. "Combatants and Noncombatants: Atrocities, Massacres, and War Crimes." In *A Companion to World War I*, edited by John Horne, 188–201. Oxford: Wiley-Blackwell, 2010.

Kuhn, A[xel]. *Die Schreckenstage von Neidenburg in Ostpreußen. Kriegserinnerungen aus dem Jahre 1914*. Minden: Wilhelm Köhler, 1914.

Leipacher, K[arl] O[tto]. *Die Russenflut in Ostpreußen. Nach amtlichen Berichten, zuverlässigen Schilderungen und eigenem Erleben*. Vol. 1: *Kämpfe um die Heimaterde*. 2nd ed. Würzburg: Curt Kabitzsch, 1916; Vol. 2: *Schicksal und Anteil*. 2nd ed. Leipzig und Würzburg: Curt Kabitzsch, 1918.

Liedtke, [Ernst]. "Erlebtes und Erfahrenes." In *Kriegserlebnisse ostpreußischer Pfarrer*, edited by C[arl] Moszeik. Vol. 2, 1–37. Berlin-Licherfelde: Edwin Runge, 1915.

["Lietuva"]. "Karo istorijai medžiaga." *Lietuva*, November 20, 1921.

Lindenberg, Paul, ed. *Hindenburg-Denkmal für das deutsche Volk. Eine Ehrengabe zum 80. Geburtstage des Reichspräsidenten*. Berlin: Vaterländischer Verlag C. A. Weller, 1927.

Liulevicius, Vejas Gabriel. *War Land on the Eastern Front. Culture, National Identity, and German Occupation in World War I*. Cambridge: Cambridge University Press, 2000.

Lohr, Eric. *Nationalizing the Russian Empire. The Campaign against Enemy Aliens during World War I*. Cambridge, MA: Harvard University Press, 2003.

———. "The Russian Army and the Jews: Mass Deportation, Hostages and Violence during World War I." *The Russian Review* 60, no. 3 (2001): 404–19.

M., J. "Už Lietuvos duoną. Vokiečių okupacijos laikų kruvini pėdsakai." *Jaunoji karta* 14 (1934): 217–18.

Moszeik, [Carl]. "Kriegserlebnisse." In *Kriegserlebnisse ostpreußischer Pfarrer*, edited by C[arl] Moszeik. Vol. 1, 1–53. Berlin-Licherfelde: Edwin Runge, 1915.

———. ed. *Kriegserlebnisse ostpreußischer Pfarrer*. Berlin-Licherfelde: Edwin Runge, 1915.

Müller, Rudolf. *Drei Wochen russischer Gouverneur. Erinnerungen an die Besetzung Gumbinnens durch die Russen August–September 1914*. 4th ed. Gumbinnen: Verlag von C. Sterzels Buchhandlung, 1915.

Nelipovich, Sergei. "Naselenie okkupirovannykh territorii rassmatrivalos' kak rezerv protivnika." *Voenno-istoricheskii zhurnal* 2 (2000): 60–69.

———. "Pereselenie nemtsev iz Vostochnoi Prussii v Rossiiu: 'vol'noplennye,' ili zlokliucheniia vostochnoprusskikh nemtsev v Rossii (1914–1917)." In *Migratsionnye protsessy sredi rossiiskikh nemtsev: istoricheskii aspekt. Materialy mezhdunarodnoi nauchnoi konferentsii, Anapa, 26–30 sentiabria 1997 g.*, 173–83. Moscow: Gotika, 1998.

Nelipovich, Sergei. "Repressii protiv poddannykh 'tsentral'nykh derzhav." *Voenno-istoricheskii zhurnal* 6 (1996): 32–42.

Nietzki, Albert. *Was wir in der Russennot 1914 erlebten*. Königsberg: Kommissionsverlag Ferd. Beyers Buchhandlung Thomas & Oppermann, 1915.

———. *Was wir in der Russennot 1914–15 erlebten*. Königsberg: Gräfe & Unzer, 1916.

Orlowski, Hubert. *"Polnische Wirtschaft": Zum deutschen Polendiskurs der Neuzeit*. Wiesbaden: Harrassowitz, 1996.

Overmans, Rüdiger. "Kriegsverluste." In *Enzyklopädie Erster Weltkrieg*, edited by Gerhard Hirschfeld, Gerd Krumeich, Irina Lenz, Markus Pöhlmann, 663–66. Paderborn u.a.: Ferdinand Schöningh, 2009.

Pakalniškis, Kazimieras. "Rusų-vokiečių karo užrašai." *Karo archyvas* 11 (1939): 101–76; 12 (1940): 95–150.

———. "Civilizuoti grobuonys plėšia Lietuvą." *Jaunoji karta* 45 (1933): 757–58.

Pakhaliuk, Konstantin. "Russkii okkupatsionnyi rezhim v Vostochnoi Prussii v 1914–15 gg." *Voenno-istoricheskii arkhiv* 6 (2012): 160–78; 9 (2012): 107–30.

"Pasisaugokime!" *Šaltinis*, May 14 (27), 1915.

[Pauliukas, Antanas] A. Uzinas. "Didžiojo karo nuotykių atsiminimai." *Panevėžio garsas*, February 16 to April 14, 1935.

Perrin, Charles. "Eating Bread with Tears: Martynas Jankus and the Deportation of East Prussian Civilians to Russia during World War I." *Journal of Baltic Studies* 48, no. 3 (2017): 363–80.

———. "Forgotten Prisoners of the Tsar: East Prussian Deportees in Russia during World War I." In *An International Rediscovery of World War One: Distant Fronts*, edited by Robert B. McCormick, Araceli Hernández-Laroche, Catherine G. Canino, 5–34. Abington, New York: Routledge, 2021.

Petkevičaitė, Gabrielė. *Karo meto dienoraštis*. Vol. 1. Kaunas: Varpo spaustuvė, 1925; Vol. 2: *1915–1916 metų okupacija*. Kaunas: Varpo spaustuvė, 1931.

———. *Karo meto dienoraštis*. Vols. 1–3. [Panevėžys]: E. Vaičekausko knygyno leidykla, 2008–2011.

Pikčilingis, Jonas. "Pergyventos valandos," *Karo archyvas* 3 (1926): 90–111.

Poehlmann, Margarete. "Aus Tilsits Russenzeit." *Die Lehrerin: Organ des Allgemeinen Deutschen Lehrerinnenvereins* 32 (1914): 242–46.

Reżat, George. *Meine Erlebnisse in der Kriegszeit und mir authentisch mitgeteilte Geschehnisse*. Tilsit: J. Reylaender & Sohn, 1917.

Richter, Klaus. "'Go with the hare's ticket' mobility and territorial policies in Ober Ost (1915–1918)." *First World War Studies* 6, no. 2 (2015): 151–70.

———. "'Seit einer Woche brennen Sumpf und Wälder'. Der Krieg in den Gouvernements Suwałki, Kovno und Kurland in der Erfahrung der Zivilbevölkerung 1915/16." In *Wielka Wojna poza linią frontu*, edited by Daniel Grinberg, Jan Snopko, Grzegorz Zackiewicz, 117–31. Białystok: Instytut Historii i Nauk Politycznych Uniwersytetu w Białymstoku, 2013.

Ruseckas, Petras. *Išniekintos vėliavos: Lietuvos atgijimo novelės*. Kaunas: Varpo spaustuvė, 1935.

———. "Kaip rašyti į Didįjį Karą." *Lietuvos aidas*, March 14, 1935.

———. ed. *Lietuva Didžiajame kare*. Vilnius: Vilniaus žodis, 1939.

Safronovas, Vasilijus. *The Creation of National Spaces in a Pluricultural Region: The Case of Prussian Lithuania*. Boston: Academic Studies Press, 2016.

———. "Neumann-Sass-Prozess als Ausdruck fundamentalen Wandels in den Beziehungen zwischen Litauen und Deutschland." *Annaberger Annalen* 21 (2013): 9–34.

Safronovas, Vasilijus, Vytautas Jokubauskas, Vygantas Vareikis, and Hektoras Vitkus. *Didysis karas visuomenėje ir kultūroje: Lietuva ir Rytų Prūsija*. Klaipėda: Klaipėdos universiteto leidykla, 2018.

Sanborn, Joshua A. "Unsettling the Empire: Violent Migrations and Social Disaster in Russia during World War I." *The Journal of Modern History* 77, no. 2 (2005): 290–324.

Sapała, Barbara. "Organisierte Erinnerung. Ein Beitrag zu Entstehungsgeschichte und Funktionen der Kriegschronik der Provinz Ostpreußen." *Studia Ełckie* 17, no. 3 (2015): 255–68.

Schöttler, Hans. *Aus Ostpreußens Kriegsnot: schlichte Bilder aus schwerer Zeit*. Potsdam: Stiftungsverlag, 1915.

Schuster, Frank M. *Zwischen allen Fronten. Osteuropäische Juden während des Ersten Weltkrieges (1914–1919)*. Vienna: Böhlau, 2004.

Schwark, Bruno. *Der Feind im Land: Berichte ermländischer Geistlicher über Ostpreussens Russenzeit 1914/15*. Braunsberg: Ermländische Zeitungs- und Verlagsdruckerei, 1915.

Senn, Alfred Erich. "The Activity of Juozas Gabrys for Lithuania's Independence, 1914–1920." *Lituanus* 23, no. 1 (1977): 15–22.

Siegfried-Jäglack, S. J. *Aus der Russenzeit Ostpreußens. Erlebnisse einer Gutsfrau*. Berlin: Hapke & Schmidt, 1915.

SG. "Vokiečių nežmoniškumas," *Viltis*, June 25 (July 8), 1915; reprinted in: *Šaltinis*, June 30 (July 13), 1915.

[Sruoga, Balys] Jurgis Plieninis, *Vokiškasis siaubas. Teisybė apie vokiečius*. s.l.: n.p., 1934.

*Steigiamojo Seimo darbai* 13 (1921).

Strazhas, Aba. *Deutsche Ostpolitik im Ersten Weltkrieg. Der Fall Ober Ost 1915–1917*. Wiesbaden: Harrassowitz, 1993.

———. "Kolonial'nyi rezhim germanskikh imperialistov v Litve v gody pervoi mirovoi voiny." *Voprosy istorii* 12 (1958): 67–85.

Strimaitis, J. "Vokiečių okupacija Kaune." *Lietuvos aidas*, March 24, 1934.

Šinkūnas, P[eliksas]. *Krašto mokslo vadovėlis (istorijos pradžiamokslis)*. 3rd ed. Kaunas: Varpo spaustuvė, 1928.

Šležas, P[aulius] and V[aclovas] Čižiūnas. *Lietuvos istorija šeštam pradžios mokyklų skyriui*. Kaunas: Sakalas, 1936.

[Šmulkštys, Antanas] Papentis. "Rašykime karo istoriją!" *Šaltinis*, May 30 (June 12), 1915.

Tiepolato, Serena. "La deportazione di civili prussiani in Russia (1914–1920)." In *La violenza contro la popolazione civile nella grande Guerra. Deportati, profughi, internati*, edited by Bruna Bianchi, 107–25. Milano: Unicopli, 2006.

———. "... und nun waren wir auch Verbannte. Warum? Weshalb? Deportate Prussiane in Russia 1914–1918." *Deportate, Esuli, Profughe. Rivista telematica di studi sulla memoria femminile* 1 (2004): 59–85.

Tumas, J[uozas]. "Rinkkime žinias karo istorijai Lietuvoje!" *Rygos garsas*, June 6 (19), 1915.

Urbšienė, Marija. "Susisiekimas, paštas ir pasai Lietuvoje Didžiojo karo metu." *Karo archyvas* 12 (1940): 63–84.

———. "Sveikatos priežiūra vokiečių okupuotoje Lietuvoje Didžiojo karo metu." *Karo archyvas* 12 (1940): 85–94.

———. "Vokiečių karo metų spauda ir Lietuva." *Karo archyvas* 8 (1937): 71–116.

———. "Vokiečių okupacijos ūkis Lietuvoje." *Karo archyvas* 10 (1938): 7–94; 11 (1939): 19–100.

Usedom, Oscar. *Im Kampf mit dem russischen Koloß*. Leipzig: Hesse & Becker, 1916.

"Užkrečiamosios ligos ir kova su jomis." *Šaltinis*, May 25 (June 7), 1915.

Überegger, Oswald. "'Verbrannte Erde' und 'baumelnde Gehenkte'. Zur europäischen Dimension militärischer Normübertretungen im Ersten Weltkrieg." In *Kriegsgreuel. Die Entgrenzung der Gewalt in kriegerischen Konflikten vom Mittelalter bis ins 20. Jahrhundert*, edited by Sönke Neitzel, Daniel Hohrath. Vol. 40 of *Krieg in der Geschichte*, 241–78. Paderborn u.a.: Ferdinand Schöningh, 2008.

V., P. "Vokiečiai Lietuvoje." *Šaltinis*, May 19 (June 1), 1915; May 25 (June 7), 1915.

*Verhandlungen des Reichstags* 311 (1918).

*Verwaltungsbericht der Militärverwaltung Litauen für die Zeit vom 1. April bis 30. September 1917.* Vol. 7. Kowno: Militärverwaltung Litauen, 1917.

Vireliūnas, Antanas. "Atsiminimai iš Didžiojo karo," *Karo archyvas* 1 (1925): 107–20.

Vitkus, Hektoras. "*Die Russen in Ostpreussen*: Rusijos ir rusų įvaizdžiai 1914–1939 m. Vokietijoje publikuotuose atsiminimuose apie Didįjį karą Rytų Prūsijoje." *Darbai ir dienos* 67 (2017): 31–67.

*Vokiečių okupacija Lietuvoje 1915–1919 m. paveiksleliuose ir trumpuose jų aprašymuose*, edited by J. Šilietis [Jaroslavas Rimkus]. Kaunas: J. Šilietis, 1922.

Watson, Alexander. "Ego Documents from the Invasion of East Prussia, 1914–1915." In *Inside World War One? The First World War and its Witnesses*, edited by Richard Bessel and Dorothee Wierling, 83–101. Oxford: Oxford University Press, 2018.

———. "'Unheard-of Brutality': Russian Atrocities against Civilians in East Prussia, 1914–1915." *The Journal of Modern History* 86, no. 4 (2014): 780–825.

Westerhoff, Christian. "Deutsche Arbeitskräftepolitik in den besetzten Ostgebieten." In *Über den Weltkrieg hinaus. Kriegserfahrungen in Ostmitteleuropa 1914–1921*, edited by Joachim Tauber. Vol. 17 of *Nordost-Archiv*, 83–107. Lüneburg: Nordost-Institut, 2009.

———. "'A kind of Siberia': German labour and occupation policies in Poland and Lithuania during the First World War." *First World War Studies* 4, no. 1 (2013): 51–63.

———. "Rekrutierung und Beschäftigung jüdischer Arbeitskräfte im besetzten Polen und Litauen während des Ersten Weltkriegs." In *Arbeit in den nationalsozialistischen Ghettos*, edited by Jürgen Hensel and Stephan Lehnstaedt, 33–51. Osnabrück: Fibre, 2013.

———. *Zwangsarbeit im Ersten Weltkrieg: Deutsche Arbeitskräftepolitik im besetzten Polen und Litauen 1914–1918*. Paderborn u.a.: Ferdinand Schöningh, 2011.

Zavadivker, Polly M. *Blood and Ink: Russian and Soviet Jewish Chroniclers of Catastrophe from World War I to World War II*. PhD diss., University of California Santa Cruz, 2013.

Žadeikis, Pranciškus. *Didžiojo karo užrašai*. Vol. 1: *1914–1915–1916 metai*. Klaipėda: Rytas, 1921.

———. *Didžiojo karo užrašai*. Vol. 2: *1917–1918–1919 metai*. Klaipėda: Rytas, 1925.

CHAPTER 3

# The Military Pogroms in Lithuania, 1919–1920

## Darius Staliūnas

The anti-Jewish pogroms that surged through Eastern Europe in 1918–1921 were the most serious outburst of anti-Jewish violence to occur between the Khmelnytsky (Chmielnicki) Uprising in Ukraine in the seventeenth century and the Holocaust.[1] To determine the precise number of such acts of violence is difficult because different concepts of the pogrom are used in historical literature. During this period, Oleg Budnitskii has calculated over one thousand five hundred pogroms and "excesses" (less serious cases of anti-Jewish violence) in Ukraine alone.[2] While Elissa Bemporad and Thomas Chopard believe that in the former territory of tsarist Russia in 1917–1921 there were over one thousand two hundred pogroms, of which 80 percent took place in Ukraine.[3] Unlike the first wave of pogroms in the Russian Empire in the beginning of the 1880s, but similarly as in 1903–1906, mass anti-Jewish violence spread into Belarus: almost two hundred pogroms occurred, taking the lives of twenty-five thousand

---

1   Lidiia Miliakova, "Vvedenie," in *Kniga pogromov. Pogromy na Ukraine, w Belorussii i evropeiskoi chasti Rossii v period Grazhdanskoi voiny. 1918–1922* (Moscow: ROSSPEN, 2007), vi; Oleg Budnitskii, "Shots in the Back: On the Origin of Anti-Jewish Pogroms of 1918–1921," in *Jews in the East European Borderlands: Essays in Honor of John D. Klier*, ed. Eugene M. Avrutin and Harriet Murav (Boston: Academic Studies Press, 2012), 187.
2   Budnitskii, "Shots in the Back," 187.
3   Elissa Bemporad and Thomas Chopard, "Introduction," *Quest. Issues in Contemporary Jewish History. Journal of Fondazione CDEC*, no. 15; "The Pogroms of the Russian Civil War at 100: New Trends, New Sources," edited by Elissa Bemporad and Thomas Chopard (August 2019): vi, accessed October 15, 2021, www.quest-cdecjournal.it//index.php?issue=15. Very recently, Jeffrey Veidlinger argued that during the Russian civil war "over 1,000 separate incidents were documented in about 500 different locales": Jeffrey Veidlinger, "Anti-Jewish Violence in the Russian Civil War," in *Pogroms. A Documentary History*, ed. Eugene M. Avrutin and Elissa Bemporad (New York: Oxford University Press, 2021), 133.

victims.[4] In the territory of the former Polish-Lithuanian Commonwealth, not including events that occurred within the framework of the Russian Civil War, William W. Hagen has calculated 279 pogroms or less serious cases of anti-Jewish violence that took the lives of 400 to 532 people.[5] If we compare this to the prewar period, not only the number of violent acts increased, but also the nature of the violence itself changed, in the opinion of a majority of contemporaries and researchers. There were more and more acts of mass violence that had genocidal features. Although it is difficult to arrive at even an approximate number of victims, the figures here vary between fifty thousand and two hundred thousand killed.[6] Thousands of Jews became victims of pogroms in Hungary as well.[7]

No doubt the war contributed to this unprecedented brutalization of the civilian population[8] not only in the sense that, as has been noticed earlier, the political vacuum, disorder and degradation of moral norms created more favorable conditions for all forms of violence, including inter-group violence,[9] but also that around fifteen million individuals had been conscripted into the Russian army. And it was precisely the tsarist army that was the institution where antisemitism had established very deep roots, and it was none other than military units, mostly Cossacks, who committed many of these pogroms in 1915.[10] They took place in Lithuania as well. However, I have not managed to find a single case where the local population and not Russian army units would have initiated this violence.[11] These acts of violence from the beginning of the war were significantly different from the spontaneous, mostly unarmed attacks that various social groups carried out against Jews up to 1914. The so-called military pogroms of 1915 were better organized, more brutal, and sent a clear message to Jews that nobody could protect them. Very often the participants of postwar

---

4   Bemporad and Chopard, "Introduction," xv.
5   Wiliam W. Hagen, *Anti-Jewish Violence in Poland, 1914–1920* (New York: Cambridge University Press, 2018), 512.
6   Miliakova, "Vvedenie," xii; Budnitskii, "Shots in the Back," 187.
7   Michael M. Miller, "The Forgotten Pogroms, 1918," *Slavic Review* 78, no. 4 (2019): 648.
8   Piotr Wróbel, "The Seeds of Violence. The Brutalization of and east European Region, 1917–1921," *Journal of Modern European History* 1, no. 1 (2003): 125.
9   Miliakova, "Vvedenie," iii, xi.
10  Eric Lohr, "1915 and the War Pogrom Paradigm in the Russian Empire," in *Anti-Jewish Violence: Rethinking the Pogrom in East European History*, ed. Jonathan Dekel-Chen et al. (Bloomington: Indiana University Press, 2011), 41–51; Budnitskii, "Shots in the Back," 189–94; Semen Goldin, *"Prinia" iskliuchitel'nye mery . . ." Russkaia armiia i evrei. 1914–1917* (Moscow: Mosty kul'tury, 2018), 285–95.
11  Darius Staliūnas, *Enemies for a Day. Antisemitism and Anti-Jewish Violence in Lithuania under the Tsars* (Budapest: Central European University Press, 2015), 204–8.

pogroms were the same people who had earlier served in the tsarist army, so, they had not only gone through a kind of anti-Jewish indoctrination, but they also "knew" that acting violently towards Jews was permitted. The motivating factors among the violent offenders in the pogroms of 1918–1921 were rather varied: a chance to profit under the conditions of an authority vacuum, economic competition, accusations against the Jews of supporting the Bolsheviks, and an absence of loyalty to the new, emerging nation states (Poland and Ukraine).[12]

The Lithuanians were creating their nation state after the war, and here we also see some anti-Jewish incidents, of which the most famous was the case of Panevėžys in 1919. The event itself has already been mentioned in historical literature; in fact, historians have made rather common descriptions, sometimes confusing the chronology of events and not going into very much detail.[13] Azriel Shohat has claimed that no pogroms occurred while the Germans controlled the situation.[14] The Lithuanian historian Aldona Gaigalaitė has actually tried to minimize the scale of this incident by using various euphemisms and claiming that the attack itself was provoked by "the Red Army's leaders' persistence in keeping Panevėžys in their hands."[15] Vygantas Vareikis stated that "in interwar Lithuania there was not a single religious, national or politically motivated altercation between the Jews and the Lithuanians during which a person would have died."[16]

War pogroms, particularly acts of mass violence enacted by military units, differ from the spontaneous incidents initiated and performed by the civilian

---

12 Budnitskii, "Shots in the Back," 187–88; Bemporad and Chopard, "Introduction," viii; Eugene M. Avrutin and Elissa Bemporad, "An Introduction," in *Pogroms. A Documentary History*, 13–14.
13 Azriel Shohat, "The Beginnings of Anti-Semitism in Independent Lithuania," *Yad Vashem Studies* 2 (1958): 44–45; Vygantas Vareikis, "Žydų ir lietuvių susidūrimai bei konfliktai tarpukario Lietuvoje," in *Kai ksenofobija virsta prievarta. Lietuvių ir žydų santykių dinamika XIX a.– XX a. pirmoje pusėje*, ed. Vladas Sirutavičius and Darius Staliūnas (Vilnius: LII leidykla, 2005), 161; Liudas Truska, *Lietuviai ir žydai nuo XIX a. pabaigos iki 1941 m. birželio. Antisemitizmo Lietuvoje raida* (Vilnius: VPU leidykla, 2005), 77; Vytautas Petronis, "Neperkirstas Gordijo mazgas: valstybinės prievartos prieš visuomenę Lietuvoje genezė (1918–1921)," *Lietuvos istorijos metraštis*, no. 1 (2015): 77–78; Tomas Balkelis, *War, Revolution, and Nation-Making in Lithuania, 1914–1923* (Oxford: Oxford University Press, 2018), 117; Eglė Bendikaitė, "'Lai kalba žygiai ir faktai': Panevėžio krašto žydai Nepriklausomybės kovose": 71–73, accessed January 3, 2020, http://www.paneveziomuziejus.lt/files/krasto_istorija/Bendikaite%20 lai%20kalba%2zygiai%202018.pdf; Hektoras Vitkus, "Žydų kariai Lietuvos (lietuvių) Nepriklausomybės kovose 1919–1923 metais. Ką žinome apie jų motyvus?" *Acta Historica Universitatis Klaipedensis* 38 (2019): 172–74.
14 Shohat, "The Beginnings of Anti-Semitism," 44.
15 Aldona Gaigalaitė, *Lietuva Paryžiuje 1919 metais* (Kaunas: Šviesa, 1999), 111–12.
16 Vareikis, "Žydų ir lietuvių susidūrimai," 162.

population. Civil violence can be just as brutal as that enacted by soldiers, as occurred in the Russian Empire in 1903–1906, for example. However, during the military pogroms, the victims are usually in a completely helpless situation, as they cannot expect protection from the government, since the government itself (or its military units) is responsible for the violence. Yet, in both types of incidents we can look for symbolic markers that allow us to better understand the intentions and world view of the perpetrators.[17]

In this chapter, I decode the symbolic meanings of the military pogroms that took place in Lithuania in 1919–1920 and explain how they reflected the interethnic relations in the postwar situation. I argue that, alongside elementary acts of theft, these incidents were also characterized by the symbolic elimination of Jews from the new political body and even their dehumanization, for example, the denial of full humanness.

## Jews and Non-Jews in Panevėžys before 1919

Before launching into an analysis of the events of 1919, Christian-Jewish relations in Panevėžys and its surroundings up to the end of the war should also be discussed.[18] Testimonials given by Jews from Panevėžys and collected after the Russian government's deportations in 1915 contain claims that before the war "relations between Jews and other ethnic groups were relatively peaceful," only "the Poles engaged in antisemitic agitation against the Jews, however this agitation never developed into an actual organized form."[19] *Nash Krai* [Our Region], a Russian newspaper in circulation in 1914 in Panevėžys, was meant to improve relations between Jews, Lithuanians, and Belarusians. However, it was but a short-term project, and there are no reasons to suggest that it would have had any tangible effect on interethnic relations.[20] It was in none other than the Panevėžys

---

17 For such an approach see: Rogers Brubaker and David Laitin, "Ethnic and Nationalist Violence," *Annual Review of Sociology* 24, no. 1 (2003): 441. One of the most recent examples of such an approach: Hagen, *Anti-Jewish Violence in Poland, 1914–1920*.
18 According to the All-Russian census of 1897, Jews made half of the population of Panevėžys (6,545 out of 12,958).
19 f. 9548, op. 1, d. 164, l. 192, *Gossudarstvennyi arkhiv Rossiiskoi Federatsii* (State Archves of the Russian Federation hereafter cited as GARF); f. 9548, op. 1, d. 167, GARF. A little bit later, in 1919, the Jewish press reported that antisemitism is stronger in the northeastern and eastern parts of Lithuania which are more Polonized: *Der Tog un di varhayt* 1731 (1919), 4.
20 Darius Staliūnas, "Rusų kalba kaip lietuvių ir žydų komunikacijos priemonė: laikraštis 'Naš kraj' (1914)," in *Abipusis pažinimas: lietuvių ir žydų kultūriniai saitai* ed. Jurgita Šiaučiūnaitė-Verbickienė (Vilnius: VU leidykla, 2010), 161–81.

and Šiauliai districts, the only regions in Lithuania, where a wave of pogroms and less serious anti-Jewish excesses occurred in the long nineteenth century (in Linkuva, Pašvitinys, and Konstantinov [Vaškai]). Such cases of blood libel, which is what prompted this violence, remained in the memory of Lithuanian society for a long time and were known to a wider circle than just the population in those specific locations.[21] The onset of war, especially the deportation of Jews and other factors, such as the conversion of the Panevėžys Jewish cemetery into a pasture for cows utilized by the tsarist intendant,[22] sent to the Christian society a clear message that Jews were viewed as second-rate subjects in the Russian Empire. If we are to believe the testimonials given by Jews, Jewish-Christian relations worsened in Panevėžys with the start of the war. Christians were suspicious of Jews for artificial price inflation and spying for the Germans,[23] while at the railway station, a random priest was heard saying that the "the time of reckoning with the Jews had come."[24] In 1915 in the larger cities of the Kaunas province, and thus also in Panevėžys, Jews had not experienced violence. Yet pogroms took place in smaller towns, also in the Panevėžys District. On Saturday July 9, 1915 in Vabalininkas, when Jews opened their shops for business, the soldiers of infantry and artillery units seized this opportunity and even paid for their goods. However, upon the arrival of the Cossacks, a pogrom broke out: the Cossacks caught Jews in the streets, beating and robbing them of any valuables, broke into their houses, and destroyed their property.[25] No such cases were recorded in Panevėžys in 1915. However, the local population did appropriate Jewish property regardless of the police's efforts to stop this.[26] Robbers appropriated not only Jewish property, but this ethno-confessional group suffered most.

## Anti-Jewish Violence in Panevėžys in May 1919

The main source of knowledge about the events in Panevėžys in 1919 are the findings of the Special Lithuanian Government Interrogation Commission

---

21  Staliūnas, *Enemies for a Day*, 57.
22  Goldin, *"Priniat' iskliuchitel'nye mery...",* 314.
23  f. 9548, op. 1, d. 164, l. 192, GARF.
24  f. 9548, op. 1, d. 163, l. 62, GARF.
25  "Iz 'chernoi knigi' rossiiskogo evreistva," *Evreiskaia starina* X (1918): 275; Goldin, *"Priniat' iskliuchite"nye mery...",* 290. According to the All-Russian Census of 1897, Jews made the majority of Vabalininkas population (1,828 out of 2,333).
26  RG80 File 1062, l. 79436, 79438, YIVO archive; Goldin, *"Priniat' iskliuchitel'nye mery...",* 311–12.

(hereafter called the Commission). Aside from one lower-ranked official, this Commission included three well known figures—the Minister of Justice Liudas Noreika, the State Attorney from the Kaunas District Court Rapolas Skipitis, and the Minister Without Portfolio for Jewish Affairs Max Soloveichik. The following analysis rests mainly on their findings thus far, and no other sources give a more detailed account of the events have been uncovered.[27] Sources from that time insinuate that censorship orders prevented the Yiddish newspaper *Yiddishe shtime* (The Jewish Voice) from publishing information about the anti-Jewish attacks.[28] The Commission's findings should not be considered solely as a "Lithuanian" interpretation of events, because, as was already mentioned, one of its members was Soloveichik. All the members were unanimous over the findings,[29] and an identical summary of the events was published in *Yiddishe shtime* several years later, probably thanks to the efforts of the minister for Jewish affairs.[30]

The situation in Panevėžys was complicated because control of the city swapped hands numerous times, and, in certain periods, the city was left without any government whatsoever. In the three months leading up to March 27, 1919, Panevėžys had been occupied by the Bolsheviks. And in some government offices, especially those that had greater contact with the local population, there were quite a few Jews who could not speak Lithuanian, making Russian the official language.[31]

Although no sociolinguistic research has been conducted, one important document does show that Jews in the cities did not speak Lithuanian as there were very few Lithuanians there. Also, up to World War I, the Lithuanian language

---

27  Back in late May 1919, when he was in Šiauliai and thus could not have known about the events apart from what he might have heard from other people, the Minister of Trade and Industry Jonas Šimkus sent a short message to the prime minister about the events in Panevėžys: "After the occupation of the city, Germans flooded the city within a few hours and together with our army started to rob the population, mostly the Jews. Soldiers were walking in gangs around the city, breaking into apartments and demanding residents to hand over all watches, shoes and money. Some of the Jews who opposed this were shot. Officers stood by and did not stop the soldiers" (Bendikaitė, "'Lai kalba žygiai ir faktai,'" 71).
28  Report from the Minister Without Portfolio for Jewish Affairs to the prime minister, December 11, 1919, f. 923, ap. 1, b. 30, l. 24, *Lietuvos valstybės centrinis archyvas* (Lithuanian State Central Archives hereafter cited as LCVA).
29  Commission's findings, June 15, 1919, f. 923, ap. 1, b. 1350, l. 14, LCVA.
30  "Der mishpet iber di ekscesn in Ponevezh," *Yiddishe shtime* 34 (1922), 3.
31  Some memoirs mention the date of March 24: P. Lelis, "Panevėžio išvadavimas 1919 m.," accessed January 29, 2020, http://www.partizanai.org/karys-1964m-1-2/5432-panevezio-isvadavimas-1919-m.

was not held to be prestigious, unlike Russian on "Jewish Street."[32] Lithuanian-Jewish communication mostly took place in Russian.[33] Prior to the war, the use of Russian in the Jewish community was one of the themes taken up by Lithuanian antisemitism. Yet compared to other topics, like supposedly harmful economic activities of the Jews, its role was only marginal at best.[34] However, once the nation state started being created, the question of languages used by national minorities in the public space became much more relevant. The mass vandalism against non-Lithuanian signs in the early 1920s and other measures taken to eliminate the use of other languages in the public space testified to the determination of that group of Lithuanians who wished to see the domination of the Lithuanian language in the nation state.[35]

In much of the same way, the identification of Jews with Bolsheviks was not a completely new phenomenon in Lithuanian society. Back in the early twentieth century, the right-wing Lithuanian press accused Jews of promoting "progressive," for instance, leftist, ideas that were condemned by the Lithuanian clerics.[36] During the Lithuanian war against the Bolsheviks, the identification of Jews with the latter became more widespread. This aspect shall be analyzed further in the chapter.

The city was taken over by the Lithuanian army on March 27, 1919 and part of it "immediately took on the attitude of the non-Jewish part of the population viewing Jews as one of pillars of the Bolshevik regime." However, there was no information about any serious anti-Jewish acts of violence, only about "tense relations among us [Lithuanians], the army, and Jewish civilians in Panevėžys."[37] Already by April 4, Lithuanian units, pressured by the Red Army, had to withdraw from the city, when they were allegedly fired upon by Jews. The Commission, despite "all the work done," could not confirm this fact, yet it did

---

32 The Commission also probably recorded testimonials in Russian. Firstly, according to the afore-mentioned Skipitis, Soloveichik did not know Lithuanian, thus Lithuanians communicated with him in Russian (Rapolas Skipitis, *Nepriklausomą Lietuvą statant. Atsiminimai* [Chicago: Terra, 1961], 357); second, certain key terms in the Commission's findings were specified in brackets in Russian, suggesting that this was the language the testimonial was given in.
33 Staliūnas, "Rusų kalba kaip lietuvių ir žydų komunikacijos priemonė," 161–81.
34 Staliūnas, *Enemies for a Day*, 77.
35 Vytautas Petronis, "The Emergence of the Lithuanian Radical Right Movement, 1922–1927," *Journal of Baltic Studies* 46, no. 1 (2015): 81–85.
36 Staliūnas, *Enemies for a Day*, 80.
37 Commission's findings, June 15, 1919, f. 923, ap. 1, b. 1350, l. 14, LCVA.

not doubt that this circumstance "was the psychological component for all the events that occurred thereafter."[38]

The image of the Jew as a traitor, always prepared to "stab in the back," had already established deep roots in imperial Russian society, especially among soldiers,[39] while later, it was prevalent in national armies.[40] Many men who had previously served in the tsarist army now made up the Lithuanian units. Oleg Budnitskii associates the aforementioned image with the conviction in Christian society in imperial times about the improper behavior of Jews. If in the event of anti-Jewish violence, a Jew used a firearm in self-defense, the dominant society would treat such behavior as not following its imagined "rules of the game," and in such cases, the brutality of the perpetrators of violence would only intensify.[41] It is not surprising that in 1919 in Panevėžys, "angered over being fired upon from windows and gateways, as those questioned alleged, during their departure, the Lithuanian soldiers shot at two Jews, one of them was 66 years old, and another woman aged 23," and they also "left with feelings of anger towards the city, speaking against the Jews that they would get even the next time they took control of Panevėžys."

The Lithuanian and German Freikorps took control of the city for the second time in the evening of May 19. According to the data collected by the Commission, the next day, fearing reprisals, the Jews did not open their shops. The new hosts of the city treated it as a sign of opposition and "on May 20 a round of looting of Jewish shops and private apartments began, and according to all witnesses, the Germans who entered the city right after the Lithuanian army began looting everywhere; and generally, in most cases, the initiators of the looting were the Germans."[42] Among the soldiers who joined German Freikorps, there were quite a few who had no permanent job and were just looking for material gains. Besides, there were problems with military discipline

---

38  Commission's findings, June 15, 1919, f. 923, ap. 1, b. 1350, l. 15, LCVA.
39  Budnitskii, "Shots in the Back," 196.
40  Christopher Gilley, "Beat the Jews, Save . . . Ukraine: Antisemitic Violence and Ukrainian State Building Projects 1918–1920," *Quest: Issues in Contemporary Jewish History. Journal of Fondazione CDEC*. no. 15 ("The Pogroms of the Russian Civil War at 100: New Trends, New Sources," ed. Elissa Bemporad and Thomas Chopard) (August 2019): 122, accessed October 15, 2021, http://www.quest-cdecjournal.it//index.php?issue=15.
41  Budnitskii, "Shots in the Back," 197. See also: John D. Klier, "Christians and Jews and the 'Dialogue of Violence' in Late Imperial Russia," in *Religious Violence Between Christians and Jews: Medieval Roots, Modern Perspectives*, ed. Anna Safir Abulafia (New York: Palgrave, 2002), 166; Staliūnas, *Enemies for a Day*, 193.
42  Commission's findings, June 15, 1919, f. 923, ap. 1, b. 1350, l. 16, LCVA.

in these units.[43] Thus, one can make an educated guess that soldiers of these German Freikorps sometimes eagerly took any opportunity for robbing. The looting continued on May 21.

By May 21, the Lithuanian and German units had withdrawn from Panevėžys. It appeared that the city was under no one's control for some time. Occasionally, Bolshevik reconnaissance units made an appearance, yet groups of German and Lithuanian soldiers were much more active in the city. According to the Commission's data, the city was ravaged by looting and killing on May 21–24. It was alleged that the Germans were mostly responsible for taking the property:

> Generally speaking, the looting was done by gangs of mostly German soldiers walking around the city, breaking into Jewish shops or into apartments mostly occupied by Jews, taking the goods and things they found, bundling them up into sacks and loading them onto their wagons which they had usually brought with them from outside the city, and took everything away to their camps. The Germans would get Lithuanian soldiers to join them. Often, separate gangs of Lithuanian soldiers would also take part in the looting. The looting soldiers would sometimes be joined by certain locals, especially women and boys, mostly from among the Old Believers who would show them which houses or shops to loot and would load their sacks with goods to drag home with themselves.[44]

Meanwhile, "in the opinion of the victims' relatives, the killings and injuries were done only by Lithuanian soldiers":

> It can be concluded that the killings and injuries were, in a majority of cases, of a meaningless, wantonly violent nature, typical of wartime looting (*maroderstva*). Among those killed and injured, of whom there were around 20, as witnesses testified, were three elderly men aged 65–70 and a 12-year-old girl. Many shots were fired at people who were simply walking down the street and at house windows, and in those cases, according to our data, only Jews were the victims.[45]

---

43 Petras Jakštas, "*Saksų savanorių dalys* Lietuvoje 1919 m.," *Karo archyvas* 6 (1935): 194–95.
44 Commission's findings, June 15, 1919, f. 923, ap. 1, b. 1350, l. 16, LCVA.
45 Commission's findings, June 15, 1919, f. 923, ap. 1, b. 1350, l. 17, LCVA. It is somewhat odd that the Commission did not identify a single victim by name.

An important stimulus to engage in violence against the Jews could also have been Lithuanian infantry regiment leader Vincas Grigaliūnas-Glovackis' order to fire at captured Bolshevik soldiers and people who had collaborated with the Bolsheviks or were suspected of doing so.[46] Grigaliūnas-Glovackis generally acted like a warlord, and the Lithuanian government had trouble controlling him. Like various warlords in Ukraine,[47] he often dealt with the civilian population without resorting to a court of law.[48]

On May 24, when the city came under the occupation of Lithuanian and German military units, the looting continued for another several days, although acts of violence against individuals decreased. Yet on May 25, two soldiers killed a Jew Golombek, a popular paramedic in the city who had allegedly attempted to poison a Lithuanian soldier a few days earlier.[49]

The poisoning both in the broader sense, when speaking about the detrimental effect of Jews on Christian society, and about the specific use of poison for malicious purposes, is a frequently reoccurring narrative in the antisemitic discourse in Eastern Europe.[50] Sometimes in these antisemitic narratives, poisoning was related specifically to Jewish paramedics.[51] The Commission could not find any data testifying that the city commandant would have taken any steps to stop the looting, except in the case where the goods of one Lithuanian were protected.[52] Incidentally, the leader of the second infantry unit, the aforementioned Grigaliūnas-Glovackis and the aforementioned city commandant Puzer von Miller released a proclamation against violence and looting.[53] Yet the

---

46  Petronis, "Neperkirstas Gordijo mazgas," 77.
47  Gilley, "Beat the Jews, Save . . . Ukraine."
48  For more on this see: Petronis, "Neperkirstas Gordijo mazgas,"69–95; Kęstutis Kilinskas, "Pulkininkas prieš vyriausybę: plk. Vinco Grigaliūno-Glovackio ir Mykolo Sleževičiaus vyriausybių santykiai 1919 ir 1926 m.," *Acta Historica Universitatis Klaipedensis* 32 (2016): 76–93; Česlovas Laurinavičius, "On Political Terror during the Soviet Expansion into Lithuania, 1918–1919," *Journal of Baltic Studies* 46, no. 1 (2015): 70, 73–74.
49  Commission's findings, June 15, 1919, f. 923, ap. 1, b. 1350, l. 17, LCVA.
50  *Rassvet* 18 (1881), 758; Hagen, *Anti-Jewish Violence in Poland, 1914–1920*, 165, 199, 250, 282, 392.
51  Hagen, *Anti-Jewish Violence in Poland, 1914–1920*, 392; The 1952–53 "Doctor's plot" in the Soviet Union is from the same narrative, see: Jeffrey Veidlinger, "Was the Doctors' Plot a Blood Libel?" in *Ritual Murder in Russia, Eastern Europe, and Beyond. New Histories of an Old Accusation*, ed. Eugene M. Avrutin, Jonathan Dekel-Chen and Robert Weinberg (Bloomington: Indiana University Press, 2017), 238–52.
52  However, the Minister of Trade and Industry Jonas Šimkus asserted that "the city commandant Milerius (Miller) kept a check on things as much as he could, stopping the looting where he could and returning stolen goods. But he alone could only do so much." Quote from Bendikaitė, "'Lai kalba žygiai ir faktai,'" 71.
53  Commission's findings, June 15, 1919, f. 923, ap. 1, b. 1350, l. 17-18, LCVA.

Commission was not convinced by the sincerity and effectiveness of that proclamation and it came to the conclusion that all these circumstances could have formed the "conviction that the Jews were not protected by the law," which is what eventually led to the "disgusting event of June 3."[54]

## Humiliation of Jews on June 3, 1919

On that day, the city commandant gave orders to the chief of the city military police Lukenski to dig up and rebury six Red Army soldiers killed in action outside the city. The soldiers had been ceremoniously buried in the city center during the Bolshevik occupation.[55] The killed soldiers were Christians, most probably Catholics, as the new city government decided to rebury them in the Catholic cemetery on the city's outskirts. The exploitation of Jewish labor in this case provoked the image of Jews as Bolsheviks. The further course of events only confirmed this argument. At first, the Jews rounded up by the militia and soldiers had to dig up the coffins containing the already partly decomposed bodies and then carry them to the cemetery outside of the city. Despite being beaten and humiliated, the Jews managed to negotiate that the coffins be transported on a wagon. However, the militia chief agreed only on the condition that the wagon to be used belonged to a Jew, not to a Christian. He also requested that one coffin still had to be carried. At the cemetery, the executors of this campaign forced a Jewish teacher believed to be a rabbi to sing religious hymns along with a few other Jews. Two people who participated in this humiliation of Jews, whom the Commission identified as deserters with a criminal history, took the opportunity to also rob them.[56] Besides the brutality of the act itself, the Commission was left surprised that the perpetrators "did not sense there was anything extraordinary in their actions, and that some of them tried to lay the blame for certain acts on one another, and that they used a

---

54 Commission's findings, June 15, 1919, f. 923, ap. 1, b. 1350, l. 18–19, LCVA.
55 In his memoirs, Grigaliūnas-Glovackis wrote about his astonishment and indignation over this burial place in the center of Panevėžys: "In the widest street in Panevėžys, Ramygala Street, almost the very city center, I saw a recently made grave surrounded by a low, wooden fence, decorated with wreaths and bouquets of fresh flowers. I thought this was a grave for the heroes of the Panevėžys battalion, who had defended the city from the Bolsheviks. I was wrong. It was a Bolshevik grave—of those who defended Panevėžys from our men" (Vincas Grigaliūnas Glovackis, *Generolo atsiminimai*, vol. 2–3 (Vilnius: Generolo Jono Žemaičio Lietuvos karo akademija, 2017), 64.
56 Commission's findings, 15 June 1919, LCVA, f. 923, ap. 1, b. 1350, l. 19–20; "Der mishpet iber di ekscesn in Ponevezh," *Yiddishe shtime* 34 (1922): 3; June 20, 1919: 44–45.

normal tone of speaking when describing the most horrific details of what happened, and of the humiliation."[57] Nor do we come across any remorse over this violence in the memoirs of Grigaliūnas-Glovackis where the events of June 3 are described using various euphemisms, in which he refers to Jews as dandies and snobs. He justified violence against the civilians and described Soloveichik contemptuously.[58] All of this reveals the deeply symbolic meaning of this act: Bolshevism was viewed as a purely Jewish phenomenon and thus Jews were nothing but pariahs.

## The Lithuanian Government and Anti-Jewish Violence

The actions of government institutions of the Republic of Lithuania that followed were an obvious demonstration of the ambiguous attitudes of Lithuanian elites towards the Panevėžys incident and the position of Jews in general within the Lithuanian nation state. Already on June 7, the Commission arrived in Panevėžys, where they worked intensively to gather information: many witnesses were interviewed, and the Commission received 192 declarations and requests in which the victims evaluated the cost of damages to the amount of 1,469,673 Russian rubles.[59] On June 15, the Commission formulated its recommendations that the guilty Puzer von Miller and Liukianski be dismissed from their offices. The compensation of damages was postponed until a court hearing, but it was decided to pay out a pension first to Golombek's family. The Commission also initiated withdrawing the illegal orders issued by Grigaliūnas-Glovackis and Puzer von Miller regarding the shootings without a court hearing.[60] The government approved these recommendations on June 18.[61] The Lithuanian government and the new Panevėžys city commandant Tadas Chodakauskas also released proclamations where they urged upholding law and order and threatened legal repercussions against those who acted violently

---

57 Commission's findings, June 15, 1919, *LCVA*, f. 923, ap. 1, b. 1350, l. 20–21.
58 Vincas Grigaliūnas Glovackis, *Generolo atsiminimai*, vol. 2–3 (Vilnius: Generolo Jono Žemaičio Lietuvos karo akademija, 2017), 64–65.
59 Commission's findings, June 15, 1919, f. 923, ap. 1, b. 1350, l. 13–14, LCVA.
60 Minutes from the Commission's meeting, June 15, 1919, f. 923, ap. 1, b. 60, l. 1–2, LCVA. This means that the Lithuanian government was only prepared to take responsibility for the events that happened after May 25, when the city was already under the total control of the Lithuanian army. Yet, it would not be held accountable for the events a few days prior.
61 Copy of the Governments' decision, June 18, 1919, f. 923, ap. 1, b. 60, l. 3–6, LCVA.

towards their fellow citizens.[62] However, according to the available data, at least until 1922, no one was ever punished for these crimes.[63] By then, Puzer von Miller had already left Lithuania, while the two convicted Lithuanian soldiers never received any punishment.[64] This kind of ambiguous situation where the offenders were condemned yet never seriously prosecuted unfolded due to a number of circumstances.

Firstly, both the Commission and the government were uneasy about the willful behavior of some of the army leaders, especially the acts of violence against the civilian population, including Jews, which certainly did nothing to increase the latter's loyalty to the Lithuanian nation state.[65] Soloveichik and other Jewish community leaders drew the attention of other government members to the number of times the acts of anti-Jewish violence were enacted and demanded that appropriate measures be taken.[66] In addition, such events severely impacted the prestige of the young Lithuanian state in the international arena,[67] especially since the Lithuanian government tried to publicize information about the anti-Jewish pogroms being performed by the Poles.[68] However, there were other obstacles in the battle against perpetrators of violence against Jews.

Historians have stated on numerous occasions that, due to the complicated international and military situation, the central government of Lithuania often had to cope with the arbitrary acts of army leaders such as Grigaliūnas-Glovackis.[69]

---

62  Proclamation "Citizens!" f. 923, ap. 1, b. 37, l. 61, LCVA; "Piliečiai!," *Lietuva*, no. 133 (1919), 1.
63  The Jewish press published in the US was complaining about this already in 1919: "Vilkomir, Ponevezh un Oniksht," *Der Tog un di varhayt*, no. 1762 (1919), 6. See also "Žydų bendruomenės suvažiavimo reikalu," *Lietuva*, no. 40 (1920), 2.
64  "Der mishpet iber di ekscesn in Ponevezh," *Yiddishe shtime*, no. 34 (1922), 3; Bendikaitė, "'Lai kalba žygiai ir faktai,'" 73.
65  Commission's findings, June 15, 1919, f. 923, ap. 1, b. 1350, l. 21, LCVA.
66  Materials collected by the Minister Without Portfolio for Jewish Affairs, f. 923, ap. 1, b. 157, l. 53–58, LCVA; Memorandum from the Lithuanian Jewish Communities to the prime minister, August 3, 1919, f. 923, ap. 1, b. 30, l. 105–108, LCVA; Resolution by the Congress of the Jewish communities, January 5–12, 1920, f. 923, ap. 1, b. 117, l. 10, LCVA. The Jewish elite in Lithuania approved of the decisions passed by the government in the summer of 1919 regarding the events in Panevėžys: Newsletter of the Ministry for Jewish Affairs, no. 2, July 22, 1919, f. 923, ap. 1, b. 30, l. 126–127, LCVA.
67  Minutes of the meeting of the Government, June 30, 1919, f. 923, ap. 1, b. 24, l. 3, LCVA; Gaigalaitė, *Lietuva Paryžiuje 1919 metais*, 111–12.
68  Notice from J. Purickas to J. Šaulys and an unidentified person by the surname of Wiker, June 20, 1919, Ms. Coll. 1243: Jurgis Saulys papers, Box 3, Folder 9, University of Pennsylvania, Kislak Center for Special Collections, Rare Books and Manuscripts. At the time, Lithuania and Poland were in conflict over Vilnius and other territories that both sides considered "their own."
69  Petronis, "Neperkirstas Gordijo mazgas," 69–95.

Additionally, the meeting of the Cabinet of Ministers held on June 30, 1919 where both the events in Panevėžys and other anti-Jewish excesses were discussed revealed that some government members were not hesitant in naming Jews as disloyal to the Lithuanian state. They put some of the blame on the anti-Jewish mood in society and the army in general, and for the violence in Panevėžys on Jews themselves. Prime Minister Mykolas Sleževičius suggested that Jews "accept part of the blame," as they "looked towards the Russians, the Germans and others," for example, that they were loyal to just about anyone except for the Lithuanian state. Meanwhile, the Chief of Defense General Silvestras Žukauskas complained that, when he arrived to Panevėžys, the Jews allegedly appealed to the Americans rather than to him, as they "wanted to show that Lithuania was still too immature for independence."[70] The army commander also asked "why does Soloveichik not tell the Jews: do not shoot," thus reminding those gathered of the image of the Jew as of someone just waiting to attack a Lithuanian from behind, while also shifting the blame, or at least part of it, upon the victims themselves.[71]

Both the government's indecisive position in fighting anti-Jewish violence, and its inability to fully control the Lithuanian army's units led to the fact that the Panevėžys pogrom was not the only case of mass anti-Jewish violence in Lithuania in 1919–1920. At least one more incident that occurred in the summer of 1919 in Ukmergė resulted in more victims (one killed and several injured). Much like in Panevėžys, it should be interpreted as an episode of the struggle against enemies of the Lithuanian state. A Zionist meeting was held in this city on July 10. It was disturbed when shooting by Lithuanian soldiers broke out. The soldiers accused the Jews themselves of firing from the hall where the meeting was held. In other words, the narrative about Jewish "provocation" was repeated in this story as well. According to the accusation, the leader of this attack, the sergeant of the Ukmergė commandant's company Aleksandras Vilavičius, decided to end the meeting as a few soldiers who were inside overheard "adverse comments against the Lithuanian government and a critique of its campaigns."[72] And the soldiers reached the conclusion that "the Jews were

---

70 Minutes of the meeting of the Government, June 30, 1919, f. 923, ap. 1, b. 24, l. 2–3, LCVA.
71 Ibid. Other sources from the time also mentioned how the Jews from Panevėžys appealed to "Americans and the English." See: Bendikaitė, "'Lai kalba žygiai ir faktai,'" 71.
72 "Apie Ukmergės Karo Komendantą karininką Kmieliauską kaltin. Baudž. Kod. 676 straipsn.," f. 483, ap. 8, b. 305, LCVA.

organizing a revolt against the Lithuanian government."[73] The patriotic motif was not the only one in this incident as some Jews were also robbed.[74]

It was none other than the appropriation of Jewish property that was the reason for the pogrom in Vabalininkas that took place on August 12, 1920 and other less serious excesses, for example, in Kaišiadorys,[75] mostly carried out by soldiers or recruits.[76] Around eight hundred new recruits arrived in Vabalininkas and "gathered in large gangs, trailed the town streets and stormed into shops, looting and damaging goods."[77] And when Leizer Kriger and his family tried to stop them from looting, "they became painfully bashed by the crowd."[78] Even though there were some shops in the town that also belonged to non-Jews, "not a single one of them was looted during this riot."[79] The minister without a portfolio for Jewish affairs also spoke about frequent cases where soldiers would act violently towards Jews in the street for no reason.[80] The sources currently available do not explain why specifically Jews were targeted in these less serious incidents, yet it is clear that the soldiers were convinced that it was permissible to act violently towards Jews in particular without fear of any punishment.

---

73  This point is not very clear. The commandant of Ukmergė granted permission to hold the meeting, but it is unlikely that he demanded it to be held in Lithuanian—a language most Jews in Ukmergė either did not know at all or could only communicate in on a very basic level. The meeting could have been held in Russian, which was used no less than Yiddish in the Zionist discourse during the imperial period. In that case, some Lithuanian soldiers could have understood the content of the speeches.
74  "Apie Ukmergės Karo Komendantą karininką Kmieliauską kaltin. Baudž. Kod. 676 straipsn.," f. 483, ap. 8, b. 305, LCVA; report from Natan Ionasevich to the minister without portfolio for the Jewish affairs (copy), July 14, 1919, f. 923, ap. 1, b. 30, l. 84, LCVA; Shohat, "The Beginnings of Anti-Semitism," 45; Šarūnas Liekis, Lidija Miliakova, and Antony Polonsky, "Prievarta prieš žydus buvusiose Lietuvos-Lenkijos žemėse 1919 m.," in *Kai ksenofobija virsta prievarta*, 246–47; Šarūnas Liekis, *1939: The Year That Changed Everything in Lithuania's History* (Amsterdam-New York: Rodopi, 2010), 246–47. The perpetrators were not punished.
75  Gaigalaitė, *Lietuva Paryžiuje 1919 metais*, 111.
76  According to the newspaper "Tauta" (The Nation), a group of recruits of Bolshevik orientation were looting Jewish shops in Ramygala: "Lietuvos žinios. Ramygala," *Tauta*, no. 34 [44] (1920).
77  Report from the minister without portfolio for Jewish affairs to the prime minister (copy), August 14, 1920, f. 923, ap. 1, b. 117, l. 41–44, LCVA.
78  Ibid.
79  Ibid.
80  Materials collected by the minister without portfolio for Jewish affairs, f. 923, ap. 1, b. 157, l. 53–58, LCVA; "Litauen," *Neue Jüdische Monatshefte*, no. 7–8 (1920), 179; Shohat, "The Beginnings of Anti-Semitism," 45–46.

## Conclusion

The military pogroms of 1919–1920 took a number of victims' lives in Lithuania. However, their exact number is unclear as the Commission that studied the incidents in Panevėžys mentioned that there were twenty Jews either killed or injured on May 21–24, 1919, without identifying how many specifically there were of each, nor listing any surnames, nor mentioning the fact that there were victims in Panevėžys both before and after the events of May 21–24, with one Jew killed in Ukmergė.

The humiliation of Jews organized by Lithuanian officials on June 3, 1919 in Panevėžys not only revealed that Jews were identified with Bolsheviks, but also that there was an intention to eliminate them from the political body of the new nation state. During the incident, they were also dehumanized (the first order to carry the coffins containing decomposing bodies over a long distance; the violent behavior towards Jews digging the grave pits and the orders to sing hymns). These acts are very reminiscent of episodes of the murder of Jews that would take place in rural Lithuania in 1941. During the infamous pogrom in Jedwabne, Poland, the offenders forced the Jews to carry a monument of Lenin whilst singing and to bury the statue later.[81] Incidentally, unlike in Jedwabne, the Jews involved in the Panevėžys campaign survived.

The critical conditions leading to mass violence in 1919 were an escalation in violent acts during World War I (with the pogroms of 1915 also serving as a kind of example) and ultimately the inability of the Lithuanian government to control its military units. Those were probably the most important factors that facilitated the emergence of such brutality.

In some of the war pogroms, it is hard to identify any other motives but looting. Yet one of the most important circumstances, for example, in Vabalininkas, was that only Jewish shops were looted, which clearly indicates the military's attitude towards Jews as a highly vulnerable group. Due to the lack of sources, it is sometimes difficult to determine whether the looting was the cause of outbreaks of violence, or just a side effect.

The events in Panevėžys cannot be interpreted as actions aroused by atavistic, anti-Judaic superstitions. They were rather part of the process of creating the nation-state. While the Jews were not completely eliminated from its political body, they nonetheless faced a clear condition—loyalty to the Lithuanian nation state. It was precisely this discourse that is evident from the government

---

81 Jan T. Gross, *Neighbors. The Destruction of the Jewish Community in Jedwabne, Poland* (Princeton: Princeton University Press, 2001), 19.

meeting of June 30, 1919, called to discuss the anti-Jewish incidents. This is also how researchers interpret the pogroms of 1918–1921 in Central Europe, for example, as the elimination of Jews from the newly created national-political Polish, Czech (Czechoslovakian), and Hungarian communities.[82]

Even though the events in Panevėžys in this sense were similar to the pogroms in Poland, Hungary, and Czechoslovakia, the scale of anti-Jewish violence in Lithuania was very small compared to other Central and East European countries. This geography of violence also needs an explanation, especially as there were certainly many expressions of brutal violence in Lithuania during the war years (the Cossack war pogroms of 1915 and the deportation of Jews).

The question of why there were not even more pogroms is a legitimate one in this case, because, as has been noted in historical literature, the potential for interethnic violence increases significantly under war and postwar conditions. Also, as mentioned in the introduction, the number of cases of mass anti-Jewish violence was very great over a large part of the former tsarist empire. The political cooperation between Lithuanian and Jewish political activists diminished antisemitic agitation among the Lithuanian population and this might have had some impact on the grassroots attitudes towards Jews. However, the pragmatic alliance between Lithuanian and Jewish political leaders in the early twentieth century may have played some role but is unlikely to be able to explain this situation alone, as similar cooperation took place also in Ukraine, and it had little impact on what unfolded in the provincial areas.[83] The fact that Lithuania was an agrarian country hardly affected by rapid urbanization and industrialization and, therefore, with less opportunities for modern forms of antisemitic agitation and mass inter-ethnic violence is an important one, if we want to explain the prewar situation. However, it does little to help explain the postwar situation, because, for example, many pogroms in Ukraine took place specifically in rural areas.[84] The role of the Jewish volunteers in the Lithuanian army might have played some role in creating a positive image of Jews among the ethnic Lithuanian soldiers, but it is hardly possible to prove such an argument empirically.[85]

The lower number of war pogroms in Lithuania after 1918, compared to other countries in the former Jewish Pale of Settlement may also be explained by the

---

82   Michael M. Miller, "The Forgotten Pogroms, 1918," *Slavic Review* 78, no. 4 (2019): 648–53.
83   For more on a pragmatic alliance between Lithuanian and Jewish public leaders, see: Vladas Sirutavičius and Darius Staliūnas, ed. *Pragmatic Alliance. Jewish-Lithuanian Political Cooperation at the Beginning of the 20th Century* (Budapest: Central European University Press, 2011).
84   Miliakova, "Vvedenie," vii.
85   On Jewish soldiers in the Lithuanian army see Vitkus, "Žydų kariai," 163–85.

fact that during the so-called Independence Wars (1918–1920) there were relatively fewer acts of lethal terror in general against the civilian population.[86] Furthermore, unlike in Belarus and even more so in Ukraine, in Lithuania there were no traditions of anti-Jewish violence. Thus, pragmatic alliance between Jewish and Lithuanian political elites and diminished antisemitic propaganda at the beginning of the twentieth century, no tradition of mass anti-Jewish violence alongside some other factors (the agrarian nature of Lithuania, less extensive brutalization in other conflicts that took place in this region, volunteering and enlistment of some Jews into the Lithuanian army) might be listed as the most probable explanations for the smaller scale of anti-Jewish violence in Lithuania as compared to other East and Central European countries.

## Bibliography

Avrutin, Eugene M., and Elissa Bemporad. "An Introduction." In *Pogroms: A Documentary History*, edited by Eugene M. Avrutin and Elissa Bemporad, 1–22. Oxford: Oxford University Press, 2021.

Balkelis, Tomas. *War, Revolution, and Nation-Making in Lithuania, 1914–1923*. Oxford: Oxford University Press, 2018.

Bemporad, Elissa, and Thomas Chopard. "Introduction." *Quest. Issues in Contemporary Jewish History. Journal of Fondazione CDEC*, no. 15 "The Pogroms of the Russian Civil War at 100: New Trends, New Sources," edited by Elissa Bemporad and Thomas Chopard (August 2019). Accessed October 15, 2021. http://www.quest-cdecjournal.it//index.php?issue=15.

Bendikaitė, Eglė. "'Lai kalba žygiai ir faktai': Panevėžio krašto žydai Nepriklausomybės kovose." Accessed January 3, 2020. http://www.paneveziomuziejus.lt/files/krasto_istorija/Bendikaite%20lai%20kalba%20zygiai%202018.pdf.

Brubaker, Rogers, and David Laitin. "Ethnic and Nationalist Violence." *Annual Review of Sociology* 24, no. 1 (2003): 423–52.

Budnitskii, Oleg. "Shots in the Back: On the Origin of Anti-Jewish Pogroms of 1918–1921." In *Jews in the East European Borderlands: Essays in Honor of John D. Klier*, edited by Eugene M. Avrutin and Harriet Murav, 187–201. Boston: Academic Studies Press, 2012.

Gaigalaitė, Aldona. *Lietuva Paryžiuje 1919 metais*. Kaunas: Šviesa, 1999.

Gilley, Christopher. "Beat the Jews, Save . . . Ukraine: Antisemitic Violence and Ukrainian State Building Projects 1918–1920." *Quest. Issues in Contemporary Jewish History. Journal of Fondazione CDEC*, no. 15 "The Pogroms of the Russian Civil War at 100: New Trends, New Sources," edited by Elissa Bemporad and Thomas Chopard (August 2019). Accessed October 15, 2021. http://www.quest-cdecjournal.it//index.php?issue=15.

Goldin, Semen. *"Priniat' iskliuchitel'nye mery . . ." Russkaia armiia i evrei. 1914–1917*. Moscow: Mosty kul'tury, 2018.

---

86 Laurinavičius, "On Political Terror," 65–76.

Grigaliūnas Glovackis, Vincas. *Generolo atsiminimai*. Vols. 2–3. Vilnius: Generolo Jono Žemaičio Lietuvos karo akademija, 2017.
Gross, Jan T. *Neighbors. The Destruction of the Jewish Community in Jedwabne, Poland*. Princeton: Princeton University Press, 2001.
Jakštas, Petras. "Saksų savanorių dalys Lietuvoje 1919 m." *Karo archyvas* 6 (1935): 181–232.
Hagen, Wiliam W. *Anti-Jewish Violence in Poland, 1914–1920*. Cambridge: Cambridge University Press, 2018.
Kilinskas, Kęstutis. "Pulkininkas prieš vyriausybę: plk. Vinco Grigaliūno-Glovackio ir Mykolo Sleževičiaus vyriausybių santykiai 1919 ir 1926 m." *Acta Historica Universitatis Klaipedensis* 32 (2016): 76–93.
Klier, John D. "Christians and Jews and the 'Dialogue of Violence' in Late Imperial Russia." In *Religious Violence Between Christians and Jews: Medieval Roots, Modern Perspectives*, edited by Anna Safir Abulafia, 157–70. New York: Palgrave, 2002.
Laurinavičius, Česlovas. "On Political Terror during the Soviet Expansion into Lithuania, 1918–1919." *Journal of Baltic Studies* 46, no. 1 (2015): 65–76.
Lelis, P. "Panevėžio išvadavimas 1919 m." Accessed January 29, 2020. http://www.partizanai.org/karys-1964m-1-2/5432-panevezio-isvadavimas-1919-m.
Liekis, Šarūnas. *1939: The Year That Changed Everything in Lithuania's History*. Amsterdam: Rodopi, 2010.
Liekis, Šarūnas, Lidija Miliakova, and Antony Polonsky. "Prievarta prieš žydus buvusiose Lietuvos-Lenkijos žemėse 1919 m." In *Kai ksenofobija virsta prievarta. Lietuvių ir žydų santykių dinamika XIX a.–XX a. pirmoje pusėje*, ed. Vladas Sirutavičius and Darius Staliūnas, 213–48. Vilnius: LII leidykla, 2005.
Lohr, Eric. "1915 and the War Pogrom Paradigm in the Russian Empire." In *Anti-Jewish Violence: Rethinking the Pogrom in East European History*, edited by Jonathan Dekel-Chen et al., 41–51. Bloomington: Indiana University Press, 2011.
Miliakova, Lidiia. "Vvedenie." In *Kniga pogromov. Pogromy na Ukraine, w Belorussii i evropeiskoi chasti Rossii v period Grazhdanskoi voiny. 1918–1922*, iii–xxviii. Moscow: ROSSPEN, 2007.
Miller, Michael M. "The Forgotten Pogroms, 1918." *Slavic Review* 78, no. 4 (2019): 648–53.
Petronis, Vytautas. "The Emergence of the Lithuanian Radical Right Movement, 1922–1927." *Journal of Baltic Studies* 46, no. 1 (2015): 77–95.
———. "Neperkirstas Gordijo mazgas: valstybinės prievartos prieš visuomenę Lietuvoje genezė (1918–1921)." *Lietuvos istorijos metraštis*, no. 1 (2015): 69–95.
Shohat, Azriel. "The Beginnings of Anti-Semitism in Independent Lithuania." *Yad Vashem Studies* 2 (1958): 7–48.
Sirutavičius, Vladas and Darius Staliūnas, ed. *Pragmatic Alliance. Jewish-Lithuanian Political Cooperation at the Beginning of the 20th Century*. Budapest: Central European University Press, 2011.
Skipitis, Rapolas. *Nepriklausomą Lietuvą statant. Atsiminimai*. Chicago: Terra, 1961.
Staliūnas, Darius. *Enemies for a Day: Antisemitism and Anti-Jewish Violence in Lithuania under the Tsars*. Budapest: Central European University Press, 2015.
Truska, Liudas. *Lietuviai ir žydai nuo XIX a. pabaigos iki 1941 m. birželio. Antisemitizmo Lietuvoje raida*. Vilnius: VPU leidykla, 2005.
Vareikis, Vygantas. "Žydų ir lietuvių susidūrimai bei konfliktai tarpukario Lietuvoje." In *Kai ksenofobija virsta prievarta. Lietuvių ir žydų santykių dinamika XIX a.–XX a. pirmoje pusėje*, edited by Vladas Sirutavičius and Darius Staliūnas, 157–80. Vilnius: LII leidykla, 2005.

Veidlinger, Jeffrey. "Anti- Jewish Violence in the Russian Civil War." In *Pogroms. A Documentary History*, edited by Eugene M. Avrutin and Elissa Bemporad, 133–38. Oxford: Oxford University Press, 2021.

———. "Was the Doctors' Plot a Blood Libel?" In *Ritual Murder in Russia, Eastern Europe, and Beyond. New Histories of an Old Accusation*, edited by Eugene M. Avrutin, Jonathan Dekel-Chen, and Robert Weinberg, 238–52. Bloomington: Indiana University Press, 2017.

Vitkus Hektoras. "Žydų kariai Lietuvos (lietuvių) Nepriklausomybės kovose 1919–1923 metais. Ką žinome apie jų motyvus?" *Acta Historica Universitatis Klaipedensis* 38 (2019): 163–85.

Wróbel, Piotr. "The Seeds of Violence. The Brutalization of and east European Region, 1917–1921." *Journal of Modern European History* 1, no. 1 (2003): 125–49.

CHAPTER 4

# Scandinavian Volunteers as Perpetrators of Violence and Crime in the Estonian War of Independence

## Mart Kuldkepp

This chapter examines the violent and criminal actions perpetrated by Finnish, Swedish, and Danish volunteers in the Estonian War of Independence (EWI). A successor conflict to World War I, the Estonian War of Independence lasted from late autumn 1918 until February 1920 and had Estonian national troops and the Red Army as its main fighting parties. Three Scandinavian volunteer detachments operated on the Estonian side, with the Finns by far the largest contingent (about four thousand men in total) and the Danish and the Swedish units substantially smaller (about two hundred men each).

I consider the character and likely causes of the crimes and acts of violence committed by the Scandinavian volunteers as related to their experiences and attitudes before and during the EWI. This task is not exhausted in this study, which engages little with primary sources and is primarily intended to provide a synthesis of the research findings of other scholars. Nevertheless, it will be possible to draw some preliminary conclusions that could benefit further research in the future.

My second area of interest is the way that volunteer violence and criminality related to the pro-interventionism of the Estonian Temporary Government and military authorities. Since the volunteers were recruited on Estonian initiative and fought under the Estonian command, it is pertinent to ask whether there was any desire to sanction them for wrongful behavior, or whether, on the contrary, the Estonian leadership's main concern was the avoidance of negative publicity if the incidents became publicly known.

I would like to note that, based on our current state of knowledge, we cannot assume that the Scandinavian volunteers were, on average, more violent or criminal than other soldiers, including the Estonians. What was different, however, was their very foreignness: most Scandinavian volunteers had little advance knowledge about Estonia or the war in which they were going to fight. Together with the fact that they had their own distinct ideological and experiential baggage (as will be detailed below), their war experiences must have been different from those of native Estonian troops. Furthermore, the sensitive questions of domestic and international political expediency, as well as considerations of jurisdiction and applicable law steered the decisions and attitudes of Estonian authorities in matters involving the volunteers probably far more than when dealing with native Estonian troops. Whether the Scandinavian volunteers behaved particularly badly or not, instances of their bad behavior certainly amounted to a special kind of headache.

## Pro-interventionism and Volunteerism

In what has been described as the "shatter zone" of old imperial borderlands in Eastern and Central Europe,[1] World War I brought about not just depopulation and economic and social disruption, but also a deep crisis of governance. With established centers of power and authority broken down in war, revolution, and under ruthless occupation regimes, the crisis unleashed a long period of violence, which lasted until the early 1920s and caused further reverberations throughout the rest of the interwar period.

The outcome of World War I gave a chance for the various successor states to the autocratic Russian and Austro-Hungarian Empires to build more democratic systems of governance, but initially the newcomers struggled to establish themselves as legitimate authorities and to take control of their territory in the face of foreign and domestic opposition. As state presence "on the ground" was often weak, the lawlessness caused by the power vacuum was difficult to contain, particularly under conditions of warfare, shortage of resources, and destruction or underdevelopment of much of the infrastructure. Trying to assert themselves,

---

1  Julia Eichenberg and John Paul Newman, "Introduction: Aftershocks: Violence in Dissolving Empires after the First World War," *Contemporary European History* 19, no. 3 (2010): 183.

the young states occasionally turned into enablers and perpetrators of violence, as they lacked other means of dealing with the challenges they were facing.[2]

Another result of successor state weakness was their appetite for interventionism: the desire to enlist foreign help to bolster the strength of their own regimes and complement lacking military capabilities (such as in naval or air power), but also to improve the faltering domestic morale, and—most generally—to internationalize the ongoing conflicts as something to be managed through international agreements and at peace conferences, not solely by the young states themselves.

The incursions into their sovereignty that pro-interventionist new states were prepared to accept could be far-reaching indeed. Drawing a few examples from the history of Estonia alone, it can be pointed out that at various times in late 1918 and early 1919, the Estonian authorities invited Sweden to bring a corps of police troops into Estonia and take control of its territory.[3] They also asked the United Kingdom to occupy Estonia and take command of the Estonian military forces[4] and proposed to Finland the establishment of a joint Finnish-Estonian state, with Estonians as the junior partner.[5] These requests were made in exceptionally difficult circumstances, but there is little doubt that they were serious. While Soviet historians certainly (and intentionally) overstated their case by designating Estonian nationalist politicians "lackeys of Western imperialism" and equating their desire for Estonian independence with submission to outside states,[6] the Estonian Temporary Government clearly preferred almost any form of foreign intervention from the West (Germany excepted) to a likely defeat at the hands of the Red Army.

Of course, none of the above plans came to fruition. The states that the Estonians turned to for assistance were not only too short of resources and war-weary but also too skeptical of the viability of Estonian statehood, and too

---

2   For Estonian examples, see Taavi Minnik, "The Cycle of Terror in Estonia, 1917–1919: On its Preconditions and Major Stages," *Journal of Baltic Studies* 46, no. 1 (2015): 42–45.

3   See Seppo Zetterberg, "Der Weg zur Anerkennung der Selbständigkeit Estlands und Lettlands durch die skandinavischen Staaten 1918–1921," in *Ostseeprovinzen, Baltische Staaten und das Nationale. Festschrift für Gert von Pistohlkors zum 70. Geburtstag*, ed. Norbert Angermann, Michael Garleff and Wilhelm Lenz (Münster: Lit Verlag, 2005), 419–20 and below.

4   "Maanõukogu protokoll nr 69-a," in *Maanõukogu protokollid: 1917–1919: 1. koosolekust 1. juulil 1917 78. koosolekuni 6. veebruaril 1919* (Tallinn: R. Tohver, 1935), 346.

5   Seppo Zetterberg, *Konstantin Päts ja Soome. Unistus kaksikriigist* (Tallinn: Varrak, 2020), 31–43.

6   See e.g., Paul Vihalem, *Eesti kodanlus imperialistide teenistuses (1917–1920)* (Tallinn: Eesti Riiklik Kirjastus, 1960).

concerned about their own domestic left wing opposition to get closely involved in the question of Estonia's—and, by extension, Russia's—future.[7] What the Estonian government was eventually able to secure was relatively modest: some weapons and ammunition and other supplies from the UK, the US, and Finland,[8] loans from Finland and the US,[9] limited British naval protection in the Gulf of Finland,[10] and permissions—amounting to half-official support in Finland[11] and an inclination to "look the other way" in Sweden and Denmark[12]—to recruit volunteer troops in Scandinavia. Thanks to this latter development, volunteerism (the practice of recruitment and enlistment of foreign volunteer soldiers) became a significant factor in EWI, although the numbers of volunteers never reached the many thousands originally envisioned.

Much of the story of Scandinavian volunteers in Estonia is already well-known. In recent years, there has been a surge in literature on Scandinavian participation in the post-World War I struggles against Bolshevism, including Mikkel Kirkebæk's impressively researched two-volume work on Danish volunteers,[13] Bernadette Preben-Hansen's and Michael Clemmesen's biography of Victor Anton Palludan[14] and Aapo Roselius's and Oula Silvennoinen's book on White

---

7   See e.g., Seppo Zetterberg, "Die schwedische Regierung und die baltische Krise im Herbst 1918," in *Reval und die baltischen Länder: Festschrift für Hellmuth Weiss zum 80. Geburtstag*, ed. Jürgen von Hehn and Janos Kenez (Marburg an Lahn: Herder-Institut, 1980), 75–89.

8   See Olavi Hovi, *The Baltic Area in British Policy, 1918–1921. Vol. 1: From the Compiègne Armistice to the Implementation of the Versailles Treaty* (Helsinki: The Finnish Historical Society, 1980); Mikkel Kirkebæk, *Den yderste grænse: danske frivillige i de baltiske uafhængighedskrige 1918–1920*, vol. 1–2 (Copenhagen: Lindhardt og Ringhof, 2019), 83–86; Seppo Zetterberg, *Suomi ja Viro 1917–1919. Poliittiset suhteet syksystä 1917 reunavaltiopolitiikan alkuun* (Helsinki: Suomen Historiallinen Seura, 1977), 151–54.

9   See Zetterberg, *Suomi ja Viro*, 151–54; Heino Arumäe, *Eesti ja Soome. Sõjast sõjani* (Tallinn: Argo, 2018), 82–83; Eduard Laaman, *Eesti iseseisvuse sünd* (Stockholm: Vaba Eesti, 1964), 341, 383–84; Eero Medijainen, "Ameerika Ühendriikide de iure tunnustus Balti riikidele 1922. aastal–väärtuspõhine otsus või majanduslik kalkulatsioon?" *Ajalooline Ajakiri*, no. 2 (2011): 141–45, Maie Pihlamägi, "Eesti 1919. aasta sõjavõlg Ameerika Ühendriikidele ja selle kustutamine," *Acta Historica Tallinnensia* 20, no. 1 (2014): 132–56.

10  Laaman, *Eesti iseseisvuse sünd*, 341–44; Hovi, *The Baltic Area in British Policy*, 64–109.

11  See Zetterberg, *Suomi ja Viro*, 155–65.

12  Niels Jensen, *For Dannebrogs ære: danske frivillige i Estland og Letlands frihedskamp 1919* (Odense: Odense Universitetsforlag, 1998), 13–26; Mart Kuldkepp, "Eesti Vabadussõja vabatahtlike värbamine Rootsis," *Õpetatud Eesti Seltsi aastaraamat/Annales Litterarum Societatis Esthonicae 2013* (2014): 195–200; Kirkebæk, *Den yderste grænse*, 1: 224, 228–31.

13  Kirkebæk *Den yderste grænse*. See also my review: Mart Kuldkepp, "Den yderste grænse: danske frivillige i de baltiske uafhængighedskrige 1918-1920," *Journal of Baltic Studies* 51, no. 2 (2020): 289–91.

14  Bernadette Preben-Hansen and Michael Clemmensen, *Bondefanget til borgerkrigen. Det danske korstog til ærkeenglen Michaels by* (Viborg: Syddansk Universitetsforlag, 2015).

Finnish volunteers in the auxiliary and successor wars after World War I.[15] Older examples include Olavi Hovi's and Timo Joutsamo's study of the social history of Finnish volunteers,[16] and Niels Jensen's journalistic account of the Danish recruitment effort.[17] Less attention has been paid to the Swedish volunteers, who have been studied by Kaido Jaanson,[18] Lars Ericson Wolke[19] and more recently by myself.[20] In my treatment of the Swedish case below, I will therefore rely more on primary sources, particularly memoirs.[21] The most important relevant unpublished studies are Vesa Leino's master's thesis on the administration of justice in the Finnish volunteer detachments[22] and Henri Rantanen's master's thesis on the Finnish volunteers' motivation to enlist.[23]

What has been mostly lacking is comparative work. Outside of some general overviews of EWI written from the Estonian point of view,[24] the various studies have usually focused on single national contingents, even though the boundaries between them were fuzzy: there were ethnic Danes fighting in the Swedish detachment, Swedes in the Finnish ones, and some Scandinavians also in purely Estonian units. This fact has been recognized by some authors, who draw parallels highlighting the shared experiences of servicemen belonging to different nationalities.[25] Nevertheless, the similarities have been insufficiently examined with a focus on violence and criminality, and little attention has been paid to the responses of the Estonian authorities to these phenomena.

---

15 Cited here in Estonian translation: Aapo Roselius and Oula Silvennoinen, *Metsik ida. Soome hõimusõjad ja Ida-Euroopa murrang 1918–1921* (Tallinn: Rahva Raamat, 2020).
16 Olavi Hovi and Timo Joutsamo, *Suomalaiset heimosoturit Viron vapaussodassa ja Itä-Karjalan heimosodissa vuosina 1918–1922* (Turu: Turun yliopisto, 1971).
17 Jensen, *For Dannebrogs ære*.
18 Kaido Jaanson, *Draakoni hambad. Rootsi ja Taani palgasõdurid 1919. aastal Eestis* (Tallinn: Eesti Raamat, 1987).
19 Most importantly Lars Ericson, *Svenska frivilliga. Militära uppdrag i utlandet under 1800- och 1900-talen* (Lund: Historiska Media, 1996).
20 Kuldkepp, "Eesti Vabadussõja vabatahtlike värbamine Rootsis"; Mart Kuldkepp," Kaks majorit kahel pool Läänemerd: Väljaöeldu ja väljamõeldu Carl Axel Mothanderi romaanis President," *Akadeemia*, no. 2 (2014): 235–70; Mart Kuldkepp, "Franchi sõbrad ja mõrvarid: Einar Lundborgi mälestused teenistusest Rootsi Korpuses," *Akadeemia*, no. 8 (2017): 1493–99.
21 Conrad Carlsson, *Okänd svensk soldat* (Stockholm: Albert Bonniers Förlag, 1937); Einar Lundborg, "Rootsi korpusega Eesti Vabadussõjas," *Akadeemia*, no. 8 (2017): 1427–93.
22 Vesa Leino, "Oikeudenhoito suomalaisessa vapaaehtoisjoukossa Viron vapaussodassa 1919" (MA diss., University of Jyväskylä, 2001).
23 Henri Rantanen, "Vapaus ja veljeys vai viha ja pelko? Suomalaisvapaaehtoisten lähtömotiivit Viron vapaussotaan vuosina 1918–1920" (MA diss., University of Helsinki, 2018).
24 See Ago Pajur et al., *Eesti Vabadussõja ajalugu* (Tallinn: Varrak, 2020).
25 See, e.g., Roselius and Silvennoinen, *Metsik ida*, 40, 172, 194; Kirkebæk, *Den yderste grænse*, vol. 1, 314–21.

## The Recruitment and Deployment of Scandinavian Volunteers

As mentioned above, Estonian leaders approached Sweden for assistance in September 1918, requesting weapons, equipment, and a corps of Swedish police troops to replace the German forces that were likely to be soon withdrawn from the Baltics. This request was rejected by the Swedish government as were the repeated follow-up efforts with British backing. With their plans for an officially sanctioned foreign intervention frustrated, in mid-December, the Estonians turned to volunteerism as the second-best opportunity. According to Estonian representatives in Sweden, there was plenty of interest in signing up.[26]

Around Christmas in 1918, a special Estonian delegation arrived in Stockholm to begin negotiations with a small cadre of Swedish officers who had fought in the Finnish Civil War and were now willing to organize a Swedish volunteer force in Estonia. These plans enjoyed the diplomatic support of the British government, and it seems that the Swedish officers were also encouraged by the Finnish regent Gustaf Mannerheim, who considered Estonia a suitable bridgehead for a broader campaign against Bolshevik Russia. Soon, however, the negotiations between the Swedes and the Estonians ran aground—not for the lack of will, but for lack of money, which had in the meantime been reallocated to Finland, where the degree of interest in volunteering was higher and the logistical circumstances for recruitment more favorable.[27]

In late November and early December, Estonian ministers Jaan Poska and Jaan Tõnisson had requested intervention with regular troops also from Finland. Lauri Ingman, the new Finnish Premier did not consider it possible to relinquish any Finnish troops, which he argued were needed at home. Nevertheless, the government did agree to provide aid in the form of weapons, money, and permission to recruit volunteers. By that time, right-wing circles had already started publicly calling for assistance to Estonia for reasons of ethnic kinship and Finland's own security which would have been under threat if the Bolsheviks had taken over the southern coast of the Gulf of Finland.[28]

---

26 Kuldkepp, "Eesti Vabadussõja vabatahtlike värbamine Rootsis," 194–96; Ericson, *Svenska frivilliga*, 77–78.
27 Zetterberg, *Suomi ja Viro*, 176–77; Kuldkepp, "Eesti Vabadussõja vabatahtlike värbamine Rootsis," 195–200; Jaanson, *Draakoni hambad*, 28; Kirkebæk, *Den yderste grænse*, 1:52–59, 64–65, 117–20; Ericson, *Svenska frivilliga*, 79.
28 Zetterberg, *Suomi ja Viro*, 152, 155–57, 172–75; Arumäe, *Eesti ja Soome*, 82–83; Roselius and Silvennoinen, *Metsik ida*, 89–91; Jaanson, *Draakoni hambad*, 32; Kirkebæk, *Den yderste grænse*, 1:109.

In the week before Christmas in 1918, a special Estonian Relief Committee (Viron Avustamisen Päätoimikunta/Centralkommittén för Estlands Undsättning) was established in Helsinki to coordinate the recruitment of volunteers. Headed by Senator Oskari Wilho Louhivuori, the organization was politically representative of radical Finnish nationalism and gave the recruitment a rightwing flavor, which resonated primarily with men who had participated on the White side in the Finnish Civil War.[29]

The military side of the movement congregated early around two officers, Hans Kalm and Martin Ekström. Kalm, an ethnic Estonian who had been a battalion commander in the Finnish Civil War, had made himself known for his extreme ruthlessness and disobedience of all authority he disagreed with, having already narrowly escaped trial in military court.[30] Amongst his other notorious feats, Kalm had been responsible for the war's worst streak of executions carried out at a POW camp in Lahti, where more than five hundred prisoners, two hundred of them women, were murdered in a matter of weeks.[31] Ekström was a Swedish military adventurer who had entered Persian service in 1911 and later fought as an officer in the Finnish Civil War, during which he was responsible for the so-called Viipuri massacre, in which two hundred Russians and their supporters were killed by the victorious White troops.[32] Both Kalm and Ekström were charismatic and ferocious leaders.

The remarkable enthusiasm for volunteering, which appeared in Finland around the turn of 1918–1919, produced in the matter of a few weeks around ten thousand applications of those willing to go to Estonia. Such numbers were far too high for the Relief Committee to handle for logistical reasons, but also for reasons of funds and political expediency. In the end, about four thousand Finnish volunteers were dispatched to Estonia, divided between Kalm's and Ekström's regiments. Initially, Finnish general Martin Wetzer was appointed as the overall commander of the Finnish contingents.[33] Ekström's unit included a third of Swedish speakers, about one hundred of them from Sweden.[34] Kalm's detachment was almost entirely ethnically Finnish.

---

29 Roselius and Silvennoinen, *Metsik ida*, 89–91; Arumäe, *Eesti ja Soome*, 83; Zetterberg, *Suomi ja Viro*, 157–59.
30 Roselius and Silvennoinen, *Metsik ida*, 91–92; Rantanen, "Vapaus ja veljeys," 31–32; Zetterberg, *Suomi ja Viro*, 159.
31 Marko Tikka, "Warfare and Terror in 1918," in *The Finnish Civil War 1918: History, Memory, Legacy*, ed. Tuomas Tepora and Aapo Roselius (Leiden: Brill, 2014), 110.
32 Roselius and Silvennoinen, *Metsik ida*, 92–93.
33 Zetterberg, *Suomi ja Viro*, 161, 164–65; Arumäe, *Eesti ja Soome*, 83–84; Roselius and Silvennoinen, *Metsik ida*, 113–15; Rantanen, "Vapaus ja veljeys," 36.
34 Jaanson, *Draakoni hambad*, 44.

The recruitment initiative in Sweden was slow to pick up after the initial setbacks. Partially, this was for ideological reasons. In Sweden, there was very little enthusiasm for helping the Estonians, who were not considered a kindred nation. Although the Swedish right-wing circles looked back to Sweden's seventeenth century Great Power era with nostalgia, they had little faith in the descendants of their former serfs building independent statehood. The Swedish left was even more skeptical, and indeed outright hostile towards any idea of military intervention against Bolshevik Russia, even on a voluntary basis.[35]

In the end, a small Swedish detachment was nevertheless organized on the private initiative of former Swedish Reserve Ensign Carl Axel Mothander, who was likely encouraged by the United States' embassy of Stockholm and Mannerheim, whom Mothander knew from his time in the Finnish Civil War. Mothander had made it to Estonia in the first days of 1919 and initially served in an Estonian unit. After a few weeks, he approached the Estonian government with his plan of forming a separate Swedish detachment of three hundred volunteers. Mothander, who had been promoted to major in Finland, was given the green light and sufficient funding. A recruitment bureau was set up in Stockholm, where it caused much controversy with left-wing Swedish newspapers.[36]

In autumn 1918, the possibility of intervention was also being discussed in Denmark. The Danish (and, for that matter, the Norwegian) government had similarly had to resist British pressure to send regular troops to the Baltics. In January, after a plea from the Estonian government and following the recommendations of Danish representatives abroad, Denmark nevertheless decided to allow recruitment of volunteers.[37]

This effort, in which the Danish state was not actively involved, came to be led by the wealthy and well-connected right-wing businessman Aage Westenholz. A Danish nationalist and anti-socialist with militaristic interests, Westenholz had established private volunteer groups already before World War I. In the final days of 1918, he discussed the formation of a Danish expeditionary force to Estonia with Danish business circles, who agreed to support the undertaking financially, and the Finnish Estonian Relief Committee, who were keen to expand their recruitment activities outside of Finland. A variety of setbacks ensued, some

---

35 About the Swedish attitudes towards Baltic independence, see Mart Kuldkepp, "Swedish political attitudes Towards Baltic Independence in the Short Twentieth Century," *Ajalooline Ajakiri*, no. 3–4 (2016): 406–12.
36 Kuldkepp, "Kaks majorit," 242–45; Roselius and Silvennoinen, *Metsik ida*, 168–69; Jaanson, *Draakoni hambad*, 45–46; Kirkebæk *Den yderste grænse*, 1:312–13; Ericson, *Svenska frivilliga*, 79.
37 Kirkebæk, *Den yderste grænse*, 1:65–77, 121–28.

due to monetary reasons or difficulties of cooperating with Estonians, others because of a fierce countercampaign organized by Danish syndicalists. In the end, only a company-size unit was sent on its way. It was headed by captains Iver de Hemmer Gudme and Richard Borgelin. Gudme, characterized by Kirkebæk as one of the "ideologues" of the Danish unit, had already fought in the Finnish Civil War. Borgelin had been a lieutenant in the Danish army. Both men were avid Danish nationalists, attracted to Estonia partly because of the role Danish crusaders had played there in the Middle Ages. Another separately recruited and privately funded small Danish unit of less than twenty men was headed by former Danish Lieutenant Victor Anton Palludan and went to Estonia on its own initiative.[38]

Out of the three contingents, the Finnish volunteers played by far the most important military role in the war, particularly in the first weeks of their deployment. Ekström's unit, officially known as the First Finnish Volunteer Corps (1 Suomalainen Vapaajouko), departed for Estonia on December 30, 1918, while Kalm's detachment followed in January.[39] Immediately after arriving in Tallinn, Ekström presented his plan of recapturing the border town Narva from the Red Army to the Estonian Supreme Command. The Estonians thought the plan reckless and unlikely to succeed, but nevertheless agreed to it in principle. After some skirmishes east of Tallinn, Ekström indeed went ahead with some Estonian support and captured Narva with an ambitious amphibious operation just a week after his arrival in the country. Along with some Estonian successes around the same time, this was a turning point in the war, with the initiative now shifting to the Estonian side. It also remained Ekström's most impressive feat in Estonia. When his unit returned to the front in February after a short respite, it accomplished little of note until leaving for Finland in March.[40]

Hans Kalm's regiment, Sons of the North (Pohjan Pojat), arrived in Estonia slightly later, remained for a while in Tallinn and was dispatched to the front at the end of January. The Estonian Supreme Commander Johan Laidoner tasked this detachment with recapturing the Latvian-Estonian border town Valga (Valka). Together with Estonian troops led by Lieutenant Julius Kuperjanov,

---

38 Kirkebæk, *Den yderste grænse*, 1:128–52, 176–83, 219–24, 226–28, 231–52, 313, 409–13; Roselius and Silvennoinen, *Metsik ida*, 189–92; Jaanson, *Draakoni hambad*, 79–83, 86–87, 89–90; Preben-Hansen and Clemmesen, *Bondefanget til borgerkrigen*, 33–37; Zetterberg, *Suomi ja Viro*, 169–70.
39 Roselius and Silvennoinen, *Metsik ida*, 121.
40 Zetterberg, *Suomi ja Viro*, 166; Arumäe, *Eesti ja Soome*, 89–90; Roselius and Silvennoinen, *Metsik ida*, 138–41, 144–45, 197–98; Kirkebæk, *Den yderste grænse*, vol. 1, 113–16; Carlsson, *Okänd svensk soldat*, 141–43.

Kalm's unit fought against Red Latvian riflemen in the Battle of Paju, one of the most famous and bloodiest battles of the war. In the end, Kalm's unit succeeded in capturing the Paju manor house, which also decided the fate of Valga. After a respite in the town, Kalm overstepped the terms of his contract with the Estonian government and proceeded to march into Latvia, where his troops attacked and sacked the town of Alūksne (Marienburg). As Kalm's obstinacy grew—he was particularly unwilling to take orders from Wetzer—his grip over his troops loosened. In mid-March, Kalm returned to Finland for consultations, leaving his unit to fight further bloody battles around Vastseliina. By the end of March, disarray in the ranks had deepened, and in April, Kalm's troops were sent home to Finland and Kalm himself was released from duty.[41]

The Swedish volunteers arrived in small groups via Finland to Tallinn, where Mothander received them and sent them on to Narva, where the Swedish detachment—the Swedish Corps in Estonia (Svenska Kåren i Estland)—was stationed. The field unit was initially headed by Captain Georg Malmberg, an adventurer and mercenary who had fought in Mexico, Belgian Congo, and Finland.[42] The strength of the Swedish Corps never quite reached the planned three hundred, remaining closer to two hundred men. Furthermore, disintegration began even before the unit had been fully formed with some men leaving already in Tallinn to join other volunteer detachments and with Mothander's authority being increasingly questioned. After the so-called Franchi affair (see below), the Swedish Corps was reorganized under the command of Major Lambert Hällén and played a minor role on the front in Setumaa region until being disbanded in May.[43]

The Danish volunteers arrived in Tallinn in early April. Gudme and Borgelin initially remained there, waiting for reinforcements that never arrived since the Estonian funds had been exhausted and Westenholz decided to pull out of the whole affair.[44] The volunteers that had made it to Estonia were organized into the so-called Danish-Baltic Auxiliary Corps (Dansk-Baltisk Auxiliær Corps, DBAC). After a period of training in Nõmme outside of Tallinn, this unit of about two hundred men was dispatched to the southern front on May 19, where it proved to be a capable force. DBAC subsequently participated in battles in

---

41　Arumäe, *Eesti ja Soome*, 90–91; Zetterberg, *Suomi ja Viro*, 166–67; Roselius and Silvennoinen, *Metsik ida*, 155–59, 161–66, 198.
42　Roselius and Silvennoinen, *Metsik ida*, 169–70.
43　Jaanson, *Draakoni hambad*, 61–63; Carlsson, *Okänd svensk soldat*, 155; Roselius and Silvennoinen, *Metsik ida*, 171–72.
44　Roselius and Silvennoinen, *Metsik ida*, 193–95.

Northern Latvia and around Pskov, remaining in Estonia until the beginning of September 1919.[45]

This Danish detachment was far from an elite military unit as it has sometimes been described, but of all the Scandinavian volunteer units in Estonia, it presented the best example of sustained and successful deployment. At the time, the Danes were some of the best equipped and armed troops in Estonia, with their 24 light Madsen machine guns giving them superior firepower in most infantry battles.[46] The Danish officers were also seemingly more professional and disciplined than those of the other volunteer units.[47] This judgement rings less true of the other Danish contingent headed by Palludan, which was attached to the Swedish Corps and participated in its sad fate.[48]

## The Causes of Volunteer Violence and Criminality: Before Arrival to Estonia

There are essentially two ways of explaining incidents of volunteer violence and criminality. The first possibility would be to put emphasis on the various circumstances affecting the men prior to their enlistment, ranging from cultural and societal factors to concrete personal experiences and character traits. Some of these factors—such as adventurousness or difficulties adjusting to civilian life—could have motivated the decision to enlist in the first place. Others, such as youth and inexperience, might have become more significant later.

The second possibility is to emphasize the circumstances present at their actual place of service, including the leadership styles of their military units, their view of allies and enemies, peer pressure from fellow soldiers, and generally what were perceived to be acceptable codes of conduct in the conditions of weak rule of law and brutal ideologically motivated warfare.

In the end, of course, the distinction between the two is mostly artificial. It was inevitable that factors of both kinds would conspire together in facilitating violence and criminality, and their relative weight and importance would be difficult to assess even if appropriate datasets existed. My evidence, detailed below, is not exhaustive and largely limited to cases mentioned in secondary

---

45  Kirkebæk, *Den yderste grænse*, 1:383–89 and Bd II 9–13, 45–69, 79–81, 93–107, 122–43, 148–50, 156–58, 184–98, 203–66, 343–47; Jaanson, *Draakoni hambad*, 104–5.
46  Kirkebæk, *Den yderste grænse*, 1:348–353, Bd II, 74–77.
47  Ibid., 442; 2:509.
48  Roselius and Silvennoinen, *Metsik ida*, 173; Jaanson, *Draakoni hambad*, 73–74, 87–88, Kirkebæk, *Den yderste grænse*, 1:316–21.

literature, but it does indicate some relevant trends, suggesting what might have been likely explanatory factors.

The existence of circumstances of the first kind—the fact that many volunteers had backgrounds or motivations that were likely to veer into violence and criminality—is easily detectable from existing sources. This was, of course, not unique to the foreign volunteers in EWI. Swedish editor Ernst Klein, who had followed another contingent of Swedish volunteers into the Finnish Civil War a few months earlier, divided the men into four types: those who had enlisted out of an immediate patriotic reaction to the Red insurgency in Finland, those who had a deeper aversion to socialism and revolutionaries, those who were adventurous and attracted to the battlefield, and those who, as Klein wrote, were such that it was better to "remain silent" about them.[49]

More statistically oriented research has been conducted on the Finnish volunteers in EWI. Out of the 206 surviving former volunteers who were interviewed by Hovi and Joutsamo, 42.6 percent indicated that their main motivation for enlistment had been a wish to help Estonia, 19 percent mentioned adventurousness, 9 percent ideological reasons, 7.4 percent hatred towards the Russians, and 2.1 percent revenge. Economic reasons were less important at 4.7 percent; 27 percent had some other reason.[50] Rantanen's later study of the contemporary enlistment applications modified these numbers somewhat, but largely confirmed their overall validity.[51] Similar studies have not been conducted of other volunteer contingents, but the Finnish volunteers were probably unique in terms of the importance they attached to helping Estonia. As Rantanen points out, it was perhaps natural given that "relief" figured prominently in the name and ethos of the Finnish recruitment effort.[52] Furthermore, the idea of "helping Estonia" is ambivalent and likely to conceal various ideological motivations.

Using a more qualitative approach, Mikkel Kirkebæk divides the Danish volunteers in EWI into five main groups: the anti-Bolshevik "ideological warriors," the mercenaries (primarily interested in their pay), the professionals (with a background in the military), the adventurers (motivated by a romantic or youthful desire for excitement) and the criminals (looking to escape or to carry out their activities where possible with impunity).[53] Overlaps existed between the categories, so they should be seen as abstractions, not descriptions of specific

---

49  Roselius and Silvennoinen, *Metsik ida*, 44–45.
50  Hovi and Joutsamo, *Suomalaiset heimosoturit*, 154; Zetterberg, *Suomi ja Viro*, 177–78.
51  Rantanen, "Vapaus ja veljeys," 57.
52  Ibid., 58.
53  Kirkebæk, *Den yderste grænse*, 1:399–400.

individuals. For my own purposes, I find it useful to apply Kirkebæk's typology to other Scandinavian volunteers and consider his five types in relation to their potential for violence and criminality.

Men of the first category proceeded from an ideological motivation, which, at least outside of Finland, had little to do with helping Estonia and more to do with the fact that Estonia was a prime location for fighting against the Red Army. The Danish and Swedish anti-Bolsheviks also tended to be better educated than other volunteers, and sometimes had university degrees. Oftentimes, they ended up enlisting repeatedly in various White forces, as was the case with Iver de Hemmer Gudme, who in 1918–1920 fought in Finnish, Estonian, Russian White, and Polish armies.[54]

The Finnish ranks likewise included dedicated ideological anti-Bolsheviks, some with higher education,[55] but many more Finnish volunteers had been ideologically radicalized only very recently in the Finnish Civil War, where they had learned to see the "Reds" as not only the enemy but also as an existential threat.[56] The Finns' readiness for uncompromising warfare against the ideological or existential enemy is substantiated by the sources. Vilho Helanen reports that already before setting their foot in Estonia, some Finnish volunteers were talking about "settling their debts" with the Reds who had killed their families and burned down their farmsteads.[57]

Kirkebæk's second category, the money-oriented mercenaries, had, at first glance, a rather straightforward motivation with no obvious connection to violence or criminality. Nevertheless, it soon became apparent that promises of compensation or supply of equipment were frequently not kept, which was a significant cause of discontent and lack of discipline in the volunteer units, and probably led to a relaxed attitude towards theft, fraud, and unlawful requisitions. Simple greed must have also played a role. More than a few volunteers tried to acquire money by fraud: either from the Estonian authorities, as did Mothander[58] and Palludan,[59] from the Scandinavian recruitment offices,[60] or just from people they came across in Estonia.[61] In the Danish case, some

---

54 Ibid., 400–1.
55 Rantanen, "Vapaus ja veljeys," 61–62.
56 Roselius and Silvennoinen, *Metsik ida*, 39–40.
57 Rantanen, "Vapaus ja veljeys," 56.
58 Lundborg, "Rootsi korpusega Eesti Vabadussõjas," 1441.
59 Kuldkepp, "Eesti Vabadussõja vabatahtlike värbamine Rootsis," 205.
60 Kirkebæk, *Den yderste grænse*, vol. 1, 430, Bd II 365.
61 Ibid., 449–50.

incidences of theft were reported already before the men had left for Estonia.[62] Others, such as the Swede Einar Lundborg, used enlistment to escape from their creditors.[63]

The category of anti-Bolsheviks overlaps to some extent with that of the professionals who had a background in the military. Some of these men volunteered to put their training into practice. Others did so out of restlessness, such as the Swedish volunteers Conrad Carlsson and Einar Lundborg, who could not readjust to civilian life in Sweden after having fought in the Finnish Civil War.[64] When Lundborg's applications to enlist in the Swedish army were repeatedly rejected, he decided that going to Estonia was the next best choice. Carlsson, for his part, deserted from active service in Sweden to do the same.[65] Others, hailing from neutral Scandinavia, might have seen EWI as a kind of substitute conflict in which to compensate for their non-participation in World War I, the greatest war of the generation. Another likely motivation was quick advancement in ranks, which was possible in places like Finland and Estonia, even if the new ranks were not always recognized at home.[66]

It also needs to be noted that while the actual professionals (trained officers and NCOs) were not very numerous in the volunteer units, many of the volunteers were already veterans of the Finnish Civil War. Of the Finns who went to Estonia, more than 90 percent had fought on the White side,[67] and many Swedish and even Danish volunteers had done the same. Frequently, there is evidence of these men's inability to readjust to the civilian life: some of them reenlisted at every opportunity and participated in a long series of wars.[68] Volunteering in Estonia could also be a form of compensatory service or proof of loyalty for those Finns who for some reason had not taken part in the Civil War or had fought on the defeated Red side.[69]

Military experience, of course, was not equal to military training. Only 63 percent of Finnish volunteers had had some training before arriving in Estonia.[70] More than 50 percent of the Danish volunteers who went to Estonia had not previously served in the Danish army, and 40 percent of the Danish privates had

---

62   Ibid., 430.
63   Ibid., 433; Lundborg, "Rootsi korpusega Eesti Vabadussõjas," 1430.
64   Lundborg, "Rootsi korpusega Eesti Vabadussõjas," 418–19.
65   Ibid., 1429–30; Carlsson, Okänd svensk soldat, 123–25.
66   Kirkebæk, Den yderste grænse, 1:419–20.
67   Hovi, Joutsamo, Suomalaiset heimosoturit, 165–66; Kirkebæk, Den yderste grænse, 2:34.
68   Roselius and Silvennoinen, Metsä itä, 37–39.
69   Rantanen, "Vapaus ja veljeys," 42, 66; Roselius and Silvennoinen, Metsä itä, 118–19.
70   Rantanen, "Vapaus ja veljeys," 41; Roselius and Silvennoinen, Metsä itä, 120.

no military experience whatsoever.[71] The officers were not always well-trained either. The head of Ekström's fourthcompany, Lieutenant Bror Dahlgren had no military training apart from having completed national service in Sweden.[72] The commander of DBAC, Iver de Hemmer Gudme, had had no military experience apart from his membership in a shooting society, when he enlisted as a volunteer in the Finnish Civil War. From Finland, he returned as a captain, and from Estonia as a lieutenant colonel.[73]

Overall, the professionals were perhaps less likely to engage in criminal behavior than the other groups, even if their restlessness, lack of experience, or misguided ambitions could be contributing factors. Volunteering in Estonia also seems to have attracted some more problematic members of the armed forces whose careers had taken a wrong turn. According to Carlsson, none of the Swedish officers in Estonia (as compared to Ekström and Kalm) were suitable for the task of putting together a functional military unit and he characterizes them as "degenerate individuals."[74] This group, which included Mothander,[75] was not limited to the Swedes. The Danes had their own share of military failures: Max Arildskov,[76] Victor Anton Palludan,[77] and likely others.

The fourth category, adventurers, brings together men with several interrelated motivations. Some simply wanted to add to their otherwise limited opportunities to travel and see the world.[78] One Finnish volunteer, for example, indicated in his application that he wanted to enlist to get a free railway ticket, which was otherwise too expensive to obtain for a poor person.[79] Others were likely motivated by some form of war romanticism, influenced by literature and war propaganda. Peter de Hemmer Gudme mentioned Lawrence of Arabia as inspiration, referring to his own trip to Estonia repeatedly as an "adventure."[80] But more broadly, many volunteers must have identified with contemporary ideals of masculinity, which included the heroization of soldiers' self-sacrifice. It is worth noting that some women also tried to enlist as nurses or as soldiers,

---

71 Kirkebæk, *Den yderste grænse*, 1:399.
72 Roselius and Silvennoinen, *Metsik ida*, 144–45.
73 Ibid., 195; Jaanson, *Draakoni hambad*, 77.
74 Carlsson, *Okänd svensk soldat*, 135–36, 151.
75 Kuldkepp, "Kaks majorit," 242.
76 Kirkebæk, *Den yderste grænse*, vol. 1, 424–25.
77 Ibid., 313.
78 Ibid., 428.
79 Rantanen, "Vapaus ja veljeys," 60.
80 Kirkebæk, *Den yderste grænse*, 1:427.

and one of them, Aino Mälkönen, ended up serving in Estonia.[81] Judging by her letters, she, too, was motivated by romantic adventurousness.[82]

Some adventurous volunteers, such as Ekström or Malmberg, seemingly found enjoyment in war itself, enlisting repeatedly and possibly with a sense of indifference towards what they were fighting for or fighting against. But in other cases, adventurousness seems to have strongly interfaced with political ideologies: the anti-Bolshevism mentioned above, and, in the Finnish case, with radical Finnish nationalism and its dreams of creating a 'Greater Finland' that would have included some areas populated by kindred Finno-Ugric nationalities.[83]

In connection with adventurousness, it is worth pointing out that many of the volunteers were also extremely young. The age of the Finnish volunteers varied from fifteen to thirty-six, with more than a half aged sixteen to twenty and with 21.1 as the average age. In most cases, the officers were just a few years older than the men.[84] The average age of the Danish applicants was older, twenty-four years, and rose to twenty-six amongst those who ended up going in Estonia. But the age differences were significant, with the youngest Danish volunteer only fifteen, and the oldest fifty-three years old.[85]

Kirkebæk's final category, criminals, included those men who were looking for a chance to escape from their country (and from the police) and possibly to take advantage of the chaotic situation in Estonia. There was good contemporary awareness of their existence. Arnold Posti, the Estonian consul in Stockholm, estimated that about 75 percent of the Swedish volunteers had had previous run-ins with the police. Lambert Hällén, the last commander of the Swedish Corps, stated in May 1919 that most of its members—including the officers—had criminal convictions from Sweden.[86] The Danish contingent likewise included some problematic men who were sent home ahead of the others.[87] Another related group were the drug addicts. One Finnish volunteer who was addicted to morphine volunteered for medical service in Estonia probably to gain better access to the drug.[88] Lundborg reports that the doctor of the Swedish

---

81  Roselius and Silvennoinen, *Metsik ida*, 39, 115–17; Kirkebæk, *Den yderste grænse*, 1:435; Rantanen, "Vapaus ja veljeys," 40.
82  Rantanen, "Vapaus ja veljeys," 60.
83  Roselius and Silvennoinen, *Metsik ida*, 42–43, 117–18.
84  Hovi, Joutsamo, *Suomalaiset heimosoturit*, 139; Rantanen, "Vapaus ja veljeys," 44; Roselius and Silvennoinen, *Metsik ida*, 40–41.
85  Kirkebæk, *Den yderste grænse*, 1:396.
86  Jaanson, *Draakoni hambad*, 159.
87  Kirkebæk, *Den yderste grænse*, 1:452.
88  Roselius and Silvennoinen, *Metsik ida*, 120.

Corps was a "degenerate cocaine addict" and, in fact, not a doctor at all.[89] There are reports of later widespread cocaine use amongst those Scandinavians who continued to fight in the Russian Civil War.[90]

Interestingly, some of the criminals later used their time in Estonia as form of excuse. A Helsinki thief who had served in Estonia went on a spree of robberies after returning to Finland, committing a murder during one of them. He justified his action by saying that after having seen all sorts of carnage in Estonia, he could no longer attach any value to human life.[91] In other similar cases, there might have been some genuine trauma behind the rampage, although it is difficult to judge in hindsight. In 1921, a former Finnish officer murdered two policemen apparently under the delusion that he was still in Estonia and was being arrested by the Bolsheviks.[92]

## The Causes of Volunteer Violence and Criminality in Estonia

The circumstances of the second kind—the experiences and attitudes acquired by the volunteers at their place of deployment—were more immediate and therefore likely even more important with respect to violence and criminality. In the following, I outline some more important factors of this kind, as reflected in ego-documents, and picked up from there by scholars. I first draw attention to the volunteers' initial impressions of Estonia, then briefly consider their units' operational and leadership styles, and, finally, discuss their attitudes towards their Estonian allies and the enemy.

As already mentioned, most Scandinavian volunteers had little knowledge about Estonia or the war that they were going to fight in. This meant that their first impressions upon arrival must have had a significant impact on their subsequent behavior and morale. Sometimes, as with some Finnish volunteers, their romantic expectations about Estonia were met by a less pleasant reality. In other cases, preexisting orientalist views about "the East" as uncivilized and barbaric must have found ready confirmation. In any case, the volunteers' first impressions of Tallinn, their port of arrival, tended to be negative. The Estonian capital looked dirty, poor, inadequately policed, and full of war refugees. One Finnish

---

89   Lundborg, "Rootsi korpusega Eesti Vabadussõjas," 1446.
90   Kirkebæk, *Den yderste grænse*, 2:382–86.
91   Roselius and Silvennoinen, *Metsik ida*, 120.
92   Rantanen, "Vapaus ja veljeys," 68.

volunteer wrote in his diary about the disappointment he felt upon encountering the multitude of languages and cultures in Tallinn, leaving the impression that the Estonians were disorderly, unnational, and probably incapable of independence: "are we not just spilling the dear Nordic blood in vain?" he asked.[93] Lundborg describes the people in Tallinn as a "mixture of Estonian ugliness and Russian filthiness."[94] The Danish volunteers referred to Tallinn as a "robber-town" where everyone goes around with a revolver in their pocket.[95]

On the plus side, alcohol and prostitutes were cheap and widely available. On his unit's day of arrival, December 30, 1918, Martin Ekström noted in his diary that "all the boys were already drunk by ten o'clock in the evening."[96] The Finnish *markka* was one of the strongest currencies in use in Tallinn, giving many young Finnish volunteers an easy way to take advantage of the permissive environment they found themselves in. The officers had to put in a serious effort to maintain discipline and to solve disputes among the volunteers and between volunteers and the locals.[97]

The Swedish and Danish volunteers, when they arrived, joined the same multinational revelry, often disappearing at night, so that Borgelin and Mothander had to go looking for them around the town. Borgelin writes that even those men who had been law-abiding citizens before would acquire a mentality of impunity, as if they stood above the local laws and customs.[98] The officers themselves also participated in the nightlife, as witnessed by ego-documents and court records.[99] Prostitution was very common, and sexually transmitted diseases proved to be a significant problem, not least from the military point of view.[100] Kalm and Borgelin stopped handing out permissions to visit downtown during the night, and Hällén later complained that venereal diseases had taken out as many of his men as had the enemy.[101]

---

93 Ibid., 64.
94 Lundborg, "Rootsi korpusega Eesti Vabadussõjas," 1435.
95 Kirkebæk, *Den yderste grænse*, 1:293–95.
96 Ibid., 303.
97 Roselius and Silvennoinen, *Metsik ida*, 147–51; Rantanen, "Vapaus ja veljeys," 50; Magnus Ilmjärv, "Soome vabatahtlikud Eesti Vabadussõjas ehk ühe legendi lõpp," *Vikerkaar*, no. 4 (1993): 61.
98 Roselius and Silvennoinen, *Metsik ida*, 193–94; Kirkebæk, *Den yderste grænse*, 1:443–46; Lundborg, "Rootsi korpusega Eesti Vabadussõjas," 1438–39.
99 Kirkebæk, *Den yderste grænse*, 1:447; Jaanson, *Draakoni hambad*, 63–64; Carlsson, *Okänd svensk soldat*, 152.
100 Carlsson, *Okänd svensk soldat*, 145–46, 166.
101 Roselius and Silvennoinen, *Metsik ida*, 153–54, 194; Jaanson, *Draakoni hambad*, 65; Kirkebæk, *Den yderste grænse*, 1:454–60, Lundborg, "Rootsi korpusega Eesti Vabadussõjas," 1748.

In Tallinn, the Scandinavian volunteers also encountered each other and exchanged stories—possibly exaggerated ones—about their frontline experiences. It seems that the newly arrived Danes were told by Finnish volunteers that it was a normal practice in Estonia to loot farmsteads and shoot prisoners. References to such "facts of life" were later used by them to excuse their own crimes and misdemeanors.[102]

After some time in Tallinn, the volunteer units headed to battle. Their operational style has been described as close to irregular or guerrilla warfare, with emphasis on taking initiative and individual bravery. Contacts with the enemy were haphazard and incidental; usually sought out by means of small-scale reconnaissance missions. One of the Finnish officers went as far as to explain the early Finnish successes in Estonia with the volunteers' lack of battle experience and recklessness unaffected by tendencies of "social democratization," which had supposedly taken root amongst the Estonians.[103] Kirkebæk describes the Danish detachment as more of a paramilitary than a military unit, with its members more amateurs than professionals, and with all the expected deficiencies in discipline, experience, and military culture.[104]

For lack of other unifying purpose, the volunteers tended to develop a strong sense of loyalty towards their leaders. This soon proved to be a problem for both Ekström's and Kalm's units, where the morale easily faltered in the face of the leader's absence or perceived lack of initiative. Ekström's unit rapidly started losing discipline after the successful capture of Narva. The same soon happened with Kalm's regiment after the battle of Paju. In a characteristic, if extreme development, the commander of Kalm's first battalion, Erkki Hannula, set up a court of sorts in a Valga restaurant, sent his men in the countryside to bring back alcohol, attempted to take the leadership of the regiment as prisoners, and eventually decided to break the terms of his contract with the Estonian government and to return to Finland.[105]

Another important guiding factor for behavior was the volunteers' negative attitudes towards Estonia and Estonians. From surviving evidence, it is quite apparent that for whatever reason they were fighting—against Bolshevism, for money, out of adventurousness or even to "help Estonia"—the volunteers tended to have a low opinion of the young state and its inhabitants.

---

102 Kirkebæk, *Den yderste grænse*, 1:33; 2:36.
103 Roselius and Silvennoinen, *Metsik ida*, 175, 158.
104 Kirkebæk, *Den yderste grænse*, 2:72.
105 Roselius and Silvennoinen, *Metsik ida*, 110, 143–44, 165.

The sources tell of some Danish officers considering the Estonians a primitive nation unprepared for independence, thinking it inevitable that the country would soon be absorbed by some "more cultured" power.[106] The volunteers also frequently assumed that they had been brought in to compensate for the failures of the Estonian army, even if their opinions about individual Estonian officers could be more positive.[107] Initially, the Finnish volunteers had so little faith in the Estonian military leadership that they were unwilling to fight under the Estonian command at all, which led to the appointment of Martin Wetzer as the chief of all Finnish forces. The initial plan, blocked by Laidoner, had even been to appoint Wetzer as the overall commander of all anti-Bolshevik forces in Estonia.[108]

The volunteers felt a similar distaste towards Estonian politics. The victory of left-wing parties in the elections to the Estonian Constituent Assembly in April 1919 was seen with deep suspiciousness. Its new Social-Democratic Speaker, August Rei, had only in January openly stated that White terror had been far worse for the country than the Red.[109] This hardly earned him any favors in the eyes of the White volunteers.

Likely the most important brutalizing factor, however, was the Scandinavian volunteers' utterly negative image of their enemy. As noted above, many of the men held strong anti-Bolshevik attitudes even before going to Estonia, and their subsequent experiences contributed further to dehumanization of the Bolsheviks and the development of a crusader mentality that was unwilling to accept defeat or compromise.[110] Several interrelated aspects of their negative image of the enemy are worth drawing attention to, including the impact of enemy and allied atrocities, orientalism, and antisemitism.

A particularly important factor behind the volunteers' negative image of the enemy was their awareness of the atrocities perpetrated by the Red Army. To some extent encouraged by Baltic representatives abroad, news of Bolshevik war crimes had made it to right-wing Scandinavian newspapers already before the volunteers' arrival. Newspaper propaganda was further corroborated by interviews with refugees from Russia and the Baltics.[111] As some of the first units to retake territory from the enemy, the Finnish volunteers also witnessed firsthand

---

106 Kirkebæk, *Den yderste grænse*, 1:293–95, 332–36.
107 Ibid., 301–03, 343; 2:70–72.
108 Arumäe, *Eesti ja Soome*, 86.
109 Ibid., 85–86; Kirkebæk, *Den yderste grænse*, 1:343–47.
110 Kirkebæk, *Den yderste grænse*, 2:321.
111 Ibid., 25–26, 28.

the mass graves in Rakvere and Tartu and heard stories about Red terror from survivors.[112]

Other Scandinavians had similar experiences, even if they arrived later. On their way to the front, the Danish detachment encountered an insane woman who had apparently been tied by the Bolsheviks to a tree trunk and forced to watch her family being murdered. This incident left an impression, and several volunteers reported it in their writings.[113] The Danes' hatred for the enemy was further deepened by the mass graves they saw in Tartu, full of corpses of people executed by the Bolsheviks,[114] and later in Latvia in Vecgulbene, where the graves reportedly also included dead children.[115] Otherwise, firsthand experiences of Bolshevik brutality were probably not very common, as the volunteers themselves also later admitted. Much of the demonization of the enemy relied on "front rumors" of atrocities not witnessed firsthand but heard about from others, possibly with extra colorful detail added. These stories also contributed to the volunteers' fear of capture and imprisonment by the enemy, and thereby added to their fighting spirit.[116]

First or secondhand experiences of Red terror also interfaced with those of White terror. The Danish General Consul Jens Christian Johansen in Tallinn wrote in his diary that the perpetrators of atrocities in Estonia had been "almost without exception" homegrown Estonian Bolsheviks—not foreign invaders— and that the likewise homegrown White troops had responded with actions in kind.[117] Even if not entirely true, such understanding of the situation normalized violence as a rational, tit-for-tat response. The Danish volunteers also claimed to have witnessed White war crimes firsthand, starting with the shooting of Red prisoners in Tallinn,[118] and followed by the hanging of civilians suspected of spying for the Red side and the shelling of civilian villages in Russia.[119]

Finally, the volunteers' image of the Red Army, referred to by Carlsson as "raw, primitive forces"[120] included a large dose of orientalist and racist othering. The claim that the Bolsheviks were using exceptionally brutal "Chinese troops" had been employed as an effective propaganda tool in Western newspapers, even

---

112 Roselius and Silvennoinen, *Metsik ida*, 142.
113 Kirkebæk, *Den yderste grænse*, 2:45.
114 Ibid., 38.
115 Ibid., 336–38.
116 Ibid., 322–29.
117 Ibid., 31–32.
118 Ibid., 37.
119 Ibid., 303–9.
120 Carlsson, *Okänd svensk soldat*, 137.

though Chinese troops formed only a very small part of the Red Army. The leaders of the Danish recruitment effort were similarly keen to evoke images of "Asiatic barbarism,"[121] and the Danish volunteers did the same. Gudme describes having seen people cut into pieces and laid in primitive mass graves by "Chinese-Russian" soldiers. Borgelin states that "Samoyeds, Kalmyks, Kyrghyz and others" were the "wild half-humans that filled the ranks of Trotsky's army."[122] The enemy's supposed oriental origin could also be used to excuse war crimes. Kalm, when writing about the aftermath of the battle of Paju, remarks that "some more were found hiding in the basement, amongst them a couple of Chinese."[123] It went without saying that he would order them to be executed.[124]

It was likewise very common to equate Bolsheviks with Jews. Some volunteers must have been familiar with the so-called Judeo-Bolshevik theory already before arrival in the Baltics, others probably adopted antisemitic views once there.[125] Einar Lundborg, who reputedly had not held antisemitic views before, acquired them during his service in the Baltics.[126] Particularly important in this respect must have been contacts with Russian White officers, who, at least according to Carlsson, seemed to believe that all Jews were Red spies.[127] The Reds' reliance on female troops was likewise perceived by the volunteers as a form of unnatural warfare and mocked in lurid stories.[128]

## Instances of Volunteer Violence and Criminality

The known instances of violence and criminality perpetrated by Scandinavian volunteers in EWI were numerous and varied. Roughly, they can be categorized into crimes against property (theft, fraud, burglary, vandalism, and so on), public order offenses (drunkenness, harassment, dereliction of duty), and offenses against the person (murder, rape, assault, robbery). However, crimes of several kinds would often be linked in concrete incidents, meaning that there is little

---

121 Kirkebæk, *Den yderste grænse*, 2:29–30, 295–96.
122 Ibid., 31, 323.
123 Hans Kalm, *Pohjan Poikain retki* (Porvoo: WSOY. 1921), 65.
124 Leino, "Oikeudenhoito suomalaisessa vapaaehtoisjoukossa," 54.
125 Kirkebæk, *Den yderste grænse*, 2:173–78; Leino, "Oikeudenhoito suomalaisessa vapaaehtoisjoukossa," 53.
126 Kirkebæk, *Den yderste grænse*, 2:453.
127 Carlsson, *Okänd svensk soldat*, 194; Kirkebæk, *Den yderste grænse*, 2:176.
128 Kirkebæk, *Den yderste grænse*, 2:298.

sense in their artificial separation and categorization. In the following, I will instead present a part-chronological, part-analytical overview.

During the volunteers' early days in Tallinn, their drunkenness easily led to fights, sometimes involving knives and guns. Weapons were used to threaten or intimidate civilians.[129] Even the officers were reputedly harassing people in the town, especially Russians. The Estonian authorities frequently had to step in. Already in the first weeks, a couple of Finnish volunteers were killed in drunken disputes, and two civilians also lost their lives.[130]

Other crimes were more directly related to battle. During Ekström's sacking of Narva, everyone who admitted to being "Red" was shot indiscriminately. According to Vilho Helanen, "all the various peoples of the Russian Bolshevik armies starting with the Finns and ending with Estonians and the Chinese" were found in the piles of bodies in the morning after the battle. Indeed, it seems that the Finnish volunteers were particularly merciless towards their compatriots in the Red Army.[131] Twenty-seven Red Finnish prisoners were murdered by Finnish volunteers in front of Narva town hall.[132] Kalm's unit behaved much in the same fashion. Immediately after the battle of Paju, his troops executed about fifty prisoners and ten civilians—the servants of the household—who had been hiding in the basement.[133]

References to shootings of Red prisoners are also found in Danish and Swedish sources, where such actions are justified as reprisals. A particularly frequently described scene by Danish volunteers was the execution of eleven men and four women in Vecgulbene in the beginning of June. However, there are no sources confirming that Danish or Swedish volunteers themselves participated in mass executions.[134]

Smaller-scale executions nevertheless likely took place. In his memoirs, Gudme reports seeing Swedish officers shooting prisoners to try out their new pistols. Lundborg describes how he himself ordered a spy to be shot, and the Danish volunteers possibly executed several people thought to be spies, one of

---

129 Kirkebæk, *Den yderste grænse*, 1:302–4.
130 Ilmjärv, "Soome vabatahtlikud Eesti Vabadussõjas," 61; Leino 2001, 43–44, 46; Roselius and Silvennoinen, *Metsik ida*, 154–55.
131 Roselius and Silvennoinen, *Metsik ida*, 140–43; Rantanen, "Vapaus ja veljeys," 69–70; Arumäe, *Eesti ja Soome*, 92.
132 Leino, "Oikeudenhoito suomalaisessa vapaaehtoisjoukossa," 53; Kirkebæk, *Den yderste grænse*, 2:34.
133 Leino, "Oikeudenhoito suomalaisessa vapaaehtoisjoukossa," 53; Roselius and Silvennoinen, *Metsik ida*, 157–58; Kirkebæk, *Den yderste grænse*, 2:34.
134 Kirkebæk, *Den yderste grænse*, 2:218, 291–92, 296–302, 331.

them an underage boy. Kirkebæk points out that these episodes seem to have occurred towards the end of the Danish volunteers' service in Estonia, and possibly constitute evidence of their deepening brutalization. Initially, they would hand suspected spies over to the Estonian authorities, but as time wore on, the Danes would instead carry out beatings and executions.[135]

Once out of battle, the volunteer units easily succumbed to problems with discipline. After the capture of Narva, the discipline in Ekström's unit rapidly deteriorated, with soldiers drinking heavily and looting during their respite.[136] Kalm's capture of Valga had similar consequences and drunken and marauding Finnish volunteers made themselves extremely unpopular.[137] An even lower point was Kalm's unauthorized capture of Alūksne with the explicit purpose of acquiring supplies. Ahead of battle, Kalm had apparently promised his men that they would get to loot the town thoroughly. Undertaken against the orders of Martin Wetzer, this raid also amounted to Kalm's rebellion against his immediate superiors, which he was only able to weather thanks to Laidoner's support.[138] On the way to Alūksne, the Finns looted several grand land estates, and took the town after a short and bloody battle under Kalm's orders of "take no prisoners and show no mercy to the Jews."[139]

The fact that looting was common is also witnessed by the Finnish volunteers' ego-documents and military court records.[140] Already early in the campaign, the Finns resorted to looting—not entirely without the approval of their officers—to compensate for the lack of supplies provided by the Estonian command.[141] Altogether twenty-three Finnish volunteers were charged by the Estonian Relief Committee's judicial authorities for property crimes,[142] but the actual number of incidents must have been higher. Most of the Finnish volunteers' further crimes against civilians, including several likely murders, also seem to have taken place in the context of looting and robbery.[143] In Kalm's regiment, self-initiated

---

135 Ibid., 312–20.
136 Roselius and Silvennoinen, *Metsik ida*, 143–44.
137 Ibid., 159; Ilmjärv, "Soome vabatahtlikud Eesti Vabadussõjas," 61.
138 Roselius and Silvennoinen, *Metsik ida*, 161–62.
139 Leino, "Oikeudenhoito suomalaisessa vapaaehtoisjoukossa," 53, 63–64; Roselius and Silvennoinen, *Metsik ida*, 163–65.
140 Rantanen, "Vapaus ja veljeys," 53.
141 Leino, "Oikeudenhoito suomalaisessa vapaaehtoisjoukossa," 61–62, 67; Ilmjärv, "Soome vabatahtlikud Eesti Vabadussõjas," 62.
142 Leino, "Oikeudenhoito suomalaisessa vapaaehtoisjoukossa," 56.
143 Ilmjärv, "Soome vabatahtlikud Eesti Vabadussõjas," 62; Leino, "Oikeudenhoito suomalaisessa vapaaehtoisjoukossa," 48–49.

requisitions and home inspections were eventually banned,[144] which put Kalm on a collision course with some of his own officers.

Possibly influenced by the Finnish example, the Danish volunteers also occasionally looted valuables that they came across in land estates. Even more common were field requisitions of food from the local civilian population, which could easily turn into outright robbery. Weapons and threats of violence were certainly used in such incidents.[145] Later, back in Denmark, other Danish officers accused Borgelin of having carried out unnecessarily harsh requisitions that had made the reputation of the Danes amongst the local people apparently worse than that of the Reds.[146]

While the legality of wartime food requisitions might be debatable, the volunteers' acquisition of valuables and antiquities clearly had a criminal character. Lundborg reports that while stationed in Petseri, the Swedish volunteers completely looted the local monastery of all the valuables. The chaplain of the unit even organized a smuggling route of valuables to Finland and Sweden, where the prices were higher.[147] There is also some evidence of the volunteers plundering dead bodies.[148]

Some volunteers also sold their own equipment, or the property of their units, or stole from their comrades. Lundborg reports that in the final days of the Swedish Corps, some men were walking around without trousers or boots, which they had sold for bread and vodka.[149] Some of the officers condemned these practices,[150] while others engaged in similar activities themselves.[151] A few Finnish officers were eventually tried for embezzlement of funds by their own military court.[152] Volunteers also tried to acquire money from their local diplomatic representatives, or from the recruitment offices back home.[153] Officers stationed away from the field units were—perhaps not groundlessly—accused of living a good life in Tallinn, while their units suffered deprivation on the front.[154]

Serious inner problems, sometimes bordering on mutiny, indeed came to characterize all Scandinavian volunteer contingents. The tensions between

---

144 Leino, "Oikeudenhoito suomalaisessa vapaaehtoisjoukossa," 62.
145 Kirkebæk, Den yderste grænse, 2:109, 112–15, 117, 365.
146 Ibid., 372.
147 Lundborg, "Rootsi korpusega Eesti Vabadussõjas," 1490.
148 Kirkebæk, Den yderste grænse, vol. 2, 119–20.
149 Lundborg, "Rootsi korpusega Eesti Vabadussõjas," 1491.
150 Kirkebæk, Den yderste grænse, 1:430–31.
151 Lundborg, "Rootsi korpusega Eesti Vabadussõjas," 1475.
152 Leino, "Oikeudenhoito suomalaisessa vapaaehtoisjoukossa," 58.
153 Kirkebæk, Den yderste grænse, 2:159.
154 Ibid., 368.

Kalm and his officers on the one hand, and Kalm and his superiors on the other have already been mentioned. The Finnish soldiers were unwilling to fulfil the orders of ethnically Swedish officers, with the consequence that desertions and unauthorized retreats from some sectors of the front became common.[155] In the Danish detachment, a group of ten officers unsuccessfully conspired to replace Borgelin with one of their own.[156] In the Swedish detachment, a mutiny against Mothander had already been brewing when the tensions came ahead in the so-called Franchi affair.

Giuseppe Franchi was a Swedish volunteer, who soon after arriving in Estonia had left Mothander's unit and instead joined the Estonian army's Baltic German battalion. There, he was asked to organize a separate Swedish artillery battery. Franchi, who had served in the Finnish Civil War, traveled to the other Swedes in Narva to convince them to join his new unit. Supposedly, he promised them that they would be allowed to rob and loot as much as they wanted and receive better pay. Even after being admonished by the officers, Franchi refused to cease his activities and advised the other soldiers to raise their weapons against their superiors, if needed. Consequently, Malmberg had Franchi arrested, organized a quick field court, and had him executed the following morning. This was all done without Mothander's permission, who went to Laidoner to accuse his officers of insubordination and insurgency. To carry out an investigation, the Swedish unit was transferred to Paldiski, delaying its deployment on the front.[157]

In the meantime, crimes against public order and the civilians continued also during the volunteers' respites in towns. Several such episodes are known from Tartu,[158] the most gruesome of which involved a Finnish Ensign, who shot and killed an Estonian prostitute who had apparently admonished the Finns for their hatred of Russians and Jews.[159] The volunteers were naturally attracted to the easier life in urban environments. Estonian Colonel Karl Parts writes that on one occasion, some three hundred to four hundred Finns had demanded a train to Tallinn, and when it was not granted to them, they hijacked one, forcing the passengers to leave and stealing their baggage.[160]

---

155 Roselius and Silvennoinen, *Metsik ida*, 144–45.
156 Kirkebæk, *Den yderste grænse*, 2:160–61.
157 Roselius and Silvennoinen, *Metsik ida*, 170–71; Jaanson, *Draakoni hambad*, 52–57; Kirkebæk, *Den yderste grænse*, 1:315–16; Ericson, *Svenska frivilliga*, 80–82; Leino, "Oikeudenhoito suomalaisessa vapaaehtoisjoukossa," 30; Lundborg, "Rootsi korpusega Eesti Vabadussõjas," 1445–67; Carlsson, *Okänd svensk soldat*, 156–63.
158 Kirkebæk, *Den yderste grænse*, 1:452; Rantanen, "Vapaus ja veljeys," 50.
159 Leino, "Oikeudenhoito suomalaisessa vapaaehtoisjoukossa," 45.
160 Ilmjärv, "Soome vabatahtlikud Eesti Vabadussõjas," 61.

The eventual process of repatriation was also fraught with criminality and tensions. Some Swedish officers, since the men had received their pay in Finnish markka, took up currency speculation before leaving for Sweden.[161] Hannula's battalion, which had befouled the hotels and restaurants in Valga, initially refused to give up their weapons and had to be loaded on train cars under the watch of Estonian machine guns.[162] In Tallinn, when Estonian customs officials wanted to search through the volunteers' baggage, they were forced to leave with raised weapons and threats. Nevertheless, the men were still searched upon their arrival in Helsinki and many prohibited goods confiscated.[163]

## The Reactions of the Estonian Authorities

The Estonian authorities were certainly aware of at least some of the instances of violence and crime perpetrated by the Scandinavian volunteers. Nevertheless, their crimes usually remained unprosecuted—possibly more than was the case with native Estonian troops, although this is difficult to prove. In the following, I examine the likely reasons why this was the case, as well as some instances where the volunteers nevertheless did face prosecution and punishment.

There is a reason to agree with Roselius and Silvennoinen, who argue that, from the outset, the Estonian authorities had turned a blind eye to the crimes and disorderly conduct of the Finnish volunteers because they were considered a vitally important military force and care needed to be taken not to antagonize them.[164] However, it is worth adding the caveat that the Finnish volunteers' likely main importance was in the boost they provided to the Estonian morale, not in concrete operational successes. In his report to the Estonian Constituent Assembly on April 30, Konstantin Päts emphasized precisely this aspect: the Finnish volunteers were living proof that the Estonians were not alone but had a kindred nation fighting alongside them.[165]

Indeed, there is evidence of early Estonian resignation to the fact that crimes and violence would occur during the volunteers' service in Estonia. Apparently, the Estonian Premier Päts himself stated to the Finns that "everything you get

---

161 Lundborg, "Rootsi korpusega Eesti Vabadussõjas," 1491.
162 Roselius and Silvennoinen, *Metsik ida*, 167–68.
163 Leino, "Oikeudenhoito suomalaisessa vapaaehtoisjoukossa," 64–65; Roselius and Silvennoinen, *Metsik ida*, 199; Rantanen, "Vapaus ja veljeys," 54.
164 Roselius and Silvennoinen, *Metsik ida*, 154–55.
165 Arumäe, *Eesti ja Soome*, 88.

as spoils of war—take it from the Bolsheviks, the money and goods."[166] Päts retained much the same mindset months later, as evidenced by a conversation between him and the Danish General Consul Johansen on April 5. Responding to Päts's observation that the Danish volunteers had behaved well, Johansen replied that the same had initially been true of the Finns and the Swedes, "but then quite a lot happened." Päts responded: "Small stuff! It doesn't matter. Let the men drink and steal a few silver trinkets. It's not a problem. As long as they help us bravely against the enemy.[167]" Johansen pointed out that even if the Estonian government did not care about the volunteers' behavior, he, as the Danish representative, nevertheless had to pay attention to it, which made Päts more serious.[168]

By that point, there was already plenty of evidence of volunteer criminality. Although the Estonian Relief Committee publicly stated that the rumors about Finnish marauding and acts of vandalism in Estonia were groundless,[169] it had nevertheless already on January 27 set up a special military court to prosecute Finnish volunteer crimes according to Finnish law. The first hearings were held on February 5 in Tartu. Previously, Ekström's unit had had its own field court, which had sentenced one volunteer to death for robbery and three more to imprisonment.[170] An ad hoc field court was also used by the Swedish Corps in the Franchi case. This was a general trend: the Estonian Government itself made frequent use of similar measures.[171]

The cases tried in the Finnish military court were not many. Leino conjectures that Estonian civilians likely thought it impossible to get justice against the Finns, so they did not bother coming forward.[172] Nevertheless, Ilmjärv estimates that more than one hundred Finnish volunteers spent some time in prison in Tallinn. Oswald Kairamo, the Finnish diplomatic representative there, wrote in early April that even several officers had been arrested, blaming them for the sorry state of the Finnish relief effort.[173] Some Swedish and Danish volunteers also found their way to Estonian prisons and one Danish soldier was even

---

166 Roselius and Silvennoinen, *Metsik ida*, 160.
167 Kalervo Hovi. *Estland in den Anfängen seiner Selbständigkeit: die Tagebuchaufzeichnungen des dänischen General konsuls in Reval Jens Christian Johansen 13.12.1918–29.5.1919* (Turu: Turun yliopisto, 1976), 117.
168 Kirkebæk *Den yderste grænse*, 1:299; Arumäe, *Eesti ja Soome*, 92.
169 Roselius and Silvennoinen, *Metsik ida*, 161.
170 Leino, "Oikeudenhoito suomalaisessa vapaaehtoisjoukossa," 26–30; Ilmjärv, "Soome vabatahtlikud Eesti Vabadussõjas," 62.
171 Kirkebæk, *Den yderste grænse*, 2:19.
172 Leino, "Oikeudenhoito suomalaisessa vapaaehtoisjoukossa," 46.
173 Ilmjärv, "Soome vabatahtlikud Eesti Vabadussõjas," 63.

sentenced to five years of prison camp for insubordination.[174] The leaders of the volunteer contingents frequently sought assistance from Estonian authorities, such as in July 1919, when the commander of DBAC requested immediate arrest of all Danish volunteers without valid travel permissions found on trains.[175]

In instances where more serious—and thus politically more inconvenient—volunteer crimes were investigated by Estonian authorities, they seemed to do so half-heartedly. In the Franchi case, which attracted major attention in Swedish newspapers, the Estonian investigation reached the conclusion that the Swedish officers had acted correctly in line with the dangerous situation so close to the front. Mothander was made the scapegoat for having raised an unfounded case against his own officers, released from duty and allowed to return to Sweden.[176] Lundborg, who was repeatedly interrogated by the Estonian investigators, reported that the latter were relatively uninterested in assigning blame for Franchi's death and more concerned about providing the Swedish detachment with more effective leadership going forward.[177]

When forced to choose between the foreign volunteers and their own, however, the Estonians would naturally support the latter. With the Finns, the tensions came to a head on April 7, right before Kalm's troops were supposed to return to Finland. Juhan Kriisa, the twenty-one-year-old commander of Valga, killed an arrested Finnish volunteer as he was trying to escape from the town prison. This incident provoked an outcry in Finland and soured the Estonian-Finnish relations when the Estonian investigation established that Kriisa's action had been justified.[178]

Behind the scenes, however, the existence of the problem was eventually recognized even by the political leadership. On March 24, Louhivuori privately admitted to Päts that looting was taking place.[179] At the end of the same month, Päts wrote to the Estonian representatives in Helsinki that the Finnish troops were behaving as if they were in a conquered land, with people suffering under their brutality and violence, and that it was therefore imperative to get rid of them.[180]

---

174 Kirkebæk, *Den yderste grænse*, 1:452; 2:158–59.
175 Ibid., 451.
176 Roselius and Silvennoinen, *Metsik ida*, 171–172; Kirkebæk, *Den yderste grænse*, 1:316.
177 Lundborg, "Rootsi korpusega Eesti Vabadussõjas," 1476.
178 Leino, "Oikeudenhoito suomalaisessa vapaaehtoisjoukossa," 50–51; Roselius and Silvennoinen, *Metsik ida*, 167.
179 Leino, "Oikeudenhoito suomalaisessa vapaaehtoisjoukossa," 64.
180 Arumäe, *Eesti ja Soome*, 92.

After the Finnish units returned to Finland in March and April, the Estonian authorities did not renew their contracts or organize new recruitment. No mention was made of any problems that the volunteers had caused: the newspapers simply stated that the Finns been sent home since their mission had been accomplished. Of course, criminality and violence were far from the only reasons to not to renew the effort. By that point, the front had already moved beyond Estonian territory and the Finnish volunteers—who were not contractually obliged to fight outside of Estonia—ceased to have a military purpose.[181] This was compounded by the Estonians' chronic lack of money, and sensitive political issues, such as some of the volunteers' worryingly close contacts with the Russian Whites and Baltic Germans.[182]

After the volunteers had already left, there was even less of an incentive to draw attention to their crimes. As Kirkebæk points out, the Estonian government had early on recognized that the story of the Danish detachment would become important for Danish-Estonian relations, making it imperative to maintain a positive image of the Danish efforts in Estonia.[183] Westenholz, likewise, later took care to dampen the mutual accusations between former DBAC officers, lest the reputation of the whole effort be undermined.[184] Ilmjärv similarly concludes that there was no official recognition of the crimes of the volunteers for foreign political reasons: after all, Estonia might have needed the help of its neighbors again in the future.[185]

## Conclusions

The Estonian experience with Scandinavian volunteers in EWI suggests that the volunteer contingents were a rather problematic fighting force. The recruitment efforts tended to attract ideological warriors prone to radicalization, adventurers and criminals, all of whom had very little knowledge about Estonia. After their arrival, the volunteers tended to be influenced by superficial impressions of local chaos and lawlessness, which encouraged criminal behavior on their part. The volunteer detachments suffered from lack of discipline, caused by inexperience, poor leadership, and weakness of local authorities. The Scandinavians'

---

181 Roselius and Silvennoinen, *Metsik ida*, 198.
182 Kirkebæk, *Den yderste grænse*, 1:376–77.
183 Ibid., 2:506–7.
184 Ibid., 374–75.
185 Ilmjärv, "Soome vabatahtlikud Eesti Vabadussõjas," 64.

often cavalier, colonialist, and dehumanizing attitudes towards both their allies and especially the enemy, also played a significant role in facilitating violence and criminality, as did the easy availability of alcohol.

The crimes and violence perpetrated by Scandinavian volunteers in EWI were thus born out of various forms of weakness. Brutality in warfare, exemplified by the shooting of prisoners and suspected spies, was an expression of their irregular operational style and leadership, but also of the lack of resources and oversight that might have prevented these incidents from happening. The many instances of looting and theft can similarly be explained by the lack of resources and weakness of local rule of law, as can their vandalism, fraud, and harassment or even murder of civilians. The volunteer units' tendency to easily lose discipline, develop inner tensions between officers, and even to disintegrate, was yet another form of weakness with many of the same causes.

Although some volunteers who had committed crimes faced prosecution in Estonia, most of them likely did not, which must have encouraged feelings of impunity. To an important degree, volunteer violence and criminality were therefore facilitated by the Estonian authorities, which lacked the ability and the political will to deal with their wrongful behavior. Over time, the authorities' perspective seems to have shifted to some degree, and in the end, the immediate problem was solved by sending the volunteers back home.

By then, the participation of Finns, Swedes, and Danes in the Estonian War of Independence had become a part of the history of—and by extension also a factor in the future of—Estonian-Finnish, Estonian-Swedish, and Estonian-Danish relations. This meant that the positive image of Scandinavian volunteers in EWI continued to be upheld, which has been the case largely to this day. Hopefully, the present study can, in line with much of the newer research on the topic, contribute to a more balanced and less politically calculating perspective on these events, helping us to better understand the phenomenon of volunteerism in EWI in its full complexity.

# Bibliography

Arumäe, Heino. *Eesti ja Soome. Sõjast sõjani.* Tallinn: Argo, 2018.
Carlsson, Conrad. *Okänd svensk soldat.* Stockholm: Albert Bonniers Förlag, 1937.
Eichenberg, Julia, and John Paul Newman. "Introduction: Aftershocks: Violence in Dissolving Empires after the First World War." *Contemporary European History* 19, no. 3 (2010): 183–94.
Ericson, Lars. *Svenska frivilliga: Militära uppdrag i utlandet under 1800- och 1900-talen.* Lund: Historiska Media, 1996.

Hovi, Olavi. *The Baltic Area in British Policy, 1918–1921. Volume 1, From the Compiègne Armistice to the Implementation of the Versailles Treaty.* Helsinki: The Finnish Historical Society, 1980.

Hovi, Olavi, and Timo Joutsamo. *Suomalaiset heimosoturit Viron vapaussodassa ja Itä-Karjalan heimosodissa vuosina 1918–1922.* Turu: Turun yliopisto, 1971.

Ilmjärv, Magnus. "Soome vabatahtlikud Eesti Vabadussõjas ehk ühe legendi lõpp." *Vikerkaar*, no. 4 (1993): 60–64.

Jaanson, Kaido. *Draakoni hambad. Rootsi ja Taani palgasõdurid 1919. aastal Eestis.* Tallinn: Eesti Raamat, 1987.

Jensen, Niels. *For Dannebrogs ære: danske frivillige i Estland og Letlands frihedskamp 1919.* Odense: Odense Universitetsforlag, 1998.

Kirkebæk, Mikkel. *Den yderste grænse: danske frivillige i de baltiske uafhængighedskrige 1918–1920.* Bd I-II. Copenhagen: Lindhardt og Ringhof, 2019.

Kuldkepp, Mart. "Eesti Vabadussõja vabatahtlike värbamine Rootsis." *Õpetatud Eesti Seltsi aastaraamat/Annales Litterarum Societatis Esthonicae 2013* (2014): 191–209.

———. "Kaks majorit kahel pool Läänemerd: Väljaöeldu ja väljamõeldu Carl Axel Mothanderi romaanis President." *Akadeemia*, no. 2 (2014): 235–70.

———. "Swedish Political Attitudes Towards Baltic Independence in the Short Twentieth Century." *Ajalooline Ajakiri*, no. 3–4 (2016): 397–430.

———. "Franchi sõbrad ja mõrvarid: Einar Lundborgi mälestused teenistusest Rootsi Korpuses." *Akadeemia*, no. 8 (2017): 1493–99.

———. "Den yderste grænse: danske frivillige i de baltiske uafhængighedskrige 1918–1920." *Journal of Baltic Studies* 51, no. 2 (2020): 289–91.

Laaman, Eduard. *Eesti iseseisvuse sünd.* Stockholm: Vaba Eesti, 1964.

Leino, Vesa. "Oikeudenhoito suomalaisessa vapaaehtoisjoukossa Viron vapaussodassa 1919." MA diss., University of Jyväskylä, 2001.

Lundborg, Einar. "Rootsi korpusega Eesti Vabadussõjas." *Akadeemia*, no. 8 (2017): 1427–93.

"Maanõukogu protokoll nr 69-a." in: *Maanõukogu protokollid: 1917–1919: 1. koosolekust 1. juulil 1917 78. koosolekuni 6. veebruaril 1919*, 343–46. Tallinn: R. Tohver, 1935.

Medijainen, Eero. "Ameerika Ühendriikide de iure tunnustus Balti riikidele 1922. aastal – väärtuspõhine otsus või majanduslik kalkulatsioon?" *Ajalooline Ajakiri*, no. 2 (2011): 123–52.

Minnik, Taavi. "The Cycle of Terror in Estonia, 1917–1919: On its Preconditions and Major Stages." *Journal of Baltic Studies* 46, no. 1 (2015): 35–47.

Pihlamägi, Maie. "Eesti 1919. aasta sõjavõlg Ameerika Ühendriikidele ja selle kustutamine." *Acta Historica Tallinnensia*, no. 20 (2014): 132–56.

Pajur, Ago, et al. *Eesti Vabadussõja ajalugu.* Tallinn: Varrak, 2020.

Preben-Hansen, Bernadette, and Michael Clemmensen. *Bondefanget til borgerkrigen. Det danske korstog til ærkeenglen Michaels by.* Viborg: Syddansk Universitetsforlag, 2015.

Rantanen, Henri. "Vapaus ja veljeys vai viha ja pelko? Suomalaisvapaaehtoisten lähtömotiivit Viron vapaussotaan vuosina 1918–1920." MA diss., University of Helsinki, 2018.

Roselius, Aapo, and Oula Silvennoinen. *Metsik ida. Soome hõimusõjad ja Ida-Euroopa murrang 1918–1921.* Tallinn: Rahva Raamat, 2020.

Tikka, Marko. "Warfare and Terror in 1918." In *The Finnish Civil War 1918: History, Memory, Legacy*, edited by Tuomas Tepora and Aapo Roselius, 90–118. Leiden: Brill, 2014.

Vihalem, Paul. *Eesti kodanlus imperialistide teenistuses (1917–1920).* Tallinn: Eesti Riiklik Kirjastus, 1960.

Zetterberg, Seppo. *Suomi ja Viro 1917–1919. Poliittiset suhteet syksystä 1917 reunavaltiopolitiikan alkuun*. Helsinki: Suomen historiallinen seura, 1977.

———. "Die schwedische Regierung und die baltische Krise im Herbst 1918." In *Reval und die baltischen Länder: Festschrift für Hellmuth Weiss zum 80. Geburtstag*, edited by Jürgen von Hehn and Janos Kenez, 75–89. Marburg an Lahn: Herder-Institut, 1980.

———. "Der Weg zur Anerkennung der Selbständigkeit Estlands und Lettlands durch die skandinavischen Staaten 1918–1921." In *Ostseeprovinzen, Baltische Staaten und das Nationale. Festschrift für Gert von Pistohlkors zum 70. Geburtstag*, edited by Norbert Angermann, Michael Garleff and Wilhelm Lenz, 415–46. Münster: Lit Verlag, 2005.

———. *Konstantin Päts ja Soome. Unistus kaksikriigist*. Tallinn: Varrak, 2020.

CHAPTER 5

# The Rich and the (In)famous: Social Conflicts and Paramilitary Violence in Hungary during the Counterrevolution, 1921–1923

## Béla Bodó

Although the armistice between the main warring parties in November 1918 officially ended World War I, armed conflicts failed to come to an end. Besides the Polish-Soviet War of 1919–1921 and the Greek-Turkish War of 1919–1922, low-intensity conflicts in the form of border clashes, ethnic strife, and civil wars continued until at least 1924.[1] The explanation for the continued conflict has taken ideological, geopolitical, cultural, and mass psychological factors into consideration. Robert Gerwarth's latest survey emphasizes the importance of ethnic nationalism, political events, such as the disintegration of three empires and, most importantly, the Bolshevik political and ideological challenge to the liberal/capitalist global order, as the main sources of conflicts in the postwar world.[2] George L. Mosse blamed the intensity of military and political conflicts

---

1 Robert Gerwarth and John Horne, ed., *War in Peace: Paramilitary Violence in Europe after the Great War* (Oxford: Oxford University Press, 2012); Ariel Roshwald, *Ethnic Nationalism and the Fall of Empires: Central Europe, Russia and the Middle East, 1914–1923* (London: Routledge, 2001).
2 Robert Gerwarth, *The Vanquished. Why the First World War Failed to End, 1917–1923* (London: Penguin, 2016).

in Europe after 1918 on the brutalization of soldiers and civilians. Wartime suffering made the population impervious to humanitarian arguments; they also led to the rise of militarized political parties and movements, which regarded compromise as a surrender, political competition as a zero-sum game, and total victory and the annihilation of opponents as legitimate goals.[3] In the same vein, Klaus Michael Mallmann and Gerhard Paul have argued that the brutalization of men in the trenches during World War I made their reintegration into civilian society in the 1920s exceedingly difficult. The participation of many of these socially uprooted and psychologically damaged war veterans in right-wing movements and their support for the Fascist Nazi states, World War II, and the Jewish genocide was a logical conclusion of their political careers and their exposure to extreme violence, which had begun in the trenches of World War I.[4] In Germany in particular, the unexpected defeat in the war and humiliation at the negotiating table in its aftermath stirred up resentment against the victors in the postwar order. The explosive mixture of mourning, political paranoia, resentment, and strong faith in the resurrection of the nation through violence gave birth to what Wolfgang Schivelbusch has called a culture of defeat. The rigid focus of the defeated on revenge and national revival had remained a major source of tension in the interwar period and contributed to the outbreak of World War II.[5] That the ideological legacy of the war and the immediate postwar conflicts, such as integral nationalism, political paranoia, anti-Bolshevism, violent antisemitism, and ethnic hatred was also present in the victorious countries (Great Britain, France, and Czechoslovakia) only made a future continental or even worldwide conflict more likely.[6] The agents of postwar violence—the nationalist militias—made a major contribution to the state-building efforts in the new countries of the Baltic region and East-Central Europe.[7] With the exception of the Communists, the postwar militias were nationalists; the majority

---

3   George L. Mosse, "Two World Wars and the Myth of the War Experience," *Journals of Contemporary History* 21, no. 4 (1986): 491–513; Piotr Wróbel, "The Seeds of Violence. The Brutalization of an Eastern European Region, 1917–1921," *Journal of Modern European History* 1, no. 1 (2003): 125–49.
4   Klaus Michael Mallmann and Gerhard Paul, eds., *Karrieren der Gewalt. Nationalsozialistische Täterbiographien* (Darmstadt: Wissenschaftliche Buchgesellschaft, 2004), 5, 16.
5   Wolfgang Schivelbusch, *Culture of Defeat: On National Trauma, Mourning and Recovery* (New York: Picador, 2001), 1–36, 289–95.
6   Rudolf Kučera, "Exploiting Victory, Sinking into Defeat. Uniformed Violence in the Creation of the New Order in Czechoslovakia and Austria, 1918–1922," *The Journal of Modern History* 88, no. 4 (2016): 827–55.
7   Tomas Balkelis, "Turning Citizens into Soldiers: Baltic Paramilitary Movements after the Great War," in *War in Peace: Paramilitary Violence in Europe after the Great War*, ed. Robert G. Gerwarth and John Horne (Oxford: Oxford University Press, 2012), 201–25.

sympathized with the proto-Fascist and Fascist Right. Emilio Gentile regards militia violence not as the manifestation of deep-seated social and economic problems, but as the expression of the ideology and political practices of paramilitary leaders and their followers, who regarded struggle as the meaning of life; it was also a *modus operandi* with which they chose to interact with the outside world, eliminate political opponents, monopolize power, and build a new and totalitarian state.[8] Many studies also point to the "retreat of the state" and the partial or complete loss of its monopoly over the means of violence as the primary cause of atrocities, particularly attacks by militias and the mob on ethnic and religious minorities. Thus, Felix Schnell blames—besides the brutality of rural life and the long tradition of peasant antisemitism—the intensity of the Russian Civil War and peasants' attacks on "class enemies" and ethnic and religious outsiders, such as Jews, for the collapse of the federal and local governments after the two revolutions.[9]

Earlier historians regarded fascism and Nazism as the "radicalism of the middle": a product of the culture of the middle and the lower middle classes. They were interested in the overlaps and continuities in ideology, personnel, and political practices between the German *Freikorps* of the post-1918 period and the Nazi SA and the SS of the 1920s and 1930s. Historians also wanted to know if the post-militias had indeed recruited their leaders and rank-and-file from the middle and the lower middle classes, which were believed to have been particularly susceptible to the Nazi message.[10] In a fascinating study on the language of the *Freikorps*, Klaus Theweleit concluded that militia violence had functioned as an outlet for the sexual frustration of young middle-class men, who both desired their victims and feared that intimate contact with working class women would lead to the contamination and disintegration of their bodies. The perpetrators of extreme violence were motivated by prejudices and hostile stereotypical images, created and reinforced by patriarchy and capitalism, about women, workers, and Jews. In Theweleit's account, economic and social factors played at best a subordinate and indirect role in the postwar atrocities.[11]

---

8   Emilio Gentile, "Paramilitary Violence in Italy: The Rationale of Fascism and the Origins of Totalitarianism," in *War in Peace. Paramilitary Violence in Europe after the Great War*, 85–106.
9   Felix Schnell, *Räume des Schreckens. Gewalträume und Gruppenmilitanz in der Ukraine 1905–1933* (Hamburg: Hamburger Edition, 2012); Dirk Schumann, *Political Violence in the Weimar Republic: Fight for the Streets and Fear of Civil War* (New York: Berghahn, 2009).
10  See Hagen Schulze, *Freikorps und Republik 1918–1920* (Boppard am Rhein: Harald Boldt Verlag, 1969), 34–69; Clifton E. Edmondson, *The Heimwehr and Austrian Politics, 1918–1936* (Athens, GA: University of Georgia Press, 1978).
11  Klaus Theweleit, *Women, Flood, Bodies, History*, vol. 1 of *Male Fantasies* (Minneapolis: University of Minnesota Press, 1987), especially 18, 41–45.

This chapter looks at the social causes of right-wing paramilitary violence in Hungary during the counterrevolution of 1919 and 1921. It stresses, in conjunction with ideology, the importance of economic and social factors as sources of aggression and the motives of the perpetrators. My main argument is that in the Hungarian White Terror, ideological and socioeconomic causes were intertwined: the perpetrators perceived their economic interests through the prism of their group and class culture, ideological obsessions, and paranoia. Jewish merchants and landowners, for example, became their main targets of aggression not only because they were well-to-do, but also, and more importantly, because they were the members of a historically disliked religious minority. The elite and the middle class, the more professional Hungarian Freikorps units (*szabadcsapatok*), which had been built around officers' companies, and the local civic militias, which drew their support mainly from civilians and the members of the middle and lower middle-classes, all used violence to vent frustration and to further the social and material interests of their members. As this study shows, some of these interests, such as the feeding of the troops, were ephemeral, and tied to the poverty of the state and the social and political chaos in Hungary after the war. Others, such as the expulsion of Jews from the universities and some professions, had been part of the political program of many social and right-wing political groups since at least the turn of the century and remained on the agenda until the Jewish genocide in 1944. Political violence was thus both ephemeral and systematic; it was informed by both economic necessities and blind passion, on the one hand, and cold calculation and long-term vision, on the other. How the interests of individuals and social classes informed political violence during the counterrevolution and what forms violence took are explored subsequently.

## The Hungarian Freikorps (*Szabadcsapatok*)

The main agents of paramilitary violence in Hungary after the collapse of the Soviet Republic in early August 1919 were the officers' detachments. There were about a dozen such units in the center of the counterrevolution, Szeged, in early August 1919: they had about three thousand five hundred members.[12]

---

12  The most important officers' companies in August 1919 included: The Prónay Company; the Ostenburg Company; the Csongrád-Csanádi 46th Infantry Regiment (which had four companies: the Szvoboda Company, the Heim Detachment, the Hammerl Company, and the Bencze Company); the Jakab Vén Company; the Third Hungarian Hussar Regiment—Liptay

During the "hot phase" of the counterrevolution in Hungary, in the fall of 1919 and early spring of 1920, the officers' detachments and the civic militias executed between six hundred and one thousand people. However, if we include the number of people executed or tortured to death in the various prisons, the toll of the victims of the White Terror would exceed three thousand and could even reach the five thousand mark.[13] Often called *szabadcsapatok*, which is the Hungarian equivalent of the German Freikorps, the officers' militias were made up of professionals or reserve officers, many of whom were highly decorated war veterans, who, for either ideological or social considerations, had refused to put down their arms in November 1918 or joined the counterrevolution in the summer and fall of 1919. The officers' detachments constituted the backbone of Admiral Miklós National Army; the elite paramilitary groups received their orders directly from Horthy or the Ministry of Defense. In early August 1919, they left the center of the counterrevolution, Szeged, with the order to cleanse the liberated counties of Communists; arrest, punish and, if warranted, execute the functionaries of the Soviet Republic; reinstate qualified administrators to their former positions; collect guns and military equipment; and requisition trucks, wagons, horses, food, clothing, and fodder for the troops. Deputy Colonel Baron Pál Prónay, the commander of the most important and deadly paramilitary group, allegedly asked Horthy and General Károly Soós, the Chief of the General Staff, to put their orders, particularly the summary execution of Communists, into writing; however, his superiors courteously denied the

---

company; the Hungarian Artillery Battalion of Szeged, which also had only one company, led by Major György Eckensberger; the Bárdoss Company; the Székely Infantry Battalion; the Simonyi Hussar Company; the Feldbach Battalion—Colonel Anton Lehár's "Army"; the Madary Company; the Seidenlist Company; the List Detachment; the Third Infantry Battalion of Mátészalka-the Rátz Company; and the Freisberger Detachment. Mihály Perneki, *Shvoy Kálmán titkos naplója és emlékirata* (Budapest: Kossuth Kiadó, 1983), 46–47.

13 Earlier studies estimated that the regime and militias had killed about five thousand people. See György Ránki, Tibor Hajdu and Lóránd Tilkovszky, eds., *Magyarország története. 1918–1919. 1919–1945* (Budapest: Akadémiai Kiadó, 1976), 397; Ignác Romsics estimates the number of people "tortured, lynched, and otherwise executed" during the counterrevolution at only slightly over a thousand. Gergely Bödők believes that the number was even lower: about 350. See Gergely Bödők, "Politikai erőszak az első világháború után: forradalmak és ellenforradalmak Magyarországon és Közép Európában," in *Az első világháború következményei Magyarországon*, ed. Béla Tomka (Budapest: Országgggyűlés Hivatala, 2015), 85–108. My higher estimate includes the number of people who died in prison or, as a result of their injuries in captivity. See Béla Bodó, *The White Terror: Antisemitic and Political Violence in Hungary, 1919–1923* (London: Routledge, 2019), 93–95.

request. At the departure, General Soós allegedly warned Prónay not to kill "too many Jews, which could create a problem, too."[14]

In the next three months, the two elite paramilitary groups, the Prónay and the Ostenburg officers' companies, grew into battalions. The battalions accumulated an enormous amount of power during the first year of the counterrevolution. Prónay and Gyula Ostenburg had direct access to Horthy who valued their advice on domestic and foreign policy. Until the spring of 1921, the two units served as Horthy's Praetorian Guards. As intelligence officers, the members of the two elite units had the right to arrest and interrogate political opponents. The members of the two battalions guarded the most important military prisons and internment camps during the counterrevolution. Prónay's and Ostenburg's militias were also tasked to combat corruption and end black marketeering, by controlling traffic through the fluid borders and arresting and punishing smugglers, currency speculators, and petty criminals. The two elite Freikorps units were popular not only with the civic militias, but also with the commanders and rank-and-file of many regular army and police units. They represented a "state within the state" and could have easily grabbed power before the fall of 1920.

The postwar social and economic crisis had a negative impact on the armed forces: officers complained constantly and bitterly about the lack of weapons and the inability of the state to provide shelter, food, and equipment.[15] Prónay claimed that he and his men acted on Horthy's orders and that they never took more than they needed. His soldiers resorted to violence rarely to requisition badly needed supplies. Wealthy Jews, like the Meyerhoffer family, who rented the estate of Prince Hohenlohe in the village of Inke, Prónay noted in his diary, "voluntarily, and [without expecting] any compensation, delivered to my troops food and fodder."[16] Others, including Prónay's fellow officers in the

---

14 Pál Prónay, "Ellenforradalmi naplójegyzeteim 1918–1921," 4.1. A-738/1, p. 174, Állambiztonsági Szolgálatok Történeti Levéltára (Historical Archives of the Hungarian State Security hereafter cited as ÁBTL). The Regent, to the end of his life, denied that he ordered the paramilitary units to kill anyone. Yet in his memoirs, he also expressed sympathy for the officers who took revenge for the torture and humiliation of their family members during the Communist interlude and vented their frustration on people, such as Jews and liberals, whom they blamed for the mutilation of their country. See Miklós Horthy, *Emlékirataim* (Budapest: Európa Könyvkiadó, 1990), 119–22, 124, 130–32, 163. Colonel Jenő Pilch, Horthy's first biographer, argued that 'pacification' and the restoration of order was, indeed, the main task of the National Army in the fall of 1919. He denied, however, that Horthy ordered the summary execution of opponents and Jews. See Jenő Pilch, *Horthy Miklós* (Budapest: Athenaeum, 1928), 140–41.
15 Anton Lehár, *Erinnerungen: Gegenrevolution und Restaurationsversuche in Ungarn 1918–1921* (Vienna: Verlag für Geschichte und Politik, 1973), 156–57.
16 Prónay, "Ellenforradalmi naplójegyzeteim 1918–1921," 4.1. A-738/1, p. 223, ÁBTL.

National Army and the victims, remember the role of the militias differently. Kálmán Shvoy, then still a young counterrevolutionary officer, for example, described Prónay and his officers in his own memoirs published after World War II as thieves.[17] As the letters of complaints sent by the victims of the requisitioning campaign to the Ministry of Defense show, the officers' detachments took far more than what they needed. In mid-June 1920, two weeks before the harvest officially began, Lieutenant Antal Molnár asked his commander Prónay to send two trucks to the Western Railway Station to pick up the grain that he and his detachment had collected in the village of Fegyvernek and its vicinity. He advised his commander that the trucks be sent at night so that the starving population of the capital would not take notice.[18] The officers' detachment did not take only what they and fellow units needed; if anything, they were more interested in consumer goods and luxury items. One squad of the Prónay Battalion, for example, ravaged the estate of Miksa Szekulecz in the outskirts of Kunszentmiklós in August 1920. The soldiers stole men's suits, hunting equipment, shoes, beddings, tobacco, and food. They also pillaged Szekulecz' cellar, taking large quantities of expensive wine. Intoxicated by alcohol and violence, the militia destroyed what they could not carry off and demolished the house's interior as well.[19] The members of the squads always pocketed part of the booty. However, Prónay also profited directly from his men's robberies. A Jewish commercial farmer by the name of Manó Rózsa recognized the highbred horses drawing Prónay's carriage in Üllői Street in Budapest as his own, taken from his farm by Prónay's men a few months earlier. In vain, he demanded that Prónay either return his property or pay compensation.[20]

Jewish commercial farmers were the main, but not the only, target of the militias. During the militia uprising in western Hungary in the summer and fall of 1921, the right-wing paramilitary groups requisitioned cars, motorcycles, pianos, oriental carpets, jewelry, clothing, and food from the mainly

---

17 Perneky, *Shvoy Kálmán titkos naplója és emlékirata*, 52.
18 Mihály Pásztor, *A fehérterror néhány jelensége: Pest megye, 1919–1920* (Budapest: Pest Megyei Levéltár, 1985), 296.
19 Attorney of the Royal Hungarian Gendarmerie Dr Schmitz. Verdict, 2 June 1922, Troops' Documents from the Horthy Era, Szeged Hunters' Battalion (Prónay), Kt. 2439–2947, 123 doboz, Hadtörténeti Intézet Levéltára (Military History Institute Archive hereafter cited as HIL), Budapest.
20 Depositions regarding the White Terror in 1919: Dr. Géza Dombováry to Ödön Beniczky, Legal Assistance Office of the Pest Israelite Community, 1921, 3110/3, Magyar Zsidó Levéltár (Hungarian Jewish Archive hereafter cited as MZSL), Budapest.

German-speaking local population.²¹ One squad of the Prónay Battalion, for example, took the grain of poverty-stricken estate servants in the village of Solt in the fall of 1919.²² Yet, archival sources also show that the officers did not much care about the social background of their victims. In the village of Nagybajom, for example, Prónay's men emptied the cellars of the local tavern keeper, Mrs. Sándor Zavagyil.²³ They also stole pigs from the estate of a noble man in the vicinity of Debrecen. They injected the poor animals with morphine to prevent them from squealing.²⁴

Requisitioning always involved the use or the threat of violence. On August 21, 1919, two officers from the Prónay Company summoned the leader of the Jewish community to the city hall in the village of Alap. They demanded that the community donate to the National Army to "cover transportation costs." The Jewish representative accepted the ultimatum without protest. After he left, Lieutenant Thiringer told the mayor, "This Jew got lucky. Had he uttered a word [of protest], I would have smashed his head with my lead baton." Thiringer then asked the mayor to name two Jews to be hanged publicly. "Without the shedding of Jewish blood," he added, "this village cannot escape." The mayor begged the officers to reconsider. Jews, he argued, had been living in the village for centuries and had always been "good Hungarians." Faced with resistance from rural administrators, the two officers then left the community, promising to return three days later to "settle scores with the Jews".²⁵

During the counterrevolution, the right-wing militias behaved in the same way as the Austro-Hungarian army units had behaved in Serbia, Ukraine, or Italy during the war. They treated Hungarian Jews as they treated natives in the occupied lands. In April 1920, Prónay dispatched an entire company to cleanse the town of Szolnok and its vicinity of Communists. On the basis, prepared by his father, of a list of suspected left-wing radical, the company commander, Lieutenant

---

21 Superintendant of the Royal Hungarian Gendarmerie Colonel Rákosy to Prónay, November 27, 1921, Troops' Documents from the Horthy Era, Szeged Hunters' Battalion (Prónay), Kt. 2439–2947, 122 doboz, HIL.
22 Superintendant of the Royal Hungarian Gendarmerie General Kontz. Verdict, April 8, 1921, Troops' Documents from the Horthy Era, Szeged Hunters' Battalion (Prónay), Kt. 2439–2947, 123 doboz, HIL.
23 Attorney of the Royal Hungarian Gendarmerie Dr Schmitz. Verdict, May 6, 1921, Troops' Documents from the Horthy Era, Szeged Hunters' Battalion (Prónay), Kt. 2439–2947, 122 doboz, HIL.
24 Ágnes Szabó and Ervin Pamlényi, eds., *A határban a halál kaszál: Fejezetek Prónay Pál feljegyzéseiből* (Budapest: Kossuth Könyvkiadó, 1963), 231.
25 Depositions regarding the White Terror in 1919: Simon Weisz's and Andor Weisz's Deposition, August 25, 1919, 3110/3, MZSL.

Antal Molnár, and his brother Ferenc arrested about fifty people upon arrival. Most of the detainees were middle and upper-class Jewish merchants and manufacturers, who had committed no crime during the Soviet Republic. The family members begged the Molnár brothers to release their loved ones; in return, they promised to make a generous donation to the National Army. A deal was soon struck; however, to Prónay's anger, the better part of the booty, more than fifty thousand koronas, ended up in the pockets of the Molnár brothers.[26]

In the cities, Prónay's men used and abused the same power allotted to them by Admiral Horthy in early August 1919 to persecute Communists and enrich themselves. Thus, Lieutenant György Schefcsik rummaged through the flat of a middle-level functionary, László Szamuely (the brother of infamous Communist Commissar, Tibor Szamuely), soon after the latter's arrest, stealing many of his valuables in the process.[27] Here, too, many, perhaps the majority, of the victims were not Communists at all. For example, Prónay's officers raided the flat of Vilmos Horeczky, a wealthy conservative shopkeeper on Aréna Street in the Seventh District of Budapest in January 1920. The detachment misappropriated jewelry and money in the value of between fourteen thousand and fifteen thousand koronas during their search. The well-connected Horeczky reported the infamy directly to Admiral Horthy's office. In the end, the Ministry of Defense forced Prónay's officers to return at least some of the stolen valuables to their original owner.[28]

The same men who pillaged apartments and kidnapped young women methodologically also worked out a system to steal motorcycles and automobiles. The chauffeur of the Prónay Battalion, János Kukucska, and two or three of his comrades, roamed the streets of the capital in search for cars and motorcycles. They reported their findings back to Lieutenant István Déván, an enforcer and infamous torturer. Déván, or someone of his ilk, then paid a visit to owners and,

---

26 Troops' Documents from the Horthy Era, Szeged Hunters' Battalion (Prónay), Kt. 2439–2947, 123 doboz; Dr. Schmitz (Attorney of the Royal Hungarian Gendarmerie). Verdict, May 16, 1922, HIL; Royal Hungarian National Defense Department. Deposition, September 18, 1920, Troops' Documents from the Horthy Era, Szeged Hunters' Battalion (Prónay), Kt. 2439–2947, 120 doboz, HIL; Hungarian National Defense Department. Deposition, June 18, 1920, Troops' Documents from the Horthy Era, Szeged Hunters' Battalion (Prónay), Kt. 2439–2947, 120 doboz, HIL.

27 Superintendant of the Royal Hungarian Gendarmerie General Kontz. Verdict in the Case against First Lieutenant György Schefcsik, April 6, 1921, Troops' Documents from the Horthy Era, Szeged Hunters' Battalion (Prónay), Kt. 2439–2947, 122 doboz, HIL.

28 First Lieutenant Wittenbarth. Assignment (Szolgálati jegy), Budapest, January 5, 1921, Troops' Documents from the Horthy Era, Szeged Hunters' Battalion (Prónay), Kt. 2439–2947, 120 doboz, HIL.

by using a transparent pretext, confiscated the vehicle.[29] The illegal confiscation of private vehicles created an outcry among the well-to-do. In mid-1920, the Ministry of Defense, under pressure from the same group, ordered Prónay to hand over six cars and one truck (one Mercedes, one Opel, one Daimler, two Benz and one Sisere-Nandin) to the Ministry. It also demanded proof that the commanders of the Battalion were in legal possession of the vehicles they had been driving. At the time of the request, Prónay owned two automobiles, a Ford and a Puch. His subordinate, Captain Victor Ranzenberger drove a Stoewer, while Lieutenant Iván Héjjas possessed a Ford in June 1920.[30] In September 1920, the increasingly frustrated Ministry of Defense decreed that no unit had the right to possess more than three cars and two motorcycles, and that the commander of each battalion should report directly to the minister about carrying out this decree.[31] The warning does not seem to have worked. Even though they theoretically followed the orders of the Minister of Defense, Prónay's men seized the Mercedes of a Greek citizen most likely of Jewish descent, Mór Schlesinger in late 1920 or in early 1921. To add insult to injury, they forced the wealthy businessman to pay thirty-nine thousand six hundred *korona*s for repairing the car that they had crashed after the seizure.[32]

The capital offered more opportunities than the villages and provincial towns for the elite paramilitary group to enrich themselves and improve their social standing. Operating like a criminal gang, the Prónay militia relied on the help of the janitors of large tenements to lead them to their victims.[33] Many of the illegal entries and robberies had unintended consequences, and violence tended to get out of hand either in response to resistance or, more often, because of the

---

29  Lieutenant István Déván. Affidavit (Jegyzőkönyv), June 9, 1920, Troops' Documents from the Horthy Era, Szeged Hunters' Battalion (Prónay), Kt. 2439–2947, 120 doboz, HIL.
30  Royal Hungarian Ministry of Defense to Prónay, June 28, 1920, Troops' Documents from the Horthy Era, Szeged Hunters' Battalion (Prónay), Kt. 2439–2947, 120 doboz, HIL.
31  Commandant of the Budapest Military District General Dáni. Decree, September 18, 1920, Troops' Documents from the Horthy Era, Szeged Hunters' Battalion (Prónay), Kt. 2439–2947, 120 doboz, HIL.
32  Colonel Rákosy (Supervisor of the Royal Hungarian Gendarmes) to Prónay, May 20, 1921, June 14, 1921, June 27, 1921, Troops' Documents from the Horthy Era, Szeged Hunters' Battalion (Prónay), Kt. 2439–2947, 122 doboz, HIL.
33  Three soldiers showed up at the apartment building at Népszinház út 42 on November 25, 1919. They went from apartment to apartment, collecting clothing and taking people's possessions. The inhabitants were called down to the janitor's apartment and asked about their religion. Those who were Jewish were beaten with the butts of their gun. The victims were convinced that the whole incident had been initiated by the janitor. Gyula Wettel, Deposition (prepared by Legal Office of the Social Democratic Party), November 25, 1919, 658. f. 10. cs. 3. őe, 1. kötet, p. 35, Politikatörténei és Szakszervezeti Levéltár (Archives of Political History and of Trade Unions hereafter cited as PIL), Budapest.

vulnerability or complete collapse of the victims. Informed by the janitor that the parents had left, the militia entered the home of three adolescent Jewish girls and two teenage boys in March 1920 in search for weapons and political documents. Predictably they found no incriminating evidence; still, the men took the oldest girl, the twenty-one-year-old Mariska Kohn, in for interrogation. The soldiers told her siblings that they would release her within a few hours, or she would return the next morning at the latest. The children waited for their sister in vain: Mariska Kohn seems to have disappeared without a trace.[34]

The blank check issued by the militia elite to the elite militias to arrest, interrogate, and punish suspected spies and political opponents at will invited extreme forms of violence. Interrogations often degenerated into orgies of aggression: the militias raped female, and occasionally even male, victims.[35] They forced inmates to have sex with each other in their presence.[36] They tortured the captives to death and mutilated their remains.[37] Prónay's men did not simply execute their prisoners: they skinned or burned them alive,[38] sawed them into two,[39] cut their stomachs open, and filled their bellies with pebbles.[40]

The robberies, not to mention the extreme forms of violence, had nothing to do with starvation or even relative deprivation. Because of their social background, the members of the elite units fared much better than the rest of society in the postwar period. In contrast to other right-wing militias in contemporary Europe, such as the German *Freikorps* or the Fascist militias in Italy, the Hungarian officers' companies, which constituted the leading element of

---

34 Ilona Kohn, Deposition (prepared by Legal Office of the Social Democratic Party), March 14, 1920, 658. f. 10.cs. 3. őe, 1.kötet, p. 297, PIL.
35 József Dundek, Deposition (prepared by Legal Office of the Social Democratic Party), December 19, 1919, 658. f. 10.cs. 3. őe, 1.kötet, p. 105, PIL.
36 "A fehérterror Magyarországon. Az angol egyesült munkás kiküldöttség teljes jelentése, 1920 május," in *Magyar pokol: A magyarországi fehérterror betiltott és üldözött kiadványok tükrében*, ed. Györgyi Markovits (Budapest, Magvető, 1964), 336–40.
37 Adolf Landau and his nephew, Géza Landau, were arrested and taken by Héjjas' men to a military base in Kelenföld in the outskirts of Budapest. The captors wanted to extort money from the Landau family. In the end, they tortured their victims. The elderly Landau was castrated and crucified; he died of his injuries. Géza Landau barely survived the maltreatment. *Pesti Napló* (Pest News), July 20, 1922.
38 Marcali Járás Főjegyzője, "Deposition. December 22, 1949, MMI. XXII. 417/1919/7," in *Iratok az ellenforradalom történetéhez*, ed. Dezső Nemes (Budapest: Szikra, 1956), 177–78.
39 Lajos Oláh to the Municipal and County Police of Kiskunfélegyháza. Denounciation, April 22, 1957, XXV. 4.a. 1798/57 FB Bttö, Fr. Kiss Mihály, p. 153–54, Budapest Főváros Levéltára (Budapest City Archive hereafter cited as BFL), Budapest.
40 István Szili, Deposition, June 7, 1957, XXV. 4.a. 1798/57 FB Bttö, Fr. Kiss Mihály, p. 340, BFL.

Admiral Miklós Horthy's National Army, had a decisively elite character. The most important paramilitary group, the Prónay Officers' Company was perhaps the most elitist paramilitary unit in the history of the European counterrevolution; yet aristocrat, nobles, and the members of the upper-middle class were overrepresented in the majority of the officers' companies gathered in Szeged in the summer of 1919.[41] They were the flowers of the Hungarian social and political elite: the rich and the famous, or the sons of the rich and the well-connected, who joined the Freikorps in the summer and fall of 1919. The reason for the atrocities that they had committed were manifold: some, a small minority, wanted to avenge personal injuries suffered during the Communist interlude; others, motivated by ideology, wanted to exterminate Communism root-and-branch; still others regarded violence as fun, an occasion to bond with fellow militia men, or as the only meaningful and successful way to interact with political opponents and revive the country after the war and the two revolutions. Yet, economic motives, such as greed, class interests, and class prejudices, also played an important role in the atrocities. Some of the militia members were large landowners or the children or relatives of large landowners. The elite militias were often invited by local aristocrats to restore order on their estates. The paramilitary groups accepted the invitation because their commanders regarded the local aristocrats as their friends; financial incentives and the promise of accommodation also played a role in the atrocities. The diary of Deputy Colonel Pál Prónay explains clearly how the process worked:

> In the above mentioned village, I stopped with my detachment on the estate of landowner Dénes Szluha. On the way [to his estate], I organized a hunt with my horsemen for Red Terrorists hiding and shooting at us from the corn fields; indeed, they brought down a few of them on the meadow. In Előszállás and also in Czecze, both in the villages and on the large estates, we had to restore order several times among the restless estate servants by using a generous amount of lashing. My main goal was to restore the good old relations between the masters and the estate servants. [We had to do this] because in an agrarian country, like Hungary, uninterrupted agricultural production was vital for both survival and existential reasons. Dénes Szluha

---

41 Béla Bodó, "The White Terror in Hungary, 1919–1921: The Social Worlds of Paramilitary Groups," *Austrian History Yearbook* 42 (2011): 133–63.

invited all of us to a sumptuous dinner; many estate owners from the vicinity were also present. Since the party lasted until early morning, we did not go to bed [that night] but continued our march towards Simontornya the next day.[42]

The attacks on the agrarian poor were motivated by interclass resentment and interests and by a determination to end the revolution and restore prewar social relations in the countryside. The assaults on Jewish estate managers and commercial farmers, on the other hand, were informed by intraclass envy and greed. Violence against wealthy Jewish capitalist entrepreneurs provided an outlet for the tension between landholding aristocrats and nobles, who had been losing ground, on the one hand, and Jewish commercial farmers, who had been buying up the estates of déclassé nobles since the 1870s.[43] Dressed in the uniforms of the National Army, the officers remained landowners at heart, locked in a competition with Jewish commercial farmers. They used the requisitioning campaign not only to line their pockets but also to remove competition and competitors permanently. In Siófok, Prónay had György Löwy, a well-to-do manager of a nearby estate, arrested on false charges in August 1919. Löwy was interrogated, tortured, and his wallet, which contained more than thirty-four thousand *korona*s, and personal belongings (a gold watch, a chain, a silver cigarette case and a pair of leather boots) were stolen by the overenthusiastic interrogators in the famous *Hullám* Hotel. Meanwhile, Prónay's men took up residence on the same estate where Löwy had been a manager for years (the estate was owned by a Jewish businessman and convert to Catholicism). In a few days, they succeeded in destroying a prosperous and successful commercial farm, by slaughtering animals and smashing equipment to pieces. On the order of the Minister of Defense, Prónay, in the end, released Löwy from captivity. The hapless manager could not return to his earlier life, however. The estate servants, incited by Prónay's officers, assaulted their formal superior and forced him to flee the county.[44]

---

42   Prónay, "Ellenforradalmi naplójegyzeteim 1918–1921," 4.1. A-738/1, p. 193–94, ÁBTL.
43   Julianna Puskás, "Zsidó haszonbérlők a magyarországi mezőgazdaság fejlődésének folyamatában (Az 1850-es évektől 1935-ig)," *Századok* 1 (1992): 35–59. See also Gábor Gyáni and György Kövér, *Magyarország Társadalomtörténete: A Reformkortól a Második Világháborúig* (Budapest: Osiris, 2006), 226–27.
44   Attorney of the Royal Hungarian Gendarmerie Dr. Schmitz. Verdict, June 1, 1922, Troops' Documents from the Horthy Era, Szeged Hunters' Battalion (Prónay), Kt. 2439–2947, 123 doboz, HIL; Prónay Pál, "Ellenforradalmi naplójegyzeteim 1918–1921," 4.1. A-738/1, p. 208, ÁBTL.

## The Civic Militias

The officers' detachments were not the only agents of violence during the counterrevolution. Local militias, organized on a voluntary basis, also killed hundreds of people; they also staged more pogroms and committed more robberies than the elite paramilitary units. Violence committed by rural militias was part and parcel of a larger event: the so-called "Green Revolution" which swept Italy, East-Central, and Eastern Europe after the war. The Green Revolution was about social justice, land redistribution, local (peasant) autonomy, and violence. Hungary experienced the Green Revolution in two phases or waves. In both phases, the rebels were anti-city, anti-elite, anti-state, anti-Communist and anti-semitic. However, they chose their victims carefully and opportunistically. In the first phase, between the spring and summer of 1919, the Greens vented their aggression on aristocrats, priests, rural administrators, and Jewish farmers and merchants. During the Soviet Republic and the counterrevolution, their focus shifted to the representatives of the hated Communist regime and Jews. In the fall of 1919, the leaders of the rural militias hailed exclusively from the local elites and middle class; a small minority was noble landowners and the rest were rural administrators, wealthy farmers, liberal professionals, and military and police officers. The rank-and-file came from the lower middle class: they were farmers, artisans, estate servants, and gendarmes.[45]

The civic militias were responsible for the majority of the more than sixty pogroms and riots in Western and Central Hungary between August 1919 and the end of 1920. The civic militias were created by the local authorities or more often by local activists (often young officers) who had occupied no position in the county and municipal administration before the war. The units normally had no direct contact with leaders of the National Army and high-ranking officials in the Ministry of Defense. The most important units, especially in Central Hungary, however, maintained close relations with the largest and most infamous Freikorps units, such as the Prónay and Ostenburg Battalion, and served as their auxiliaries. The hard core involved in the pogroms was the leaders and members of paramilitary groups; the hastily recruited local mob provided the onlookers and the foot soldiers only. Many of these outsiders, especially women and children, were attracted by the opportunity to steal with impunity; others saw the pogroms as a kind of *Volksfest* to wonder, be entertained, and find an

---

45  Bodó, *The White Terror*.

outlet for their deep-seated ethnic hate and aggression. The pogroms always involved verbal abuse and physical violence.

In mid-May of 1920, a squad of the Héjjas militia arrived in the town of Kiskunmajsa. With the help of local fanatics, all members of the Fascist patriotic association, the Alliance of Awakened Hungarians (Ébredő Magyarok Egyesülete or ÉME), organized a public demonstration on the town square. The first speaker, an officer, greeted the crowd that had gathered with "praise Jesus Christ and beat the Jews." He then told the people that "we should not be satisfied with the smashing of the Jews' windows; we have to kill them, too. We have to exterminate the Jews to the last man." The demonstration was followed by a ball in the evening during which free alcohol was distributed. While the crowd was dancing, a drunken mob made up of officers and young peasants pillaged the houses of Jews, seriously wounding a shoemaker and a merchant, striking women and children alike, destroying property, and stealing valuables. After this horrific event, every Jewish family left the community.[46] Radicalization seems to have been encoded in every riot. The mob that attacked Jews in the villages of Diszel and Marcali in late summer of 1919, for example, seem to have only wanted to rob their victims' houses and stores. In the end, however, the group of soldiers and civilians brutally murdered two families and gang raped a young woman and a thirteen-year-old child.[47]

Pogroms always involved not only stealing and robberies but also verbal abuse and physical assaults as well as the wanton destruction, often through fire, of property. The goal of the pogroms, irrespective of the motives of those involved, was to intimidate and terrorize individuals and the entire Jewish community. The armed robberies, which were normally carried out at night, on the other hand, were clearly about financial gain. Armed robberies served to perpetuate the existence of the militias and to enrich and improve the social status of their members. One of Iván Héjjas' men told the court that they thought they had been carrying out Horthy's and the government's orders and that their commander, Héjjas told him they could take the valuables of their victims as a form of salary.[48] Like the officers' detachments, the civic militias worked out a

---

46  The People of Kiskunmajsa, Deposition, Legal Office of the Israelite Community of Budapest, May 27, 1920, Depositions regarding the White Terror in 1919, 3110/3, MZSL. "A pesti Izr. Hitközösség Jogsegítő Irodájának felvételei," *Egyenlőség,* July 8, 1922
47  Flóra Breuer, "Deposition (Kihallgatási Jegyzőkönyv), September 12, 1919," in *Együttélés és kirekesztés: Zsidók Zala megye Társadalmában 1919–1945,* ed. László Németh and Zoltán Paksy (Zalaegerszeg: Zala Megyei Levéltár, 2004), 87–88.
48  Mihály Danics, Affidavit, Kecskemét, April 27, 1945, Héjjas és társai Bp. Nb VII5e 20630/49, pp. 78–80, BFL.

system to maximize their gains and avoid surprises. The most infamous of all civic militias, the Héjjas Detachment, roamed the streets of Kecskemét and the neighboring villages during the day in early 1920, painting the houses and stores red that they intended to rob at night.[49] Unlike the Freikorps units, which focused their attention on luxury items, the peasants in the civic militias stole everything from cash and food items to bed linen and clothing. In places where the militias enjoyed the full support of local administrators, the robberies often took place in broad daylight and were accompanied with other types of violence aimed at material gain, such as extortion. In the town of Soroksár, for example, Héjjas' men forced the manager of a local bank to resign from his position; his job was taken over by one of Héjjas' friends. Simultaneously, the detachment pillaged Jewish homes and businesses in the town, injuring several people in the process. When begged by one of the Jewish victims to reign in the militias and put an end to the atrocities, the local mayor, who was also a member of the ÉME, responded, "Why don't you Jews just hand over your businesses to Christians?"[50]

Like pogroms, armed robberies tended to degenerate into sexualized and "autotelic violence" (*autotelische Gewalt*), when the perpetrators used force for the sake of violence and their goal was destroy the body of their victims completely.[51] On May 7, 1920, in the village of Abony, a squad of Héjjas' unit broke into the house of a widow, Mrs. László Verhovay, and forced her to hand over one thousand six hundred koronas. The next evening, they forced their way into the home of Ignác Deutsch; under duress, Deutsch gave them one thousand two hundred koronas, two pairs of gold earrings and a few pieces of collectors' coins. Militia men then raped the seventeen-year-old Margit Deutsch and the servant girl, Róza Mucsi; they took the gold ring off the half conscious Margit Deutsch's hand and stole her gold earrings as well. The same night, the gang ransacked the house of Manó Pick; they got away with nine thousand koronas in cash, forty liters of rum, twenty liters of wine and a few kilograms of sweets. On May 28, the same group broke into the houses of Jakab Albert, Sámuel Rechtschaffer and Miksa Véli. They killed Sámuel Rechtschaffer and seriously injured Albert, whom they beat with a lead baton. To their disappointment, however, the night netted only a few hundred koronas, two hand watches, and other small valuables.

---

49  János Faragó. Affidavit (prepared by Legal Office of the Social Democratic Party), May 17, 1920, 658. f. 10.cs. 3. őe, 1. kötet, p. 362, PIL.
50  Lipót Blau, Affidavit (prepared by Legal Office of the Social Democratic Party) May 18, 1920, 658. f. 10. cs. 3. őe, 1.kötet, p. 364, PIL.
51  See Jan Philip Reemtsma, *Vertrauen und Gewalt: Versuch über eine besondere Konstellation der Moderne* (Hamburg: Pantheon, 2009), 103–33.

Significantly, none of the victims had anything to do with Communism or with politics.[52]

After the entry of Horthy and the national army into Budapest on November 19, 1919, some of the local militias also set up residence in either military bases or, more often, in luxury hotels in the heavily Jewish business center of the capital. From their headquarters, which also served as interrogation and torture centers, they visited banks, jewelry shops, boutiques, and retails stores of all kinds to pillage them or extort money from their owners.[53] Sometimes, they forced, at gunpoint, the hapless owners to sell their business to them at a nominal price.[54] The militias were mainly interested in financial gain. Like the pogroms in the countryside, the violence used during arrests, kidnappings, and robberies tended to get out of control. What often started out as a crime with a rational and limited goal in mind, often degenerated into an orgy of violence, which led to heinous crimes, such as the torture of elderly men and women.[55]

## Student Militias

In the capital, two student battalions (one from the regular and the other from the technical university) represented a serious political and police force. Students distributed pro-government, antisemitic, and anti-socialist flyers produced by the Ministry of Propaganda and the ÉME. The right-wing fraternities and the militias organized publicity campaigns to convince readers to boycott socialist, liberal, and "Jewish" newspapers, and subscribe only to "Christian" dailies.

---

52 Attorney of the Royal Hungarian Gendarmerie Dr. Schmitz. Investigation Order, September 5, 1921, Troops' Documents from the Horthy Era, Szeged Hunters' Battalion (Prónay), Kt. 2439–2947, 123 doboz, HIL.

53 Thus, Manó Svirszki was forced to hand over his candy shop in the Eötvös Street in Budapest to Héjjas' men in the fall of 1920. Cf. Dr. Strache Gusztáv, Királyi Főügyész. November 29, 1920, 115240 sz. k. ü. 1920, 4.1 A-830, pp. 19–23, ÁBTL.

54 *Népszava*, November 12, 1920.

55 On November 8, 1919, two militiamen in civilian dress detained, for no reason, the eighty-year-old Dávid Weisz. The elderly peddler, who traded in goose feathers, was brought into the cellar of the Hotel Britannia, which housed the Babarczy and Héjjas militias. There he was tortured repeatedly. Only after he had agreed to pay one hundred fifty kronen to his kidnappers and torturers, who included Lieutenant György Schefcsik and Attila Rumbold, was the elderly man able to leave the building. Rumbold—a university student, reserve officer, and one of the founders of the ÉME—was later sentenced to death in criminal court in 1920. Cf. Court of Justice. Warrant. December 9, 1920, VII 18 15/119-120/1920 Royal Hungarian Office of Prosecution. Trial Documents. Szili-Török Miklós and Company, 214–17, BFL. Horthy reduced his sentence, and he was released from captivity in 1921.

They also helped the officers' detachments and the civic militias to enforce the ban on the distribution of "destructive" newspapers and periodicals. In the fall of 1919, radical students spearheaded the campaign to cleanse the university and public libraries of the works of socialist, democratic, and Jewish authors. In the absence of a regular police force, the university militias, on the order of the Military Command of Budapest, helped to maintain order in Budapest in the fall and winter of 1919. Students acted as strikebreakers, spied upon and helped to monitor the mood of the population in poor neighborhoods, organized counterdemonstrations, and campaigned for pro-government parties during elections. For their services, the members of the student militias drew a monthly stipend from the state.[56] Armed with revolvers and bludgeons, the student militias periodically invaded lower class districts to provoke fights with, and terrorize, workers.[57]

The main targets of nationalist students, however, remained their Jewish classmates and professors. The student militias killed few people. While individual students, as members of the civic militias and the Freikorps units, committed horrendous crimes (indeed, some of the most infamous torturers, such as Dénes Bibó, were students), the university battalions were not involved in armed robberies, kidnappings, and extortions. The scope of their aggression remained limited and subordinated to a political goal. Its purpose was to permanently cleanse, or at least drastically reduce the presence of Jews at institutions of higher learning. The student militias were confiscating and destroying the report cards (the so-called indexes) of Jewish classmates to prevent them from taking exams and continuing their studies. At the two universities in Budapest, radical students periodically disrupted the lectures and seminars of Jewish professors, loudly demanding that only people "filled with Christian-nationalist spirit" should be allowed to teach at Hungarian institutions of higher learning.[58] In the fall of 1919, the student militias guarded the gates of the university buildings in Budapest and large provincial towns, blocking the entry of Jews and women (the latter were also perceived as competitors for places in the lecture rooms and for future jobs). They demanded the screening of the entire student body by a five-member committee, made up entirely of members of the student militias.

---

56  Róbert Kerepeszki, *A Turul Szövetség, 1919–1945. Egyetemi ifjúsági és jobboldali radikalizmus a Horthy-korszakban* (Máriabesnyő: Attraktor, 2012), 42–43.
57  Andor Ladányi, *Az egyetemi ifjúság az ellenforradalom első éveiben* (Budapest: Akadémiai Kiadó, 1979), 100–110.
58  The police burned fifteen thousand volumes of printed material taken from the shelves of the Budapest Municipal Library, famous for its social science collection. József Pogány, "A kultúr terror," in *Magyar pokol*, 303–04.

This committee would determine who would be allowed to enroll at university and take their exams. Because of pressure on university administrators and Jewish students, and the chaos produced by the radical students' attempts to control admission, the number of Jewish students in Budapest plummeted in the fall and winter of 1919.[59]

The cleansing of the universities of "Jewish spirit" and the reduction of the share of Jews in the student body had been an old demand of nationalist students. Universities had been a hotbed of antisemitism, right-wing radicalism, and militarism: the first university militias had been founded by one of the most infamous antisemitic ideologues, Miklós Szemere, in the early twentieth century. However, Hungary's liberal governments did not give in to the students' demands. The situation changed drastically after the war. With the return of students from the trenches, the closing of Hungarian universities in annexed territories, and the influx of thousands of refugee students produced a serious bottleneck in the education system. Overcrowding, unprecedented misery, a lack of shelter and food, gloomy job prospects (exacerbated by the entry of tens of thousands of doctors, lawyers, and civil servants from the occupied territories),[60] combined with the wrong lessons drawn from the Communist dictatorship (which the Christian middle class falsely and conveniently equated with Jews) suddenly made the nationalist students' demands look reasonable.[61] Nationalist students were also apt at portraying their special interests and career ambitions as national concerns. In public speeches and newspaper articles, student activists and their supporters argued that the overproduction of journalists and lawyers and the rise of a large intellectual proletariat of mainly Jewish origin had paved the way for the October Revolution of 1918 and Communist dictatorship. The planned *numerus clausus* legislation, they contended, was to prevent the repetition of a similar tragedy.[62]

---

59  As a result of this vetting, only twelve Jewish students were enrolled at the University of Budapest in the second half of the 1919/1920 academic year; this was just 0.25 percent of the student population. At the Technical University, the number was higher: the percentage of Jewish students was at 12.25. At the national level, the percentage was 5.14 percent. Ladányi, *Az egyetemi ifjúság az ellenforradalom első éveiben*, 139.

60  Because of the refugee problem, by the early 1920s Hungary had more doctors and lawyers per capita than any state in Europe. See Mária Kovács, *Liberalizmus, Radikalizmus, Antiszemitizmus. A magyar orvosi, ügyvédi és mérnöki kar politikája 1867 és 1945 között* (Budapest: Helikon Kiadó, 2001), 72–75.

61  Ladányi, *Az egyetemi ifjúság az ellenforradalom első éveiben*, 1–16, 49–55, 80–82.

62  Gusztáv Gratz, *A Forradalmak Kora: Magyarország Története, 1918–1920* (Budapest: Magyar Szemle Társaság, 1935), 334–35.

The main function of student violence was to terrorize Jews and keep them out of university buildings; yet it also served to draw attention to students' plight and create sympathy among, and support for, their cause among the social, political, and cultural elite to pass legislations favorable to students' interests. In the end, they were able to enlist the support of leading Right-radical journalists, the members of the right-wing patriotic associations and secret societies, religious dignitaries, such as the Catholic bishop of Székesfehérvár and Christian socialist activist, Ottokár Prohászka, ex-prime minister István Friedrich, the head of the influential veterans' organization the Hungarian National Defense Association (*Magyar Országos Véderő Egyesület* or MOVE), Gyula Gömbös, the conservative peasant politician Gyula Rubinek, and, most importantly, Prime Minister Pál Teleki.[63] Student organizations launched a well-organized publicity campaign to gain the assistance of parliamentary representatives in early 1920. They did not have to lobby aggressively to find sympathetic ears; the parliament in 1920 was full of passionate antisemites who sought to reverse Jewish emancipation and confine Jews to the periphery of the nation's economic, social, and cultural life.[64]

At the end of September 1920, the parliament passed the infamous *numerus clausus* legislation, which stated that only people whose patriotic credentials and morals were beyond doubt could be admitted to institutions of higher learning. It also urged administrators to take into consideration "that the ratio among students of individual races and nationalities living within the state should as far as possible be equal to the countrywide ratio of the races or nationalities involved." The mentioning of other "races and nationalities" was meant to cover up the real intent behind the new law: the *numerus clausus*' sole purpose was to significantly reduce the share of Jews and women in the student body and remove future competitors.[65]

The *numerus clausus* law was the first of its kind in interwar Europe; similar legislation was passed in Nazi Germany only in the spring of 1933.[66] The legislation marked a watershed in the history of Hungarian universities, students,

---

63  Balázs Ablonczy, *Teleki Pál* (Budapest: Osiris, 2005), 146–49, 402–08.
64  Krisztián Ungváry, "A Szociálpolitika Ethnicizálása," in *Gróf Bethlen István és kora*, ed. Zsejke Nagy (Budapest: Osiris, 2014), 171–73.
65  Randolph L. Braham, *The Politics of Genocide: The Holocaust in Hungary*, vol. 1 (New York: Columbia University Press, 1981), 29–31; Rudolf Paksa, "A numerus clausus és módosítása," in *Gróf Bethlen István és kora*, 137–57; Mária M. Kovács, *Törvénytől sújtva. A numerus clausus Magyarországon* (Budapest: Napvilág Kiadó, 2012).
66  Géza Komoróczy, *A zsidók története Magyarországon II. 1849-től a jelenkorig* (Pozsony: Kalligram, 2012), 421–22.

and Jews. It ended the liberal era in Hungarian history and legitimized the new form of antisemitism and political extremism that emerged after World War I. The law ended free competition on the academic market, reversed the process of emancipation, and permanently excluded Jews from the nation by defining them as an ethnic group or race. The implementation of the law led to a decline in the Jewish share of the university population from about one-third in 1914 to between 8 and 10 percent in the interwar period. The new law triggered a mass migration of talented young Jewish men and women to German, Italian, and French universities. Some of these students, including some of the greatest future scientists of the twentieth century, such as Karl Mannheim, Leó Szilárd, János (John) von Neumann, Ede Teller, and Jenő (Eugen) P. Wigner, never returned.[67] The majority, however, came back after graduation. Paradoxically, the state continued to accept university degrees acquired abroad; many companies, in fact, preferred men and women with foreign degrees and international experience. To the frustration of student activists and their supporters, Jewish competition refused to disappear. Between 1920 and 1930, the share of Jewish lawyers in Budapest declined from 57 percent to just 55.7 percent, the percentage of Jewish physicians from 47.8 to 40.2 and of journalists from 39.5 to 36.1.[68] In the long run, the impact was more serious: by 1939, the share of practicing lawyers in Budapest had fallen to 39.5 percent, and that of Jewish physicians to 31 percent.[69]

The anti-Jewish alliance, which had been formed among representatives of various social groups—such as provincial administrators; army and police officers; better-off farmers; non-Jewish artisans and shopkeepers; university students; radical clergy; and liberal professionals, such as "Aryan" doctors, journalists, dentists, and so on—also had survived the counterrevolution, and continued to serve as the popular basis of support for the Horthy regime until 1944. It was the same social alliance that continued to demand the extension of the *numerus clausus* legislation into every aspect of life and every profession in the 1920s and early 1930s, and which pushed for the anti-Jewish laws after 1938.[70] The *numerus*

---

67  Komoróczy, *A zsidók története Magyarországon*, 426–27; Tibor Frank, "'All modern people are persecuted.' Intellectual exodus and the Hungarian trauma, 1918–1920," in Victor Karady and Peter Tibor Nagy, eds., *The numerus clausus in Hungary. Studies on the First Anti-Jewish Law and Academic Anti-Semitism in Modern Central Europe* (Budapest: Central European University Press, 2012), 176–205.
68  Andrew C. Janos, *The Politics of Backwardness in Hungary, 1825–1945* (Princeton: Princeton University Press, 1982), 226.
69  Kovács, *Liberalizmus, Radikalizmus, Antiszemitizmus*, 84–86.
70  See Mária M. Kovács, "The Hungarian Numerus Clausus: Ideology, Apology and History, 1919–1945," in *The Numerus Clausus in Hungary: Studies on the First Anti-Jewish Law and*

*clausus* put universities, cultural institutions, and professional organizations on a fateful track, which led to the complete expulsion of Jews from economic and cultural life and to their marginalization and social seclusion in the late 1930s and early 1940s, and ultimately to their genocide in 1944.[71]

# Conclusion

This chapter stressed the importance of economic and social factors as the generators of violence during the counterrevolution in Hungary between August 1919 and the end of 1921. Revolution, and its counterpart, counterrevolution, are normally seen as conflict between social classes: between the rich and the poor, the powerful and the powerless, employers and employees, workers and the bourgeoisie, as well as between their respective ideologies (socialism, anarchism, and communism, on the one hand, and liberalism, conservatism, and fascism, on the other). Counterrevolutionary violence is conceived as a response to the social and political pretension of the lower classes and outsiders and as a reaction to violence used by the same groups and their political representatives to overturn the established order.

There was plenty of interclass conflict and violence during the counterrevolution in Hungary: the majority of people killed or imprisoned after August 1919 had supported or sympathized with the Soviet Republic. However, the White Terror was not only about interclass violence; neither was it simply a reaction to the Red Terror. Violence during the counterrevolution was generated by, and gave an outlet to, already existing tensions and hostility between subgroups in the middle class and the elite. The White Terror was not produced by the "retreat" or partial collapse of the state, and the state's loss of its monopoly on the use of violence alone: chaos only favored the violent resolution of already existing conflicts. Ideology was certainly important; however, anti-Communism and even antisemitism were often as much pretexts and covers for material interests and greed, as they were the "first movers." Postwar misery and deprivation, combined with national humiliation and injured pride ("Culture of defeat") were tension-generators; yet, particularly in the case of the aristocratic and upper middle-class members of the elite paramilitary groups who continued to live

---

*Academic Anti-Semitism in Modern Central Europe*, ed. Victor Karady and Peter Tibor Nagy (Budapest: Central European University Press, 2012), 27–55.
71 Ablonczy, *Teleki*, 172–82, 402–10; Randolph H. Braham, *The Politics of Genocide. The Holocaust in Hungary* (New York: Columbia University Press, 1981), 140–91.

the life of the leisure class, they were of secondary importance. Young aristocrats joined the militias to restore order on their estates, punish poor peasants, and avenge the wrong that they had suffered at the hands of the representatives of the Soviet Republic. Yet they also assaulted Jewish commercial farmers and wealthy merchants, who had been their economic competitors since the late nineteenth century.

The White Terror also favored the violent resolution of conflicts between civil servants and liberal professionals. Civil servants, particularly rural administrators but also army officers, had been moving to the radical and antisemitic right since the 1880s; they were statist and resented the high living standards of successor lawyers, doctors, engineers, and other free professionals. That Jews, for historical reasons, were overrepresented in many professions, which had remained liberal or even, as it was the case with many doctors, artists, and journalists, embraced leftists causes, only exacerbated tensions between the civil service class and the liberal professionals. The competition between Jewish and non-Jewish members of the same liberal professions, especially when the latter had come from noble, rural, and civil-service families, only reinforced the already existing fault line between the Christian and the Jewish middle classes. Against the background of postwar chaos and the Communist dictatorship, in which journalists, low-ranking bankers, doctors, artists, and teachers of Jewish decent had played an important role, the conflict between the two segments of the middle class acquired violent forms. This was especially true in the countryside, where Jewish commercial farmers competed not only with aristocrats, who had often neglected their responsibilities as landowners, but also with non-Jewish and upwardly mobile commercial farmers, who resented the wealth and success of Jewish agricultural entrepreneurs. The sons of wealthy farmers and rural administrators in civic militias not only sought to line their pockets; they also wanted to eliminate competition and competitors either by robbing and killing them or forcing them to leave their communities permanently.

Student violence in the cities served the same end, even if it took on much milder forms. The *numerus clausus* law of 1920 had been long in coming; yet, it would not have been possible without the civil war, postwar chaos, misery, antisemitism, and, most importantly, student radicalism, terrorism (directed in part against academic administrators), and violence. It was this law, more than any other product of or event during the counterrevolution, which proved to be the most fateful legacy of the White Terror. The *numerus clausus* legislation provided the model for the even more restrictive anti-Jewish laws of the late 1930s and early 1940s, which rapidly impoverished and marginalized Hungarian Jews, and paved the way to their deportation and genocide in 1944.

# Bibliography

Ablonczy, Balázs. *Teleki Pál*. Budapest: Osiris, 2005.
Balkelis, Tomas. "Turning Citizens into Soldiers: Baltic Paramilitary Movements after the Great War." In *War in Peace: Paramilitary Violence in Europe after the Great War*, edited by Robert G. Gerwarth and John Horne, 201–25. Oxford: Oxford University Press, 2012.
Bodó, Béla. "The White Terror in Hungary, 1919-1921: The Social Worlds of Paramilitary Groups." *Austrian History Yearbook* 42 (2011): 133–63.
———. *The White Terror. Antisemitic and Political Violence in Hungary, 1919-1921*. London: Routledge, 2019.
Bödők, Gergely. "Vörös- és Fehérterror Magyarországon (1919-1921)." PhD diss., Károly Eszterházy University, 2018.
Braham, Randolph L. *The Politics of Genocide: The Holocaust in Hungary*. Vol. 1. New York: Columbia University Press, 1981.
Edmondson, Clifton E. *The Heimwehr and Austrian Politics, 1918-1936*. Athens, GA: University of Georgia Press, 1978.
Gentile, Emilio. "Paramilitary Violence in Italy. The Rationale of Fascism and the Origins of totalitarianism." In *War in Peace. Paramilitary Violence in Europe after the Great War*, edited by Robert Gerwarth and John Horne, 150–76. Oxford: Oxford University Press, 2012.
Gerwarth, Robert, and John Horne, ed. *War in Peace. Paramilitary Violence after the Great War*. Oxford: Oxford University Press, 2012.
Gerwarth, Robert. *The Vanquished: Why the First World War Failed to End, 1917–1923*. London: Penguin Books, 2016.
Karady, Victor and Peter Tibor Nagy. *The Numerus Clausus in Hungary. Studies on the First Anti-Jewish Law and Academic Anti-Semitism in Modern Central Europe*. Budapest: Central European University Press, 2012.
Katzburg, Nathaniel. *Zsidópolitika Magyarországon, 1919–1943*. Budapest: Bábel Kiadó, 2002.
Kerepeszki, Robert. *A Turul Szövetség, 1919–1945. Egyetemi ifjúsági és jobboldali radikalizmus a Horthy-korszakban*. Máriabesnyő: Attrakto, 2012.
Komoróczy, Géza. *A zsidók története Magyarországon II. 1849-től a jelenkorig*. Pozsony: Kalligram, 2012.
Kovács, Mária M. *Törvénytől sújtva. A numerus clausus Magyarországon, 1920–1945*. Budapest: Napvilág, 2012.
Kučera, Rudolf. "Exploiting Victory, Sinking into Defeat: Uniformed Violence in the Creation of the New Order in Czechoslovakia and Austria 1918-1922." *Journal of Modern History* 88, no. 4 (2016): 827–55.
Ladányi, Andor. *Az egyetemi ifjúság az ellenforradalmi első éveiben (1919–1921)*. Budapest: Akadémiai Kiadó, 1979.
Perneky, Mihály. *Shvoy Kálmán titkos naplója és emlékirata, 1918–1945*. Budapest: Kossuth Könyvkiadó, 1983.
Ránki, György, Tibor Hajdu, and Lóránd Tilkovszky. *Magyarország története, 1918–1919, 1919–1945*. Budapest: Akadémiai Kiadó, 1976.
Schivelbuch, Wolfgang. *The Culture of Defeat: On National Trauma, Mourning, and Recovery*. New York: Picador, 2004.

Schnell, Felix. "Ukraine 1918: Besatzer und Besetzte in Gewaltraum." In *Gewaltträume. Soziale Ordnungen im Ausnahmezustand,* edited by Jörg Baberowski and Gabriele Metzler, 135–68. Frankfurt am Main: Campus Verlag, 2012.

Schulze, Hagen. *Freikorps und Republik 1918–1920.* Boppard am Rhein: Harald Boldt Verlag, 1969.

Theweleit, Klaus. *Women, Flood, Bodies, History.* Vol. 1 of *Male Fantasies.* Minneapolis: University of Minnesota Press, 1978.

Zinner, Tibor. *Az Ébredők Fénykora 1919–1923.* Budapest: Akadémiai Kiadó, 1989.

CHAPTER 6

# The Polish Central Government, Regional Authorities, and Local Paramilitaries during the Battle for the Western Borderlands, 1918–1921

## Jochen Böhler

The year 1918 marked the beginning of independent statehood for the Polish-speaking population of Central Europe after more than one hundred years of non-Polish rule. In Polish national historiography, November 11, 1918 assumes the function of a zero hour in which the state institutions of the Second Polish Republic were brought into being, as it were, overnight. However, while a so-called Regency Council of the Kingdom of Poland (Rada Regencyjna Królestwa Polskiego) set up by the German occupiers in 1916 at least laid the foundations for a postwar Polish government—admittedly as a mere satellite state of the German *Reich*—by the end of 1918, the Polish Army proved to be far from a functioning, disciplined, uniformed, or well-equipped military apparatus. Rather, until 1918, the 3.5 million Polish-speaking soldiers who fought in World War I fought in the armies of the three partitioning powers: the tsarist army, the German army, and the Habsburg army.[1] Indeed, special Polish units had been

---

1 For the "Partitions of Poland," see Jerzy Lukowski, *The Partitions of Poland: 1772, 1793, 1795* (London: Longman, 1999).

formed within the latter two—such as the Puławy Legion and the First Polish Corps in Russia, or the Polish Legions in Galicia.[2] However, despite massive attempts at recruitment, the creation of a Polish army under German command towards the end of the war to avert defeat proved to be a failure.[3]

Of course, until November 1918, no single Polish-speaking veteran of World War I had fought in the service of a Polish state; the units that came closest to the idea of an organized Polish army at that time were not even stationed in Central Europe. Rather, thousands of miles to the west in France, approximately eighty thousand Polish prisoners of war who had fought in the Central Powers' armies were grouped together in the so-called Blue Army (Błękitna Armia) under the command of general Józef Haller to fight on the side of the entente. In November 1918, these units were impatiently waiting for the green light to move to Poland, where their combat power was badly needed.[4] By the end of that year, the Warsaw government managed to recruit an army of about one hundred thousand men; mostly from the ranks of the Polish Legions and the Polish Military Organization (Polska Organizacja Wojskowa, POW). These men were therefore by nature loyal to their wartime commander, marshal Józef Piłsudski.[5]

From the very start, the borders of the nascent Polish state were fiercely contested. In the east, Polish and Ukrainian paramilitaries clashed in Lviv as early as November 1, 1918, fighting street battles over the course of three weeks, the outcome of which could only be decided in favor of the Polish side by sending more Polish troops into Eastern Galicia. The battle for the region, however, did not end there. It continued into the summer of 1919, growing into the undeclared, but nevertheless full-blown Polish-Ukrainian War. Once more, only the deployment of additional Polish troops led to victory for the Second Polish Republic.

---

2   Wojciech Jerzy Muszyński, *Białe legiony 1914–1918: Od Legionu Puławskiego do I Korpusu Polskiego* (Warsaw: IPN, 2018); David R. Stefanic, "Piłsudski's Polish Legions: The Formation of a National Army Without a Nation State," in *Armies in Exile*, ed. David R. Stefancic (New York: Columbia University Press, 2005), 103–15; Andrzej Chwalba, *Legiony Polskie, 1914–1918* (Kraków: Wydawnictwo Literackie, 2018).

3   Jochen Böhler, *Civil War in Central Europe, 1918–1921: The Reconstruction of Poland* (Oxford: Oxford University Press, 2018), 51–58.

4   Mieczysław Wrzosek, "Problem przyjazdu armii generała Hallera do kraju (listopad 1918–czerwiec 1919)," in *Polska i jej wschodni sąsiedzi w XX wieku*, ed. Hanna Konopka and Daniel Boćkowski (Białystok: Wydawnictwo Uniwersytetu w Białymstoku, 2004), 53–65; Paul S. Valasek, ed., *Haller's Polish Army in France* ([Naples, FL]: Whitehall Printing, 2006). On General Haller, see Krzysztof Kaczmarski, Wojciech Jerzy Muszyński, and Rafał Sierchuła, *Generał Józef Haller 1873–1960* (Warsaw: Instytut Pamięci Narodowej, 2017).

5   Kazimierz Badziak, *W oczekiwaniu na przełom: Na drodze od odrodzenia do załamania państwa polskiego, listopad 1918-czerwiec 1920* (Łódź: Ibidem, 2004), 52–54; Böhler, *Civil War in Central Europe, 1918–1921*, 51–54.

At the beginning of 1919, the entente allowed the Blue Army to enter Poland on the condition that it would not participate in fighting in the region. However, the Polish head of state and commander in chief Piłsudski ignored this condition to secure the eastern territories for the Polish state.[6]

It is thus obvious that it was not a regular Polish army that created the Second Polish Republic. The proclamation of a Polish state in November 1918 necessitated and initiated the creation of a Polish army, and this very army was only forged in the fires of Poland's border conflicts between late 1918 and the summer of 1920, when the young Polish state faced an invasion of the Soviet Red Army. Consequently, the creation of a regular army in Poland—as in all other emerging nation states in Central Europe at the time—was rather improvised and chaotic than planned and organized. Even more so, since in late 1918 Poland was politically divided into two major political factions operating from different bases: the leftist Piłsudski government in Warsaw, central Poland, and the right-wing National Democrats (Endecja, from the acronym ND) in Poznań, western Poland.[7] This further complicated matters because while Piłsudski's camp claimed political power in the country, the National Democrats and their leader Roman Dmowski controlled the Polish National Committee (Komitet Narodowy Polski, KNP) in Paris, which represented Polish interests towards the entente. This split also ran through Poland's armed forces, with the Blue Army following the orders of the KNP and an Army of Greater Poland (Armia Wielkopolska) gathering under the command of General Józef Dowbor-Muśnicki (who considered himself a nonaffiliated nationalist) in the Poznań area. Soldiers from the Polish Legions, however, who had fought under Piłsudski during World War I remained loyal to their commander when he became head of state. For a brief moment in December 1918, Dmowski even contemplated deploying the Blue Army for a coup against the Warsaw government, which undoubtedly would have brought the country to the brink of a civil war. At some rare occasions in 1918 and 1919, Piłsudskite legions and units from the Army of Greater Poland even exchanged fire.[8]

---

6    Damian Markowski, *Lwów or Lviv? Two Uprisings in 1918* (Frankfurt am Main: Peter Lang, 2018); Serhy Yekelchyk, "Bands of Nation Builders? Insurgency and Ideology in the Ukrainian Civil War," in *War in Peace: Paramilitary Violence in Europe After the Great War*, ed. Robert Gerwarth and John Horne (Oxford: Oxford University Press, 2012), 107–25; Böhler, *Civil War in Central Europe, 1918–1921*, 76–83.
7    It is worth noting, though, that in late 1918, critics of Piłsudski's leftish government were not only found within the National Democratic Party, but generally in the conservative, right-wing, anti-socialist, and anti-Bolshevik circles of Polish society.
8    Böhler, *Civil War in Central Europe, 1918–1921*, 183.

The battle for the historic eastern borderlands was very much on Piłsudski's agenda—he himself was born there, in the vicinity of the Polish-Lithuanian city of Vilnius. In mid-1919, Piłsudski and Haller had laid their animosities aside to fight the Ukrainians, a conflict which the entente did not approve of, but did not interfere with substantially either. In the west, at the frontier to defeated Germany, the situation was completely different. The German-Polish border was a matter of international security and power policies, with British and French interests differing widely. In the area of Poznań and Greater Poland, the Warsaw central government was sidelined by the National Democrats who exhibited an anti-German attitude and dominated the regional political representative body, the Supreme People's Council (Naczelna Rada Ludowa, NRL). Further to the south in Upper Silesia, governmental and Endecja forces had to reckon with interallied troops that were sent in to secure the region while it was preparing for a plebiscite. While there was strong regional support for Upper Silesian autonomy within Polish state borders, there was also another movement striving for a separatist future where Upper Silesia would belong to neither Germany nor Poland. Yet this movement played only a minor a role on the course of events.[9]

Given this highly complicated situation, it becomes obvious that simplistic depictions of the Polish border wars between 1918 and 1921 as a united struggle of *one* Polish army commanded by *one* national government are far from reality. The situation was complicated even more by the presence of paramilitary units in addition to regular troops in both the east and in the west of Poland. While the Polish regular troops by and large—despite severe disciplinary problems— obeyed orders from above, Polish paramilitary formations often followed their own agendas which could either harmonize or come into conflict with the will of the regional or central Polish authorities.

It therefore seems appropriate to take a closer look at such paramilitary units which in the past have been treated rather as mere extensions of the regular Polish army. The circumstances of their formation, the nature of their deployment, as well as their relationship to higher authorities and local populations may all suggest a new interpretation of the activities which such paramilitary groups undertook. Political sociology has introduced the concept of so-called spin-off groups which often appear in the context of civil war. The term applies to paramilitary units which usually emerge and operate within the framework of state-sanctioned military action and violence, and thereby partially follow their own agenda and operate outside the realm of governmental control. "In situations in

---

[9] Andrea Schmidt-Rösler, "Autonomie- und Separatismusbestrebungen in Oberschlesien 1918–1922," *Zeitschrift für Ostmitteleuropaforschung* 48, no. 1 (1999): 1–49.

which governments feel they cannot exclusively rely on their army, they tend to either tolerate or deliberately create other informal armed forces," writes Klaus Schlichte, "Like a royal court society, they produce their own symbolic world and work as socializing institutions for their members."[10]

This contribution argues that some Polish paramilitary formations that took part in the conflicts over the western borderlands in the wake of World War I acted as spin-off groups rather than as the Polish army's auxiliaries. This change of perspective is, however, not simply a matter of taxonomy. It underlines the initiative and scope of action these very formations disposed of and explains why their agenda would sometimes deviate from what regional or central authorities expected of them. While this contribution starts with an overview of the deployment of Polish paramilitaries in Greater Poland at the turn of the year 1918–1919 as a point of reference, its main focus will be directed on the Polish Military Organization of Upper Silesia (Polska Organizacja Wojskowa Górnego Śląska, POW GŚ) as a case study. It will then address the question of how the Polish military leadership in hindsight evaluated the operations and actions of the POW GŚ and its leaders after Poland's takeover of Silesia. And, finally, it will summarize what can be gained from viewing the triangle of the central government, regional authorities, and local paramilitaries in the western borderlands as an example of conflicting interests rather than of concerted action.

## Polish Local Paramilitaries, Regional Institutions, and the Government in Poznań, 1918–1919

The battles over the eastern and western borderlands of the nascent Polish republic erupted spontaneously. In Lviv, the proclamation of a Western Ukrainian People's Republic and the occupation of the city by Ukrainian-speaking soldiers of the Habsburg army on November 1, 1918 was the starting signal.[11] In Poznań, the visit of famous pianist, composer, advocate of the Polish national cause in the US, and spokesman of the KNP in Paris, Ignacy Paderewski, was the spark that ignited the powder keg. The situation in the Poznań region, however, differed significantly from that in Eastern Galicia, where two emerging national groups were fighting over the Habsburg legacy. Greater Poland had been part

---

10  Klaus Schlichte, *In the Shadow of Violence: The Politics of Armed Groups* (Frankfurt am Main: Campus, 2009), 48–56, quotes: 51, 18.
11  In late October 1918, though, the Polish Liquidation Commission (*Polska Komisja Likwidacyjna*) in Galicia had planned a similar take-over from the Polish side.

of the German Empire (until 1871 belonging to the state of Prussia) since the partitions of Poland at the end of the eighteenth century, and thus was state territory of the Weimar Republic which had come into being in November 1918. However, at the same time it was historically claimed by the Second Polish Republic. The new German government was not prepared to hand over the country's eastern territories to its Polish neighbor without a fight. But with the German Imperial Army in the process of dissolution, and the new democratic government still in the making, the only regular military force at the Berlin government's disposal was the German Ober Ost troops that the entente had allowed to remain in the north-east of Poland as a buffer to Soviet Russia. Therefore, German paramilitary forces for the defense of Greater Poland—the Free Corps (Freikorps)—had to be recruited from scratch within Germany and transported to the region. In contrast, the Polish side was much better prepared for the armed struggle against the Germans.[12]

Because the Central Powers had controlled almost all Central Europe until late 1918, the sudden eclipse of their reign—as a consequence of the total defeat at the Western Front—came as a surprise. Nevertheless, a quite rigorous Germanization policy in Greater Poland in effect since the late nineteenth century had only strengthened the Polish national movement in the region which had been preparing for military action long before the armistice. In prewar Eastern Galicia, Polish gymnastic clubs, scouting organizations, and rifle associations had preceded the formation of Piłsudski's Polish Legions in 1914. Following this example, in 1917–1918, Polish nationalist activists in and around Poznań mobilized some thousands of scouting, gymnastic, and rifle club members. These activists had been clandestinely working for the national Polish cause during the war, and some were Polish speaking soldiers of the German Army who had avoided conscription, had deserted, or had been demobilized. In November and December 1918, they were joined by Polish security forces that had been set up by the new regional authority, the NRL. The NRL had been created in 1916 as a Polish national representative body in the Prussian partition zone and cooperated closely with the KNP in Paris. Towards the end of 1918, it still favored a smooth takeover of the territory by the Polish state, while within the paramilitary organizations, it was the Polish Military Organization of the Prussian Partition Zone (Polska Organizacja Wojskowa Zaboru Pruskiego, POW ZP) under the leadership of Mieczysław Paluch which pressed for armed

---

12 Böhler, *Civil War in Central Europe, 1918–1921*, 97–99. For a history of Germany at the end of World War I, see Mark Jones, *Founding Weimar: Violence and the German Revolution of 1918–1919* (Cambridge: Cambridge University Press, 2016).

action. When Paderewski's arrival in Poznań on December 26 triggered the Polish insurrection against the German forces in the city, the Silesian activist Wojciech Korfanty was responsible within the NRL for the organization and functioning of the paramilitary forces, which in the whole area of Greater Poland numbered between eight thousand and ten thousand men.[13] In Upper Silesia, Korfanty would become the political leader of the three insurrections that shook the region between 1919 and 1921, with Paluch commanding the paramilitary forces in the second of these in 1920.

Since Piłsudski's interest in the western borderlands was rather limited—he preferred to leave the decision over the area's fate to the entente—the political momentum was with the NRL. It tried to streamline its diverse troops—which lacked discipline and fought with partisan tactics—and to unify its command structure. To this purpose, on December 28, 1918 an officer of the Polish General Staff who accidentally happened to be in Poznań, was appointed the rank of major and established a High Command which soon assumed control of the Polish armed forces in Greater Poland. In the spring of 1919, their transformation into the already mentioned regular Army of Greater Poland, numbering about one hundred twenty thousand men under the command of General Dowbor-Muśnicki, was completed.[14] Nevertheless, since by May 1919 the German forces outweighed the Polish forces by a factor of two, the ultimate integration of Greater Poland into the Polish state was not decided on the battlefield but by the entente in Paris.[15]

Despite all appearance, the Polish side did not manage the conflict over Greater Poland cohesively. At the outset of the crisis, the NRL favored negotiations with the Germans, while the POW ZP pressed for armed insurrection. Furthermore, the NRL only recognized the authority of the KNP in Paris. What actually happened in January 1919 was that the Endecja tried to erect its own Polish government in Poznań and to overthrow the leftist government in Warsaw. They

---

13  Jacek Macyszyn, "Powstanie Wielkopolskie 1918–1919," *Niepodległość i Pamięć* 22, no. 1 (2015): 81–101, here 88. One has to keep in mind, though, that a clean-cut division between "Polish" and "German" loyalties is difficult to make in an ethnically mixed region like Greater Poland. This point has been convincingly made by Jens Boysen, "Simultaneity of the Un-simultaneous: German Social Revolution and Polish National Revolution," in *Germany 1916–23: A Revolution in Context*, ed. Klaus Weinhauer, Anthony McElligott, and Kirsten Heinsohn (Bielefeld: Transcript, 2015), 229–50.

14  Macyszyn, "Powstanie Wielkopolskie 1918–1919," 72. On General Dowbor-Muśnicki, see Rafał Sierchuła and Wojciech Jerzy Muszyński, *Józef Dowbor-Muśnicki, 1867–1937* (Poznań, Warsaw: IPN, 2018).

15  Benjamin Conrad, *Umkämpfte Grenzen, umkämpfte Bevölkerung: Die Entstehung der Staatsgrenzen der Zweiten Polnischen Republik 1918–1923* (Stuttgart: Steiner, 2014), 118–25.

even planned to release the soldiers of the Army of Greater Poland from their oath sworn to Warsaw and pledge allegiance to the NRL as the only legitimate government instead.[16] On the other hand, something was achieved in Greater Poland which the Polish side lacked in the Upper Silesian conflict from the very start: the unification and alignment of the deployed paramilitary forces within a regular army. It is important to note that two of the major players in Upper Silesia had gained crucial experience in Greater Poland: Korfanty at the regional level in the NRL, and Paluch within the local paramilitary forces.

## Polish Local Paramilitaries, Regional Institutions, and the Central Government's Engagement in Upper Silesia, 1919–1921

Further to the south, in Upper Silesia, things took a different path. Historically, the region had not belonged to any Polish state for centuries, so that—although having a mixed German-Polish population—towards war's end it was regarded as historically German territory. Much more than in the case of Greater Poland, all Polish representative bodies would—at least officially—acknowledge the entente's authority in Upper Silesian affairs. As a result, the only regular military, which would be stationed in the area in early 1920, was an international security force made up of French, British, and Italian soldiers.[17] On the other hand, all German and Polish units operating in the area between 1919 and 1921 were made up of paramilitaries, although clandestinely supported by their respective governments. And while at the beginning of the year 1919, the rivalry between Piłsudski's, Haller's, and Dowbor's troops complicated the picture here as well, it was clarified during the summer when the Polish government managed to place them all under the command of the War Ministry (Ministerstwo Spraw Wojskowych, MSW) in Warsaw.[18] Furthermore, in December 1918, in stark contrast to what was happening simultaneously in Poznań, neither a paramilitary nor a regular Polish force was yet fit for action in Upper Silesia.[19]

---

16  Böhler, *Civil War in Central Europe, 1918–1921*, 141–42.
17  Alun Thomas, "The British Upper Silesia Force ('UPSI' Force), May 1921–July 1922," *Journal of the Society for Army Historical Research* 95, no. 384 (2017): 338–64, depicts the deployment of British troops in Upper Silesia in 1921.
18  Badziak, *W oczekiwaniu na przełom*, 65. By early 1919, Paderewski had managed to convince Piłsudski and Dmowski to temporary bury their hatches, and a unity government was built.
19  Ryszard Kaczmarek, *Powstania Śląskie 1919–1920–1921: Nieznana wojna polsko-niemiecka* (Kraków: Wydawnictwo Literackie, 2019), 37. This most recent and without a doubt best

Nevertheless, events in Upper Silesia were closely connected to adjacent Greater Poland; not only through key personnel—such as Korfanty or Paluch—but also through institutions. The region's political representation, the Sub-Commissariat of the Supreme People's Council for Silesia (Podkommissariat Naczelnej Rady Ludowej dla Śląska, PNRL), was installed in Upper Silesia in early 1919 as a subbranch of the NRL in Poznań. The main paramilitary force of the Polish insurrection in the region was a branch of the POW as well; namely, the POW GŚ which not only was created by the NRL in early 1919 but was even obligated to consult it in all political matters before taking any action. Recruits of the POW GŚ were sworn in by the NRL, not by the Warsaw government, which in any case had no connection to the Upper Silesian fighters in early 1919.[20] Like in Greater Poland, dissent over the chain of command and timing accompanied the Polish planning from the very start. This was even true within the POW GŚ's leadership. In March 1919, in a report to Korfanty, we read:

> There is division within the organization: [Stanisław] Wiza, [Józef] Grzegorzek and [Adolf] Lampner press for upheaval. [Kazimierz] Jesionek supported by [Józef] Dreyza wants a good organization and then waits for the orders from Poznań. [Kazimierz] Czapla, through Jesionek, demands that the NRL give an order that an armed action cannot begin without permission. In the field, the district commanders say that they will not be able to take control without the intervention of the regular [Polish] army. [Hence] The method of organization has been changed: Jesionek creates a special contact office between Upper Silesia and Poznań in Sosnowiec (maintains contact with district commanders). We need a senior officer here, who would give a factual account of the whole organization, because so far there is no such unification and everyone organizes and orders on their own, just as it was in the first days in Poznań.[21]

It is worth noting that, despite their differing attitudes, all named POW GŚ officers were from Greater Poland or Upper Silesia. Thus, those three commanders who pushed for the uprising shared the same regional background as, but

---

comprehensive monograph on the three Polish insurrections in Upper Silesia has proved extremely helpful in developing the main arguments of this subchapter.
20  Ibid., 38, 105, 109–10.
21  Ibid., 111.

were in direct opposition to, Korfanty, who himself was very skeptical about the prospect of a premature uprising, and therefore favored a political solution. Accordingly, localism was not a decisive factor of the differing strategical choices at play here, and they surely had nothing to do with any animosities between the Poznanian-Upper Silesian and Warsawian camps within the POW GŚ.

In April, the commander of the Polish armed forces in Poznań Dowbor-Muśnicki and Korfanty—who was also eager to coordinate the developments on the ground with diplomatic negotiations in Paris—repeatedly had to rein in the POW GŚ commanders who were pressing for armed action, despite the fact that their men were poorly armed and outnumbered by German paramilitaries in the region.[22] Obviously, the degree of the insurrectionists' determination contrasted starkly with the degree of their organization and military potential.

Most remarkably, although the POW GŚ's model had been the wartime POW which had acted as a secret paramilitary organization under Piłsudski's command in the German and Austrian occupation zones, its loyalties were mainly with the powers in Poznań, rather than Warsaw.[23] Clearly, political and ideological orientation were not the major factors here. When, as a result of the unification process of the Polish armed forces, the Upper Silesian insurgents were subordinated to Warsaw, the POW GŚ's leadership protested vehemently against the decision. The liaison officer between the insurgents' staff and the NRL, Zygmunt Parski, was informed in late June 1919 that Upper Silesia now fell under the jurisdiction of the General Staff in Warsaw. The POW GŚ explained its disagreement with the decision in a detailed report to the NRL: In the weeks preceding the decision, the General Staff had used POW GŚ fighters for sabotage operations in Upper Silesia which had been—due to the lack of experience of the dispatched military personnel from Warsaw—a complete failure and resulted in the exposure and subsequent dissolution of several regional POW GŚ cells. Military instructors from the "Kingdom"—a deliberate reference to the former German puppet state (Kingdom of Poland, 1916–1918)—were not welcome any longer in Upper Silesia. The POW GŚ would have instead preferred to remain under the command in Poznań than to be transferred to the Warsaw command.[24] In

---

22 Ibid., 112–16.
23 The foundation of the POW GŚ at the turn of 1918–1919 is more nuanced than can be elaborated here. In fact, its units were built up partly from the POW ZP in Poznań, partly from the Polish High Command in Warsaw. By March 1919, they were placed under the roof of the POW's Executive Committee (*Komitet Wykonawczy*). See Edward Długajczyk, *Wywiad polski na Górnym Śląsku 1919–1922* (Katowice: Muzeum Śląskie, 2001), 84–91.
24 See the letter of the executive committee of the POW GŚ to the NRL commissariat in Poznań, Bytom, July 1, 1919, Centralne Archiwum Wojskowe (Central Military Archive

another document dated the same day, the POW GŚ even openly stated that this was the only logical choice because the military people in Poznań knew the Upper Silesian operational area much better, and because of the political conflict between Endecja dominated Greater Poland and leftist-oriented Warsaw, which was, itself at strife with Upper Silesia's most prominent representative, Korfanty. "The entire population of [Upper] Silesia gravitates more strongly to Poznań than to Warsaw," the writing concluded, "and the severing of the thread with Poznań may cause dissatisfaction and apathy." Furthermore, how could POW GŚ paramilitaries be expected to serve the Warsaw government if they had taken their oath to the government in Poznań?[25]

The conflict over who was commanding the Upper Silesian paramilitaries significantly weakened the Polish position in the area because in August 1919, monitored from Poznań, it necessitated a complete reorganization of the POW GŚ's leadership. The goal was to sideline the war hawks within the organization's mid-level commanders who still impatiently pushed for combat. The result, however, was the opposite. In open violation of orders from the new POW GŚ leadership, as well as the Poznań and Warsaw authorities' orders, the mid-level commanders cut loose, starting the first Upper Silesian insurrection against the vastly superior Germans, which in the end led to a disastrous failure for the Poles. Piłsudski for his part did not support the insurgents in Upper Silesia because—as he told an Endecja politician on August 21—the international situation did not allow for any kind of interference from the Warsaw government.[26] Instead of sending the Polish Army to Upper Silesia, when failure was unavoidable, Warsaw called in vain for an allied intervention to clear up the mess the POW GŚ's single-handed attempt had created.[27]

Thus, during the summer of 1919, to rise up against the Germans, the local Upper Silesian insurgents first had to revolt against their own superiors at regional and state levels in Poznań and Warsaw; a fact which perfectly illustrates the discord in the Polish political landscape at the time. It is little wonder that, after the failed first insurrection, the central government in Warsaw made it perfectly clear who would decide on military action at the western (and at all other) borders of the Second Republic of Poland. As the MSW put it in late 1919, it intended "to exploit the existing secret military organizations in the plebiscite

---

hereafter cited as CAW), *Laudański Files*, vol. 16 (I.440.12.16), 53. Most ironically, by that time Psarski himself was already on the payroll of the High Command in Warsaw, see Kaczmarek, *Powstania Śląskie 1919–1920–1921*, 121.
25  Kaczmarek, *Powstania Śląskie 1919–1920–1921*, 122–23, quote: 122.
26  Ibid., 144–50, quote: 150.
27  Ibid., 178.

areas, for example, the contested area of Upper Silesia, which have completely passed under the authority of the Second Department [of the General Staff]."[28] Since the POW GŚ had proven unreliable, this went hand in hand with a total reorganization of its structure, including key personnel. To this purpose, from early 1920 onwards, officers and foot soldiers from the Haller Army were sent to Upper Silesia. Since General Haller had aligned his forces with governmental troops in mid-1919, his men were now regarded as more reliable than local mercenaries. Thus, the ranks of the POW GŚ were supplemented with personnel that had been trained in France and within the ranks of the Polish army, thus changing the ratio between locals and non-locals.[29] Since the region had been singled out for a plebiscite by the entente, in February 1920 Korfanty set up camp in a Polish Plebiscite Commissariat (Polski Komisariat Plebiscytowy, PKP) in Hotel Lomnitz in Bytom. Within the next months, he wrestled with the Warsaw MSW over the control of the POW GŚ:

> Korfanty demands to remove [Alfons] Zgrzebniok and to hand over the whole POW [GŚ] to him instead. We do not and never will agree to both. Korfanty accuses the POW [GŚ] during the [May 1 and 3] celebrations of cowardice and throws a whole series of slanders at the organization and its leaders. He sends such letters to all ministries.[30]

In the end, Korfanty and the MSW compromised on leaving Zgrzebniok—who was responsible for the contact between the POW GŚ and the High Command in Warsaw[31]—in charge, but appointing the Upper Silesian Jan Ludyga-Laskowski, an officer of Korfanty's choice, the POW GŚ's chief of staff.[32]

---

28 Letter of the Second Department of the MSW to the commander of the Upper Silesian Front, General Franciszek Latinik, [Warsaw], 1919 [after the opening of the Silesian Front on October 19], CAW, *Baczyński Files*, vol. 37 (I.476.1.37), 1. The Second Department of the Polish General Staff was responsible for military intelligence and counterintelligence.
29 Kaczmarek, *Powstania Śląskie 1919–1920–1921*, 257–59.
30 Letter, probably from First Lieutenant Tadeusz Puszczyński, to the POW GŚ leadership, May 15, 1920, quoted from Długajczyk, *Wywiad polski na Górnym Śląsku 1919–1922*, 219, annotation: 37. In early 1920, Puszczyński (pseudonym "Konrad Wawelberg") was responsible for Upper Silesia within the information department of the MSW. In 1921, during the third insurrection, he would command the Polish General Staff's sabotage troop "Wawelberg." His memoirs have recently been edited, see Tadeusz Puszczyński, *Polskie działania destrukcyjne na Górnym Śląsku w latach 1920–1921*, ed. Edward Długajczyk (Katowice: Śląsk, 2019).
31 Kaczmarek, *Powstania Śląskie 1919–1920–1921*, 194.
32 Długajczyk, *Wywiad polski na Górnym Śląsku 1919–1922*, 219.

In the summer of 1920, with the anniversary of the first insurrection approaching, tensions between Germany and Poland were once more on the rise in Upper Silesia. On August 17, Katowice witnessed German mass demonstrations, in the course of which the Polish plebiscite office was vandalized and Polish activist Dr. Andrzej Mielęcki was killed. Korfanty, once more, hesitated to call for insurrection. The German demonstrators had chosen Poland's weakest moment: by mid-August, the Red Army stood at the gates of Warsaw, and the Polish army had to throw in all available resources to prevent a Soviet victory, one which would have sealed the fate of the Second Polish Republic. Internationally, the country was isolated, because Piłsudski's failed Kiev Offensive in April 1920 was seen as provocation for the Soviet advance.[33]

Under pressure from the POW GŚ commanders, Korfanty called for a general strike. As far as armed actions were concerned, he still preferred to hold back and keep that option as a bargaining chip with the Interallied Governmental and Plebiscite Commission that had been sent to Upper Silesia to mediate between Poland and Germany. Korfanty's strategy foresaw the dissolution of the German police forces to enable the Polish side to clandestinely extend its paramilitary network in Upper Silesia. He thus found himself again in opposition to most of the POW GŚ commanders who favored an immediate and full-blown second insurrection. He ordered another restructuring of the POW GŚ leadership, but his hand was forced when the commander of the POW GŚ's Katowice branch, Walenty Fojkis, started the second insurrection on August 18, 1920. Korfanty now had little choice but to put himself at the head of a movement which, once set in motion, he was unable to stop. But, although he took over the command, the difficulties did not end, because the insurgents continued to act autonomously and beyond his control. On August 23, 1920, Korfanty visited Hołdunowa (Anhalt), a predominantly German town that had been torched and plundered by the POW GŚ. To limit the political damage caused by the marauding insurgents, he wrote the inhabitants a check of thirty-two thousand Reichsmark as compensation.[34] When after twelve days of fighting the insurrection ran out of steam, he quickly cut a deal with the Germans, brokered by the entente. The results were far from impressive. The German dominated security forces in Upper Silesia were replaced by a German-Polish Plebiscite Police

---

33 On the Polish-Soviet War 1919–20 see Norman Davies, *White Eagle, Red Star: The Polish-Soviet War, 1919–20* (London: Orbis Books, 1983) (first published: 1973); Stephan Lehnstaedt, *Der vergessene Sieg: Der Polnisch-Sowjetische Krieg 1919–1921 und die Entstehung des modernen Osteuropa* (Munich: Beck, 2019); Böhler, *Civil War in Central Europe, 1918–1921*, 123–28.
34 Kaczmarek, *Powstania Śląskie 1919–1920–1921*, 300–3.

(Abstimmungspolizei, APO), an outcome which for sure could have been achieved by just following Korfanty's political agenda. The French troops, which meanwhile had been stationed in the area as a neutral force, would have had no difficulties at all nipping the second Polish insurrection in the bud if only their superiors would have wanted to. Instead, barely hiding its anti-German stance, France explained its inaction by alleging that the Polish insurgents were a superior force, which the French troops in the region could not match.[35]

As events had shown, the POW GŚ was still divided in a pro-Warsaw camp—which had issued a call to arms, hoping in vain for military support from the Polish army—and a Korfanty camp, which only approved paramilitary support of the Plebiscite in Poland's favor. With peace restored, the renewed insubordination of the local POW GŚ commanders against Korfanty did not go without consequences. As early as August 25, 1920, he had the entire leadership of the organization disbanded. As a next step, he dissolved the whole POW GŚ and restructured it as a Physical Education Center (Centrala Wychowania Fizycznego, CWF) under the command of his close confident Paluch. According to Ryszard Kaczmarek, this was not only a change in name but also indicated a future use of the paramilitaries for more civilian purposes. Nevertheless, Paluch allowed commanders loyal to the government in Warsaw—like Zgrzebniok and his sort—to join the CWF, where they immediately set about rebuilding the paramilitary structures and preparing for the next uprising.[36] Here a pattern emerges: for the third time, the Upper Silesian paramilitary's higher ranks were filled with personnel from outside. Only Zgrzebniok was a local (but the central government's choice), whereas Paluch and Mieczysław Chmielewski were from Greater Poland, Tadeusz Puszczyński and Wiktor Przedpełski from central Poland (both near Warsaw), Michał Grażyński was from southern Poland, and Stanisław Baczyński from eastern Poland. And still, under the leadership of Paluch—who had served in the German Army at the Western Front and then participated in the Poznań street fights in late 1918—they developed an autonomous agenda that was more radical than the political planning in Katowice, Poznań, and Warsaw. They even bypassed Korfanty by addressing Head of State and Commander in Chief Piłsudski to get the support of the Polish army for another insurrection, and indeed managed to bring in military instructors from Warsaw. Another purge of the paramilitaries in Upper Silesia was looming, with Korfanty convincing the MSW at the end of 1921 to cede the command again to the Poznań military district under the condition that "all military organizational

---

35   Ibid., 316–17.
36   Ibid., 330–31.

authorities must act in the closest possible understanding with [Plebiscite] Commissar Korfanty." With Paluch and Zgrzebniok, the two highest ranking officers within the CWF were fired. The organization got a new name as well: Plebiscite Defense Command (Dowództwo Obrony Plebiscytu, DOP).[37]

Now, two years after the events in Poznań, the paramilitaries in Upper Silesia were—not nominally, but factually—transformed into something like a regular armed force resembling the Army of Greater Poland. At the same time, more than twenty thousand reservists—mostly refugees from the plebiscite area and other embattled territories—were trained in combat and stationed along the Polish western border to Upper Silesia. All fighters were organized under the auspices of and reported to the Polish Army. Finally, with almost fifty thousand men under arms, this was the largest, best organized and equipped Polish force in the conflicted area so far. The fact that its command center was shifted from Warsaw to Poznań only moved it closer to the operational area. Politically, this did not matter anymore since the differences between the two power houses had been solved and their forces united in the course of 1919.[38]

In the meantime, the Germans were building up their own combat force of volunteers—the Upper Silesian Self Defense (Oberschlesischer Selbstschutz, OS)—which was organized, commanded, and equipped by the German army. Although officially still no regular army was involved, the conflict developed into an "undeclared unconventional war."[39] What the Poles and Germans—in order not to appall the entente which had the last say in a political solution of the conflict—had done has been called pointedly "an outsourcing of actual state power."[40] The paramilitaries they deployed in the area were classic spin-off groups.

The third Polish insurrection in Upper Silesia was launched on May 3, 1921, after the plebiscite had resulted in a majority vote for the German side. Kaczmarek calls the ensuing battles, which lasted until the end of the month, a "Polish-German War."[41] Indeed, it makes little sense to analyze the third armed escalation of the conflict in terms of the use of paramilitaries by the Polish

---

37  Ibid., 357–59, quote: 359.
38  Ibid., 360.
39  James E. Bjork, *Neither German nor Pole: Catholicism and National Indifference in a Central European Borderland* (Ann Arbor: University of Michigan Press, 2008), 355–56.
40  Peter Haslinger et al., "*Frontiers of Violence*: Paramiliärs als Gewaltgemeinschaften im Ostmitteleuropa der 1920er Jahre," in *Gewaltgemeinschaften in der Geschichte: Entstehung, Kohäsionskraft und Zerfall*, ed. Winfried Speitkamp et al. (Göttingen: Vandenhoeck & Ruprecht, 2017), 233–54, here: 235. See also Böhler, *Civil War in Central Europe, 1918–1921*, 109–10.
41  Kaczmarek, *Powstania Śląskie 1919–1920–1921*, 376–523.

government—it officially denied any engagement in the fighting in Upper Silesia. The Polish troops deployed in the "Third Uprising" had not much in common with the paramilitary force that had emerged in late 1918 and early 1919. They were a well-developed army with a functioning chain of command and intelligence service acting on the order of the MSW. The decision to launch the hostilities was made by Korfanty, and he had the full support not only of the Polish Army, represented by Major Roman Abraham (who had himself gained experience as the leader of a paramilitary spin-off group in Eastern Galicia in 1918–19), but also of the local DOP commanders, now headed by colonel Maciej Mielżyński from Greater Poland.[42]

Nevertheless, differences between Korfanty's defensive and the DOP commanders' offensive strategy resurfaced again during the fighting. After the conflict's most famous battle towards the end of May 1921, the Battle of Annaberg, Mielżyński still harbored the unrealistic hope of turning this Polish defeat into a victory and expressed dissatisfaction with Korfanty's attitude to stop the fighting as soon as possible.[43] A few days later, other commanders—amongst them Michał Grajek from Greater Poland and Grażyński—harshly criticized Korfanty, blaming him for tactical mistakes which, in their eyes, had allowed the Germans to regroup their forces. Without hesitation, Korfanty relieved both commanders of their posts and replaced them with more compliant officers.[44] Although these were quarrels over single military decisions and not the overall strategy, the underlying current still reflected the tug-of-war between a cautious politician and a military cadre pressing him for action. But in contrast to 1919 and 1920, in 1921 there was no sign of a joint commanders' revolt against Korfanty's leadership. Other than the two preceding insurrections, the third was successful insofar as in the end, the partition of Upper Silesia sanctioned by the entente largely ceded the territory occupied by the Polish "insurgents" to the Polish state, which was much more than the outcome of the plebiscite would have suggested.[45]

In hindsight, even specialists have difficulties in saying who decided the timing and outcome of the conflict in Upper Silesia: Polish mid- and high-level politicians, the entente, or the paramilitaries on the ground. One thing, however, is certain: without the quasi-official support of the Polish army in 1921, the Polish

---

42　Ibid., 376–81. On Abraham's engagement in Eastern Galicia see Böhler, *Civil War in Central Europe, 1918–1921*, 166–70, 186, 191.
43　Kaczmarek, *Powstania Śląskie 1919–1920–1921*, 443, 451.
44　Ibid., 457–58. Jan F. Lewandowski, *Wojciech Korfanty*, Biografie Sławnych Ludzi (Warsaw: Państwowy Instytut Wydawniczy, 2013), 111–14.
45　Conrad, *Umkämpfte Grenzen, umkämpfte Bevölkerung*, 164–80.

cause would have been lost.[46] Prior to that, the differences between local commanders, regional political representatives, and the central government turned out to be too grave to guarantee smooth cooperation between the three levels. Divergent planning, rivalry, and a drive for autonomy at the leadership level of the POW GŚ constantly caused trouble. This last fact in particular requires an explanation. The interpretation that the leadership of the POW GŚ pursued an autonomous Upper Silesian agenda is inconclusive insofar as the insubordination and the urge to fight continued even after a complete change of personnel and the infiltration of foreign commanders, while the local Polish-speaking population generally rejected an armed conflict.[47]

Other explanations must be found for this, which would certainly be worth pursuing in the future. The most obvious is the assumption that the POW GŚ, as a spin-off group of the Polish government, developed its own agenda which, to a certain extent, prevailed as *esprit de corps* even under new leadership brought in from outside. Historical research has amply demonstrated that paramilitary fighters at the end of World War I sought continuation of the struggle as an end in itself. This was true for German Free Corps fighters as well as for Czech, Lithuanian, and Ukrainian paramilitaries.[48] A similar attitude may be assumed among the paramilitary fighters of the POW GŚ, most of whom had gained their first military experience in World War I and in military intelligence and subversion. They were by no means representative of most of the Polish speaking population in Central Europe by the time, but highly politicized fighters for the national cause. This conviction let them to rebel even against their own leadership if, in their view, it did not support the national struggle decisively enough. This conviction was apparently so strong that it made the Polish paramilitaries estimate their own military power unrealistically. Korfanty—who had no military training whatsoever—was to be proved right every time in his divergent assessments.

The feeling of belonging to an avant-garde group of so-called companions of fate was presumably also reinforced by joint attacks against the local

---

46   Kaczmarek, *Powstania Śląskie 1919–1920–1921*, 7–10.
47   Ibid., 301.
48   Robert Gerwarth, "Fighting the Red Beast, Counter-Revolutionary Violence in the Defeated States of Central Europe," in Gerwarth and Horne, *War in Peace*, 52–71; Rudolf Kučera, "Exploiting Victory, Sinking into Defeat: Uniformed Violence in the Creation of the New Order in Czechoslovakia and Austria, 1918–1922," *Journal of Modern History* 88, no. 4 (2016): 827–55; Tomas Balkelis, "From Defence to Revolution: Lithuanian Paramilitary Groups in 1918 and 1919," *Acta Historica Universitatis Klaipedensis* 28 (2014), 43–56; Yekelchyk, "Bands of Nation Builders?"

German-speaking population. Between 1918 and 1921, Polish paramilitaries looted Upper Silesia and terrorized the non-Polish civilian population. Even such incidents were judged completely differently by the POW GŚ leadership and Korfanty, who on several occasions harshly criticized the encroachments of POW GŚ commanders and their subordinates.[49] It is important to emphasize, however, that German paramilitaries, like their Polish counterparts, attacked and terrorized the Upper Silesian population in the same manner. As Tim Wilson has shown, paramilitary violence of conflicting parties against the "ethnic foe" in Upper Silesia served the goal of forging a national community out of a national rather than an indifferent mixed population.[50] There is reason to believe that acts of collective violence were the glue that held together the Polish and the German paramilitary milieus.[51]

## Historical Engineering by the Military Historical Office in the Early 1930s

Immediately with the founding of the Second Polish Republic, the General Staff of the Polish Army made sure to control its military history. For this purpose, in September 1919, the Third Department of the High Command opened a historical-operational department, which after some operational changes in 1927 became the Military Historical Office (Wojskowe Biuro Historyczne, WBH), editing its own journal, the *Historical-Military Review* (*Przegląd Historyczno-Wojskowy*, PHW).[52] But by the mid-1920s, several cases of negligent handling of files became public. When Piłsudski—who was not only a gifted military commander and politician, but also self-promoter—wrote his version of the Battle of Warsaw, he had file transcripts delivered from the military archive to his residence in Sulejów on the outskirts of Warsaw. Some files, however, went missing. Obviously, some officers had treated the archive as a kind of self-service shop. An investigative commission was even established to clarify the affair.[53]

---

49  Böhler, *Civil War in Central Europe, 1918–1921*, 111–12.
50  Tim Wilson, *Frontiers of Violence: Conflict and Identity in Ulster and Upper Silesia 1918–1922* (Oxford: Oxford University Press, 2010).
51  Wojciech Pieniazek, "Subversive Kriegsführung in Oberschlesien 1920–1921," in *Spór o Górny Śląsk 1919–1922: W 90 rocznicę wybuchu III powstania śląskiego*, ed. Marek Białokur and Adrian Dawid (Gdańsk: Regionalny Zarząd Gospodarki Wodnej, 2012), 191–95.
52  Konrad Paduszek and Witold Rawski, "Wojskowe Biuro Historyczne i jego kadra w 1939 roku," *Przegląd Historyczno-Wojskowy* 2011: 69–96, here: 69.
53  Józef Piłsudski, *Year 1920 and its climax battle of Warsaw, during the Polish-Soviet War, 1919–1920: With the addition of Soviet Marshal Tukhachevski's March beyond the Vistula* (London:

In May 1926, Piłsudski seized power in Warsaw and ruled the country with a hard fist until his death in 1935. Behind him he gathered former comrades-in-arms from World War I and the Polish border wars of 1918–1921, mainly former legionnaires and members of the POW.[54] Piłsudski showed great personal interest in the work of the WBH and was apparently determined to clean up and control the military archive. Poland, with him as commander-in-chief, had emerged victorious from the border wars. Now it was to be ensured that official historiography honored his achievement. In 1927, the WBH was made independent from the General Staff, some new personnel and departments were added, and it received its own budget and residence. As the WBH chief General Julian Stachiewicz—who in February 1919 had been Chief of Staff within the Supreme Command of the Army of Greater Poland in Poznań—put it in 1928: "In the last reporting year, the WBH has grown from a small institution with a strictly limited scope of work to an institution that unifies all issues of military history."[55]

One of the WBH's first tasks was to "unify" the complex history of the Polish Army's engagement in the Upper Silesian conflict between 1918 and 1921. This project was entrusted in 1930 to none other than Baczyński, who in 1920 had headed the DOP's Third Department on behalf of the Warsaw High Command. Obviously, nothing was left to chance. Baczyński was born in Lviv in 1890, he had been a member of a socialist youth organization and joined the POW during World War I. He thus was neither close to the Endecja's political agenda nor did he exhibit local patriotism to Upper Silesia. After his deployment in Upper Silesia—he left office after some quarrels within the DOP—he dedicated himself to high literature and to the cultural life of interwar Poland. After the WBH had addressed him in 1930 for researching and writing the military history of the Upper Silesian conflict from 1918 to 1921, he collected the relevant

---

Piłsudski Institute of London, 1972) (Polish first edition: 1924). On the book's genesis and the ensuing affair see "Minutes of the Meeting of the Commission of Experts October 9, 1925 at 5 p.m.: Hearing of General Stachiewicz, Mokotow Hospital," Archive of the Archiwum Instytutu Józefa Piłsudskiego w Ameryce (Archive of the Józef Piłsudski Institute in America hereafter cited as AJPI), 701/1/69, 2–6; letter from General Stachiewicz criticizing General Kukiel's work at the Historical Office, undated [1926], AJPI, 701/1/70, 3–58. The affair even made the pages of the *Kurier Poranny* in early October 1925.

54  Joseph Rothschild, "Marshal Józef Piłsudski's Concept of State Vis-à-Vis Society in Interwar Poland," in *East Central European War Leaders: Civilian and Military*, ed. Béla K. Király and Albert A. Nofi (Boulder: Social Science Monographs, 1988), 289–303.

55  Arkadiusz Tuliński, "Oficerowie Biura Historycznego i Wojskowego Biura Historycznego w latach 1922–1939: Część 1," *Przegląd Historyczno-Wojskowy* 270, no. 4 (2019): 157–89, here: 157–58, quote: 158.

files from the Foreign Office, from the Council of Ministers, and the Second Department of the General Staff and set to work. The result was a manuscript on the Upper Silesian paramilitary organizations, which he handed over to the WBH in 1931, and which since then has—together with his transcripts of relevant files—become a stand-alone record group called the Baczyński Files (*Teki Baczyńskiego*) within the Central Military Archive (*Centralne Archiwum Wojskowe*, CAW) in Warsaw.[56]

Although there are indications that Baczyński was critical of Piłsudski's eastern policies in 1920, these are either exaggerated or the antagonisms had been overcome at the beginning of the 1930s.[57] In any case, there is nothing to be read of a critical standpoint toward the Piłsudski camp in Baczyński's account. On the contrary, in his assessment, written a decade later, of Korfanty's relation to the POW in 1921, he perfectly mirrored Piłsudski's. In the first postwar years, Korfanty had become one of Upper Silesia's most prominent politicians and even a congressman who strongly advocated for the voivodship's autonomy within the Polish state. Even a Silesian Parliament (Sejm Śląski) and treasury had been established in the early 1920s.[58] Korfanty's regional opponent after Piłsudski's coup d'état in May 1926 was Grażyński, who had been the marshal's man in Upper Silesia during the conflict, and now had become the Silesian voivode. With the authoritarian turn of Piłsudski's sanction (*sanacja*) regime in the second half of the 1920s, the air became thinner for the proponents of Silesian autonomy. The Silesian Parliament was dissolved in 1930, and in the course of a political purge, Korfanty was incarcerated in the infamous Brest Fortress in Eastern Poland, where he was physically and psychologically tortured, only to be released in 1931.[59] In other words, while Baczyński noted down his assessment of Korfanty's role as a political and military leader in 1921, the latter became public enemy number one and the personal adversary of Piłsudski,

---

56 Editor's note in Stanisław Baczyński, "Tajne organizacje wojskowe na Górnym Śląsku w latach 1918–1921 na tle sytuacji ogólnej," *Najnowsze Dzieje Polski. 1914–1939* 13 (1968): 113–16; Bożena Panecka, "Źródła do dziejów Powstań Śląskich (1919–1921) przechowywane w Centralnym Archiwum Wojskowym," *Biuletyn Wojskowej Służby Archiwalnej* 13–14 (1985): 73–85.

57 Such insinuations are based on hearsay and were published in the 1960s in Communist Poland, where Piłsudski was *persona non grata*, not least because of the Polish-Bolshevik War of 1919–1920, see Edmund Semil, "Ojciec i syn," in *Żołnierz, poeta, czasu kurz...: Wspomnienia o Krzysztofie Kamilu Baczyńskim*, ed. Zbigniew Wasilewski (Kraków: Wydawnictwo Literackie, 1967), 13–60; here: 28.

58 Franciszek Serafin, *Województwo Śląskie, 1922–1939: Zarys monograficzny* (Katowice: Wydawnictwo Uniwersytetu Śląskiego, 1996).

59 Lewandowski, *Wojciech Korfanty*, 152–71.

who would therefore without a doubt read this very assessment with utmost attention.

Baczyński certainly knew what was at stake and did what he thought was expected of him by describing Korfanty's role in Upper Silesia in the darkest colors. The plebiscite commissar had been, according to Baczyński, not only a hardcore Endecja politician who fought the leftist government in Warsaw with a vengeance, but also a capitalist enemy of the Upper Silesian population which was mostly working class. Thus, Baczyński concluded that, in reality, Korfanty had been an ally of the German enemy. He failed to explain, however, how this ludicrous fairytale resonated with his allegation that Korfanty was a separatist whose intention, on the order of Poznań, had been to cut Upper Silesia from the body of the Polish state.[60] Why would Korfanty try to separate a region from the Polish state whose population by and large considered him an enemy of the working class? And, if he was working for the Germans, would it not have made much more sense if he simply had changed sides? One can leave it at that, because since Baczyński's insinuations, the historiography has proven beyond the shadow of a doubt that Korfanty was a Polish nationalist who, when it came to the erection of an independent Polish state in 1918, put aside his conservative agenda—just like Piłsudski had put aside his socialist one.

More interesting in our context, though not much closer to the truth, is Baczyński's explanation of the discrepancies between Korfanty and the officer corps of the Upper Silesian paramilitary organizations. "Commissar Korfanty," he wrote:

> in order to preserve his sole authority and maintain the course of his policy, was constantly trying to undermine the work of the Ministry of Military Affairs' [MSW] organization and to penetrate the intelligence secrets of the Second Department of the [General] Staff, while at the same time conducting a strenuous fight against the influx of officers and volunteers, especially from Lesser Poland [*Małopolska* in Southern Poland] and the former Kingdom, which created an atmosphere of resentment towards them. As a result, in the later period, from December 1920 to the termination of the [third] uprising, there were constant intrigues

---

60 Stanisław Bacyzński, "Secret military organizations in Upper Silesia in the years 1918–1921 under consideration of the general situation," 1931 (unpublished manuscript), CAW, *Baczyński Files*, vol. 28 (I.476.1.28), 15–18. This part of Baczyński's manuscript has been omitted in the publication of the same title in 1968 (see annotation 56).

and breakdowns in the military organization based on district antagonisms, riots within the DOP before the third uprising between the officers from Poznań and from Warsaw, and during the third uprising an attempted coup against Korfanty by Grażyński, Przedpełski, and others.[61]

As we have seen, things were not as simple as that. Of course, animosities and a division between Poznań and Warsaw officers in the DOP's upper ranks are likely to have occurred. On the other hand, they probably would have surfaced without any interference from Korfanty's side. More importantly, the strife between POW and DOP commanders and Korfanty were not repercussions of a rivalry between officers from Upper Silesia and Poznań on the one hand, and from Warsaw on the other. As has been shown, in all three cases of insubordination, the commanders came from both sides of this politico-geographical divide. In Baczyński's example from 1921, he fails to mention Grajek, one of Korfanty's major critics, who was immediately removed by him. But Grajek happened to be from Greater Poland and thus did not fit into Baczyński's narrative. Even less so for Paluch, the most prominent commander of the Poznań upheaval and leader of the second insurrection in Upper Silesia. How does Baczyński's analysis explain that Paluch, a son of Greater Poland and one of Korfanty's closest confidants, was part of the conspiracy against him in 1920 and therefore dismissed by Korfanty without further ado? In fact, the paramilitary commanders that took part in the three revolts between 1919 and 1921 represented all geographical and political layers of contemporary Poland. This leaves no other explanation than to conclude that they were not driven by political ideology or localism. They were rather acting like a kind of paramilitary "warrior class," whose assessment of the military situation in their eyes surpassed that of the "civilian" Korfanty.

The narrative runs like a red thread through Baczyński's description. The separatist and conservative opponents of Piłsudski in Poznań and Upper Silesia had done anything to sabotage the efforts of the Polish General Staff to integrate Upper Silesia into the Polish state. Of course, as we have seen, he did not simply make up differences between Warsaw and the western periphery, between Endecja and leftist circles, between Korfanty and the paramilitary commanders, nor amongst them—those tensions existed between 1918 and 1921, and more than once they diminished the prospect of a Polish victory. But what Baczyński

---

61 Baczyński, "Tajne organizacje, wojskowe na Górnym Śląsku w latach 1918–1921 na tle sytuacji ogólnej" (unpublished manuscript), 16.

did—and what his old adversaries probably would have also done in his place—was blaming the other side for all the ills and taking all the credit for his own camp. We may assume that his general settlement was not only based on the intention to ingratiate himself with Piłsudski. Personal animosities may have also played a role. With barely concealed indignation, Baczyński noted that the opposing side had regarded the paramilitary commanders as "a bunch of undisciplined half-wits."[62]

Be that as it may, he may have exaggerated somewhat with his over-simplistic portrayal of the complex conflict over Upper Silesia. A marginal note on the cover page of the file, explicitly referring to the part of the manuscript wherein Baczyński described the Polish inner quarrels, asked: "Polish War [sic]. Is this work based on sources and worthy of further detailed study?"[63]

## Conclusion

From its inception, the Second Polish Republic was involved in border battles that would determine the territory of the new state. However, a powerful regular army was not at hand. Rather, it had to be built while the fighting continued. In parallel, paramilitary combat units were formed from Polish speaking veterans of World War I, primarily from members of Polish nationalist units within the imperial armies—like the Polish Legions—and Polish secret organizations, first and foremost, the POW. However, the use of these paramilitary units in the national struggle varied depending on the area of operation. In the contested area in eastern Poland, they existed primarily during the military conflict with Ukrainian and Bolshevik forces in 1918–1920.[64] At the western border in Greater Poland, the integration of paramilitary forces into the regular Polish army was realized within a few weeks. In Upper Silesia, on the other hand, the paramilitary POW GŚ existed from the beginning of the conflict until its very end. It was a classic spin-off group that the Polish government deployed in the area because the use of regular Polish troops on German territory would have been tantamount to a declaration of war. Analogously, the German government

---

62  Ibid.
63  Ibid., title page.
64  My forthcoming article for the *Slavic Review* titled *Special Task Forces or Loose Cannons? Paramilitary Groups in Polish Service as Agents of Violence, 1918–1921* (ca. 2023) describes the deployment of spin-off groups in Poland's embattled eastern borderlands.

sent mainly its paramilitary Free Corps to the region and held back from deploying regular troops.

As events in Western Poland, especially in Upper Silesia, showed, the use of paramilitary troops in local conflicts created great difficulties for the Polish government. The paramilitaries on the ground often developed their own agenda, which differed from that of the Polish government. The situation was further complicated by the fact that at the beginning of independence there were several competing power centers in Poland, which also sought to gain influence over the paramilitaries. In Greater Poland and Upper Silesia, therefore, we are dealing with a three-way constellation consisting of the central government, the regional Endecja camp, and the local paramilitaries. These three had an extremely complicated and conflictual relationship that defies simplistic explanations. Thus, from the spring of 1919 onward, the greatest tension was no longer between the central government in Warsaw and the regional Endecja stronghold Poznań, but between the commanders of the Upper Silesian paramilitaries and the political leader of the Upper Silesian insurrection, Korfanty.

These tensions can best be explained by the fact that the Upper Silesian paramilitaries behaved like a spin-off group of the regional and central power centers. More so than troops of a regular army, they tended to develop their own ideas on how to achieve the common goal of integrating Upper Silesia into the Polish state. Having their own agenda brought them into conflict primarily with the regional leadership which, more so than the Warsaw government, determined the specific choice of means and the timing of their deployment. As has been shown, these tensions had little to do with divergent political views and more to do with the confrontation of a paramilitary warrior caste with its civilian command center.

Since the mid-1920s, during the authoritarian turn under Piłsudski, some of his former opponents from the border struggles of 1918–1921 were persecuted as political opponents. Therefore, in the early 1930s an attempt was made within the Polish military to rewrite the inner-Polish conflict during the struggle with Germany over Upper Silesia as a purely political confrontation between the Piłsudski government in Warsaw and the Endecja forces in Poznań and Upper Silesia—and especially with Korfanty. This version, however, does not stand up to closer historical scrutiny. Rather, it had been the complicated and conflicted relationship between local paramilitaries, a regional political leadership, and the central government in Warsaw that determined the course of events in Greater Poland and Upper Silesia between 1918 and 1921.

# Bibliography

## Archival Sources

Bacyzński, Stanisław. "Secret military organizations in Upper Silesia in the years 1918–1921 under consideration of the general situation." 1931 (unpublished manuscript). Baczyński Files, vol. 28 (I.476.1.28). Central Military Archive in Warsaw (CAW).
Letter of the executive committee of the POW GŚ to the NRL commissariat in Poznań, Bytom. July 1, 1919. Laudański Files, vol. 16 (I.440.12.16), 53. CAW.
Letter of the Second Department of the MSW to the commander of the Upper Silesian Front, General Franciszek Latinik. [Warsaw], 1919 [after the opening of the Silesian Front on October 19]. Baczyński Files, vol. 37 (I.476.1.37). CAW.
Letter from General Stachiewicz criticizing General Kukiel's work at the Historical Office. [1926]. 701/1/70, 3–58. Archive of the Józef Piłsudski Institute in America (AJPI).
"Minutes of the Meeting of the Commission of Experts October 9, 1925 at 5 p.m.: Hearing of General Stachiewicz, Mokotow Hospital." 701/1/69, 2–6. AJPI.

## Secondary Literature

Baczyński, Stanisław. "Tajne organizacje wojskowe na Górnym Śląsku w latach 1918–1921 na tle sytuacji ogólnej." *Najnowsze Dzieje Polski. 1914–1939* 13 (1968): 113–56.
Badziak, Kazimierz. *W oczekiwaniu na przełom: Na drodze od odrodzenia do załamania państwa polskiego, listopad 1918-czerwiec 1920*. Łódź: Ibidem, 2004.
Balkelis, Tomas. "From Defence to Revolution: Lithuanian Paramilitary Groups in 1918 and 1919." *Acta Historica Universitatis Klaipedensis* 28 (2014): 43–56.
Bjork, James E. *Neither German nor Pole: Catholicism and National Indifference in a Central European Borderland*. Ann Arbor: University of Michigan Press, 2008.
Böhler, Jochen. *Civil War in Central Europe, 1918–1921: The Reconstruction of Poland*. Oxford: Oxford University Press, 2018.
Boysen, Jens. "Simultaneity of the Un-simultaneous: German Social Revolution and Polish National Revolution." In *Germany 1916–23: A Revolution in Context*, edited by Klaus Weinhauer, Anthony McElligott, and Kirsten Heinsohn, 229–250. Bielefeld: Transcript, 2015.
Chwalba, Andrzej. *Legiony Polskie, 1914–1918*. Kraków: Wydawnictwo Literackie, 2018.
Conrad, Benjamin. *Umkämpfte Grenzen, umkämpfte Bevölkerung: Die Entstehung der Staatsgrenzen der Zweiten Polnischen Republik 1918–1923*. Stuttgart: Steiner, 2014.
Davies, Norman. *White Eagle, Red Star: The Polish-Soviet War, 1919–20*. London: Orbis Books, 1983.
Długajczyk, Erward. *Wywiad polski na Górnym Śląsku 1919–1922*. Katowice: Muzeum Śląskie, 2001.
Gerwarth, Robert. "Fighting the Red Beast, Counter-Revolutionary Violence in the Defeated States of Central Europe." In *War in Peace: Paramilitary Violence in Europe After the Great War*, edited by Robert Gerwarth and John Horne, 52–71. Oxford: Oxford University Press, 2012.

Haslinger, Peter et al. "Frontiers of Violence: Paramiliärs als Gewaltgemeinschaften im Ostmitteleuropa der 1920er Jahre." In *Gewaltgemeinschaften in der Geschichte: Entstehung, Kohäsionskraft und Zerfall*, edited by Winfried Speitkamp et al., 233–54. Göttingen: Vandenhoeck & Ruprecht, 2017.

Jones, Mark. *Founding Weimar: Violence and the German Revolution of 1918–1919*. Cambridge: Cambridge University Press, 2016.

Kaczmarek, Ryszard. *Powstania Śląskie 1919–1920–1921: Nieznana wojna polsko-niemiecka*. Kraków: Wydawnictwo Literackie, 2019.

Kaczmarski, Krzysztof, Wojciech Jerzy Muszyński, and Rafał Sierchuła. *Generał Józef Haller 1873–1960*. Warszawa: Instytut Pamięci Narodowej, 2017.

Kučera, Rudolf. "Exploiting Victory, Sinking into Defeat: Uniformed Violence in the Creation of the New Order in Czechoslovakia and Austria, 1918–1922." *Journal of Modern History* 88, no. 4 (2016), 827–55.

Lehnstaedt, Stephan. *Der vergessene Sieg: Der Polnisch-Sowjetische Krieg 1919–1921 und die Entstehung des modernen Osteuropa*. Munich: Beck, 2019.

Lewandowski, Jan F. *Wojciech Korfanty, Biografie Sławnych Ludzi*. Warsaw: Państwowy Instytut Wydawniczy, 2013.

Lukowski, Jerzy. *The Partitions of Poland: 1772, 1793, 1795*. London: Longman, 1999.

Macyszyn, Jacek. "Powstanie Wielkopolskie 1918–1919." *Niepodległość i Pamięć* 22, no. 1 (2015): 81–101.

Markowski, Damian. *Lwów or L'viv? Two Uprisings in 1918*. Frankfurt am Main: Peter Lang, 2018.

Muszyński, Wojciech Jerzy. *Białe legiony 1914–1918: Od Legionu Puławskiego do I Korpusu Polskiego*. Warsaw: IPN, 2018.

Paduszek, Konrad and Witold Rawski, "Wojskowe Biuro Historyczne i jego kadra w 1939 roku." *Przegląd Historyczno-Wojskowy* (2011): 69–96.

Panecka, Bożena. "Źródła do dziejów Powstań Śląskich (1919–1921) przechowywane w Centralnym Archiwum Wojskowym." *Biuletyn Wojskowej Służby Archiwalnej* 13–14 (1985): 73–85.

Pieniazek, Wojciech. "Subversive Kriegsführung in Oberschlesien 1920–1921." In *Spór o Górny Śląsk 1919–1922: W 90 rocznicę wybuchu III powstania śląskiego*, edited by Marek Białokur and Adrian Dawid, 191–95. Gdańsk: Regionalny Zarząd Gospodarki Wodnej, 2012.

Piłsudski, Józef. *Year 1920 and its climax battle of Warsaw, during the Polish-Soviet War, 1919–1920: With the addition of Soviet Marshal Tukhachevski's March beyond the Vistula*. London: Piłsudski Institute of London, 1972.

Puszczyński, Tadeusz. *Polskie działania destrukcyjne na Górnym Śląsku w latach 1920–1921*, edited by Edward Długajczyk. Katowice: Śląsk, 2019.

Rothschild, Joseph. "Marshal Józef Piłsudski's Concept of State Vis-à-Vis Society in Interwar Poland." In *East Central European War Leaders: Civilian and Military*, edited by Béla K. Király and Albert A. Nofi, 289–303. Boulder: Social Science Monographs, 1988.

Schlichte, Klaus. *In the Shadow of Violence: The Politics of Armed Groups*. Frankfurt am Main: Campus, 2009.

Schmidt-Rösler, Andrea. "Autonomie- und Separatismusbestrebungen in Oberschlesien 1918–1922." *Zeitschrift für Ostmitteleuropaforschung* 48, no. 1 (1999): 1–49.

Semil, Edmund. "Ojciec i syn." In *Żołnierz, poeta, czasu kurz . . .: Wspomnienia o Krzysztofie Kamilu Baczyńskim*, edited by Zbigniew Wasilewski, 13–60. Kraków: Wydawnictwo Literackie, 1967.

Serafin, Franciszek. *Województwo Śląskie, 1922–1939: Zarys monograficzny*. Katowice: Wydawnictwo Uniwersytetu Śląskiego, 1996.
Sierchuła, Rafał and Wojciech Jerzy Muszyński. *Józef Dowbor-Muśnicki, 1867–1937*. Poznań, Warsaw: IPN, 2018.
Stefanic, David R. "Piłsudski's Polish Legions: The Formation of a National Army Without a Nation State." In *Armies in Exile*, edited by David R. Stefancic, 103–15. New York: Columbia University Press, 2005.
Thomas, Alun. "The British Upper Silesia Force ('UPSI' Force), May 1921–July 1922." *Journal of the Society for Army Historical Research* 95, no. 384 (2017): 338–64.
Tuliński, Arkadiusz. "Oficerowie Biura Historycznego i Wojskowego Biura Historycznego w latach 1922–1939: Część 1." *Przegląd Historyczno-Wojskowy* 270, no. 4 (2019): 157–89.
Valasek, Paul S., ed. *Haller's Polish Army in France*. Naples, FL: Whitehall Printing, 2006.
Wilson, Tim. *Frontiers of Violence: Conflict and Identity in Ulster and Upper Silesia 1918–1922*. Oxford: Oxford University Press, 2010.
Wrzosek, Mieczysław. "Problem przyjazdu armii generała Hallera do kraju (listopad 1918–czerwiec 1919)." In *Polska i jej wschodni sąsiedzi w XX wieku*, edited by Hanna Konopka and Daniel Boćkowski, 53–65. Białystok: Wydawnictwo Uniwersytetu w Białymstoku, 2004.
Yekelchyk, Serhy. "Bands of Nation Builders? Insurgency and Ideology in the Ukrainian Civil War." In *War in Peace: Paramilitary Violence in Europe After the Great War*, edited by Robert Gerwarth and John Horne, 107–25. Oxford: Oxford University Press, 2012.

# CHAPTER 7

# *Eisenbahnfeldzug:* Railway War in East Central Europe

## Maciej Górny

In his autobiography, as popular as it is untruthful, Lev Trotsky devoted an entire chapter to a train:

> For two and a half years, except for comparatively short intervals, I lived in a railway-coach that had formerly been used by one of the ministers of communication. The car was well fitted out from the point of view of ministerial comfort, but it was scarcely adapted to work. There I received those who brought reports, held conferences with local military and civil authorities, studied telegraphic dispatches, dictated orders and articles. From it I made long trips along the front in automobiles with my co-workers. In my spare time I dictated my book against Kautsky, and various other works. In those years I accustomed myself, seemingly forever, to writing and thinking to the accompaniment of Pullman wheels and springs.[1]

A mobile command post proved immensely useful for an army engaged in several wars at the same time on many faraway fronts. Yet, the credit for discovering the key role of railways in wars in the east of Europe does not lie with Trotsky. It was the Germans and Austro-Hungarians who initiated the railway

---

1   Leon Trotsky, *My Life: An Attempt at an Autobiography* (New York: Pathfinder Press, 1970), 413.

war (*Eisenbahnkrieg*) in the East. It started during the pause in the Brest-Litovsk negotiations when, in direct answer to the Soviet negotiating strategy, German troops headed to the East along the main railways. They were small in number but appeared at the right time and place to take control over the land.[2] What they had initiated soon evolved into an astonishingly multifaceted phenomenon, far more complicated than a simple attempt to quickly transport troops and goods. Thus, the war in East Central Europe acquired a special dimension contributing to the chaotic coexistence of soldiers and civilian populations in the highly unstable conditions of the region's political reconstruction.[3]

Research into the relationship between railway and war is rich, though unbalanced.[4] Michael Freeman, a specialist in human geography and the history of transport, noticed in his 1999 article that "with only a few exceptions (econometrics being one), much writing on railway history has been undertaken in isolation from, or in ignorance of, debates and changes in the nature of discourse in the humanities and the social sciences."[5] This critical observation remains largely valid also in the context of World War I studies. Attempts at analyzing connections between railway history and general histories of the war remain rather superficial. This may come as a surprise given the symbolism of the steam engine and its meaning for the history of warfare. While research into the topic grows steadily, groundbreaking histories of the epoch told through the specific perspective of railway that could be compared to Manu Karuka's seminal recent

---

2 Peter Leib, "Aufstandsbekämpfung im strategischen Dilemma. Die deutsche Besatzung in der Ukraine 1918," in *Die Besatzung der Ukraine 1918. Historischer Kontext–Forschungsstand–wirtschaftliche und soziale Folgen*, ed. Wolfram Dornik and Stefan Karner (Graz, Wien, Klagenfurt: Verein zur Förderung der Forschung von Folgen nach Konflikten und Kriegen, 2008), 111–39, here 116. On the theoretical considerations over the role of railway within the German command see David T. Zabecki, "Railroads and the Operational Level of War in the German 1918 Offensives," in *Finding Common Ground: New Directions in First World War Studies*, ed. Jennifer D. Keene and Michael S. Neiberg (Leiden: Brill, 2011), 161–86.

3 The passage from the war into the multilateral postwar conflicts are topic to Jochen Böhler, *Civil War in Central Europe, 1918–1921: The Reconstruction of Poland* (Oxford: Oxford University Press, 2020); Tomas Balkelis, *War, Revolution, and Nation-Making in Lithuania, 1914–1923* (Oxford: Oxford University Press, 2018).

4 For a recent overview of the history of railway and infrastructure in East Central Europe on the eve of the war see Steffi Marung, Matthias Middell, Uwe Müller, "Multiple Territorialisierungsprozesse in Ostmitteleuropa," in *Handbuch einer transnationalen Geschichte Ostmitteleuropas. Band I. Von der Mitte des 19. Jahrhunderts bis zum Ersten Weltkrieg*, ed. Frank Hadler and Matthias Middell (Göttingen: Vandenhoeck & Ruprecht, 2017), 448–52.

5 Michael Freeman, "The railway as cultural metaphor 'What kind of railway history?' revisited," in *The Journal of Transport History* 20, no. 2 (1999): 160–67.

monograph, are largely missing.⁶ Instead of being a "window" through which complex and interconnected phenomena can be viewed, and—perhaps—better understood, the topic mostly appears on the margins of studies devoted to other phenomena.

To be sure, the political meaning of the railway gets proper recognition, particularly in the context of German expansionism into the Balkans and Middle East, as well as, more generally, of the German and French investment in new infrastructure preceding the outbreak of hostilities.⁷ Military history has long focused on the strategic role of railway transport, especially as a support for army's mobility.⁸ Within this framework, 1914 mobilization plans and their implementation, particularly in the Habsburg empire, offer extremely interesting insight into the importance of railway transport.⁹ The overwhelming majority of existing publications, however, concentrate on the immediate war effort and strategy—figuratively speaking, they have situated their focus between Trotsky's coach and the German *Eisenbahnkrieg*.¹⁰ Some aspects of military history, such as armored trains, attract attention among military historians, and generate countless minor studies devoted to this weapon, to individual war episodes, or units.¹¹ Railway junctions, food and munition depots, and other

---

6   Manu Karuka, *Empire's Tracks: Indigenous Nations, Chinese Workers, and the Transcontinental Railroad* (Oakland: University of California Press, 2019).
7   See for example Allan Mitchell, *The Great Train Race: Railways and the Franco-German Rivalry* (New York: Berghahn Books, 2000); Jonathan S. McMurray, *Distant Ties: Germany, the Ottoman Empire, and the Construction of the Baghdad Railway* (Westport: Praeger, 2001); Sean McMeekin, *The Berlin-Baghdad Express: The Ottoman Empire and Germany's Bid for World Power, 1898–1918* (Cambridge, MA.: Harvard University Press, 2010).
8   David Stevenson, "War by Timetable? The Railway Race before 1914," *Past & Present* 162 (1999): 163–94.
9   Norman Stone, "Die Mobilmachung der österreichisch-ungarischen Armee 1914," *Militärgeschichtliche Mitteilungen* 16, no. 2 (1974): 68–77, 83. For a brief summary, see Alexander Watson, *Ring of Steel: Germany and Austria-Hungary in World War I* (New York: Basic Books, 2014), 112–14.
10  Klaus-Jürgen Bremm, *Armeen unter Dampf. Die Eisenbahnen in der europäischen Kriegsgeschichte 1871–1918* (Hövelhof: DGEG Medien, 2013); Christian Wolmar, *Engines of War: How Wars Were Won & Lost on the Railways* (New York: Atlantic Books, 2010); J. A. B. Hamilton, *Britain's Railways in World War 1* (London: George Allen and Unwin Ltd., 1967); Andreas Knipping, *Eisenbahnen im Ersten Weltkrieg* (Freiburg: EK-Verlag, 2004); Martin van Creveld, *Supplying War: Logistics from Wallenstein to Patton* (Cambridge: Cambridge University Press, 1977); David Wragg, *Wartime on the Railways* (Stroud: The History Press, 2006). General narratives of the First World War also offer a similar perspective.
11  See, for example, Stephen J. Zaloga, *Armored Trains* (Osprey: Bloomsbury, 2008).

infrastructure are part of a broader field of research on refugees, especially in the context of the Russian evacuation in 1915.[12]

In turn, the social history of railway construction and railway workers has formed an autonomous segment of World War I studies deeply connected with the rich tradition of nineteenth-century social history. Whereas trade unions, railway workers, and labor history form the main actors tackled by social historians, research has basically detected instances of workers' unrest, strikes, and riots. Such research raised, among others, the vital question of railway men's participation in the Russian revolutions.[13] Against this background, recent publications have relied upon cultural history to investigate railway infrastructure as knots of exchange, social life, and human emotions on the one hand, and social emancipation and experts' cultures, on the other.[14]

The metaphors present in most of these studies go beyond the typical nineteenth-century visions of technical progress of humankind symbolized by the steam engine swallowing mile after mile (a picture complementary to rising factory smoke).[15] In the context of the modern war effort, the railway is associated with the state organism through images of arteries, veins and—as in Trotsky's memories—unstoppable mobility without which the whole pursuit of military operations would be impossible. Through tracks, as through blood vessels, the war effort can be maintained, armies supplied with men and materiel, wounded transported to the rear, and goods distributed among the civilian population.

---

12  Peter Gatrell, *A Whole Empire Walking: Refugees in Russia during World War I* (Bloomington: Indiana University Press, 2011); Peter Gatrell, "War, Population Displacement and State Formation in the Russian Borderlands, 1914–1924," in *Homelands: War, Population and Statehood in Eastern Europe and Russia, 1918–1924*, ed. Nick Baron and Peter Gatrell (London: Anthem Press, 2004), 10–34; Liubov Zhvanko, *Bizhentsi pershoi svitovoi viini. Ukrains'kii vimir, 1914–1918 rr.* (Kharkiv: Virovets' A. P. 'Apostrof', 2012; Giuseppe Motta, "The Great War and the Jewish Refugees in Russia: Research in the Documents of the Joint Distribution Committee," in *Unknown Fronts: The "Eastern Turn" in First World War History*, ed. Elka Agoston-Nikolova et al. (Groningen: Nederland Rusland Centrum, 2017), 183–206; Katarzyna Sierakowska, *Śmierć, wygnanie, głód w dokumentach osobistych. Ziemie polskie w latach Wielkiej Wojny 1914–1918* (Warsaw: Instytut Historii PAN, 2015).

13  Anthony Heywood, "Spark of revolution? Railway disorganisation, freight traffic and Tsarist Russia's war effort, July 1914–March 1917," *Europe-Asia Studies* 65, no. 4 (2013): 753–72.

14  Adrian Gregory, "Railway stations," in *A Cultural History*, vol. 2 of *Capital Cities at War: Paris, London, Berlin 1914–1919*, ed. Jay Winter and Jean-Louis Robert (Cambridge: Cambridge University Press, 2007), 23–56; *1914–1918-online. International Encyclopedia of the First World War*, s.v. "Railways (Russian Empire)," by Roland Cvetkovski, last modified October 8, 2014, https://encyclopedia.1914-1918-online.net/article/railways_russian_empire; Christopher Phillipps, *Civilian Specialists at War. Britain's Transport Experts and the First World War* (London: University of London Press, 2020).

15  Jerzy Jedlicki, *Świat zwyrodniały. Lęki i wyroki krytyków nowoczesności* (Warsaw: Wydawnictwo Sic!, 2000).

In the initial phase of war and every major offensive their role was vital for the mobilization and concentration of troops and artillery on the front. Major stations functioned as exchange and communication hubs, pumping blood cells in various directions (or, in the parlance of many railway historians, being the 'lifeblood of the war').[16]

This suggestive picture has solid fundaments in wartime realities and thus deserves serious consideration. In the following pages, I will consider it while comparing selected cases of post-1918 reconstruction in East Central Europe. The analyzed cases have a common element—the confrontation between the military and civilian population which, quite often, culminated in outbursts of violence between various military units (even formally allied), common soldiers, military returnees, military police, and armed and unarmed civilians. By focusing on this aspect, I will try to add a new perspective on the history of World War I in East Central Europe and, simultaneously, identify the role played therein by the railway.

My goal could seem quite bizarre. In East Central Europe, the railway played a paradoxical role. Compared to France or Belgium, the network was sparse, and the specific Russian broader track further complicated any transport. However, it was precisely this sparsity that increased the significance of existing railway in a period—beginning in 1918—in which offensives and counteroffensives in East Central Europe's numerous wars were led mostly, oftentimes solely, by train. These circumstances gave towns like Kovel' or Baranovichi an importance they had never had before.

## Armored Trains

Military logistics necessary to bring troops to the front obviously constituted a great part of railway transport in East Central Europe during World War I. Echelons travelled in both directions along the lines which sparsely crossed the region's underdeveloped and repeatedly vandalized railway network. From the first weeks of the war, on the one hand, it was imperative to the losing party to blow up bridges, burn down stations, and destroy railway lines. On the other hand, temporary track repair, and the restoration of rail connections were among the first activities to be undertaken by invading forces. In areas that changed

---

16 See for example Jeremy Higgins, *Great War Railwaymen: Britain's Railway Company Workers at War 1914–1918* (Chicago: Uniform Press, 2014); Julian Thompson, *The Lifeblood of War: Logistics in Armed Conflict* (London: Macmillan,1991).

hands several times, such works—which, unlike digging trenches, attracted remuneration, at least in the first months of the war—provided employment and wages to locals and professionals alike.[17]

While, on the whole, military operations remained highly dependent on railway transport, around 1918 a change of balance could be observed. The steady though uneven pulse of military transports was interrupted by destruction resulting from major offensives that heretofore dominated the actual war on the rails. The German and Austro-Hungarian offensive of 1918 paved the way for a new phase of the war to be carried out mostly or solely along the main railway lines. Most of the battles between armored trains, a supreme weapon in these struggles, took place in sparsely populated areas with only a few railway lines. Armored trains were crucial for the fights around Archangelsk between the Bolsheviks, Frenchmen, and Americans fought largely along the line to Vologda with its 262 bridges destroyed and rebuilt almost on a daily basis by both sides.[18] Purpose-built armored trains were obviously more imposing than the improvised variety that Americans used in northern Russia. A Czechoslovak officer, František Petr, became fully aware of that in 1919, when he was given the command of one such unit, numbered eight:

> The handover of an armored train is not a game. The train consists of a railway unit, an artillery unit, an infantry unit, one or more locomotives, cars, cannons, machine guns, grenades, hundreds of thousands of shells, and so on, and so forth. Furthermore, it contains workshops, depots, and a chancellery tasked with compiling various registries, book-keeping, and many other affairs.[19]

Armored trains duels were a characteristic feature of the offensive of Hungarian Bolsheviks to Slovakia in 1919. Contrary to the skirmishes in northern Russia, these fights took place in and for the main transport hubs and they carried serious danger to civilian town dwellers. The Hungarians kept initiative there as long as they dominated on track. It took Czechoslovaks a couple of weeks to introduce their own armored trains and regain the initiative. The armored trains were especially crucial in the fight in Nové Zamky, a town with a Magyar majority and

---

17 Włodzimierz Borodziej, Maciej Górny, *Forgotten Wars: Central and Eastern Europe, 1912–1916* (Cambridge: Cambridge University Press, 2021), 249–51.
18 Benjamin D. Rhodes, "The Anglo-American Railroad War at Archangel, 1918–1919," *Railroad History* 151 (1984): 70–83.
19 František Stanislav Petr, *Pod rakouskou orlicí a českým lvem* (Praha: Gasset, 2015), 214.

predominantly Hungarian loyalties. General Eugène Mittelhauser who led the action on the Czechoslovak side described this fight vividly:

> My train was still some three kilometers from the train station when a massive explosion shook the car, shattering several windows. Convinced that the detonation must have taken place to the east of Nové Zámky, I immediately thought that the railway bridge over the Nitra was blown up. A few minutes later, I found Major Bonneau, who confirmed that the bridge was blown up just as our armored train was crossing it . . . Through my spyglass, I saw the cloud of smoke disperse to reveal the train on the other side of the destroyed bridge. Its vicious barrage testified to the vigor of the crew. Suspended from the remnants of a span, its wrecked tank engine indicated that the train could no longer move ahead nor back. Covered with the condensed drumfire of the artillery, it seemed sluggish as a tank, stopped in its tracks by the defenders, and yet fighting to the last with its cannons and machine guns. Then, Major [Jiří] Jelínek . . . requested permission to charge toward the bridge to defend the armored train . . . The dispersing smoke from the detonation, the intense fusillade attracted by the train, the unceasing rattle of machine guns—all this transformed the clash by the bridge at Nové Zámky into a scene from any major French battle. In this critical time, Major Jelínek did not hesitate to look death herself in the eye. Within fifteen minutes, news arrived that Major Jelínek was wounded . . . the bullet hit him a hand's breadth below the heart. We immediately knew the wound was mortal.[20]

Besides casualties and the immediate destruction of vital infrastructure, the Hungarian Bolshevik offensive caused major disruption of civilian transport in Slovakia reducing available connections to Bohemia. Newspapers in the summer of 1919 regularly informed their readers about cancelled connections and other disturbances.[21]

---

20  Quote from *World at War*, "Válka Československé republiky s Maďarskou republikou rad (1919)," accessed April 25, 2016, http://worldatwar.eu/index.php?esid=197928614b8e6e effdfa121cb30b3a37&lang=12&refcode=0&location=article&articleid=377&categoryid=4&showcomms=1. See also "Generál Mittelhauser o Sokoloch," *Slovenský Denník*, June 26, 1929, 2.
21  See, for example, "Úradná časť," *Slobodný Slovák*, June 7, 1919, 3.

Yet, the largest field of action for this modern weapon was the eastern provinces of the former Russian Empire. In 1919, the Estonian offensive against the Bolsheviks was supported by several armored trains, while the harshest fights took place at railway stations in Paju (a village) and Võru (a medium-size town). Gaining control over Paju meant that the red Latvian riflemen would not be able to get the support of the armored trains in their fights in Latvia and southern Estonia.[22] Hundreds of kilometers to the south of Estonia, the war between Poles and Ukrainians in Galicia was also a railway war. Reading military reports gives a Wild West association with a slight change concerning the booty: the mustangs and buffalos were replaced by wagons and engines.

> The armored train no. 16 followed by a cavalry unit took Powórsk [Povors'k] and pushed the enemy to the eastern bank of the Stochod [Stokhod] river. The railway bridge has been damaged. In Powórsk we won 60 broad track wagons, ammunition and weapons… The armored train no. 15 moved to Hołoby [Holoby] which is controlled by Ukrainian railway men and a small police unit. The bridge had been destroyed by the Germans. In Hołoby we can expect a lot of railway material (more than 1,000 wagons and 10 locomotives are reported). The Ukrainians keep desperately trying to repair the bridge.[23]

In the war on the former Russian territory, the trains were both the weapon and booty. Moreover, locomotives and railways were subject to reconnaissance. Incidentally, trains were used to get rid of typhoid patients who were simply transferred towards the enemy lines.[24] During the fights in Belarus, Eastern Poland, Ukraine, Latvia, and Estonia the sight of dueling trains was not a rarity. The significance of the railways for the war in Lithuania, Belarus, and Ukraine remained undiminished even when other formations came to the forefront. In April 1919, Vilnius was taken thanks to a daring maneuver by the Polish cavalry,

---

22  Jürgen von Hehn, "Der baltische Freiheitskrieg – Umrisse und Probleme 1918–1920," in *Von den baltischen Provinzen zu den baltischen Staaten. Beiträge zur Entstehungsgeschichte der Republiken Estland und Lettland 1918–1920*, ed. Jürgen von Hahn, Hans von Rimscha, and Helmuth Weiss (Marburg: Herder-Institut, 1977), 17–18.

23  "Komunikat z 7 lutego 1919 roku," *O niepodległą i granice*. Vol.1 *"Komunikaty Oddziału III Naczelnego Dowództwa Wojska Polskiego 1919–1921,"* ed. Marek Jabłonowski and Adam Koseski (Warszawa–Pułtusk: Akademia Humanistyczna im. A. Gieysztora, 1999), 47.

24  I would like to thank Łukasz Mieszkowski for this information based on the Polish archival material.

rather than a train charge, but the main objective of the assault was naturally the railway station:

> The train station, including an enormous amount of railway materiel, was claimed without firing a shot on the 5 [April 19]. The assault was so unexpected that 400 [soldiers—MG] about to be dispatched toward Lida gave themselves up inside their cars without a peep. A train sent immediately for infantry brought a foot battalion of the second [first—MG] division of the Legions to Vilnius by noon, in Bolshevik cars. Thus far, the cavalry took 13 engines, several hundred cars, substantial amounts of guns and ammunition, 14 machine guns, and over 1,000 prisoners... Trains made up of cars taken from the enemy are already running on the Lida-Vilnius line.[25]

The repercussions of fighting for railway hubs within cities such as Vilnius were serious. The taking of Vilnius by the Poles was followed by a pogrom killing up to eighty people.[26] Among the victims was Ajzyk Meir Dewernicki, a writer and member of the Bund party, while Szymon An-ski, author of the most influential description of anti-Jewish violence in Eastern Europe during the war published under the title *The Enemy at His Pleasure: A Journey Through the Jewish Pale of Settlement During World War I*, who was in Vilnius at the time, was arrested. Nojech Pryłucki, deputy to the Parliament (sejm) and son of the editor of the major Yiddish news daily *Der Moment*, convinced the Polish authorities to release him and allow him to leave for Warsaw.[27] The perpetrators claimed to have been assaulted by armed Jewish civilians during their fight for the city.

As in Slovakia, the fighting along main railway lines disrupted transport for the army and civilians alike. Polish divisional commissar Stanisław Burnagel saw the collapse of transport infrastructure as one of the gravest issues he faced while in service:

---

25 "22 kwietnia 1919 roku," in *O niepodległą i granice*, 1:170.
26 Szymon Rudnicki, Jarosław Gorliński, "The Vilna Pogrom of 19–21 April 1919," *Polin. Studies in Polish Jewry* 33 (2021): 463–94.
27 Cwi Pryłucki, *Wspomnienia (1905–1939)* (Warsaw: Archiwum Ringelbluma, 2015), 111–12.

Whoever had the opportunity to travel to Vilnius by rail in those days [that is, in 1919] surely recalls the incredible unwieldiness of the broad-gauge railway. "Running time between the right wing of the Sixth Brigade of Infantry of the Legions and Vilnius is likely to amount to 4 to 5 days," said the briefing of the divisional staff for 4 December 1919. And that's no surprise, since trains departed from Vilnius with a delay of as many as six hours—sometimes five, sometimes even twelve—and made their longest stop at Nowoświęciany [Švenčionėliai], where the locomotive left for the engine house for fuel and water, broke down, and remained out of service until the driver returned from the city. The briefing of the divisional staff for 4 November 1919 states that "the passenger train Vilnius-Turmont [Turmantas] arrives from Vilnius to Dukszty [Dūkštas] between 7 p.m. and 3 a.m., and departs from Dukszty toward Vilnius between 23 p.m. and 6 a.m." In these conditions, a trip to Vilnius turned into a serious expedition lasting at least two days. The snail's pace of the trains did nothing to help increase car turnover, meaning that if an axle of a loaded car caught fire, it became the worst of calamities. Such a car would then have to return from Podbrodzie [Pabradė] or Nowowilejka [Naujoji Vilnia] to Vilnius to be reloaded, thus delaying the delivery of the given material for another two days.[28]

While the situation gravely affected civilian traffic, not less serious was its impact on the army. The transportation of wounded soldiers under such conditions was a challenge, even though Poland and Czechoslovakia made heavy investments in sanitary trains. When Polish uhlan Jan Fudakowski got wounded in a skirmish against the Bolsheviks, he initially had to wait several hours for treatment. Then, a truck took him to the nearest train station, where he and other wounded were loaded onto a freight car. "The trip to Kovel' took a very long time, the train stopping on small stations or in the middle of nowhere to let through military transports heading to the front."[29] At Kovel', the wounded were placed in a warehouse and given coffee and soup, but no one even bothered to change the bandages of the lightly wounded. Still, after a few more days, the seriously wounded were driven deeper into the country. The others stayed for

---

28  Stanisław Burnagel, *Wspomnienia wojenne intendenta dywizji* (Warsaw: n.p., 1934), 26.
29  Jan Fudakowski, *Ułańskie wspomnienia z roku 1920* (Lublin: Towarzystwo Naukowe KUL, 2005), 90.

another week or so in the dim warehouse, unwashed and with no running water. Fudakowski remembered:

> One evening, out of boredom and incessant itching, I and my lightly wounded neighbor made a macabre bet which one of us would collect more lice from his shirt in fifteen minutes. We put two candles between the stretchers and, half-naked, began our hunt in front of a few onlookers. Once a louse was caught, you had to put it to the candle flame, and each time the flame rose with a characteristic hiss. Our audience counted and when fifteen minutes passed, they announced my victory; I picked out a hundred and some lice.[30]

Lice-ridden, the lightly wounded then travelled briefly from Kovel' to Brest. It was only then that Fudakowski embarked on a hospital train, which left him awestruck after his previous experiences:

> It was a newly furnished train from Poznań, with medical and railway staff in tow, dispatched for the first batch of wounded from the front. Inside, it felt almost like heaven. The pristine condition of the cars, the clean blankets and pillows on stretchers hanging in three tiers by the sides of the car—what luxury! In the passageway between the stretchers, attentive orderlies and sisters of the Red Cross milled about.[31]

Not before did the giant Soviet offensive of 1920 change this situation, and the war seemingly turned away from the railway lines. The reason for a final shift was surely not the absence of armored trains during the Tukhachevski's offensive. On the contrary, they were mobilized in full. But in the mass war of 1920, they no longer played a central role being instead one of the many weapons at hand. While growing in numbers their relative role diminished. Now, war machinery entered the civilian life on all possible routes.

---

30  Ibid., 91.
31  Ibid., 92.

## Returnees

While most dire and immediate consequences of the new art of fighting were immediately felt by civilians living in proximity to the main railway stations, other threats were evenly distributed throughout the lines and were not directly connected to fighting. The greatest railway-related menace for the societies of East Central Europe came initially not from military action but, somewhat surprisingly, from military returnees. Coming back from the fronts was complicated and the way led through countries whose boundaries had changed over wartime. In late 1918, the map of East Central Europe was fairly unstable—European empires had collapsed, and their place was being taken over by new state structures in the making. The changing political status of many territories increased chaos even further. For new states in the region, transportation by rail of the returnees represented an existential threat, given the relative power of the dissolving military units. Jędrzej Moraczewski, the socialist prime minister of Poland in 1918, considered it the hardest test for the young state:

> The swift functioning of railway was the precondition of our country's existence. And everything took place just at the very moment when our people kicked out every single bloody foreign railway official together with their spouses and children. The people's government did everything it could to stand up to the task. The takeover of the railway network took place in an excellent tempo. The operational brake caused by the change of personnel took no more than couple of hours. We soon got full control over the railway. The army and POW transfer was conducted so swiftly that one hardly noticed the mass of people who travelled through our country.[32]

While Moraczewski proudly announced his success, his fear of the returnees could not be covered by this official optimism. A socialist politician eager to flatter railway trade unionists failed to notice major disruptions described by Burnagel. Neither did he mention that most of the German returnees came home from the Eastern front not across Poland but on the shortest way directly to Eastern Prussia. Prisoners of war, in turn, had been largely exchanged between Soviet Russia and the Central Powers already prior to November 1918 and

---

32 Jędrzej Moraczewski, *Przewrót w Polsce* (Warsaw: Muzeum Historii Polski w Warszawie, 2015), 59.

thus they could not be justifiably claimed to be a major challenge for the Polish authorities.

Things did not go so smoothly everywhere. Austria tells an utterly different story. When the Isonzo front broke down in October 1918, soldiers of the monarchy returned in droves, mostly via rail. Their trip back home got close to a humanitarian catastrophe:

> Soldiers rushed to the trains, broke the windows to get in, the roofs of the railway carriages were packed with men. In the Tirol ... the tired out soldiers fell asleep on the roofs and rolled down at the curves if not knocked down by their comrades, owing to lack of space. Most of the soldiers on the roofs, however, were knocked down and killed passing the tunnels, the rails being lined with dead all along.[33]

Such travels put not only the travelers at risk but also law and order along their way home. In early November 1918, the main Austrian junctions, such as Gnigl bei Salzburg or Amstetten, saw scenes of fighting between the returnees and the Home Defense Force (Heimwehr) for control over depots. The local press typically blamed Hungarians and praised the behavior of German Austrians, though there is no reason to claim that nationality played a major role in such conflicts.[34] It goes without saying that less important and less attended lines remained much calmer. In the spring of 1918, a Czech soldier, Antonín Záruba, traveled home with a German sanitary train from the Sarajevo military hospital. He appreciated mostly the fact that Germans were given food at every stop. A couple of months later, Záruba took a train again—this time from his unit in Kotor, Montenegro, to newly created Czechoslovakia—smuggling a bag of tobacco. During the journey, he was repeatedly checked, yet soldiers were interested in his weapons and left his personal belongings untouched. In Bohemia, travel conditions changed. Here the main source of danger to him—a demobilized smuggler—was not the military police or local army command, but civilians. Close to his home, Záruba was almost caught by local members of Sokols organization who controlled

---

33 Quotation in F. L. Carsten, *Revolution in Central Europe 1918–1919* (London: Maurice Temple Smith Ltd, 1972), 23.

34 Hannes Leidinger and Verena Moritz, *Gefangenschaft, Revolution, Heimkehr. Die Bedeutung der Kriegsgefangenenproblematik für die Geschichte des Kommunismus in Mittel- und Osteuropa 1917–1920* (Wien: Vandenhoeck Ruprecht Verlage, 2003), 595.

military transportation. He luckily found his way out by jumping on another train full of armed Germans who were clearly too dangerous to be checked.[35]

Journeys back home from Ukraine and Belarus were different, though not necessarily less dramatic. In early 1919, the German army there, until that very moment paramount to any other side in the local conflicts, turned into a bunch of would-be civilians desperate to get back home. Their position, heretofore privileged, deteriorated rapidly—many ended up robbed and, sometimes, killed by Communists and anti-Communists, local warlords and peasants.[36] In the territories controlled by the Poles, the German return was rather civilized, but even there some misunderstandings with bloody outcomes took place (for instance, a German bombardment of the railway station in Chełm/Kholm and an attempt at establishing military occupation of the station Łapy in eastern Poland by the German soldiers' council of Białystok as a retaliation for the Polish insurrection in Prussian Posen/Poznań).[37] Being aware of possible complications, the Germans decided to pay a private security force which controlled the railway and its immediate surroundings all the way to Germany.[38]

## Disciplinary Issues

For the states experiencing further conflicts and for civilians in the *Hinterland*, the railway was a serious threat. In fact, travelling soldiers posed serious disciplinary problems. This became evident as early as late 1918 when, alongside the soldiers' journeys back home, fights for the main railway knots occurred. In railway stations, fights took place repeatedly in a tense atmosphere. The so-called anabasis of the Czechoslovak legions across Russia started with an unexpected fight on a railway station and culminated with that unit's control over the whole length of the Siberian line. Extreme as it was, it was just one of many similar incidents. In the autumn of 1918 in Kharkiv, the formally allied Western Ukrainians and Russian Whites, resting in trains on parallel tracks, started to shoot at each other without a particular reason and had to be immediately brought apart from

---

35 Pavla Horáková and Jiří Kamen, *Přišel befel od císaře pana. Polní pošta–příběhy Čechů za první světové války* (Prague: Argo, 2015), 268–70.
36 Reinhard Nachtigal, "Krasnyj Desant: Das Gefecht an der Mius-Bucht. Ein unbeachtetes Kapitel der deutschen Besatzung Südrußlands 1918," *Jahrbücher für Geschichte Osteuropas* 53, no. 2 (2005): 240–43.
37 "Komunikat z 9 stycznia 1919 roku," in *O niepodległą i granice*, 1:16–17.
38 "Komunikat z 1 lutego 1919 roku," in *O niepodległą i granice*, 1:44.

the station in opposite directions. One of the Ukrainian participants in the clash recalled the event:

> Then, the riflemen in our *sotnya* decided to take matters into their own hands. They dragged a few Russian volunteers into our cars and beat them badly. There were corpses, too. The volunteers took a few of ours in return. Then, both sides grabbed their rifles, and a shoot-out began. My machine-gunner dragged his weapon to the door. Then, our train moved ahead and the one the volunteers were on moved back, but the machine guns had already begun firing. Both trains filled with screams of the wounded and the whistling of officers calling for ceasefire.[39]

The returnees from the new fronts were not less dangerous than the giant wave of 1918. In July 1920, the transfer of one hundred fifty Polish soldiers suffering from sexually transmitted diseases caused massive problems alongside the track to Kraków. Irrespective of the prohibition to leave the train, diseased soldiers tried to get off the train at every station. In Rzeszów, such an attempt led to a shooting with the military police.[40]

Even bigger was the danger related to new recruits travelling to the front. In Romania and Poland, their route was marked by robberies in proximity to railway stations, the victims being mostly local Jews. Profiting from train stops on their way to the front, some regiments—in Poland, primarily those from Poznań and Pomerania, where right-wing propaganda was running rampant—used them as an opportunity to pillage stores in the vicinity of railway stations. Both in the Congress Kingdom and in East Galicia, these stores were typically owned by Jews. Thus, it is rather difficult to establish which of the robberies were inspired by simple banditry and which by antisemitic impulses.

However, doubts about their motivations dissolve when considering cases when nothing to steal had been left or the transported soldiers did not go beyond the station. It was precisely under these circumstances that most assaults on Jews took place. In early 1920, the Viennese railway station in Warsaw (located

---

[39] Quotation from Grzegorz Skrukwa, *Formacje wojskowe ukraińskiej „rewolucji narodowej" 1914–1921* (Toruń: Wydawnictwo Adam Marszałek, 2008), 313.

[40] "2 lipca 1920 roku, Komunikat informacyjny (sprawy wojskowe) nr 37 (104) z okręgów warszawskiego, krakowskiego, łódzkiego, kieleckiego, pomorskiego," in *O niepodległą i granice*, vol. 2, "Raporty i komunikaty naczelnych władz wojskowych o sytuacji wewnętrznej Polski 1919–1920," ed. Marek Jabłonowski, Piotr Stawecki, and Tadeusz Wawrzyński (Warszawa–Pułtusk: Akademia Humanistyczna im. A. Gieysztora, 1999–2000), 482.

in the area now occupied by the Śródmieście railway station and the Centrum station of the Metro) provided the setting for similar actions. The culprits typically evaded punishment, even when security services became involved. Events at the Dęblin station in March 1920 followed a similar pattern: "During the anti-Jewish excesses at the Dęblin station, a military police patrol that tried to arrest the culprits was surrounded by about 60 soldiers from Greater Poland, who helped the culprits evade the pursuers. The commander of the transport did not react to these outrages."[41]

Military documents describing similar cases convey the impression that in the eyes of the culprits, anti-Jewish violence was, if not a patriotic deed, at least allowed and justifiable. The view of some of the Polish soldiers passing through the Kovel's railway junction in March 1920 was similar:

> A group of soldiers surrounded a Jew and proceeded to cut his beard. The commanding officer at the square, Cpt. Witkowski, who hastened to the city when he heard of the commotion, arrived when the act was already complete. Yet he managed to arrest the culprits and lead them to the city commandant's headquarters. One of the soldiers refused to comply, then cast off his coat and jacket, stood against a wall and shouted at the others that he would rather be shot than go to jail over a Jew. Once he was arrested and incarcerated at the headquarters, however, a crowd of soldiers soon gathered, demanding his release. The order for the release came too late; by then, the guards were overpowered, the doors knocked down, and the prisoners set free. Captain Witkowski, who tried to prevent these acts from being perpetrated, was shot at. A military relief force was terrorized by the overwhelming number of troopers from Poznań, who turned to the recently arrived commandant of the city with a request to hand Jewish officers over to them. After much persuasion and effort from the commandant, the chief of the regional deputation, and several officers, the mass of agitated soldiers was talked out of enacting a Jewish pogrom.[42]

---

41 "11 marca 1920, Komunikat informacyjny nr 18 (85) z okręgów warszawskiego, kieleckiego, lubelskiego, lwowskiego, krakowskiego, poznańskiego, pomorskiego," in *O niepodległą i granice*, 2:390–91.

42 "8 kwietnia 1920, Komunikat informacyjny nr 21 (88) z okręgów warszawskiego, łódzkiego, lwowskiego, poznańskiego," in *O niepodległą i granice*, 2:401.

The emotions accompanying such outbursts of anti-Jewish violence were rooted in the same mechanisms of moral economy that regulated social unrest analyzed by Ota Konrád in the early months of the Czechoslovak statehood.[43] In the eyes of the perpetrators, all of this was about justice.

## Violence on the Commuter Trains

This railway-related menace could be—and, indeed, has been—seen as a coincidence, given that most of the towns in this area were inhabited by large Jewish communities who dominated in petty trade. However, quite a lot of antisemitic attacks took place under rather different circumstances—in commuter or even long-distance trains. Jewish deputies of the first Polish parliament received dozens of letters from Jewish countrymen who had been victims or witnesses to appalling instances of military violence against Jews either in trains or railway stations. Thanks to the documents collected by Jewish representatives and their parliamentary speeches, we now know how those assaults looked:

> The Orthodox Representatives' Club was visited by Srul Rotbard of 33 Gęsia St. in Warsaw, who asked that the following be recorded: Today, on March 25 [1920], at 6 am, I arrived on foot to the railway station in Łochów (Warsaw-Petersburg line) and acquired a second-class ticket. As I made my way into the car, an officer of Haler's Army [the "Blue Army" commanded by Józef Haller] denied me entry. I was thus forced to find a spot in one of the overcrowded third-class cars. The journey went by uneventfully until the Targówek station, because the ticket inspector closed the car we were in. For reasons unknown, as he left, the inspector left the door ajar; this fact was exploited by the soldiers, who marched into the cars and beat Jewish passengers nearly to death, cut their beards with knives, knocked me about viciously and cut off my beard—my heart aches—and cut off another Jew's beard and beat him very badly. We cried for help, but none of the railway guards bothered to show up.[44]

---

43   Ota Konrád, "Jenseits der Nation? Kollektive Gewalt in den böhmischen Ländern 1914–1918," *Bohemia* 56, no. 2 (2016): 328–61.
44   Fund 3, File. 180: Documents on national minorities, 1919–1920, p. 22, Archiwum Akt Nowych (Archive of Modern Acts hereafter cited as AAN), Warsaw.

The primary locations for these assaults were the most crowded railway lines and train stations. In their accounts, the victims repeatedly mention places like Warsaw, Siedlce, Kovel', and Koluszki, a major railway junction near Łódź. It was in the latter that Mindla Ehrlich had the dubious pleasure of crossing paths with Polish soldiers on their way to the east:

> In the lobby in Koluszki the Jews, especially the beardy ones, were beaten by soldiers. They were beaten and their beards were cut with scissors ... This took a couple of hours without any break. The same story repeated itself when we got off in Skierniewice in the lobby ... In Skierniewice the Rabbi of Wolbórz was heavily offended. The soldiers wanted to tear his beard with their bare hands. They also beat Jews at the counters without respect for age or gender. When I tried to speak for the Rabbi from Wolbórz I also got a punch in my face.[45]

Acts of violence against the Jews perpetrated by regular soldiers of the Polish army far from the front pushed the limits of violence further than any other phenomena described above—these events could no more be described as random incidents, casualties, or destruction immediately connected with the context of fighting. William W. Hagen notes that the attacks on travelling Jews had deeper, symbolic roots. As he notes, "Jewish presence in this setting of technological modernity—and of public community and individual equality within passenger classes—clearly unleashed aggression."[46] In this context, he quotes another report offering a rare opportunity to see the emotions of by-standers (and co-offenders):

> The peasant sitting next to me shouted from the train window to a passing Haller's soldier: "a Jew's sitting here!" The soldier jumped into the train, demanding that I get out immediately. A lady asked the soldier not to beat anyone in the train, whereupon the soldier pulled me from it. Fleeing, I ran through the fence, trying to get to town. The train-station guard chasing me demanded I return; otherwise he threatened to shoot. Running, I got caught on the barbed-wire, ripping all my clothes: pants, linen, overcoat.[47]

---

45   Extract from the Ehrich's testimony, 15 March 1920, Fund 3, File 180, p. 27, AAN.
46   William W. Hagen, *Anti-Jewish Violence in Poland, 1914–1920* (Cambridge: Cambridge University Press, 2018), 318.
47   Ibid., 318.

These "railway pranks" could not be easily explained with the counteraccusations of Jewish treason or collaboration with the Bolsheviks. Together with other acts of systematic antisemitic violence they posed a grave danger to the fundamental values of the newly born state, to law and order.

The Jewish elites were aware of this challenge, and they reacted both through their parliamentary representation and other channels. Their grievances found perhaps the most powerful expression in an address to the Head of State and the Polish government by a group of Jewish social activists from Lviv, a few months after the pogrom of November 1 1918. The short span of time—nearly three months from the eruption of anti-Jewish violence—clearly influenced the arguments of the Jewish charitable committee members:

> Where does all this lead? Is this systematic barbarism ever going to end? We are on the brink of the gravest misfortune ever to have visited a major social group; we are completely powerless in the face of the tyranny of unruly troopers and a kind of pathological mood of the local Polish opinion . . . We are no strangers in this land, no Helots nor slaves; we are as autochthonous as Poles and Ruthenians and we do not intend to become the slaves of any of the nationalities living here.[48]

If such appeals fell on deaf ears, other arguments spoke even to antisemites among the military and civilian elites. Antisemitic violence in Poland in general and brutal attacks on Jewish passengers in particular were reported and commented upon by international media. The Central Union of German Citizens of Jewish Faith (*Central-Verein deutscher Staatsbürger jüdischen Glaubens*) and the weekly *Allgemeine Zeitung des Judenthums* were probably the most vocal representatives of the victims.[49] In the long run, the state could not tolerate this.

---

48  Letter by the Jewish Relief Committee in Lvov, 26 January 1919, Fund 3, File 179, p. 187, AAN.
49  William W. Hagen, "Murder in the East: German-Jewish Liberal Reactions to Anti-Jewish Violence in Poland and Other East European Countries," *Central European History* 34, no. 1 (2001): 1–30.

# Conclusion

Irrespective of widespread perception, in 1918–1920 East Central European rail transportation and railway stations represented veritable foci of violence. As in a drop of water, the strains of violence on the tracks reflected the wider picture of bloodlands in miniature. Some of these pictures were obviously exaggerated or not representative of the situation in inner regions. Nonetheless, this story holds true. There is no doubt that mass migrations disrupted the states at their very early stages. The war spread along the main railway routes, and in the *Hinterland* it was railway, again, that contributed to the spread of violence including antisemitic violence. While in general it would be an overstatement to call the post-1918 conflicts in East Central Europe a total war, the railway made it almost omnipresent, at least in proximity to the rail. Without railways, such an immediate transfer of violence from the battlefield, a conquered town, or a burning *shtetl* onto the seemingly peaceful *Hinterland* would have been impossible or at least much slower.

Most of the existing research on the role of the railway in World War I focuses on the regular war. Imperial armies in East Central Europe did not deviate much from the Western Front in that respect, with railways connecting the front to the rear and keeping armies fed and supplied. The year 1918 opened a new chapter. First, the war itself moved virtually onto the tracks. Small and middle-size detachments fought along railway lines, main battles as at Nové Zámky, took place for main transport hubs, affecting nearby living civilians and disrupting civilian transport. Skirmishes were fought for the main railway stations, as in Vilnius, and over locomotives and wagons in sparsely populated areas of Belarus and Ukraine. The war came even closer when groups of soldiers travelling from or to the front assaulted civilians on station platforms and in trains. In Poland, such acts were particularly widespread, and they affected the country's center as much as its peripheries. The railway was the main channel through which a wave of anti-Jewish violence spread throughout the country. Thus, its role changed decisively. While still supplying the army on the front—despite all the obstacles caused by the state of infrastructure—it helped to transfer violence from the war area into the *Hinterland*. If, prior to 1918 railway could be compared to blood vessels helping to keep alive the war effort, in post-1918 East Central Europe it started to push infected blood back to the heart of the country.

# Bibliography

Balkelis, Tomas. *War, Revolution, and Nation-Making in Lithuania, 1914–1923*. Oxford: Oxford University Press, 2018.

Böhler, Jochen. *Civil War in Central Europe, 1918–1921: The Reconstruction of Poland*. Oxford: Oxford University Press, 2020.

Borodziej, Włodzimierz, and Maciej Górny. *Forgotten Wars: Central and Eastern Europe, 1912–1916*. Cambridge: Cambridge University Press, 2021.

Bremm, Klaus-Jürgen. *Armeen unter Dampf. Die Eisenbahnen in der europäischen Kriegsgeschichte 1871–1918*. Hövelhof: DGEG Medien, 2013.

Burnagel, Stanisław. *Wspomnienia wojenne intendenta dywizji*. Warsaw: Główna Drukarnia Wojskowa, 1934.

Carsten, F. L. *Revolution in Central Europe 1918–1919*. London: Maurice Temple Smith Ltd., 1972.

Creveld, Martin van. *Supplying War: Logistics from Wallenstein to Patton*. Cambridge: Cambridge University Press, 1977.

Cvetkovski, Roland: "Railways (Russian Empire)." In *1914–1918: International Encyclopedia of the First World War*. https://encyclopedia.1914-1918-online.net/article/railways_russian_empire.

Freeman, Michael. "The railway as cultural metaphor 'What kind of railway history?' revisited." *The Journal of Transport History* 20, no. 2 (1999): 160–67.

Fudakowski, Jan. *Ułańskie wspomnienia z roku 1920*. Lublin: Towarzystwo Naukowe KUL, 2005.

Gatrell, Peter. *A whole empire walking. Refugees in Russia during World War I*. Bloomington: Indiana University Press, 2011.

———. "War, Population Displacement and State Formation in the Russian Borderlands, 1914–1924." In *Homelands: War, Population and Statehood in Eastern Europe and Russia, 1918–1924*, edited by Nick Baron and Peter Gatrell, 10–34. London: Anthem Press, 2004.

Gregory, Adrian. "Railway stations." In *A Cultural History*. Vol. 2 of *Capital Cities at War. Paris, London, Berlin 1914–1919*, edited by Jay Winter and Jean-Louis Robert, 23–56. Cambridge: Cambridge University Press, 2007.

Hagen, William W. "Murder in the East: German-Jewish Liberal Reactions to Anti-Jewish Violence in Poland and Other East European Countries." *Central European History* 34, no. 1 (2001): 1–30.

———. *Anti-Jewish Violence in Poland, 1914–1920*. Cambridge: Cambridge University Press, 2018.

Hamilton, J. A. B. *Britain's Railways in World War 1*. London: George Allen and Unwin Ltd., 1967.

Hehn, Jürgen von. "Der baltische Freiheitskrieg – Umrisse und Probleme 1918–1920." In *Von den baltischen Provinzen zu den baltischen Staaten. Beiträge zur Entstehungsgeschichte der Republiken Estland und Lettland 1918–1920*, edited by Jürgen von Hahn, Hans von Rimscha, and Helmuth Weiss, 1–42. Marburg: Herder-Institut, 1977.

Heywood, Anthony. "Spark of revolution? Railway disorganisation, freight traffic and Tsarist Russia's war effort, July 1914–March 1917." *Europe-Asia Studies* 65, no. 4 (2013): 753–72.

Higgins, Jeremy. *Great War Railwaymen Britain's Railway Company Workers at War 1914–1918*. Chicago: Uniform Press, 2014.

Horáková, Pavla, and Jiří Kamen. *Přišel befel od císaře pana. Polní pošta–příběhy Čechů za první světové války*. Praha: Argo, 2015.

Jedlicki, Jerzy. *Świat zwyrodniały. Lęki i wyroki krytyków nowoczesności*. Warsaw: Wydawnictwo Sic!, 2000.
Karuka, Manu. *Empire's Tracks: Indigenous Nations, Chinese Workers, and the Transcontinental Railroad*. Oakland: University of California Press, 2019.
Knipping, Andreas. *Eisenbahnen im Ersten Weltkrieg*. Freiburg: EK-Verlag, 2004.
Konrád, Ota. "Jenseits der Nation? Kollektive Gewalt in den böhmischen Ländern 1914–1918." *Bohemia* 56, no. 2 (2016): 328–61.
Leib, Peter. "Aufstandsbekämpfung im strategischen Dilemma. Die deutsche Besatzung in der Ukraine 1918." In *Die Besatzung der Ukraine 1918. Historischer Kontext–Forschungsstand–wirtschaftliche und soziale Folgen*, edited by Wolfram Dornik and Stefan Karner, 111–39. Graz, Wien, Klagenfurt: Verein zur Förderung der Forschung von Folgen nach Konflikten und Kriegen, 2008.
Leidinger, Hannes, and Verena Moritz. *Gefangenschaft, Revolution, Heimkehr. Die Bedeutung der Kriegsgefangenenproblematik für die Geschichte des Kommunismus in Mittel- und Osteuropa 1917–1920*. Wien: Vandenhoeck Ruprecht Verlage, 2003.
Marung, Steffi, Matthias Middell, and Uwe Müller. "Multiple Territorialisierungsprozesse in Ostmitteleuropa." In *Handbuch einer transnationalen Geschichte Ostmitteleuropas. Band I. Von der Mitte des 19. Jahrhunderts bis zum Ersten Weltkrieg*, edited by Frank Hadler and Matthias Middell, 448–52. Göttingen: Vandenhoeck & Ruprecht, 2017.
McMurray, Jonathan S. *Distant Ties: Germany, the Ottoman Empire, and the Construction of the Baghdad Railway*. Westport: Praeger, 2001.
McMeekin, Sean. *The Berlin-Baghdad Express: The Ottoman Empire and Germany's Bid for World Power, 1898–1918*. Cambridge, MA: Harvard University Press, 2010.
Mitchell, Allan. *The Great Train Race: Railways and the Franco-German Rivalry*. New York: Berghahn Books, 2000.
Moraczewski, Jędrzej. *Przewrót w Polsce*. Warsaw: Muzeum Historii Polski w Warszawie, 2015.
Motta, Giuseppe. "The Great War and the Jewish Refugees in Russia: Research in the Documents of the Joint Distribution Committee." In *Unknown Fronts: The "Eastern Turn" in First World War History*, edited by Elka Agoston-Nikolova et al., 183–206. Groningen: Nederland Rusland Centrum, 2017.
Nachtigal, Reinhard. "Krasnyj Desant: Das Gefecht an der Mius-Bucht. Ein unbeachtetes Kapitel der deutschen Besatzung Südrußlands 1918." *Jahrbücher für Geschichte Osteuropas* 53 no. 2 (2005): 221–46.
*O niepodległą i granice*. Vol.1, "Komunikaty Oddziału III Naczelnego Dowództwa Wojska Polskiego 1919–1921," edited by Marek Jabłonowski and Adam Koseski. Warszawa–Pułtusk: Akademia Humanistyczna im. A. Gieysztora, 1999.
*O niepodległą i granice*. Vol. 2, "Raporty i komunikaty naczelnych władz wojskowych o sytuacji wewnętrznej Polski 1919–1920," edited by Marek Jabłonowski, Piotr Stawecki, and Tadeusz Wawrzyński. Warszawa–Pułtusk: Akademia Humanistyczna im. A. Gieysztora, 1999–2000.
Petr, František Stanislav. *Pod rakouskou orlicí a českým lvem*. Praha: Gasset, 2015.
Phillipps, Christopher. *Civilian Specialists at War. Britain's Transport Experts and the First World War*. London: University of London Press, 2020.
Pryłucki, Cwi. *Wspomnienia (1905–1939)*. Warszawa: Archiwum Ringelbluma, 2015.
Rhodes, Benjamin D. "The Anglo-American Railroad War at Archangel, 1918–1919." *Railroad History* 151 (1984): 70–83.

Rudnicki, Szymon, and Jarosław Gorliński. "The Vilna Pogrom of 19–21 April 1919." *Polin. Studies in Polish Jewry* 33 (2021): 463–94.

Sierakowska, Katarzyna. *Śmierć, wygnanie, głód w dokumentach osobistych. Ziemie polskie w latach Wielkiej Wojny 1914–1918*. Warsaw: Instytut Historii PAN, 2015.

Skrukwa, Grzegorz. *Formacje wojskowe ukraińskiej „rewolucji narodowej" 1914–1921*. Toruń: Wydawnictwo Adam Marszałek, 2008.

Stevenson, David. "War by Timetable? The Railway Race before 1914." *Past & Present* 162 (1999): 163–94.

Stone, Norman. "Die Mobilmachung der österreichisch-ungarischen Armee 1914." *Militärgeschichtliche Mitteilungen* 16, no. 2 (1974): 68–77, 83.

Thompson, Julian. *The Lifeblood of War: Logistics in Armed Conflict*. Oxford: Macmillan, 1991.

Trotsky, Leon. *My Life: An Attempt at an Autobiography*. New York: Pathfinder Press, 1970.

Watson, Alexander. *Ring of Steel: Germany and Austria-Hungary in World War I*. New York: Basic Books, 2014.

Wolmar, Christian. *Engines of War: How Wars Were Won & Lost on the Railways*. New York: Atlantic Books, 2010.

Wragg, David. *Wartime on the Railways*. Stroud: The History Press, 2006.

Zabecki, David T. "Railroads and the Operational Level of War in the German 1918 Offensives." In *Finding Common Ground: New Directions in First World War Studies*, edited by Jennifer D. Keene and Michael S. Neiberg, 161–86. Leiden: Brill, 2011.

Zaloga, Stephen J. *Armored Trains*. Osprey: Bloomsbury, 2008.

Zhvanko, Liubov. *Bizhentsi pershoi svitovoi viini. Ukrains'kii vimir, 1914–1918 rr.* Kharkiv: Virovets' A. P. 'Apostrof', 2012.

CHAPTER 8

# Beyond Comparison? The Challenges of Applying Comparative Historical Research to Violence

## Julia Eichenberg

Comparing forms of violence is mined territory. Until now, genocide and Holocaust studies have been most progressive in introducing comparative studies while at the same time being the battlefield of the most ardent disputes over the feasibility—and ethics—of comparison. Recent escalations include the debate about the possibility to compare the crimes of National Socialism and Communism–Socialism and the 2021 debate about Australian historian's Dirk Moses' book "The problems of genocide," discussing the Shoah in the context of colonial mass murders.[1] While the question of the uniqueness of the Shoah is a topic in itself, there seems to be an overall challenge in comparing violence. How to apply measures when dealing with transgressions, how to handle motivations, how to compare perpetrators, bystanders, or victims?

The last fifteen years have seen an increased interest in the mostly neglected history of violence during and after World War I in East Central Europe. New approaches have pointed out that instead of reading both as distinctive units (a world war versus regional border wars by mostly new national states), both conflicts are intertwined and, in many cases, share protagonists, strategies, and

---

1   Dirk A. Moses, *The Problems of Genocide. Permanent Security and the Language of Transgression* (Oxford: Oxford University Press, 2021); Jörg Baberowski and Anselm Doering-Manteuffel, *Ordnung durch Terror. Gewaltexzeß und Vernichtung im nationalsozialistischen und stalinistischen Imperium* (Bonn: Dietz, 2006).

tactics. Most importantly, their motivations were mostly intertwined, as issues central to the emergence of violence between 1918–1923 resulted from structural challenges. Some were raised by, and some not sufficiently settled by World War I. The (re)emergence of national states accelerated transgressions because the rise of nationalism was linked to the alleged need and definite political will of who would belong to a future nation and who would not. As so often in history, the construction of a common identity was inextricably linked to the exclusion of minority groups.

Furthermore, a certain openness to violence as a legitimate tool stemmed from the conviction of many individuals involved that this was a "tabula rasa" moment which offered a once-in-a-lifetime chance to achieve certain interests. The idea of legitimized violence in the name of new national states was, of course, no new invention, but simply the adaptation of a sometimes violent rule of the old empires the region had been submitted to.[2] Accordingly, it is useful to follow new attempts to integrate these years in an extended history of the world war, as suggested by the "Greater War" concept[3] and the integrative understanding of the Eastern European wars as introduced by many of the authors of this book.[4]

Comparing different case studies seems like the logical step to engage with these questions. By comparing them, we can find out what is a widespread phenomenon of the time and what is a particularity of the region; we can engage with European or global factors (for example, the war experience) and measure them against the specific impact (for example, economic factors, mobilizing warlords, borderlands, and so on).[5] All these aspects give us good reason to make comparative history the norm in writing a history of violence. At the same time, while comparative history is thriving in other fields of history (for example, institutions, social movements, and so on), only a few methodological historical comparisons exist, and many projects have been abandoned or adjusted.[6]

---

2 Compare Galtung's definition of structural violence: Johan Galtung, *Strukturelle Gewalt. Beiträge zur Friedens- und Konfliktforschung* (Reinbek bei Hamburg: Rororo, 1982).
3 Compare the "The Greater War" Series with Oxford University Press, edited by Robert Gerwarth, and John Horne, eds., *War in Peace: Paramilitary Violence in Europe after the Great War* (Oxford: Oxford University Press, 2012).
4 Recent central publications include Tomas Balkelis, *War, revolution, and nation-making in Lithuania, 1914–1923* (Oxford: Oxford University Press, 2018), Jochen Böhler, *Civil War in Central Europe, 1918–1921: The Reconstruction of Poland* (Oxford: Oxford University Press, 2019); Włodzimierz Borodziej and Maciej Górny, *Der vergessene Weltkrieg: Europas Osten 1912–1923* (Darmstadt: wbg Theiss, 2018).
5 Ideological and socioeconomic factors were also often intertwined, as pointed out in this volume by Béla Bodó.
6 Based on personal observations.

Why is it so difficult to apply comparative history to violence? To discuss this question, I first summarize what comparative history was and what it is today. I then take Eastern Europe of 1914–1923 as a specific example of the challenges of comparing violence. I also discuss alternative approaches, like a transnational, or a *histoire croisée* perspective.

This chapter will pick up on a range of key questions defined in this volume, which might be summarized under three headings. The first focus is on structural circumstances (revolutions, shortages, and so on) and includes long-term trajectories, summarized here as "society and structure." Secondly, a range of questions engages with perpetrators and victims, which I will summarize under the heading "Identities" (including both social background and identification). The third set of questions deals with practices and types of violence. In the second part of this article, I will use these three sets as examples to discuss the merits and challenges of the comparative or transnational study of violence.

## Historical Comparison—Sub-Discipline or Perspective?

For Marc Bloch, comparing was one of the three main methodological aspects of the historian (summarized by Peter Schöttler as 1. *voir–découvrir–interroger* (see–discover–question); 2. *comparer* (compare); 3. *comprendre–expliquer* (understand–explain).[7] These were contrasted to the mere activity of collecting or telling of facts (*collectionner / raconter*), which to Bloch had no analytical value.

Historical comparison was at the same time one of the important steps to escape a too narrow focus of national history, yet it was and still is mostly inseparably linked to national history as an analytical framework. The approach of the classic comparative history analysis is to define two entities (often national states, sometimes cities, less commonly social groups, very rarely ideas) and to compare them during a specific experience (for example, war) or development/ change (for example, industrialization). Kaelble even defined the comparison between nations as the gold standard of historical comparison.[8] The most common variation is the synchronic comparison, comparing two entities at the same

---

7   Quoted in Peter Schöttler, "Marc Bloch. Die Lehren der Geschichte und die Möglichkeit historischer Prognosen," *Österreichische Zeitschrift für Geschichtswissenschaft* 16, no. 2 (2005): 104–25, 110.
8   "Historische Vergleiche sind üblicherweise Vergleiche zwischen Nationen"; Hartmut Kaelble, *Der Historische Vergleich. Eine Einführung zum 19. und 20. Jahrhundert* (Frankfurt am Main-New York: Campus, 1999), 17.

time (for example, three cities during World War I).⁹ Less common is an anachronic comparison, which compares two entities at two different times or maybe one entity at different points in time.¹⁰

Maybe not surprisingly, so far, the high time of historical comparison was closely linked to the high time of social history in the 1980s and 1990s. Social history and historical comparison seemed like two birds of a feather: social history produced a history backed by numbers and statistics, but mostly referring to closed containers: cities, villages, countries, regions, nations. The closed containers as well as the seemingly neutral statistics provided a perfect starting point for comparison, questioning, and testing how far the results were unique or representative. Historical comparison, on the other hand, gave more meaning to social history case studies. Historical comparison thrived and was a welcome subject in particular with regard to classical PhD projects: to provide a German history approach with a European twist, mostly comparing it to similar events in British or French history.¹¹

In Germany, historical comparison was introduced by and is still closely linked to the names of Hartmut Kaelble, Jürgen Kocka, and Heinz-Gerhard Haupt, all three of whom were born during the war (1941, 1940, and 1943, respectively), had clearly defined interest in social history, studied and completed their PhDs at Freie Universität Berlin while also spending time abroad, and were Francophile and decidedly pro-European. Comparative history to them seemed like a way to broaden the horizon and go beyond national history, asking for more general phenomena, while not completely questioning the nation as such, which was still the backbone of their approach to writing history. Kaelble used the comparative method to explore social inequality; Kocka analyzed worker's movements; Haupt discussed class.¹²

---

9   Jay Winter and Jean-Louis Robert, *Capital Cities at War. Paris, London, Berlin 1914–1919* (Cambridge: Cambridge University Press, 1997).
10  Sebastian Conrad, *Auf der Suche nach der verlorenen Nation: Geschichtsschreibung in Westdeutschland und Japan, 1945–1960* (Göttingen: Vandenhoeck & Ruprecht, 1999). Wencke Meteling, *Ehre, Einheit, Ordnung. Preußische und französische Städte und ihre Regimenter im Krieg, 1870/71 und 1914–1919* (Baden-Baden: Nomos, 2010).
11  For an overview, see: Hartmut Kaelble, "Historischer Vergleich," Version: 1.0, in *Docupedia-Zeitgeschichte*, last modified August 14, 2012 DOI: http://dx.doi.org/10.14765/zzf.dok.2.271.v1.
12  Their first big publications using this approach were: Hartmut Kaelble, Social *Mobility in the 19th and 20th Centuries: Europe and America in Comparative Perspective* (Leamington Spa: Berg Publishers, 1985) (German edition Göttingen: Vandenhoeck & Ruprecht, 1983); Jürgen Kocka, ed., *Europäische Arbeiterbewegung im 19. Jahrhundert. Deutschland, Österreich, England und Frankreich im Vergleich* (Göttingen: Vandenhoeck & Ruprecht, 1983); Geoffrey

The ascent of cultural history on the one hand and the increasing deconstruction of statistics in social history on the other hand questioned and weakened this formerly winning pairing. Case studies could no longer rely on units or containers, as these were now increasingly regarded as artificially constructed. Cultural history introduced ambiguity; deconstructing statistics showed that social history was messier than it pretended to be. A disillusion in social history and comparative history alike ran parallel to a rise in interest in transnational history, histoire croisée and, finally, global history. Leaving the latter aside for a moment, transnational history and histoire croisée were able to accommodate cultural history into their analysis, as well as a history of transfer of ideas and values, transfer of practices.[13] All of these were (and are) difficult to grasp with a historical comparison approach. They were also less demanding in their discipline. Historical comparison had insisted on being a discipline, developing its own methodology and vocabulary. Transnational history, on the other hand, often insisted on being a perspective rather than a methodology, thus remaining even more open to interpretation and adaptation.[14]

Many arguments support the impact of transnational history and histoire croisée for the analysis of violence in our region and time period. A case in point is the detailed portrayal of World War I in Eastern Europe by Maciej Górny and Włodzimierz Borodziej in *Nasza Wojna* and others.[15] These approaches focus on the similar phenomenon of a broader region, on the transfer of knowledge and practices, on joint experiences and underline the limits of a national approach which neglects phenomena dominating a broader region. However, comparisons should not be ruled out too easily. Selecting the comparative object, defining units for comparison, choosing a synchronous or diachronous comparative approach can help to provide further insight into the research question. To give but one example, working in a collaborative research group on paramilitary violence after World War I, consisting of a selection of case studies on different national and regional occurrences of violence, provided us with a comparison and a foil against which to check our respective findings.

---

Crossick and Heinz-Gerhard Haupt, *The Petite Bourgeoisie en Europe 1780–1914. Entreprise, Family and Independence* (London: Routledge, 2016) (German edition 1998).
13 Michael Werner and Bénédicte Zimmermann, eds. *De la comparaison à l'histoire croisée* (Paris: Seuil, 2004).
14 Patricia Clavin, "Defining Transnationalism," *Contemporary European History* 14, no. 4 (2005): 421–39; Kiran Klaus Patel, "An Emperor without Clothes? The Debate about Transnational History Twenty-Five Years On," *Histoire@Politique* 26 (mai-août 2015), accessed August 2, 2021, http://www.histoire-politique.fr.
15 Borodziej and Górny, *Der vergessene Weltkrieg*.

At the same time, working in these contexts seemed to prove that comparative research of violence, while fruitful in discussion, was challenging to develop a coherent narrative. Some have persisted and managed to produce monographs comparing different case studies,[16] others have either completely abandoned one of the two comparative case studies and focused solely on one or several aspects of the comparison for articles but abandoned the idea of a monograph on the topic. There are several reasons for this with regard to history in general, but, as pointed out above, even more so when researching violence. Cultural history, relying more on concepts and ideas, seems more difficult to compare than social history, dealing with statistics and numbers. As both military history, international relations, history of violence, and the history of international law are increasingly interpreted in a "new," usually meaning more cultural way—and rightly so—this also adds complexity to the opportunity of comparison.

Historical comparison might have seemed outdated for some time, overcome by a transnational, entangled, or global approach, but has recently been rediscovered to great avail.[17] Rather than the implied evolution of approaches (which would probably read national history, comparative history, transnational history, global history), we should reconsider the strengths and weaknesses of each approach depending on what we want to enquire.

## Comparing Violence in Eastern Europe, 1914–1923

Focusing on violence and the crisis of governance in East Central Europe during 1914–1923 means scrutinizing violence in newly emerged national states in the aftermath of a world war and on the territory of dissolving empires. The agents of violence are military formations on a broad range from state to improvised, including banditry, partisans, military, and paramilitary forces as well as anti-state and pro-state paramilitary formations. There were formations under leadership and those who run wild, those well-equipped and those with leather wrapped around their feet for lack of shoes, carrying guns and ammunition which does not necessarily work together. Most of this violence has been committed under the guise of national (or ethnic) interests, committed for a

---

16 Like the excellent comparison of regional histories of violence in Ireland and Poland by Tim Wilson, *Frontiers of Violence: Conflict and Identity in Ulster and Upper Silesia, 1918–1922* (Oxford: Oxford University Press, 2010).

17 Angelika Epple, Walter Erhart and Johannes Grave, eds., *Practices of Comparing. Towards a New Understanding of a Fundamental Human Practice* (Bielefeld: Transcript, 2020).

seemingly greater good. Occasionally, violence was committed on a local level amongst communities, even neighbors, covering up for interests much more personal than expected. The hesitation to compare violence is an understandable human threshold, trying to keep the uniqueness of human suffering.

When trying to analyze the origins of paramilitary violence in the first quarter of the twentieth century, central to the discussion is its connection to World War I. Was it a prolonging of fighting with other means? Was it triggered by the war experience of the soldiers? Was it all about the Russian Revolution and failing empires in the East? What made this time so much more ruthless towards civilians than the preceding years? There are several frequent theories to explain the emergence and rise of paramilitary violence. To understand their concomitance, and their simultaneous right to exist, one must reflect on the geographic case studies which brought them into being.

## 1. Structure

Engaging with the structural circumstances of violence means engaging with the framework, the setting, which spurs transgressions. This is, firstly, state-related: the stability of the state, the control of the monopoly of force, and power of independent legislation, jurisdiction, and execution have an immediate effect on whether violent transgressions will take place (or whether they can be contained). Other structural circumstances include economic or social factors like food shortages or disputes over land ownership, as well as ideological factors like rising nationalism, mobilized religion, or ideological belief in radical revolutions. All chapters of this book mention socioeconomic hardship, caused by general living conditions, the experience of war, or established injustice because of land distribution under the old regimes, as destabilizing societies and laying ground for the rise of violence. These conditions are crucial in whether violence can emerge, whether it can spread or be contained, and how it can be ended: how society can be reconciled and what kind of long-term legacies persist.

Political and military events during World War I led to a breakdown of imperial and state authority which in its turn created a power vacuum. This was the case in vast regions over the globe, but most dominantly so in Eastern Europe, turning it into "a transnational zone of paramilitary violence."[18] Within this power vacuum left by crumbling empires and failing states, violent actors and groups

---

18 Robert Gerwarth, "The Central European Counter-Revolution: Paramilitary Violence in Germany, Austria, and Hungary after the Great War," *Past and Present* 200 (2008): 177.

took power into their own hands, profiting from lacking state control in military as well as political terms. This was especially true in imperial "shatter-zones," regions at the edge of empires with mixed population.[19] While reducing paramilitary violence after 1918 to a simple prolongation of the World War would be wrong, the war certainly provided fertile soil for the rapid emergence and spiraling of violence in many regions.[20] During the postwar period, in the newly emerging national states, governance and/or the lack of it was central to the development of violent transgressions. While some countries (like Czechoslovakia) managed the transfer to the postwar period not without military conflict, but overall did not see a rise of violence, other countries were less successful in maintaining a state monopoly of violence—or successfully controlling the military in their execution of state violence.[21]

The end of World War I, with its revolutions and tumbling empires, had given rise to the idea of a *tabula rasa*, of maps being drawn from scratch, of nations emerging, of lands being there just to be seized by the strongest and quickest. Pursuing their own interests, paramilitary groups employed violence, often considering themselves a para-state or even pre-state (preceding the new political and social order) force.[22] The opportunity to reshape the political as well as the demographic landscape was especially strong in the aforementioned shatter-zones, where land was contested, and different communities were in competition to gain majority and domination. It was here that violence became most easily employed by all sides striving to gain control and power. In regions of ethnically and religiously mixed population, the spiral of violence rapidly accelerated and could take the form of pogroms and purges. Only reinstating a state

---

Robert Gerwarth and John Horne, "The Great War and Paramilitarism in Europe, 1917–23," *Contemporary European History* 19, no. 3 (2010): 267–73.

19  See Julia Eichenberg and John Paul Newman, "Introduction: Aftershocks. Violence in Dissolving Empires after the First World War" in *Contemporary European History* 19, no. 3 (2010): 183–94; Omer Bartov and Eric D., Weitz, eds., *Shatterzone of empires. Coexistence and violence in the German, Habsburg, Russian, and Ottoman borderlands* (Bloomington: Indiana University Press, 2013).

20  Robert Gerwarth and Erez Manela, eds., *Empires at War, 1911–1923* (Oxford: Oxford University Press, 2014).

21  Political science has engaged with the question of violence in regions of remote state control, compare Teresa Koloma Beck and Klaus Schlichte, *Theorien der Gewalt zur Einführung*, 3 ed. (Hamburg: Junius, 2020); Sven Chojnacki and Fabian Namberger, "Die »neuen Kriege« im Spiegel postkolonialer Theorien und kritischer Friedensforschung: Ein Plädoyer für die Befreiung von der Last der Vereinfachung," *Zeitschrift für Friedens- und Konfliktforschung* 3, no. 2 (2014): 157–202.

22  Julia Eichenberg, "Consent, Coercion and Endurance in Eastern Europe: Poland and the Fluidity of War Experiences," in *Legacies of Violence. Eastern Europe's First World War*, ed. Jochen Böhler et al. (Munich: Oldenbourg, 2014), 235–58.

monopoly of the use of force could end this violence. Since most of these effects can be traced back to the war, the eruption of violence after 1918 has been described as an "aftershock" of World War I.[23] While in theory, clear differences exist between military warfare conducted by regular soldiers and paramilitary fighters, reality was more complicated. This was due in part to parallel timelines and to the mixed nature of some fighting formations, who differed in their self-definition and occupations. Finally, it was also due to state acceptance (or lack of control) of these paramilitary organizations.

Different timeframes have been set to describe and analyze the period of the "war after the war," as Peter Gatrell has put it. Gatrell himself referred to conflicts between 1919 and 1923 as such. Others have seen the beginning of this period in 1917, with the outbreak of the Russian Revolution, lasting either until 1922 or until 1923. End points of this period have been seen 1923, the end of conflicts produced by the Russian revolution, the end of the Irish Civil War in May 1923, or the Treaty of Lausanne of the same year, finally settling the succession of the Ottoman Empire by defining the boundaries of the new Republic of Turkey. The timeframe chosen here, from 1914 to 1923, begins with the outbreak of the war and violence almost all over the European continent, and ends in 1923 with the Treaty of Lausanne, which officially settled the post-war conflict in Turkey.[24]

While this periodization helps define postwar violence, it is only partly helpful when dealing with and trying to understand "postwar" paramilitary violence. Both the paramilitary formations and the violence did rise but did not originally emerge out of the blue after November 1918. Winston Churchill famously said, "The war of the giants is over; the wars of the pygmies have begun."[25] Looking closer, however, one realizes that the pygmies had started quarreling long before the giants cared to notice.

In most regions under what was considered foreign and/or imperial reign, elites longed for an occasion to turn the tables. "Self-determination" was a promise and hope long before Wilson as the US President introduced it as a war aim in his fourteen-point speech on 8 January 1918. In parts of Eastern Europe, for

---

23 Eichenberg and Newman, "Introduction," in *Legacies of Violence. Eastern Europe's First World War*, ed. Jochen Böhler et al. (Munich: Oldenbourg, 2014).

24 Peter Gatrell, "War after the War: Conflicts, 1919–23," in *A Companion to World War I*, ed. John Horne (Hoboken: Wiley-Blackwell, 2010), 558–75. Also book series "The Greater War, 1912–1923," edited by Robert Gerwarth (Oxford: Oxford University Press, 2018–).

25 Repeated by him after World War II, "As I observed last time, when the war of the giants is over, the war of the pygmies will begin," telegram from Winston Churchill to President Roosevelt, 18 March 1945, 20/199/76–77, Churchill Archives.

example, elites had longed for a war between the large European empires, hoping a conflict between them would break up their system of dividing the continent between them and would give room to the suppressed nations to reemerge. Erez Manela has described the excitement about the future, the restlessness inspired by Wilson's promise as "The Wilsonian Moment."[26] This is a very helpful and concise term; however, one needs to keep in mind that the Wilsonian Moment described by Manela was just the peak of a longer process of countries and people longing for self-determination. The reasons and the foundations for the violence emerging after 1918 therefore often originated in the experience of the war or in issues for which the war had served as a catalyst.

Some theories, originating from case studies in Eastern Europe and Central Eastern Europe, have focused on the impact of revolutions and counterrevolutions.[27] The Russian Revolution produced an immense number of victims due to the battles between Red and White formations, but also had a distinctive impact on other countries in Eastern and Central Eastern Europe and even beyond, raising violence in a reaction to the fear of revolution, as Horne and Gerwarth have pointed out.[28]

Historians of Russia were also first among those introducing the failed state concept theory originating in political science to explain the events in Eastern Europe. As Jörg Baberowski stresses, some of the worst excesses of violence in the twentieth century took place far from regions of urban settling. It was the absence of a central control of power that facilitated the emergence of brute force, which allowed "scrupulous perpetrators to realize their destructive and belligerent fantasies."[29] Accordingly, a "Hobbesian space" came into being, which confronted all human beings in it with the choice of being victim or perpetrator.[30] Space had its effect also in terms of topography, as often border regions, and detached settlements, close to forests, out of reach of state or police

---

26  Erez Manela, *The Wilsonian Moment: Self-Determination and the International. Origins of Anticolonial Nationalism* (New York: Oxford University Press, 2007).
27  Gatrell, "War after the War," 558–75; Robert Gerwarth, "The Central European Counterrevolution: Paramilitary Violence in Germany, Austria and Hungary after the Great War," *Past and Present* 200, no. 1 (2008): 175–209.
28  Robert Gerwarth and John Horne, "Bolshevism as Fantasy: Fear of Revolution and Counter-Revolutionary Violence, 1917–1923," in *War in Peace*, 40–51.
29  Jörg Baberowski,"Gewalt verstehen," *Zeithistorische Forschungen / Studies in Contemporary History* 5, no. 1 (2008): 5–17.
30  Felix Schnell, *Räume des Schreckens. Gewalt und Gruppenmilitanz in der Ukraine, 1905–1933* (Hamburg: Hamburger Edition, 2012).

control, were most likely to see a rise of violence.[31] Accordingly, connections like railways became central not only to communication and warfare mobilization, but also to the spread of violence.[32]

Secondly, scrutinizing the history of governance and of failed governance is inseparably linked to the history of legal systems and, in particular, of international law, humanitarian law, and criminal law. If and how societies and nations decided to legitimize or prosecute violence (in particular, against civilians, women, and minorities) is a central part of governance during the crisis. Similarly, if and whether they do so after the war, speaks of their ability to demobilize and stabilize peace. Comparative analysis of different legal cultures in the affected countries can test existing hypotheses about the impact of international law on warfare and will enhance our understanding of the period.

The focus on structural circumstances of violence seems to provide the best conditions for historical comparison, as the role of social history is central. Aspects of landownership and social conditions can be compared both in synchronic and anachronic comparison, amongst cities, regions, or nation states. Even revolutions have been successfully compared, be it to provide an overview of a certain period or to confront two specific revolutions, their ideology and their adaptation.[33] At the same time, the notion of revolution and counter-revolution is difficult to treat within national containers, as ideologies and movements rapidly spread over borders. With regard to an approach closer to a history of ideas and mobilization, historical analysis would profit from looking at transnational transfers of both.[34]

## 2. Identities and Ideologies

The second key question of analyzing violence is to focus on protagonists and their identities. Did identity or identification lead to the rise of violence and

---

31  See chapter by Vytautas Petronis, "Wartime Banditry in Lithuania, 1914–1920" in this volume.
32  See chapter by Maciej Górny, "*Eisenbahnfeldzug*. Railway war in East Central Europe" in this volume.
33  Respectively Jürgen Osterhammel, *The Transformation of the World: A Global History of the Nineteenth Century*, trans. Patrick Camiller (Princeton: Princeton University Press, 2014) and Arno J. Mayer, *The Furies: Violence and Terror in the French and Russian Revolutions* (Princeton: Princeton University Press, 2000).
34  Gerwarth and Horne, "Bolshevism as Fantasy," 40–51.

transgression of restraints? This is relevant both for self-defined as well as for attributed identities, both for perpetrators and for victims.

Analyzing identity also discusses the positioning of violent actors vis-à-vis state authorities (against state, on behalf of state, or weakness of state). Did states treat violent actors as proxies, auxiliaries, or competitors? Identities not only give us information about the perpetrators and victims, but also about their connection to the wider society and community, relating closely to the role of support and of bystanders. What was the social profiles of violent actors, what were networks of their support? Were they war veterans, newly mobilized civilians, middle class or peasants, urban or rural? Did victims stand a chance to be protected by the wider community or was violence met with tolerance or even popular support? Did violence beget violence? Did former victims become perpetrators and vice versa? Regarding long-term trajectories, we also need to ask how violence affected the identities of violent actors and victims.

Many paramilitary groups engaged in what might be described as a rather classical form of warfare, meaning that some formations identified as national armies even when they did not yet serve an independent national state. In this case, two or more rather clearly defined paramilitary formations fought each other, and to a certain extent resembled military formations or even armies in battle, in terms of the composition of the group as well as of the violence employed. In the case of the "para-state war," the paramilitary formation would be structured very close to a military formation. Because of the imperial history of the men and areas in question, "para-state" is suggested here as a useful definition of extra-military forces which considered themselves "proto-national" armies fighting to establish their own nation-state.[35]

They would usually be composed of combatants who were in possession of at least a basic equipment of arms and ammunition. At the end of World War I, people (mostly men) with some kind of battle experience had a dominant presence in Eastern European societies, with conscripts of the Russian army alone are estimated at about fifteen million.[36] They would wear uniforms or a kind of standardized clothing and often try to have some kind of signifier of the formation they belong to (armband, cap, or the like) and maybe even signifiers of ranks. Most importantly, these paramilitary formations mostly understood themselves as being legitimate forces. This belief was based on one of the

---

35 Robert Gerwarth and John Horne, "Paramilitarism in Europe after the Great War: An Introduction," in *War in Peace*, 1–18.
36 See chapter by Darius Staliūnas, "The Military Pogroms in Lithuania, 1919–1920" in this volume.

following assumptions: either they were an auxiliary formation of an existing army, or they were a formation of a dissolved army continuing battle, basing their legitimacy on experience and proper military leadership, or else they were a formation fighting for independence and the existence of a new national state. This last variation was the most frequent one to be found in the period in question. These formations drew their legitimacy from the fact that they planned to become the core of a new national army, once their national community (re)gained national independence, which was to be secured by their fighting against the existing state or against other communities competing for self-determination within the same region. This belief to be a national legitimized army motivated their actions and strengthened loyalty as well as dedication to the cause. It also seemed to legitimize all violence necessary to reach these goals, which is why these pre-state formations also frequently engaged in the other forms of violence. However, prominent examples of paramilitary groups engaging in "para-state" warfare and soldier-on-soldier battle were the following (it has to be noted that in all of the following conflict settings there were also occasions where violence afflicted civilians, which will be discussed below): the battle of Lviv between Polish and Ukrainian troops;[37] many of the battles between Red and White troops during the Russian Revolution, Yugoslav IMRO fighting the new Yugoslav army in the South, battles fought by the Legions (Polish, Czechoslovak, Croat, Jewish, and so on).

The highly heterogeneous nature of the groups and the blurred boundaries between civilian population and combatants repeatedly led to the occurrence of "irregular violence": excesses against civilians, transgressions of any code of military conduct and explosions of collective violence. Violence was used to form and to define groups; to include and to ostracize; in most cases to strengthen a national group and to externalize those who were considered no part of it.[38] In the case of foreign volunteers, as for example Scandinavians in Estonia, the combatants felt alienated from the local population which was often perceived as inferior, thus lowering moral thresholds of engaging in violence.[39]

Accordingly, different historiographical approaches have offered new perspectives on the origin of paramilitary violence. Following a history of ideas,

---

37 Polish paramilitary units in Lviv numbered between four thousand and six thousand men. There is, however, evidence, that some 'volunteers' had to be drawn at gunpoint. During the next nine months, ten thousand Polish and fifteen thousand Ukrainian soldiers were killed in battle. Both sides committed atrocities against civilians.
38 As excellently displayed in his study on Silesia and Ulster by Wilson, *Frontiers of Violence*.
39 See chapter by Mart Kudkepp, "Scandinavian Volunteers as Perpetrators of Violence and Crime in the Estonian War of Independence" in this volume.

one must consider the impact of nationalism and racism and especially the increasing conflation between "ethnic" and "civic" notions of nationality. While civic nationality, based on an inclusionary relationship with the state based on political and legal rights and obligations, was theoretically open, ethnic nationality as an exclusionary notion of kinship defined by factors such as language, religion, and descent provided arguments to exclude minorities by political and sometimes violent means.[40] In this way, many paramilitary and para-state groups saw the removal or destruction of other ethnic groups as a seemingly necessary stage in creating their national state. This nationalist violence could be directed against the communities representing the occupying power, for example German minorities in Eastern Europe.[41] Mostly, however, it turned against the Jewish communities, leading the way to a broad range of antisemitic transgressions and atrocities. Perpetrators often rightly felt that these transgressions would not be prosecuted, that violence against the Jewish communities "was permitted" at the time.[42]

Cultural history of warfare has introduced the concept of a "culture of war," militarizing whole societies and creating a mindset in which inflicting violence might seem a valid and tempting option.[43] Acts of violence could also have served to establish authority or create a sense of community, as pointed out above, by ostracizing others and bonding over the experience of committing violence. Only a process in which this culture of war was slowly dissolved, in which not only the military, but the society itself was demobilized, could end the readiness and potential to commit violence. If this process failed, or was inhibited, the rise and persistence of violence was facilitated. Defeat in war and the feeling that the end of the war and its outcomes were unjust inhibited cultural demobilization and provided fertile ground for further political radicalization—not necessarily everyone, but enough to allow violence to rise.[44]

Social historians on the other hand have focused on more mundane reasons for paramilitary violence and the collective violence often linked to it. They have stressed that in these regions tragically marked by the war years, or

---

40 Michael Mann, *The Dark Side of Democracy: Explaining Ethnic Cleansing* (Cambridge: Cambridge University Press, 2005), 10–11.
41 See chapter by Jochen Böhler, "The Polish Central Government, Regional Authorities, and Local Paramilitaries during the Battle for the Western Borderland, 1918–1921" in this volume.
42 See chapter by Staliūnas, "The Military Pogroms" in this volume.
43 John Horne, "Demobilizing the Mind: France and the Legacy of the Great War, 1919–1939," *French History and Civilization. Papers from the George Rudé Seminar* 2 (2009): 101–19.
44 Wolfgang Schivelbusch, *Culture of Defeat* (New York: Picador, 2004); Robert Gerwarth, *The Vanquished: Why the First World War Failed to End, 1917–1923* (London: Allen Lane, 2016).

socioeconomically challenged, the reasons for taking up arms could be of a very simple nature, such as "organizing" food, clothes, or shelter in order to survive.[45]

All these theories have strong points, and all have weak spots. As in most theories, they might work perfectly for a certain case study or with regard to a broader phenomenon but are less easily transferred as a general rule to different regions. Others work as long as one stays on a more general level but are challenged by individual histories of the people involved, since even though there are exceptions to every rule, sometimes the number of exceptions challenges the validity of the rule itself. Most importantly, any theory on paramilitary violence is challenged by the fact that not everyone became violent. The "theory of brutalization" argued that the long-term experience of war numbed the combatants, making them more prone to accepting violence as a legitimate tool to achieve their goals, while also excluding them from civil, democratic society, thus undermining interwar democracies. However, it overlooks the fact that many soldiers who experienced cruel violence during the war years did not continue fighting, but, on the contrary, this experience was exactly what made them invest much time and effort to fight for peace.[46] To think that a culture of defeat was the basis for continued fighting neglects that many of the troubled regions at least eventually belonged to states that were allied, and thus victorious (for example, Italy, Poland, Ireland, Serbia). At the same time, the broadening of the spectrum from states to empires has challenged the thesis that Western European states like France and Great Britain have remained completely peaceful.[47] The "failed state theory" works in many cases, but not in those where violence was directed against a government still in power (for example, Ireland, most colonial case studies) or in those cases where paramilitary violence was committed by state troops (for example, British auxiliary formations in Ireland, Palestine).

As so often, it is worthwhile to take all these theories into account and to ponder their validity with regard to each case study. All in all, the history of paramilitary violence after 1918 is a history of continuation and of new phenomena. It is the history of soldiers returning to uprooted societies in a setting where postwar conditions were less than desirable, both for material reasons as in

---

45 Jost Augusteijn, *From Public Defiance to Guerrilla Warfare: The Experience of Ordinary Volunteers in the Irish War of Independence 1916–1921* (Dublin: Irish Academic Press, 1996).
46 Based on George Mosse, *Fallen Soldiers. Reshaping the Memory of the World Wars* (Oxford: Oxford University Press, 1990), still dominant in some approaches as Ángel Alcalde, "War Veterans and the Transnational Origins of Fascism (1917–1919)," *Journal of Modern Italian Studies* 21, no. 4 (2016): 561–79, and others. This approach has, however, been mostly countered as too one-sided by many of the works cited in this article.
47 See Robert Gerwarth and Erez Manela, "Introduction," in *Empires at War*, 1–16.

terms of ideology. At the same time, the state was challenged, weak, or already failed. A promise of new national independence beckoned or might have to be defended against those neighbors who tried to ensure their own independence with violent means and at the cost of the civil population. Paramilitaries partly also emerged as "spin-off groups" of former military formations, increasingly engaging in violence and plunder, tolerated by a weak state lacking control.[48] Additionally, some sought personal gain by plundering or settling old rivalries. New combatants, mobilized by a culture of war but not yet war-weary, joined those who had nothing to go home to and who had decided to continue fighting. For all these different reasons, the temporary use of radical violence seemed an adequate choice to make the postwar expense, but sometimes also with the acceptance (or toleration) of parts of the broader civilian population. Those most afflicted and most suffering were usually minorities. The combination of these coefficients led to a completely new situation which is best described by Michael Geyer. He noted that the question was "not or no longer who is right (and hence uses force) and who is wrong (and hence uses violence). Rather, it is the more fundamental question that defines sovereignty: who has the right over life and death and who does not? If the contentions of the past concerned issues of legality (who is right and who is wrong), the new concern is over legitimacy (who has rights and who has none)."[49]

Gender history, still underrepresented as a discipline, has so far been regarded as a part of a cultural history approach, speaking about perceptions and roles. However, there is much to be done for a stronger integration of gender aspects into a history of war and violence. Following Klaus Theweleit's analysis of male fantasies, several studies like Robert Gerwarth's have discovered the importance of certain understanding of masculinity of the perpetrators on the one hand and of ascribed femininity as a trait of the victims on the other hand. More recently, this aspect has been broadened by studies engaging with women as supporters, enablers, and even perpetrators of violence. Applying comparative historical analysis of different national and/or regional case studies in a combination of social history and cultural history would deepen our understanding of underlying concepts determining social practice—not only in terms of a dichotomy of victim and perpetrator, but in a broader understanding of how societies accept

---

48  See chapter by Jochen Böhler, "The Polish Central Government" in this volume. He is using the concept introduced by Klaus Schlichte, *In the Shadows of Violence: The Politics of Armed Groups* (Frankfurt am Main: Campus, 2009).
49  Michael Geyer, "Some Hesitant Observations Concerning 'Political Violence,'" *Kritika. Explorations in Russian and Eurasian History* 4, no. 3 (2003), 695–708, here 707–08.

violence, mobilize and demobilize, and integrate victims and perpetrators by remembrance, forgiveness, and active forgetting after the end of conflicts.

Regarding identities, it becomes more challenging to apply historical comparison. Of course, we can compare minorities and their status in different countries, we can contrast prevailing concepts of nation, gender, and ethnicity, but overall, these are abstract concepts more difficult to pin down, and thus, more difficult to make tangible as an object of comparison—although some historians have fruitfully compared similar situations of regional violence.[50] In many cases, approaching these topics with methods linked to histoire croisée or entangled history (regarding, for example, borderlands), or a transnational perspective (like the study of antisemitism) has been more efficient.

## 3. Practices

A third key topic discusses the types and practices of violence. What were forms and types of violence? Why did they predominate and not the other forms? How was this violence related to the violence of World War I or earlier precedents? Was violence used for state and nation-building purposes?

The shooting of civilians was a frequent form of lethal violence. However, apparently the perception that such killings were wrong remained, as the shooting of civilians was repeatedly blamed on the enemy, who was thereby presented as ruthless. This tactic was frequent, but less common than other forms of violence which served as punishment in not only a physical but also in a symbolic way. The cutting, shearing, and shaving of hair was a form of violence frequently used, especially following accusations of betrayal. In Poland, this form of violence was used by paramilitaries of the Haller Army, but also POW and Polish Legions, in collaboration with the local population, predominantly against Jews, whose sidelocks or beards were shorn. Arson was another very frequent form of violence, serving as the ultimate pragmatic attack in a paramilitary war. It was easy and cheap. It allowed secrecy and publicity at the same time: secrecy for the perpetrator, who could get away in the shadow of the night—and publicity, since the fire would be noticed from far away. Even after the flames were extinguished, the charred ruins were a significant landmark, carrying a message and a warning.

---

50 As, for example, Tim Wilson with regard to Ulster and Upper Silesia in their own regional identity.

The power vacuum and absence of state control, general preconditions for the rise of paramilitary forces, naturally also encouraged warlordism, peasant uprisings, the forming of bands of marauders and criminal gangs.[51] Insufficient chains of command, lack of discipline, and the abundant use of alcohol further worsened the situation.[52] While incidents occurred within almost all paramilitary formations, especially the "Green" formations in Eastern Europe earned themselves a negative reputation, which is accounted for by case studies like Bodó's chapter in this book, discussing the "green revolution" not only as a social justice movement but also describing civic militias as involved in a majority of pogroms and atrocities.[53]

Irregular violence could include pogroms, atrocities, and retaliation on broader scale, as well as banditry and criminality. Sometimes, banditry evolved as a reaction to a repressive occupational regime, like in the case of Lithuania. First emerging in isolated incidents, it quickly became an established practice among soldiers and civilian criminals in particular when these actions were not reprimanded but tolerated in a mix of lacking control and military carte blanche for combatants. Pillaging and looting were common practices, fueled at first by the combatants' economic hardship but quickly nourishing greed. Foreign paramilitaries seemed to have regarded it as war booty.[54] At the same time, it also manifested a profound contempt for the local civilian population and in particular for minorities, women and alleged traitors (sometimes these categories were even considered as synonymous, with a deep-rooted mistrust in particular against the Jewish communities).[55] Diminishing "the others," disregarding them as equals, as well as describing deliberately employed violence in terms of natural

---

51 Compare Josh Sanborn, "The Genesis of Russian Warlordism: Violence and Governance during the First World War and the Civil War," *Contemporary European History* 19, no. 3 (2010): 195–213; Ryan Gingeras, "Beyond Istanbul's 'Laz Underworld': Ottoman Para militarism and the Rise of Turkish Organized Crime, 1908–1950," *Contemporary European History* 19, no. 3 (2010): 215–30; Piotr Wróbel, "The Seeds of Violence. The Brutalization of an Eastern European Region, 1917–1921," *Journal of Modern European History* 1, no. 1 (2003): 125–49.
52 Schnell, *Räume*, 163; Dietrich Beyrau, "Der Erste Weltkrieg als Bewährungsprobe. Bolschewistische Lernprozesse aus dem «imperialistischen» Krieg," *Journal of Modern European History* 1, no. 1 (Special Issue "Violence and Society after the First World War") (2003): 96–124, here 101, 105.
53 Bodó, "The Rich and the (In)famous."
54 See chapter by Mart Kuldkepp, "Scandinavian Volunteers as Perpetrators of Violence and Crime in the Estonian War of Independence" in this volume. Looting is also mentioned in the Hungarian case by Bodó, "The Rich and the (In)famous."
55 Staliūnas, "The Military Pogroms" in this volume.

catastrophes seemingly legitimized transgressions and made those considered outside the national and social peer group easy prey.[56]

An increasing politicization and rising anti-bolshevism as well as constant lack of control due to ongoing border wars radicalized the means of violence, leading to killings, sometimes fueled even further when anti-bolshevism was combined with antisemitism. Once this level of lethal violence had been reached, it was even more difficult to contain.[57]

Given the omnipresence of looting, it might almost be considered a gateway into more substantial and dangerous violence. Some looting might have been caused exclusively by socioeconomic hardship, but mostly it also manifested social, ethnic, and gender hierarchies, it was not only about the war booty but also about humiliation, manifesting power, and terrorizing civilian populations to establish dominance.[58]

Misogynistic violence, the mistreatment of women, and sometimes rape were often linked to pillaging and looting and the invasion of private space it mostly entailed. On some occasions, it is referred to as a looting situation getting out of hand, but it should probably rather be regarded as a way of tactical humiliation and submission (of women, their male relatives, and the community), sometimes also escalating to "orgies of aggression."[59]

Reprisals and hostage-taking became common techniques especially in the Eastern theater of war, used by all combatant sides.[60] Almost all parties fighting in East-Central Europe engaged in antisemitic violence. In Ukraine alone, between 1918 and 1920 about one thousand five hundred anti-Jewish pogroms cost the life of between fifty thousand and two hundred thousand people.[61] In Lviv, the rather traditional battle in November 1918 (as described earlier) was followed by a pogrom against the Jewish population. As has been pointed out,

---

56 Ibid.
57 Petronis, "Wartime Banditry"; Kuldkepp, "Scandinavian Volunteers"; Staliūnas, "The Military Pogroms."
58 Compare Jean-Paul Azam and Anke Hoeffler "Violence against Civilians in Civil Wars: Looting or Terror?" *Journal of Peace Research* 39, no. 4 (Special Issue on Civil War in Developing Countries) (2002): 461–85.
59 What Bodó calls "autotelic violence." Bodó, "The Rich and the (In)famous"; Raphaëlle Branche and Fabrice Virgili, eds., *Rape in Wartime* (New York: Palgrave Macmillan, 2012).
60 Alexander V. Prusin, *The Lands Between: Conflict in the East European Borderlands, 1870–1992* (Oxford: Oxford University Press, 2010), 41–44.
61 Sanborn, "The Genesis of Russian Warlordism," 208–9. See also Alexander V. Prusin, *Nationalizing a Borderland: War, Ethnicity, and Anti-Jewish Violence in East Galicia, 1914–1920* (Tuscaloosa: University of Alabama Press, 2005); Piotr Wróbel, "The Kaddish Years: Anti-Jewish Violence in East Central Europe, 1918–1921," *Jahrbuch des Simon-Dubnow-Instituts* 4 (2005): 211–36.

most collective violence reflects a form of social control.[62] In many cases of paramilitary excesses against civilians, collective violence, inflicted on victims by the paramilitaries themselves or by a crowd encouraged by paramilitaries, was used to have an impact on public discourse and to transport political and social messages. While at first sight, some excesses might give the impression to be arbitrary, they served a purpose in transferring these messages, a process which might be referred to as "semiotics of violence."[63]

In many ways, the violence of this period defined the structure of the new post-1918 states, their political culture, and their relations to minorities and to their neighbors. Reasons for this were rooted in the interconnection of violence and aggressive and nationalist discourse. Violence proved to be part of the discourse out of which the national community was fashioned. The symbolic use of violence both marked and expressed the social, ethnic, and religious dichotomies that underlay national identities. By employing forms of violence that served as a symbol and a message, nationalist paramilitaries manifested this discourse in the social communities in which they were embedded or to which they came from outside. In this sense, "semiotics of paramilitary violence" were used to construct communities, maybe even nations.[64]

After 1923, paramilitary and para-state protagonists were usually absorbed into regular national military formations and even into politics.[65] Yet, the role of paramilitaries in forming the nation also left an awkward, subversive legacy. After the end of the postwar independence conflicts, most countries experienced processes of consolidation and purges that reasserted the monopoly of force on the part of the new state. Paramilitary forces, which before had helped gain independence, were now a potential threat to political stability, especially as they were not centrally controlled and were usually loyal first and foremost to their immediate leader. In the absence of functioning state authorities, or in opposition to authorities that were regarded as illegitimate, paramilitary formations defined themselves as legitimate forces. Especially women's participation as combatants and the blurring of gender boundaries in irregular warfare in some countries presented a major challenge. While reestablishing "normality" after the fighting was over, traditional dichotomies had to be reinstated. Paramilitary forces

---

62  Roberta Senechal de la Roche, "Collective Violence as Social Control," *Sociological Forum* 11, no. 1 (March 1996): 97–128.
63  Eichenberg, "Dark Side of Independence," 233, 237 ff; Wolfgang Sofsky, *Traktat über die Gewalt* (Frankfurt am Main: Fischer, 2005).
64  Eichenberg, "Dark Side of Independence," 233, 237 ff; Sofsky, *Traktat über die Gewalt*.
65  Apart from the more complicated case of foreign volunteers, who were hardly ever held accountable. See chapter of Kuldkepp, "Scandinavian Volunteers."

that fought for independence were now regarded as a potential threat to political stability, both because they embodied these transgressions of social roles and because they remained an alternative source of national myth and self-legitimization. As the national struggle was reconstructed in hindsight as a legitimate, conventional war, the figure of the irregular remained troubling and, in many ways, was. While most paramilitary combatants and formations were eventually demobilized, dissolved, and integrated into society, others remained active and continued to challenge states and society. Not only Germany was haunted by ghosts of the paramilitary experience. The march on Rome in 1922 was only the first step to prove the impact of paramilitaries on interwar Italy. Piłsudski's Polish Legions backed his military coup in 1926. The question of how and how quickly states and societies managed to demobilize militarily and culturally, or at least to externalize the violence, was fundamental to their political stability in the following decades. In this post-conflict period, writing official histories was one method of establishing—and imposing—national narratives which aimed to cover up cleavages created by war and violence. National institutions like the Polish Military Historical Office (Wojskowe Biuro Historyczne) were central to this attempt to gain the monopoly of telling a unified narrative of the conflict (and thereby mostly blending out the experience of minorities).[66] But these collections of evidence, often started during the war and conflict, were also essential for propaganda, information, and sometimes even prosecution, used either to address an international audience or national courts. They could also help to give a voice to minority groups, as in the case of the Jewish Historical-Ethnographic Society which published evidence of violence against Jews, if only after the war.[67]

Focusing on practices, finally, allows us to apply historical comparative methods, comparing types of violence as well as symbolism and underlying messages encoded in the violence employed. At the same time, it opens possibilities to analyze the transfer of certain violent practices, as for example between colonial and European settings, between different theaters of war, or between abroad and the motherland.[68]

---

66  See chapter by Böhler, "The Polish Central Government" in this volume.
67  Staliūnas, "The Military Pogroms" in this volume.
68  As argued, respectively, by Isabel Hull, *Absolute Destruction: Military Culture and the Practices of War in Imperial Germany* (Ithaca: Cornell University Press, 2005); Sven Reichhardt, *Faschistische Kampfbünde. Gewalt und Gemeinschaft im italienischen Squadrismus und in der deutschen SA* (Köln-Weimar-Wien: Böhlau, 2002); James Kitchen, "The Indianisation of the Egyptian Expeditionary Force: Palestine 1918," in *The Indian Army in the Two World Wars*, ed. Kaushik Roy (Leiden: Brill, 2011), 165–90.

## Conclusions—Comparing the Incomparable? Transferring of the Exceptional?

Summing up, despite all pitfalls of comparative historical analysis and despite all promises of transnational history and histoire croisée, there are several aspects where a comparative approach can be useful to further study of the history of violence, and in particular in the early twentieth century Eastern Europe and when trying to integrate current strands of interest in academic research as new fields for violence studies. When looking at the three key topics of this book, structure, identities, and practices, historical comparison seems to be able to contribute to all three, while most efficiently it is used to analyze structural circumstances and practices. In all three parts, comparative approaches may be best used without a too narrow understanding: instead of restricting the approach to comparing containers (a city, a region, a state), more is gained in opening said containers to a transnational or entangled perspective. Picking up on Patricia Clavin's concept of transnational history as a honeycomb, we can well compare the individual cells within the honeycomb, as long as we understand that they are all interconnected.[69] With regard to violence in Eastern Europe in the first quarter of the century, this means regarding the protagonists as forming cells within a broader honeycomb of violence linked to a broader European context of war and revolution, linking separate occurrences in a larger story. Historical comparison can help us define the cells within this larger framework or honeycomb. Rather than reducing the uniqueness of the individual cases, it can help us understand the broader phenomenon.

## Bibliography

Alcalde, Ángel. "War Veterans and the Transnational Origins of Fascism (1917–1919)." *Journal of Modern Italian Studies* 21, no. 4 (2016): 561–79.

Azam Jean-Paul, and Anke Hoeffler. "Violence against Civilians in Civil Wars: Looting or Terror?" *Journal of Peace Research* 39, no. 4 (Special Issue on Civil War in Developing Countries) (2002): 461–85.

Augusteijn, Jost. *From Public Defiance to Guerrilla Warfare: The Experience of Ordinary Volunteers in the Irish War of Independence 1916–1921*. Dublin: Irish Academic Press, 1996.

Balkelis, Tomas. *War, Revolution, and Nation-making in Lithuania, 1914–1923*. Oxford: Oxford University Press, 2018.

---

69   Clavin, "Defining Transnationalism," 465.

Baberowski, Jörg. "Gewalt verstehen." *Zeithistorische Forschungen/Studies in Contemporary History* 5, no. 1 (2008): 5–17.

Baberowski, Jörg, and Anselm Doering-Manteuffel. *Ordnung durch Terror. Gewaltexzeß und Vernichtung im nationalsozialistischen und stalinistischen Imperium*. Bonn: Dietz, 2006.

Bartov, Omer, and Eric D. Weitz, eds. *Shatterzone of Empires. Coexistence and Violence in the German, Habsburg, Russian, and Ottoman Borderlands*. Bloomington: Indiana University Press, 2013.

Beyrau, Dietrich. "Der Erste Weltkrieg als Bewährungsprobe. Bolschewistische Lernprozesse aus dem «imperialistischen» Krieg." *Journal of Modern European History* 1, no. 1 (Special Issue "Violence and Society after the First World War") (2003): 96–124.

Böhler, Jochen. *Civil War in Central Europe, 1918–1921: The Reconstruction of Poland*. Oxford: Oxford University Press, 2019.

Borodziej, Włodzimierz, and Maciej Górny. *Der vergessene Weltkrieg: Europas Osten 1912–1923*. Darmstadt: wbg Theiss, 2018.

Branche, Raphaëlle, and Fabrice Virgili, eds. *Rape in Wartime*. New York: Palgrave Macmillan, 2012.

Chojnacki, Sven, and Fabian Namberger. "Die »neuen Kriege« im Spiegel postkolonialer Theorien und kritischer Friedensforschung: Ein Plädoyer für die Befreiung von der Last der Vereinfachung." *Zeitschrift für Friedens- und Konfliktforschung* 3, no. 2 (2014): 157–202.

Clavin, Patricia. "Defining Transnationalism." *Contemporary European History* 14, no. 4 (2005): 421–39.

Conrad, Sebastian. *Auf der Suche nach der verlorenen Nation: Geschichtsschreibung in Westdeutschland und Japan, 1945–1960*. Göttingen: Vandenhoeck & Ruprecht, 1999.

Crossick, Geoffrey, and Heinz-Gerhard Haupt. *The Petite Bourgoisie en Europe 1780–1914. Entreprise, Family and Independence*. London: Routledge, 2016 (first edition 1995).

Eichenberg, Julia. "Consent, Coercion and Endurance in Eastern Europe: Poland and the Fluidity of War Experiences." In *Legacies of Violence. Eastern Europe's First World War*, edited by Jochen Böhler et al., 235–58. München: Oldenbourg, 2014.

Eichenberg, Julia, and John Paul Newman. "Introduction: Aftershocks. Violence in Dissolving Empires after the First World War." *Contemporary European History* 19, no. 3 (2010): 183–94.

Epple, Angelik, Erhart, Walter, and Johannes Grave, eds. *Practices of Comparing. Towards a New Understanding of a Fundamental Human Practice*. Bielefeld: Transcript, 2020.

Galtung, Johan. *Strukturelle Gewalt. Beiträge zur Friedens- und Konfliktforschung*. Reinbek bei Hamburg: Rororo, 1982.

Gatrell, Peter. "War after the War: Conflicts, 1919–23." In *A Companion to World War I*, edited by John Horne, 558–75. Hoboken: Wiley-Blackwell, 2010.

Gerwarth, Robert. "The Central European Counterrevolution: Paramilitary Violence in Germany, Austria and Hungary after the Great War." *Past and Present* 200, no. 1 (2008): 175–209.

———. *The Vanquished: Why the First World War Failed to End, 1917–1923*. London: Allen Lane, 2016.

Gerwarth, Robert, and John Horne, eds. *War in Peace: Paramilitary Violence in Europe after the Great War*. Oxford: Oxford University Press, 2012.

———. "The Great War and Paramilitarism in Europe, 1917–23." *Contemporary European History* 19, no. 3 (2010): 267–73.

Gerwarth, Robert, and Erez Manela, eds. *Empires at War, 1911–1923*. Oxford: Oxford University Press, 2014.
Geyer, Michael. "Some Hesitant Observations Concerning 'Political Violence.'" *Kritika. Explorations in Russian and Eurasian History* 4, no. 3 (June 2003): 695–708.
Gingeras, Ryan. "Beyond Istanbul's 'Laz Underworld': Ottoman Paramilitarism and the Rise of Turkish Organized Crime, 1908–1950." *Contemporary European History* 19, no. 3 (2010): 215–30.
Horne, John. "Demobilizing the Mind: France and the Legacy of the Great War, 1919–1939." *French History and Civilization. Papers from the George Rudé Seminar* 2 (2009): 101–19.
Hull, Isabel. *Absolute Destruction: Military Culture and the Practices of War in Imperial Germany*. Ithaca: Cornell University Press, 2005.
Kaelbe, Hartmut. *Der Historische Vergleich. Eine Einführung zum 19. und 20. Jahrhundert*. Frankfurt am Main-New York: Campus, 1999.
―――. *Social Mobility in the 19th and 20th Centuries: Europe and America in Comparative Perspective*. Leamington Spa: Berg Publishers, 1985.
―――. "Historischer Vergleich," Version: 1.0. In *Docupedia-Zeitgeschichte*. Last modified August 14, 2012.
Kitchen, James. "The Indianisation of the Egyptian Expeditionary Force: Palestine 1918." In *The Indian Army in the Two World Wars*, edited by Kaishuk Roy, 165–90. Leiden: Brill, 2011.
Kocka, Jürgen, ed. *Europäische Arbeiterbewegung im 19. Jahrhundert. Deutschland, Österreich, England und Frankreich im Vergleich*. Göttingen: Vandenhoeck & Ruprecht, 1983.
Koloma Beck, Teresa, and Klaus Schlichte. *Theorien der Gewalt zur Einführung*. 3 ed. Hamburg: Junius, 2020.
Manela, Erez. *The Wilsonian Moment: Self-Determination and the International. Origins of Anticolonial Nationalism*. New York: Oxford University Press, 2007.
Mann, Michael. *The Dark Side of Democracy: Explaining Ethnic Cleansing*. Cambridge: Cambridge University Press, 2005.
Mayer, Arno J. *The Furies: Violence and Terror in the French and Russian Revolutions*. Princeton: Princeton University Press, 2000.
Meteling, Wencke. *Ehre, Einheit, Ordnung. Preußische und französische Städte und ihre Regimenter im Krieg, 1870/71 und 1914–1919*. Baden-Baden: Nomos, 2010.
Moses, Dirk A. *The Problems of Genocide. Permanent Security and the Language of Transgression*. Oxford: Oxford University Press, 2021.
Mosse, George. *Fallen Soldiers. Reshaping the Memory of the World Wars*. Oxford: Oxford University Press, 1990.
Osterhammel, Jürgen. *The Transformation of the World: A Global History of the Nineteenth Century*, translated by Patrick Camiller. Princeton: Princeton University Press, 2014.
Patel, Kiran Klaus. "An Emperor without Clothes? The Debate about Transnational History Twenty-five Years On." *Histoire@Politique* 26 (mai-août 2015). Accessed August 2, 2021. http://www.histoire-politique.fr.
Prusin, Alexander V. *The Lands Between: Conflict in the East European Borderlands, 1870–1992*. Oxford: Oxford University Press, 2010.
―――. *Nationalizing a Borderland: War, Ethnicity, and Anti-Jewish Violence in East Galicia, 1914–1920*. Tuscaloosa: University of Alabama Press, 2005.

Reichhardt, Sven. *Faschistische Kampfbünde. Gewalt und Gemeinschaft im italienischen Squadrismus und in der deutschen SA.* Köln-Weimar-Wien: Böhlau, 2002.

Sanborn, Josh. "The Genesis of Russian Warlordism: Violence and Governance during the First World War and the Civil War." *Contemporary European History* 19, no. 3 (August 2010): 195–213.

Schivelbusch, Wolfgang. *Culture of Defeat.* New York: Picador, 2004.

Schnell, Felix. *Räume des Schreckens. Gewalt und Gruppenmilitanz in der Ukraine, 1905–1933.* Hamburg: Hamburger Edition, 2012.

Schöttler, Peter. "Marc Bloch. Die Lehren der Geschichte und die Möglichkeit historischer Prognosen." *Österreichische Zeitschrift für Geschichtswissenschaft* 16, no. 2 (2005): 104–25.

Senechal de la Roche, Roberta. "Collective Violence as Social Control." *Sociological Forum* 11, no. 1 (March 1996): 97–128.

Sofsky, Wolfgang. *Traktat über die Gewalt.* Frankfurt am Main: Fischer, 2005.

Werner, Michael, and Bénédicte Zimmermann, eds. *De la comparaison à l'histoire croisée.* Paris: Seuil, 2004.

Winter, Jay, and Jean-Luis Robert. *Capital Cities at War. Paris, London, Berlin 1914–1919.* Cambridge: Cambridge University Press, 1997.

Wilson, Tim. *Frontiers of Violence: Conflict and Identity in Ulster and Upper Silesia, 1918–1922.* Oxford: Oxford University Press, 2010.

Wróbel, Piotr. "The Kaddish Years: Anti-Jewish Violence in East Central Europe, 1918–1921." *Jahrbuch des Simon-Dubnow-Instituts* 4 (2005): 211–36.

———. "The Seeds of Violence. The Brutalization of an Eastern European Region, 1917–1921." *Journal of Modern European History* 1, no. 1 (2003): 125–49.

# Contributors

**Tomas Balkelis** is a senior research fellow at the Lithuanian Institute of History in Vilnius. He received his PhD in history at the University of Toronto in 2004. After graduating, he worked at the Universities of Manchester and Nottingham. In 2009–2013, he was a European Research Council postdoctoral research fellow at University College Dublin. He also led a Lithuanian Research Council funded team of historians based at Vilnius University working on the population displacement in Lithuania in the twentieth century. In 2015–2016, he was a visiting fellow at Stanford University. He is the author of *The Making of Modern Lithuania* (Routledge, 2009) and *War, Revolution, and Nation-Making in Lithuania* (Oxford University Press, 2018). His articles have been published by *Past and Present* and other academic journals. His research fields include nation-building, forced migrations, population displacement, and paramilitary violence.

**Béla Bodó** was born in Hungary and completed his undergraduate education at the University of Debrecen and the University of Toronto in 1990. He received his PhD from York University, Canada in 1998. He got tenure and promotion to Associate Professor at Missouri State University in 2011. Since 2015, he has held the same title at the University of Bonn, Germany. He has published three monographs and more than two dozen articles. His last monograph, entitled *The White Terror: Antisemitic and Political Violence in Hungary, 1919–1923* (Routledge, 2019), won the first prize of the Hungarian Studies Association in 2021. His next study, *Black Humor and the White Terror: Jewish Responses to Antisemitic Violence in Hungary, 1918–1923*, is scheduled to be published by Routledge in 2023.

**Jochen Böhler** is the director of the Vienna Wiesenthal Institute for Holocaust Studies. He received his PhD in history at the University of Cologne in 2004. He has worked at the German Historical Institute in Warsaw (2000–2010), at the Imre Kertész Kolleg in Jena (2010–2019), and as acting chair for Eastern European History at the Friedrich-Schiller-University in Jena (2019–2022). He was a fellow at the United States Holocaust Memorial Museum in Washington, DC (2004), at Yad Vashem—The World Holocaust Remembrance Center in

Jerusalem (2007–2008), and a visiting professor at Sorbonne in Paris (2017). He is co-editor with Włodzimierz Borodziej and Joachim von Puttkamer of *The Routledge History Handbook of Central and Eastern Europe in the Twentieth Century*, vol. 4, *Violence* (Routledge, 2022); with Robert Gerwarth of *The Waffen-SS: A European History* (Oxford University Press, 2017), and author of *Civil War in Central Europe. The Reconstruction of Poland, 1918–1921* (Oxford University Press, 2018). His articles have been published by the *Journal of Contemporary History*, the *Journal of Modern European History*, *Dapim: Studies on the Holocaust*, and *Yad Vashem Studies*. His research fields include the two world wars, the Holocaust, nation building, and the history of violence.

**Julia Eichenberg** is a senior lecturer in modern European history at the University of Bayreuth, where she leads a research project on collaboration in London exile during the Second World War (Volkswagen Foundation, 2014–2023). She received her PhD in modern history at the University of Tübingen in 2008. In 2008–2011, she was a postdoctoral research fellow at Trinity College, University College Dublin. From 2011 to 2020, she lectured at Humboldt University Berlin. She is the author of a monograph on Polish World War I Veterans (Oldenbourg, 2011) and co-editor of *The Great War and Veterans' Internationalism* (Palgrave Macmillan, 2013) and of special issues on paramilitary violence (*Journal of Contemporary European History*, 2010), Contemporary Legal History (Zeithistorische Forschungen, 2019), and on the U. N. W. C. C. (*Journal of the History of International Law*, 2022). Her research fields include a cultural and social history of war and paramilitary violence, diplomacy, and legal cooperation.

**Maciej Górny** is deputy director of the Institute of History "Tadeusz Manteuffel" at the Polish Academy of Sciences, and a professor thereof. Between 2014 and 2019, he was editor in chief of *Acta Poloniae Historica*. From 2006–2010, he was research fellow at the Centrum Badań Historycznych PAN—Zentrum für Historische Forschung in Berlin. His research interests encompass East Central Europe in the nineteenth and twentieth century, history of historiography, discourses on race and World War I. His latest publications include *Science Embattled: Eastern European Intellectuals and the Great War* (Ferdinand Schöningh, 2019) and *Polska bez cudów. Historia dla dorosłych* (Agora, 2021). Together with Włodzimierz Borodziej he is the author of a synthesis of World War I history in East Central Europe, *Forgotten Wars: Central and Eastern Europe, 1912–1916* (Cambridge University Press, 2021).

**Andrea Griffante** is a senior research fellow at the Lithuanian Institute of History in Vilnius. He received his MA at the University of Trieste and his PhD in history at Klaipėda University in 2011. After graduating, he worked at Vytautas Magnus University in Kaunas. From 2016–2018 he was the Gerda-Henkel-Stiftung Research Fellow at the University of Padua. His last monograph is *Children, Poverty, and Nationalism in Lithuania, 1900–1940* (Palgrave, 2019). His research fields include history of humanitarianism, nation-building, history of childhood, and social history of medicine.

**Mart Kuldkepp** is associate professor of Scandinavian History and Politics at University College London (UCL). He received his PhD from the University of Tartu, Estonia. His research mainly concerns Baltic and Nordic history in the first decades of the twentieth century, especially Baltic-Nordic political and diplomatic contacts. Some of his works have also been devoted to the social and political history of World War I and the Estonian War of Independence.

**Vytautas Petronis** is a researcher at the Lithuanian Institute of History and chief editor of *Lithuanian Historical Studies*. His interests include the history of cartography, nationalism and right wing radicalism in the Russian Empire and interwar Lithuania, and political and societal violence in Lithuania during WWI and the early postwar years. He is the author of *Constructing Lithuania: Ethnic Mapping in Tsarist Russia, ca. 1800–1914* (Stockholm University, 2007) and numerous academic articles.

**Vasilijus Safronovas** is a research professor at Klaipėda University. He has published widely on issues of memory, identity, nationalism, mental geography, conceptual history, and cultural contacts. His study *The Creation of National Spaces in a Pluricultural Region: The Case of Prussian Lithuania* (Academic Studies Press, 2016) received honorable mention from the Association for the Advancement of Baltic Studies (Book Prize 2018). In 2015–2018, he led the research project on the remembrance of the First World War. Together with Vytautas Jokubauskas, Vygantas Vareikis, and Hektoras Vitkus, he compared the Lithuanian and East Prussian experiences and memories of the Great War and their social and cultural impact in the interwar period. Since then, he has authored several articles on these topics and edited *The Great War in Lithuania and Lithuanians in the Great War: Experiences and Memories* (Klaipėdos universiteto leidykla, 2017). He is currently the head of the Institute of Baltic Region History and Archaeology at Klaipėda University.

**Darius Staliūnas** is senior research fellow at the Lithuanian Institute of History, Vilnius and a lecturer at Vilnius University. He is the author of *Making Russians: Meaning and Practice of Russification in Lithuania and Belarus after 1863* (Rodopi, 2007); *Enemies for a Day: Antisemitism and Anti-Jewish Violence in Lithuania under the Tsars* (Central European University Press, 2015); and, with Dangiras Mačiulis, *Lithuanian Nationalism and the Vilnius Question, 1883–1940* (Herder-Institut, 2015). His research interests include issues of Russian nationality policy in the so-called Northwestern Region (Lithuania and Belarus), ethnic conflicts, problems of historiography, and places of memory in Lithuania.

**Vygantas Vareikis** is a researcher and professor at the Institute of Baltic Region History and Archaeology of Klaipėda University. His main research fields include the military history and the history of paramilitary organizations in Lithuania; and Jewish-Lithuanian and German-Lithuanian relations in the twentieth century. He co-authored *The Preconditions for the Holocaust: Anti-Semitism in Lithuania* (Margi raštai, 2004), a monograph issued by the International Commission for the Evaluation of the Crimes of the Nazi and Soviet Occupation Regimes in Lithuania. He recently participated in a three-year research project devoted to the comparative analysis of World War I memory in Lithuania and East Prussia in the interwar period. In this project, he focused on how images of the German occupation were produced and maintained in Lithuania through memories, fiction, and historical writing.

**Hektoras Vitkus** is a researcher at the Institute of Baltic Region History and Archaeology of Klaipėda University. His main research interests include discourse analysis and memory sites related to the Holocaust and other traumatic events of the twentieth century. From 2015–2018, he participated in a research project which compared the Lithuanian and East Prussian experiences and memories of the First World War in the interwar period. Within this project, he focused on how the images of the Russian invasion into East Prussia and its subsequent occupation were produced and maintained in Germany through memories, fiction, and historical writing.

# Index

Abony, 151
Abraham, Roman, 176
Africa, 50
Alap, 143
Albert, Jakab, 55, 151
Alūksne, 112, 126
Americans, 96, 193
Amstetten, 200
An-ski, Szymon, 196
Annaberg, 176
antisemitism, 84, 89, 122, 137–38, 154, 156–58
Archangelsk, 193
Arendt, Hannah, 2, 4, 9, 12
Arildskov, Max, 117
Armenians, 2
Astashov, Aleksandr, 17n9
Austria, 200
Austrians, 200
Austro-Hungary, 15

Baberowski, Jörg, 220
Baczyński, Stanisław, 174, 179–83
Balkans, 190
Balkelis, Tomas, 49
Baltics (Baltic States), 5n25, 11, 45, 108, 110, 122, 124, 128, 137
Balys, Jonas, 64
banditry, 10–12, 15–17, 22–24, 27–33, 35–39, 202, 216. *See also* criminality
Baranovichi, 192
Basanavičius, Jonas, 59
Batocki, Adolf von, 56
Belarus, 6, 45, 83, 100, 195, 201, 207
Belarusians, 86

Belgian Congo, 112
Belgium, 50–51, 61, 192
Bemporad, Elissa, 83
Berlin, 166, 214
Beyrau, Dietrich, 4
Białystok, 201
Bibó, Dénes, 153
Bloch, Marc, 213
Blue Army (Błękitna Armia), 162–163, 219
Bodó, Béla, 12, 212n5
Bohemia, 194, 200
Böhler, Jochen, 12
Bolsheviks, 31–33, 39, 85, 88–89, 92–93, 98, 108, 119, 122–24, 130, 193, 195, 197, 206
Bolshevism, 33, 94, 106, 121
Borgelin, Richard, 111–12, 120, 124, 127–28
Borodziej, Włodzimierz, 215
Brackmann, Jakab, 55–56
Brest, 180, 198
Brest-Litovsk, The Treaty of, 31, 39, 189
brutalization, 9, 75, 84, 100, 126, 137
Budapest, 142, 144, 152–54, 156
Budnitskii, Oleg, 83, 90
Bugailiškis, Peliksas, 59
Bulgaria, 6–7
Bund Party, 196
Burnagel, Stanisław, 196, 199
Bytom, 172

Carlsson, Conrad, 116–17, 123–24
casualties, 3, 12, 19, 44, 46, 194, 205
Catholicism, 26, 148

Catholics, 20, 52, 93
central government, 59, 95, 164–65, 171, 174, 177, 184
Chełm, 201
Chmielewski, Mieczysław, 174
Chmielnicki Uprising, 83
Chodakauskas, Tadas, 94
Chopard, Thomas, 83
Christians, 87, 93, 151
Churchill, Winston, 219
civil wars, 5, 136
civilians, 2–5, 7, 10–12, 18–21, 25, 28, 33, 38, 43–44, 46–55, 58–62, 64, 66, 68–71, 75, 89, 94, 123, 125–26, 128, 130, 133, 137, 139, 150, 192, 196, 199–201, 207, 217, 221–23
Clemmesen, Michael, 106
Communism, 147, 152, 157, 211
Communists, 137, 140, 143–44, 201
Compiègne, The Armistice of, 45
Cossacks, 69, 84, 87
counter-revolution, 139–41, 143, 147, 149, 156–58, 221
criminality, 4, 8, 10, 15–16, 20, 22–24, 28, 33, 36, 38–39, 103, 107, 113–15, 119, 124, 129–30, 132–33. *See also* banditry; robberies; violence
crisis of governance, 4–5, 9–12, 104, 216
Czapla, Kazimierz, 169
Czechoslovakia, 99, 137, 197, 200, 218
Czechoslovaks, 193

Dahlgren, Bror, 117
Danes, 107, 113, 117, 121, 123, 126–27, 133
Daugava, 45
David, Eduard, 50n25
Debeiki (Debeikiai), 52
Dęblin station, 203
Debrecen, 143
Democrats, 163–64
Denmark, 106, 110, 127

Deutsch, Ignác, 151
Deutsch, Margit, 151
Déván, István, 144
Dewernicki, Ajzyk Meir, 196
discipline, 17, 19, 24, 46–47, 73, 90, 115, 120–21, 126, 132–33, 167, 215
Diszel, 150
Dmowski, Roman, 163
Dowbor-Muśnicki, Józef, 163, 167–68, 170
Dreyza, Józef, 169
Dubnov, Simon, 61
Dukszty (Dūkštas), 197

Ehrlich, Mindla, 205
Eichenberg, Julia, 9, 12
Ekström, Martin, 109, 111, 117–118, 120–21, 125–26, 130
Előszállás, 147
Endecja (National Democrats), 163–64, 167, 171, 179, 181–82, 184
Estonia, 7, 9, 11, 104–6, 108–119, 121–23, 126, 128–30, 132–33, 195, 223
Estonians, 11, 104–5, 108, 110–111, 120–22, 125, 129, 131–32
ethnic conflict, 9, 10n43
Europe, 1, 3, 8–9, 11, 44, 60, 83, 92, 99, 104, 137, 146, 149, 155, 161–63, 166, 177, 188–89, 192, 196, 199, 207, 211, 213, 215–17, 219–20, 224, 229
executions, 10, 15, 23, 44, 109, 125–26
Eybert, Georges, 63

Fegyvernek, 142
Finns, 103, 115–16, 125–26, 128–33
First World War (Great War). *See* World War I
Fojkis, Walenty, 173
France, 50, 63, 137, 162, 172, 174, 192
Franchi, Giuseppe, 112, 128, 130–31

Freeman, Michael, 189
Freikorps, 45, 90–91, 138–41, 146–47, 149, 151, 153, 166
Friedrich, István, 155
Fudakowski, Jan, 197–98

Gabrys, Juozas, 60
Gaigalaitė, Aldona, 85
Galicia, 162, 165–66, 176, 195, 202
Gatrell, Peter, 51, 219
Gause, Fritz, 46–47
Geneva, 2
Gentile, Emilio, 138
Germans, 2–3, 11, 15, 18–20, 22, 25–30, 33, 35–36, 38, 43–45, 47, 50–53, 58, 61, 65–66, 68–75, 85, 87, 88n27, 90–91, 96, 132, 166–67, 171, 173, 175–76, 181, 188, 195, 200–201
Germany, 1–3, 9, 25n33, 28, 50–51, 55, 57, 59, 61–67, 71, 74, 105, 137, 155, 164, 166, 173, 184, 201, 214, 231
Gerwarth, Robert, 9, 136, 220
Geyer, Michael, 7n30, 8, 226
Gintneris, Antanas, 65n83
Glaser, Stefan, 49
Gnigl bei Salzburg, 200
Goldin, Semion, 51
Golombek family, 92, 94
Gömbös, Gyula, 155
Górny, Maciej, 12, 215
Grajek, Michał, 176, 182
Grand, 126
Grażyński, Michał, 174, 176, 180, 182
Great Britain, 137
Griffante, Andrea, 70
Grigaliūnas-Glovackis, Vincas, 92, 93n55, 94–95
Grodno, 45
Grunwald, Battle of, 70
Grzegorzek, Józef, 169
Gulf of Finland, 106, 108

Habsburg, 161, 165, 190
Hagen, William W, 84, 205
Hague Convention, The, 2
Hällén, Lambert, 112, 118, 120
Haller, Józef, 162, 164, 168, 172, 204–5
Hannula, Erkki, 121, 129
Haupt, Heinz-Gerhard, 214
Héjjas, Iván, 145, 150–51
Helanen, Vilho, 115, 125
Helsinki, 109, 119, 129, 131
Hemmer Gudme, Iver De, 111, 115, 117
Hindenburg, Paul von, 25, 66
Hitler, Adolf, 72
Hohenlohe, prince, 141
Hołdunowa, 173
Holoby, 195
Hołoby, 195
Holocaust, 83, 211
Horeczky, Vilmos, 144
Horne, John, 47, 220
Horthy, Miklós, admiral, 140–41, 144, 147, 150, 152, 156
hostages, 18
Hovi, Olavi, 107, 114
Hull, Isabel V, 49
Hungarians, 143, 150, 193, 200
Hungary, 5–7, 9, 12, 84, 99, 139–40, 142, 147, 149, 154, 157

Ianushkevich, Nikolai, 52
Ilmjärv, Magnus, 130, 132
Ingman, Lauri, 108
Isonzo, front, 200
Ireland, 216n16, 225
Italy, 55, 143, 146, 149

Jaanson, Kaido, 107
Jedwabne, 98
Jelgava, 45
Jelínek, Jiří, 194
Jensen, Niels, 107
Jesionek, Kazimierz, 169

Jews, 2, 12, 43–44, 47, 52–53, 60–61, 75, 84–100, 124, 126, 128, 138–39, 141, 143, 149–51, 153–58, 202–5
Johansen, Jens Christian, 123, 130
Joniškėlis, 30
Joutsamo, Timo, 107, 114

Kaczmarek, Ryszard, 174–75
Kaelble, Hartmut, 213–14
Kairamo, Oswald, 130
Kairys, Steponas, 33
Kaišiadorys, 97
Kalm, Hans, 109, 111–12, 117, 120–21, 124–28, 131
Kalmyks, 124
Kalyvas, Stathis, 8
Karuka, Manu, 189
Katowice, 173–74
Kaunas, 21–22, 34, 45, 63, 65, 87–88
Kavarskas, 35
Kecskemét, 151
Kharkiv, 201
Kiev, 173
Kirkebæk, Mikkel, 106, 111, 114–15, 118, 121, 126, 132
Kiskunmajsa, 150
Klaipėda, 19, 45, 64
Klein, Ernst, 114
Klimas, Petras, 73
Kocka, Jürgen, 214
Kohn, Mariska, 146
Koluszki, 205
Königsberg, 42, 55, 57
Konrád, Ota, 204
Konstantinov, 87
Korfanty, Wojciech, 167–78, 180–82, 184
Kotor, 200
Kovel', 192, 197–98, 203, 205
Kovno, 45, 52–53, 65, 73
Kraków, 202
Kriger, Leizer, 97
Kriisa, Juhan, 131

Kukucska, János, 144
Kuldkepp, Mart, 12
Kunszentmiklós, 142
Kuperjanov, Julius, 111
Kurland, 26
Kurlandiia, 53
Kuzhe (Kužiai), 52
Kyrghyz, 124

Lahti, 109
Laidoner, Johan, 111, 122, 126, 128
Lampner, Adolf, 169
landlords, 37
Łapy, 201
Latvia, 5, 7, 21, 26, 112–113, 123, 195
Latvians, 11
Lausanne, The Treaty of, 219
Lawrence of Arabia, 117
legitimate use of violence, 6
Leino, Vesa, 107, 130
Lemke, Mikhail, 17–18
Lenin, Vladimir, 98
Libau, 19
Libava, 45
Lida, 196
Liepaja, 19, 45
Linkuva, 87
Liškiava, 31
Lithuania, 5–7, 9, 11–12, 15–16, 21–24, 31–33, 36–38, 43–46, 48–49, 50n25, 52–54, 57, 59, 62–66, 71–72, 74–75, 84–87, 94–96, 98–100, 195
Lithuanian Council. See *Taryba*
Lithuanians, 11, 21, 32, 38, 53, 58–60, 74–75, 85–86, 88–89
Liukianski, 94
Liulevičius, Vėjas, 49
Łochów, 204
Łódź, 205
Lohr, Eric, 51
Louhivuori, Wilho, 109, 131

Löwy, György, 148
Ludendorff, Erich, 66
Ludyga-Laskowski, Jan, 172
Lundborg, Einar, 116, 118, 120, 124–25, 127, 131
Lviv, 162, 165, 179, 206, 223

Mälkönen, Aino, 118
Mallmann, Klaus Michael, 137
Malmberg, Georg, 112, 118, 128
Małopolska, 181
Manela, Erez, 220
Mannerheim, Karl Gustav, 108, 110
Mannheim, Karl, 156
Marcali, 150
Marienburg, 112
Masurian lakes, 45
Mažeikiai, 25
Memel, 19, 45, 64, 69, 73
Mexico, 112
Meyerhoffer family, 141
Mielęcki, Andrzej, 173
Mielżyński, Maciej, 176
Mieszkowski, Łukasz, 195n24
Miklós, admiral, 140, 147
Miller, Puzer von, 92, 94–95
Mitau (Mintauja), 19
Mitava, 45
Mittelhauser, Eugène, 194
mobilization, 50, 58, 190, 192, 221
Molnár, Antal, 142, 144
Montenegro, 200
Moraczewski, Jędrzej, 199
Morozov, Ivan, 30
Moses, Dirk, 211
Mosse, George L., 136
Mothander, Carl Axel, 110, 112, 115, 117, 120, 128, 131
Mucsi, Róza, 151

Nagybajom, 143
Narva, 111–12, 121, 125–26, 128

nationalism, 109, 118, 136–37, 212, 217, 224
Naumiestis, 43
Nazism, 138
Nelipovich, Sergei, 51
Nemunėlis, river, 26
Neumann, John von, 156
Nicholas II, emperor, 52
Nitra, 194
Nõmme, 112
Noreika, Liudas, 88
Nové Zámky, 193–94, 207
Nowoświęciany, 197
Nowowilejka, 197

Ober Ost, 15–16, 22, 25, 27–28, 45, 50, 59, 166
officers, 19, 48, 65, 73, 108–9, 113, 116–18, 120–22, 124–33, 139–44, 146–50, 153, 156, 158, 169, 172, 175–76, 178, 181–82, 202–3
Old Believers, 91
Onikshty (Anykščiai), 52
Orthodox, 25–26, 204
Ostenburg, 141, 149
Ottoman Empire, 2, 51, 219

Paderewski, Ignacy, 165, 167
Paju, Battle of, 112, 121, 124–25, 195
Pakalniškis, K., 26n40
Pakhaliuk, Konstantin, 46–47
Paldiski, 128
Pale of Settlement, 60–61, 99, 196
Palludan, 106
Palludan, Anton, 106, 111, 113, 115, 117
Paluch, Mieczysław, 166–69, 174–75, 182
Panevėžys, 25, 27, 29–30, 52, 85–91, 93n55, 94, 96, 98–99
paramilitary troops, 184
Paris, 2, 163, 165–67, 170
Parski, Zygmunt, 170
Pasvalys, 36

Pašvitinys, 87
Päts, Konstantin, 129–31
peasants, 24, 26, 31, 138, 150–51, 158, 201, 222
Petkevičaitė-Bitė, Gabrielė, 29, 74n124
Petr, František, 193
Petronis, Vytautas, 12
Petrov, Grigorii (Grishka), 34
Petseri, 127
Pilch, Jenő, 141n14
Piłsudski, Józef, marshal, 162–64, 166–68, 170–71, 173–74, 178–84
Podbrodzie (Pabradė), 197
Poehlmann, Margarete, 73
pogroms, 10–11, 52, 83–87, 95, 98–99, 149–52, 218
Poincaré, Raymond, 63
Poland, 6–7, 9, 11–12, 36–37, 85, 98–99, 161–71, 173–76, 179–84, 195, 197, 199, 201–3, 206–7, 215n16
Poles, 11, 18, 37, 86, 95, 171, 175, 195–96, 201, 206
Pomerania, 202
Posen, 201
Poska, Jaan, 108
Posti, Arnold, 118
Powórsk (Povors'k), 195
Poznań, 163–71, 174–75, 179, 181–82, 184, 198, 201–3
Preben-Hansen, Bernadette, 106
prisoners of war, 3, 11, 16n6, 17, 23–28, 30–31, 33, 36, 38–39, 55, 58–59, 162, 196, 199
Privislinskii Krai, 52
Prohászka, Ottokár, 155
Prónay, Pál, baron, 140–49
Protestant, 20
Prussia, 3, 9, 18–22, 34, 38, 42–48, 51, 54–57, 61, 65–70, 72–75, 166, 199
Prussians, 61, 69
Pryłucki, Nojech, 196
Przedpełski, Wiktor, 174, 182

Pskov, 113
Puławy Legion, 162
Puszczyński, Tadeusz, 174

railways, 17, 24nn32–33, 188–89, 195, 207, 221
Rakishki (Rokiškis), 52
Rakvere, 123
Rantanen, Henri, 107, 114
Ranzenberger, Victor, 145
Rechtschaffer, Jakab Sámuel, 151
Reds, 11, 115, 124, 127
refugees, 3–4, 33, 42, 53–54, 56, 61, 119, 122, 175, 191
Rei, August, 122
Reich, German, 42–43, 59, 66, 161
Rennenkampf, general, 18
requisitions, 8, 10–11, 15, 18–19, 21, 23, 32–33, 38, 46, 49–50, 58–59, 72, 115, 127
revolution, 1–2, 6, 60, 104, 148–49, 154, 157, 217, 219–21, 223
Richter, Klaus, 49
Riga, 19
Rimkus, Jaroslavas, 62–63, 71
riots, 12, 149, 182, 191
robberies, 10–11, 15, 23, 29, 35, 38, 119, 142, 145–46, 149–53, 202
Romania, 6–7, 202
Romanov Empire, 1, 44, 51
Roselius, Aapo, 106, 129
Rotbard, Srul, 204
Rózsa, Manó, 142
Rubinek, Gyula, 155
Ruseckas, Petras, 65, 72
Russia, 1–5, 11, 18, 20, 32–33, 43–44, 50–51, 53, 60–63, 69–70, 83, 106, 108, 110, 122–23, 162, 166, 193, 199, 201, 220
Russians, 19–20, 22, 25–30, 36–38, 43, 46, 61, 67–68, 71, 73, 96, 109, 114, 125, 128

Ruthenians, 206
Rzeszów, 202

Safronovas, Vasilijus, 12
Salzburg, 200
Samogitia, The Diocese of, 57
Samsonov, general, 18
Sanborn, Joshua, 4, 51
Sarajevo, 200
Scandinavia, 106, 116
Scandinavians, 107, 119, 123, 132, 223
Schefcsik, György, 144
Schirwindt, 42–43
Schivelbusch, Wolfgang, 137
Schlesinger, Mór, 145
Schnell, Felix, 138
Schöttler, Peter, 213
self-determination, 219–20
Senn, Alfred E, 60
Serbia, 143
Setumaa, 112
sexual violence, 50
Shoah, 211
Shohat, Azriel, 85
Shvoy, Kálmán, 142
Šiauliai (Shavli), 22, 45, 62, 87, 88n27
Siedlce, 205
Silvennoinen, Oula, 106, 129
Šimkus, Jonas, 88n27, 92n52
Simontornya, 148
Skaudvilė, 32
Skierniewice, 205
Skipitis, Rapolas, 88, 89n32
Skuodas, 62
Sleževičius, Mykolas, 96
Slovakia, 193–94, 196
Smetona, Antanas, 66
socialism, 114, 157, 211
Sokols organization, 200
Solferino, Battle of, 2
Soloveichik, Max, 88, 94–96
Solt, 143

Soós, Károly, 140–41
Soroksár, 151
Sosnowiec, 169
sovereignty, 105
Social order, 218
Śródmieście, 203
Stachiewicz, Julian, 179
Staliūnas, Darius, 12
Steponaitis, Vytautas, 63
Stochod, river, 195
Stockholm, 108, 110, 118
Stoewer, 145
Stokhod, river, 195
Strazhas, Abba, 16, 25, 49–50
Suboch' (Subačius), 52
Sulejów, 178
Suvalki (Suwałki), 45, 52
Sweden, 55, 105–6, 108–110, 116–18,
    127, 129, 131
Swedes, 107–8, 117, 128, 130, 133
Switzerland, 60
Szamuely, László, 144
Szamuely, Tibor, 144
Szeged, 139–40, 147
Székesfehérvár, 155
Szekulecz, 142
Szemere, Miklós, 154
Szilárd, Leó, 156
Szluha, Dénes, 147
Szolnok, 143

Tallinn, 111–12, 119–21, 123, 125,
    127–30
Targówek, 204
Tartu, 123, 128, 130
Taryba (Lithuanian Council), 23, 27, 59,
    62
Teleki, Pál, 155
Teller, Ede, 156
terror, 3–5, 10–11, 18–20, 30, 32, 44, 69,
    100, 122–23, 139–40, 157–58
Theweleit, Klaus, 138

Thiringer, 143
Tilly, Charles, 6
Tilsit, 69, 73
Tirol, 200
Tõnisson, Jaan, 108
Trashkuny (Troškūnai), 52
Trąmpczyński, Wojciech, 50n25
Trotsky, Lev, 124, 188, 190–91
Tukhachevski, marshal, 198
Turkey, 219
Turmantas, 197

Ukmergė, 27, 96, 97n73, 98
Ukraine, 5–6, 11–12, 83, 85, 92, 99–100, 143, 195, 201, 207
Ukrainians, 164, 195, 201
Ulster, 223n38, 227n50
Upper Silesia, 164–65, 167–76, 178–84
Urbšienė, Marija, 48–49

Vabalininkas, 87, 97–98
Valga, 111–12, 121, 126, 129, 131
Valka, 111
Vareikis, Vygantas, 12, 85
Vaškai, 87
Vastseliina, 112
Vecgulbene, 123, 125
Veidlinger, Jeffrey, 83n3
Véli, Miksa, 151
Veliuona, 35
veterans, 116, 137, 140, 155, 183, 222
Verhovay, László, 151
Vidziuny (Vidžiūnai), 52
Viipuri, 109
Vilavičius, Aleksandras, 96
Vilna, 45, 53, 58
Vilnius, 11, 37, 45, 65, 164, 195–97, 207
violence, 1–12, 15, 19, passim. See also criminality
Vishinty (Viešintos), 52
Vistula land, 52

Vitkus, Hektoras, 12
Vladislavov, 42–43
Voboľniki (Vabalininkas), 52. See also Vabalininkas
Vologda, 193
volunteers, 12, 45, 99, 103–4, 106–112, 114–33, 175, 181, 202, 223
Võru, 195

warlords, 10, 92, 201, 212
Watson, Alexander, 47–48
Weber, Max, 6
Weimar Republic, 166
Westenholz, Aage, 110, 112, 132
Westerhoff, Christian, 49
Western Dvina, 45
Wetzer, Martin, general, 109, 112, 122, 126
Wigner, Jenő (Eugen) P., 156
Wilhelmine, 50–51
Wilson, Tim, 178, 219–20
Windheim, Ludwig von, 67n89
Witkowski, captain, 203
Wiza, Stanisław, 169
Wolbórz, 205
Wolke, Lars Ericson, 107
women, 59, 70–71, 75, 91, 109, 117, 125, 138, 144, 149–50, 152–53, 155–56, 221
workers, 138, 153, 157, 191
Wróblewski Library, 58
World War I, 2–3, 15, passim

Žadeikis, Pranciškus, 62
Záruba, Antonín, 200
Zavagyil, Sándor, 143
Žemaitija, 26n40
Zgrzebionek, 175
Zgrzebniok, Alfons, 172, 174
Zhilinskii, general, 18
Žukauskas, Silvestras, 96

Printed in the USA
CPSIA information can be obtained
at www.ICGtesting.com
JSHW012222080724
66059JS00003B/23